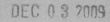

Anthony Quinn 604

604

Your Guide to the Most

ENVIRONMENTALLY FRIENDLY

Information, Products, and Services

ADRIA VASIL

ECOHOLIC

W. W. NORTON & COMPANY
New York · London

CONTENTS

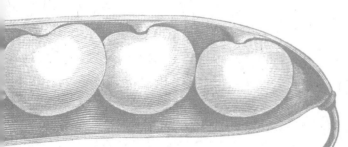

INTRODUCTION

You know, it's funny—the US has so many damn natural outdoor MVP of the year. But when thousands of trees aside from a few folk singers and some placard-bearing

no. Observers declared environmental consciousness dead. Earth Day marches had long been canceled. There was but a faint green pulse left in us as we dragged our recyclables to the curb then hopped into our gas guzzlers with the AC blasting and Bell Biv DeVoe cranked. Memories of acid rain, dead lakes, and the *Exxon Valdez* had faded to black, along with any recollection of feathered hair and shoulder pads.

Then, sometime in the last few years, someone somewhere pulled out the defibrillators and called "clear," and suddenly we joined a giant global episode of *ER*. We started waking up to the fact that the planet needs saving. Was it the spike in the price of oil, forcing us to reconsider the value of spending 80 bucks a tank just to drive ourselves to the corner store? Was it the increased alarm ringing by battalions of climate change scientists? The starving polar bears? The breaking levees? The freak storms? The ever-climbing utility bills? Maybe it was the reports that DDT is still swimming in our children's bloodstreams decades after it was banned or that nonstick chemicals are sticking to bald eagles and floating in breast milk. More realistically, it was all of the above: a perfect storm of factors that made us sit up and say, "Holy Toledo, Dorothy, we're not in Kansas anymore."

What's exciting about this surge, this outpouring of interest in all things green, is that everyone, from the trucker up the street to the CEO of Wal-Mart and, yes, even the president *attractions that you'd think the country would qualify as fall in our national forests, does anyone really care? Well, enviro groups, my answer just a few years ago was a reluctant*

of the United States of America is taking notice. And whether you're expressing your concern for the planet by reaching for organic milk, turning off the tap while you brush, driving a little less, or not driving at all, it all adds up to a movement.

Sure, sticking to a 5-minute shower rule may seem fruitless in the face of a melting planet and relentless emissions from the coal plant two towns down. But are we to throw up our hands and bury our heads in the sand? Every drop of water you conserve, each watt of power you save, every tomato you purchase from a local organic grower sends a message. To paraphrase football dads everywhere, if you want to be on a winning team, you have to think like a winner. And sometimes, when that team is slacking, you've gotta step up and take the lead. You don't have to take to the streets to make a statement (though hey, if you're itching to try out a megaphone, go ahead). Start small. Start by leading by example. Get your workplace to turn the lights off at night and the thermostat up in the summer. Tell your grocery store manager you don't need Mexican peppers vacuum-packed on polystyrene when he should be pushing local ones, loose. Tell your brother that idling is just burning up gas (not to mention the planet), and tell your government representative you support tough action on greenhouse gas emissions after, oh, eight years of federal foot-dragging.

The tough part is that figuring out what's green and what's greenwash, what's eco-friendly and what's climate-deadly, can be downright dizzying. This is where knowledge comes in to play. The more you know, the more effective your choices, actions, and movements can be. And if knowing is half the battle, just picking up this book (and reading it cover to cover, of course) should turn you into a finely trained eco warrior. In all honesty, we can't buy our way out of this mess. But we *can* vote with our dollars, and with them, vote for genuine sustainability, vibrant local economies, and, you know, maybe some green cleaning products that actually work better than spit and a rag. Don't worry—you don't have to give up shaving and chain yourself to a tree to be green. Just do what you can, one step at time—until you're a full-blown ecoholic.

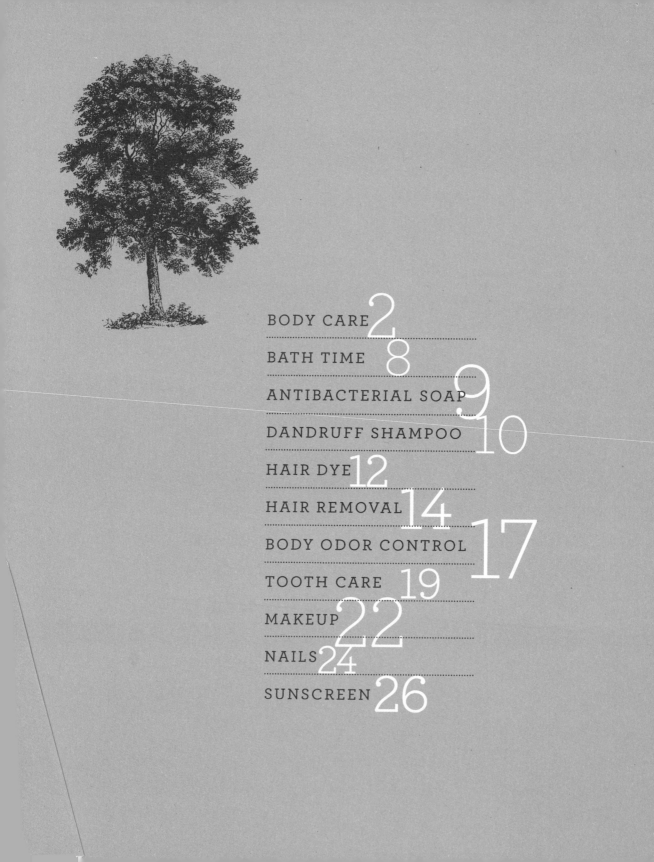

BATHROOM
CONFIDENTIAL

Human beings are so evolved, aren't we? Where a cat uses spit and a tongue to clean itself, we have hundreds of products to preen every part of our bodies. Where a duck is stuck with the feathers the universe gave it, we can pluck and paint ourselves into glorious swans. But how evolved are we really? You can scoff at those wacky Victorians for powdering their noses with lead, yet there are embalming fluids in our nail polish and hormone disrupters in our hair spray. Talk about dying to be beautiful. But don't stress—going natural doesn't mean giving up your grooming habits, no matter what you might have seen in the '60s.

BODY CARE

It's morning. You're standing in the shower and belting out the BeeGees/Britney/Bowie (you decide). You might pause to think about the toast you burned or the meeting you're late for, but never would you dream that a dab of this and a spritz of that are turning your daily routine into a chemical bath. Alas, the average adult uses nine personal-care products a day, containing a grand total of 126 chemical ingredients, according to a report by the Environmental Working Group (EWG). The synthetic slather is even more intense for the one in four women who use more than 15 products daily. The next time you get ready in the morning, do your own count. Facial wash, shampoo, shaving cream, moisturizers, lip gloss—they add up quickly. And while the roughly $20 billion beauty care industry likes us to believe its shampoos and creams are oh so natural, thanks to well-advertised ingredients like ginger and ylang-ylang, the truth is that you're drenching your lips, cheeks, and hair in a largely untested and lengthy list of petroleum-derived, genetically modified, animal-tested or animal-based ingredients.

Over 10,000 chemical ingredients are stirred into the personal-care products that line store shelves. It's a mind-boggling number really, but it gets even scarier when you consider that the government admits it doesn't require safety tests for these products before they hit stores. That's right, the Food and Drug Administration (FDA) lets you be the guinea pig, ladies and gents. The result? Only about 11% of these products have been tested for safety, according to the EWG. And those tests are done not by federal labs, but by the cosmetics companies themselves and the industry-funded Cosmetic Ingredient Review.

Dodgy Chemicals: Sure, some personal-care products leave your skin itchy and eyes a little red, but that's the least of your worries. Carcinogenic formaldehyde and estrogenic parabens are commonly used as preservatives. And although you'll rarely see the word "phthalate" on a label (it's often one of the thousands of chemicals represented by the word "fragrance"), these hormone-disrupting plastic softeners are in almost everything with a synthetic scent. Despite industry assurances about their safety, many hospitals are banning one type of phthalate, DEHP, from medical equipment because of its ties to reproductive changes in infant boys. And in 2008, the US signed the Consumer Product Safety Improvement Act, which, among other things, will purge six phthalates from children's toys.

Do our regulators care, though, that virtually every person monitored by the Centers for Disease Control and Prevention in 2005 tested positive for phthalates (they've even made their way into breast milk), and that these chemicals are turning

You're drenching your lips, cheeks, and hair in a largely UNTESTED and lengthy list of petroleum-derived, genetically modified, ANIMAL-TESTED or animal-based ingredients.

up in our waterways, soil, and wildlife, with inconclusive long-term impacts? Guess not, because they're still allowed in all the products we adults slather on our skin and hair every day. Some companies, such as L'Oréal and Revlon, have announced that they're voluntarily withdrawing two (but not all) types of phthalates from their products. It's a start.

Besides phthalates, there's more lurking inside your favorite products that you won't find on the label. The Campaign for Safe Cosmetics found the carcinogenic contaminant 1,4-dioxane in products like Herbal Essence shampoo and Olay body wash at or above FDA maximums in 2007. In 2008, the Organic Consumers Association found equally high levels in a few natural body washes. The results were enough to prompt California's attorney general to sue Whole Foods, Avalon, Alba, and NutriBiotic for failing to warn consumers that some of their products contain ingredients that may cause cancer, according to California's avant-garde warning-label system, Proposition 65. If you catch one of the following ingredients listed on your shampoo bottle, you might be sudsing up with 1,4-dioxane: sodium laureth sulfate, polyethylene, polyethylene glycol (PEG), polyoxyethylene, polyethoxyethylene—basically anything with "eth" in it.

Unfortunately, the FDA's only response to recent scares about contaminants in beauty products (including lead in lipstick; see page 23) wasn't to announce stricter monitoring regulations but to develop tools for companies to better assess *themselves*. That's kind of like asking the fox to watch the henhouse, no?

Body Care Solutions: So how do you stay away from all this junk? Look for goods with as many naturally derived and certified organic ingredients as possible, but don't sink your dollar into just any products labeled "natural" or "organic." Many of the shampoos and creams in health stores aren't as pure as you'd think—even a lot of the ones that cleverly build the word "organic" or "organics" into their name brand. They might have more earth-given ingredients than the drugstore type, but that doesn't make them angels and they can still contain plenty of questionable chemicals. And an ingredient like coconut-derived sodium lauryl sulfate is still irritating to many, even though it comes from coconuts.

Read ingredient lists carefully. You can generally spot chemical names pretty easily in so-called natural products (though some natural ingredients might go by their Latin names). Not all of them are necessarily harmful, of course; but when in doubt, look up an unfamiliar term online (**cosmeticsdatabase.com** * is a good centralized place to look) or ask the health store salesclerk. Easier still, just avoid products in which only a few ingredients are actually organic and the rest are synthetic.

Which products get the green thumbs-up? If it's purity you're looking for, high praise goes to **Dr. Bronner's**, **Terressentials**, **Organic Essence**, **Trillium Organics**, and **Vermont Soap Organics** for putting out some of the only beauty products to score the USDA organic seal (see the sidebar on organic labels). Another manufacturer that gets

WHAT'S THAT SMELL?

Your signature scent might drive your lover wild, but there's nothing sexy about squirting yourself with hormone-disrupting phthalates (found in 35 of 36 perfume samples that Greenpeace tested) and hundreds of undisclosed chemicals. Health stores should carry natural scents like **Ecco Bella**'s delicate eau de parfum with essential oils from fruits, herbs, flowers, and spices in natural grain alcohol. **Aura Cacia** is another sweet-smelling fragrance maker. **Aubrey Organics** fragrances are said to contain at least 95% certified organic ingredients, but both Aubrey and Aveda were singled out in a 2007 *Consumer Reports* study that tested eight fragrances for the presence of phthalates—even though both companies advertised themselves as being phthalate-free. A guaranteed way to smell good without all this nasty stuff is to make your own scents by blending pure essential oils (the kind you find at health stores, not synthetic-heavy Body Shop types) like vanilla and orange.

*The prefixes "http://" and "www" are omitted from the URLs in this book. Most browsers will automatically supply the required prefix for Internet addresses, but if you have trouble accessing a particular website with the URL provided, try adding "www" (followed by a period) in front of the address—in this case, www.cosmeticsdatabase.com.

10 BEAUTY PRODUCT INGREDIENTS TO AVOID

Diethanolamine (DEA): This suspected carcinogen is common in shampoos, body wash, and makeup. Cocamide DEA, MEA, and TEA may be contaminated with DEA.

Formaldehyde: You might not see it on your ingredient list, but this carcinogen is found in imidazolidinyl urea, DMDM hydantoin, and quaternium-15. Formaldehyde can evaporate into the air when the product is wet.

Parabens: All types of parabens (methyl-, ethyl-, etc.) have been found to be mildly estrogenic—meaning they mimic female hormones. Parabens have been found in breast tumor samples but haven't been conclusively linked to cancer. Parabens have been detected in the bloodstream hours after paraben-containing cream was applied.

Petrolatum: Petrolatum comes from nonrenewable crude oil, kind of like tanking up at the pump. It's not breathable. Mineral oil is also petroleum-based.

p-Phenylenediamine (PPD): PPD also goes by the name of paraphenylenediamine, 1,4-diaminobenzene, or 1,4-phenylenediamine (among others). Found in permanent hair dyes, it has been tied to increases in bladder cancer in long-term frequent users.

Phthalates: You'll rarely see this controversial family of hormone disrupters listed on labels. It's often tucked away under the ingredient "fragrance." The best way to avoid phthalates is to look for fragrance-free products, but even a "fragrance-free" label is no guarantee that fragrance wasn't added. These have been banned from baby toys.

BHA: This preservative, antioxidant, and fragrance ingredient is considered a possible human carcinogen and suspected hormone disrupter. It must come with a warning label if it's used in products sold in California. Low doses are also linked to liver damage in lab rats and immune system toxicity.

Talc: This powder is found in everything from eye shadow and blush to baby powder and deodorant. Although talc may be contaminated with asbestos fibers, the industry says that cosmetic-grade talc is asbestos-free. Still, several studies, including one on 3,000 women published in the *International Journal of Cancer* in 2007, have linked powdering your, ahem, nether regions with talc to elevated uterine cancer rates in women (in fact, in 2008 the chairs of the Cancer Prevention Coalition and the Health & Medicine Policy Research Group asked the FDA yet again to put a warning label about this on talc). The US Department of Health's National Institutes of Health (NIH) voted to have all talc (even the non-asbestos-tainted stuff) categorized as a probable carcinogen, but the proposed measure was voted down by another government body. Regardless of the cancer connection, talc mining has been responsible for some pretty serious habitat destruction in India (for more details, see page 18 on talc in deodorants).

(continued)

Toluene: This powerful solvent is found in nail polishes. Long-term exposure affects the nervous system, liver, and kidneys. It can also contribute to smog, making it an all-around bad guy.

Triclosan (a.k.a. Microban): This antibacterial chemical is used in pretty much everything. It's building up in our rivers, fish, and breast milk; and it can turn into carcinogenic dioxins when exposed to sunlight in water. Scientists say it also messes with thyroid function in frogs. It's been banned by UK supermarkets. Triclosan has been found in 75% of Americans tested. Triclocarbon should also be avoided. (See page 9 for more details.)

high marks is **GratefulBody**, which has a cool 30Plus line and Environmental Impact line for those with multiple chemical sensitivities. Australia's **Miessence** brand also carries the USDA seal and probably offers the most extensive range of clean, green, high-performance personal-care products, including firming eye and neck serum, styling gel, foundation, and more (but they're mostly available direct to consumer, so you'll have to get them online from sites like **myorganicfamily.com**).

Next are products that don't quite make the USDA cut but get serious kudos for their kick-ass performance and quality ingredients. If you have a few extra dollars to spend on top-of-the-line body, hair, and skin care products (including makeup) endorsed by the likes of Madonna and Julia Roberts, **Dr. Hauschka** grows its own organic ingredients in line with planetary rhythms and biodynamic principles. **Suki** and **Lavera** are two other top-notch makers of skin care products (including antiaging products) and more. **Weleda** is well known for using a high percentage of quality organic as well as biodynamic and fair-trade ingredients. **Pangea Organics** is a wonderfully wholesome Colorado-based maker of skin care products, body washes, and lotions crammed with organic herbal extracts and essential oils.

If you're looking for African American hair care products, the good news is that most companies took estrogen-heavy placenta out of their conditioners a few years ago after they were linked to early puberty in girls. But their products are still loaded with incredibly harsh chemicals. Better to reach for more natural hair conditioners and styling balms by companies like **Ébène** (**ebenenaturals.com**).

So they put bananas in their shampoo. Great. But despite what you might think, the Body Shop, which was bought out by L'Oréal, and Aveda aren't entirely earthy. Look at the ingredients list at **thebodyshop.com** and you'll notice that papaya shower gel (for example) is chock-full of questionable chemicals like parabens, synthetic fragrances, and sodium laureth sulfate (which can be contaminated with 1,4-dioxane). The Body Shop does have its advantages over drugstore brands: its products aren't tested on animals, its stores are reducing their carbon footprint, and 65% of its products contain at least one fairly traded ingredient.

Aveda (now owned by Estée Lauder) claims to include plant-derived ingredients "whenever possible" and has comprehensive sustainability practices, though its products can still contain some pretty suspect synthetics. Aveda says it's trying to phase out parabens. It's best to do your own ingredient check. An eyeliner might pass, but a shampoo might not.

BATH TIME

Who doesn't love a soak in the tub? But what's the point if you're just marinating yourself in carcinogens and estrogen mimickers? Ditch the dodgy synthetics and splurge on some organic bath oils and bath teas, or just reach into your kitchen cupboards and drizzle 2 tablespoons of organic almond oil or olive oil into the water. Add a few drops of your fave essential oils to sweeten things up.

Drop the petrochemical- and fragrance-filled soap in favor of a naturally zesty bar like **Pangea**'s **Indian Lemongrass soap**. Bath salts like **Little Moon Essentials**' **Tired Old Ass Soak** will get you grinning while you give your body a break. Or whip up your own natural soaks, salts, and scrubs with yummy recipes like Cinnamon Sugar Scrub and Cucumber Coconut Skin Softener (made with fresh cucumber and coconut oil!) from **makeyourcosmetics.com**·

Even our lathering tools can froth up nature's balance. Sea sponges aren't just lying around the ocean floor waiting to be used on your elbows, you know. They're living organisms with lives of their own. If you want to use them, make sure you're not buying from a source that may be overharvesting them. Or better yet, scrub your conscience with abrasive **plant-based brushes** made from jute, coconut, sisal, or loofah (which, wouldn't you know it, comes from a relative of squash). **Pumice stones**, by the way, are made of dried, hardened lava—they're actually a type of glass. I've yet to come across any pumice protection societies, so you should be in the clear with these.

ANTIBACTERIAL SOAP

They're everywhere. Lurking on every doorknob and lingering on every sponge. No, not germs—antibacterial products, silly. After news programs started scaring the bejesus out of us with footage of microscopic particles hovering in our midst, we freaked. No one could look at a damp dishcloth the same way again. Pretty much every company in North America took notice and started adding antibacterial ingredients (mostly triclosan) to anything and everything. Now commercials instruct you to spray the air around your children's toys with antibacterial mists, and every hand, dish, and floor soap kills 99.99% of anything that comes in its path. But is this really a good idea?

By now you may have heard about how antibacterial mania is lowering our defenses against germs. But there's also accumulating evidence that our obsession with these ingredients could breed drug-resistant bug strains. Research out of Tufts University found that *E. coli* that survived being treated with triclosan became resistant to 7 of 12 antibiotics. Great—like we need more supergerms in our lives.

Despite the ick factor of sharing tight spaces with coughing strangers, you should be aware that our germ phobia is wreaking serious havoc on the environment as well. Triclosan and triclocarbon, the active ingredients in a lot of antibacterial soaps, are scarily finding their way into rivers, streams, and lakes, according to a US Geological Survey, not to mention breast milk (they're actually in 75% of Americans tested). Even though the stuff is supposed to quickly break down in water, research out of Johns Hopkins University indicates that about 75% makes it down our drains and past

> **I**f your municipality is spreading sewage sludge on farmers' fields, as many are, **ANTIBACTERIAL CHEMICALS** *are essentially fertilizing the crops in your area.*

sewage treatment plants. The thing is, researchers at the University of Minnesota found that when these chemicals are exposed to sunlight in water, they create a mild dioxin (a carcinogenic hormone disrupter that accumulates in the food chain even at low levels). And when you throw chlorinated water into the mix, the result could be a much nastier form of the pollutant. If your municipality is spreading its sewage sludge on farmers' fields, as many are, triclosan and triclocarbon are essentially fertilizing the crops in your area. Indeed, Johns Hopkins researchers estimate that about 200 tons of the compounds are spread on farms every year. And these chemicals accumulate in soil. Forget field to table; this is sink to field.

British supermarkets decided to ban triclosan from their products in 2003. No word yet from American officials on this. Bottom line: read labels and stay away from soaps and other products containing triclosan or triclocarbon. They'll be listed. And why bother using antibacterial soaps at all when an FDA panel and the American Medical Association have said that antibacterial soaps and washes don't reduce household infections any more than washing with regular soap does?

Hand Sanitizers: In our quest to be germ-free, portable hand sanitizers have become the adult equivalent of baby wipes. The good news is that those sanitizing gels don't generally have triclosan in them; ethyl alcohol (a grain alcohol used for hundreds of years as a natural antiseptic) and synthetic isopropyl alcohol (a.k.a. rubbing alcohol) are the main germ killers. Antibacterial soap critic and Columbia University prof Elaine Larson says that alcohol-based hand gels kill germs without contributing to antibiotic resistance, as triclosan might. But mainstream sanitizers also contain artificial perfumes, coal tar–derived dyes, and a few petroleum-based ingredients.

Instead, reach for an all-natural hand sanitizer. **EO** makes hand-sanitizing gel and wipes with organic alcohol (though disposable wipes should really be avoided because of all the waste they create). Do you want to use these all the time, or instead of soap? No, but for the occasional extra sticky situation when a sink's nowhere in sight, they're not so bad.

DANDRUFF SHAMPOO

You know those annoying commercials that use snow as a metaphor for dandruff? Well, their solution to your scalp's weather woes is about as helpful as George Bush's response to global warming.

First of all, mainstream dandruff shampoos are loaded with supertoxic ingredients, like coal tar—the black liquid distilled from coal (which is found in Neutrogena Therapeutic T/Gel shampoo). The stuff has long been linked to cancer in miners, asphalt workers, and chimney sweeps, but the FDA says there's nothing to worry about when it's used in such small quantities. Even if you don't mind the notion of rubbing coal juice into your scalp, slicing off Appalachian mountaintops to get at coal is never a good thing and coal mining has a history of contaminating groundwater long after a mine is in use.

Another common flake-busting ingredient is zinc pyrithione (found in Head & Shoulders). What could be wrong with zinc, you ask? Well, in this form, lots. A report by the Swedish Society for Nature Conservation states that when researchers poured 3 milliliters of dandruff shampoo with 0.8% zinc pyrithione into a 1,000-liter aquarium, waited 24 hours, and then added fish, half the fish died within 4 days. This despite the fact that the ingredient is said to degrade quickly in water. The study also found that 1% to 2% of the added zinc could still be detected 80 days later. Considering that (depending on whom you ask) anywhere from 50% to 97% of North Americans experience dandruff at some point, a hell of a lot of the stuff washes down our drains every morning.

Another big "snow" buster is selenium disulfide, which is classified as very toxic to aquatic organisms, with long-term environmental effects. It's also, according to the Environmental Protection Agency (EPA), a probable human carcinogen. Tsk-tsk.

"Second-generation" flake fighter piroctone olamine is considered about 100 times less toxic for aquatic life than zinc is. Sulfur and salicylic acid are other active dandruff shampoo ingredients that aren't considered toxic to water critters. No similar data could be found on ketoconazole (patented by Nizoral), but taking this potent antifungal internally has been linked to birth defects in animals. It's not recommended for use by pregnant women or nursing mothers.

Dandruff Solutions: Ironically, lots of dandruff hair washes contain a notorious skin and scalp irritant: sodium lauryl/laureth sulfate (SLS). It actually dries out your skin. Before you buy a dandruff shampoo, make sure your regular shampoo doesn't contain SLS, which might be at the, ahem, root of your problem.

Most dandruff is caused by a yeast or fungus. Try cutting back on sugar and refined foods, taking antifungal **oregano oil** internally, and washing your hair with natural **tea tree oil** shampoos, available at health stores. You can even add a few drops of tea tree oil or essential **rosemary oil** to a palmful of regular shampoo. Some people swear by using one part **apple cider vinegar** to three parts warm water every

> Make sure your regular shampoo DOESN'T CONTAIN SLS, which might be at the, ahem, root of your dandruff problem.

few days. Let it soak into your scalp before shampooing with a really mild shampoo. You can also use the pH-balancing vinegar straight, if you can take the pungent wake-up call.

If you see flurries only in winter, you have a dry-skin problem, not a fungal issue. Pop extra **omega fatty acids** and **vitamin B$_6$** and consider a humidifier. Rubbing pure **aloe vera** into your scalp is another soothing remedy.

HAIR DYE

To dye or not to dye? The answer must have been so much simpler in Shakespeare's time, before highlights, lowlights, and frosted tips. A shot of color can really liven up your locks, and it seems as if everyone and her uncle (yes, more and more men like to transform their tufts too) head to the nearest drugstore or hair salon to do just that. But what is the eco-conscious color craver to do? Of course, you should love what Mother Nature gave you, but if you're looking for a little enhancement, there are several earth- and body-friendly alternatives out there.

Mainstream Dyes: If you're tinting your tresses with conventional dyes, it might be time to rethink things. Made up of a sordid stew of chemicals that definitely don't do the planet or your body much good, rivers of these dyes are washed down the drain on a regular basis by over a third of North American women and one in 10 men.

What's in these dyes that makes them so spooky? Besides all the well-known allergens like ammonia and peroxide, ingredients such as PPD (*p*-phenylenediamine, a.k.a. paraphenylenediamine, 1,4-diaminobenzene or 1,4-phenylenediamine) are definitely toxic to the chemically sensitive, and even people who've been dyeing for years can suddenly develop reactions to them. Then there's the whole cancer link. Sure, many of the worst carcinogens have been removed from mainstream formulas since the '80s, but in the '90s the National Cancer

Studies show that women who have been darkening their hair with PERMANENT DYES since before the '80s may have INCREASED THEIR RISK of non-Hodgkin's lymphoma.

Institute declared that deep-colored dyes (like brown or black) may increase the risk of non-Hodgkin's lymphoma and multiple melanomas when used every month over a prolonged period of time. (And you thought bleaching was bad!) Those findings were confirmed by

WASH THAT LEAD RIGHT OUT OF YOUR HAIR
(I'M TALKING TO YOU, BOYS)

Guys, beware of the lead (yes, lead) in products like Grecian Formula, GreyBan, and Youthair! There are plenty of other, less toxic dyes for you to use.

2004 and 2008 Yale studies of women who had been darkening their hair with permanent dyes since before the '80s.

Regardless of color (you blonds should listen up here), one study published in the *International Journal of Cancer* found that women who dye their hair more than once a month using permanent shades are more than twice as likely to develop bladder cancer (thanks to PPDs seeping into your skin and making their way to your bladder before you pee them out; some of us eliminate them without a problem, but others, not so much). If you've been dyeing for more than 15 years, your chances of getting cancer, according to the study, jump to three times above nondyers, and longtime hairdressers are five times more likely to develop cancer. Semipermanent and temporary dyes don't share that risk. Remember, though, that whatever doesn't penetrate your hair shaft and scalp is being washed down the sink, polluting water supplies at the end of the pipe.

Bleaching: As glaringly unnatural as stripping dark hair down to a blinding shade of blond can look, bleach may be the least of your worries. Chemical lighteners use hydrogen peroxide (HP), which, in more diluted solutions, is even marketed as an eco-friendly cleaning product. The EPA says HP breaks down rapidly into water and air. In concentrations of 35% and above, it's extremely corrosive and irritating to the skin, eyes, and mucous membranes, but the peroxide brushed onto your hair is usually only 6% (the kind you put on paper cuts is usually 3%). The biggest problem is that HP is often mixed with ammonia, and ammonia is not only a potent skin and lung irritant, it's also toxic to fish and aquatic life.

Hair Dye Solutions: What are the alternatives? Know that all permanent dyes, even health store brands, contain PPD—it's supposedly the only way to get the color to stick to your hair shaft. And those that say they don't contain PPD? Well, either they're using one of its derivative names (see page 6 sidebar on ingredients to avoid) or they're using toxic metals such as lead or mercury instead.

Clairol's Natural Instincts line of semipermanent dyes is free of ammonia and is lower in peroxide than other brands, which is great, but the colorant hardly comes from nature. According to its safety data sheet, inhaling its vapors may still cause respiratory irritation.

Herbatint is a biodegradable, ammonia- and cruelty-free herbal hair color gel that has very low concentrations of PPD and peroxide. Its semipermanent line, as with most vegetable-based semipermanent dyes, is PPD-free. **EcoColors** uses small amounts of ammonia and peroxide in a soy and flax base. **Naturcolor** is an ammonia- and cruelty-free plant-based option low in PPD that contains therapeutic herbs such as rosemary and lavender. I've tried both Naturcolor and EcoColors to darken my hair, and they worked just as well as hair salon chems, without the nasty toxic scent wafting from your head.

Aubrey Organics makes one of the only permanent hair dyes that's totally natural and PPD-free (Color Me Natural), though it comes in only two shades of brown (dark brown and mahogany).

HAIR REMOVAL

If you believe the old stereotype, every good green boy and girl rejects our cultural obsession with being follicle-free and has the grizzly beard of hairy legs to prove it. Sure, the birth of the environmental movement kind of coincided with the explosion of hairy hippies, but this is the new millennium. Just because you shave your face or sugar your legs doesn't mean you're into waxing the planet. Of course, if you lather up with chemically laden shaving foams and reach for a disposable blade every other day, it's time to shape up.

Shaving: According to Gillette, the largest supplier of disposable and reusable razor blades, over 1.7 billion men over the age of 15 remove hair daily. Since about 80% of them use razors, that's a hell of a lot of waste. And that doesn't factor in the women! Even if only a quarter of adult Americans threw out a razor blade once a week, we'd be tossing nearly 3 billion every year!

If you're hooked on razors, at the very least go for the reusable kind. Why throw out a handle every time you shave? And skip the megabrands with excess packaging—most of that plastic is not commonly recycled. Even their blade refills come with a mountain of plastic (and cost more than the original razor!). Some also have a history of animal testing. Back in the '90s, Woody Harrelson grew a beard to protest Gillette's testing practices. In 1996, Gillette instituted a moratorium on animal testing, but it hasn't issued a complete ban on using it in the future.

OLD-SCHOOL BARBERING

Both blades and electric razors lose in the ring against good old-fashioned straight razors. These classic barber-style blades can be sharpened and reused indefinitely. Imagine that! Okay, so they're a little scary. If you're not up to living on the edge, you can order old-school metal safety razors with replaceable blades online (both available at **classicshaving.com**).

Razors manufactured by **Preserve**, on the other hand, are truly, well, hair-raising. The handles are 100% recycled plastic, including Stonyfield Farm yogurt cups (which once housed organic yogurt), and they may be recyclable in towns with #5 recycling. If your municipality doesn't take them, you can mail your handle back to the company for recycling. They make lubricated double and triple blades with replaceable heads.

Electric razors are a great alternative. The downside is that they're filled with much more potentially toxic hardware than a simple plastic razor is, but they last for years. (Mine finally died recently, but it was from the early '80s!) If it's the rechargeable type and the battery just isn't holding its juice, look into replacing the battery rather than buying a whole new razor. You can avoid the battery problem altogether by getting the kind that plugs straight into a socket. (See page 185 for more on electronics.)

Shaving Creams: Whatever type of blade you choose, you're not ecologically groomed until you stop with the stinky synthetic shaving creams and gels. The canned kind aren't only filled with dodgy phthalate-heavy fragrances and petrochemicals; you're also lathering up with formaldehyde-releasing DMDM hydantoin and chemicals that have to be labeled as cancer causers in California, like BHA. Hardly worth all the foaming action, now is it?

You're not ECOLOGICALLY GROOMED until you stop with the STINKY SYNTHETIC shaving creams and gels.

Luckily, there are all kinds of all-natural shaving creams out there for both men and women, like **Aubrey Organics ginseng mint cream**. Many health store brands make healing aftershave balms and tonics. For old-fashioned types, **Herban Cowboy** offers sweatshop-free ceramic shaving mugs (made with nontoxic glazes) and unbleached wooden shaving brushes, as well as a purer line of shaving cream, aftershave balm, and cologne called Organic Grooming.

Shaving Oil: Grizzly boys give rave reviews to **all-natural shaving oils** made from essential oils. They tend to come in tiny bottles that last a crazy long time because you need only a drop or two. Shaving oils are great for preventing razor bumps and skin irritations. They're not all free of synthetics, though, so read the ingredients.

Waxing: Next time you're howling on the beautician's table, think about this: most waxes are petroleum-based, so all of the eco problems associated with digging up oil for your car are pretty much hanging off your skin. Avoid the problem by looking for natural waxes such as **beeswax** or **tree resin–derived products** (like those made by **Parissa**). But even then, because of the nature of the sticky resin, strips used to tear off hair are not reusable. If you prefer to get someone else to do your yanking for you, look for spas or salons in your area that use **paraffin-free waxes**.

Sugaring: Think the ancients were hairy? Think again. The Egyptians were yanking body hair with a sugary mix of what was in their pantries. The sticky stuff rinses away with water, making your cloth hair removal strips reusable for years. **MOOM** products are made of sugar, chamomile, lemon, and tea tree oil, and they come with reusable cotton strips. Or make your own (see the recipe at pioneerthinking.com/bodysugaring.html). Some spa and waxing salons offer pro sugaring services, so keep your eyes, well, peeled.

Creams: These freaky hair shaft dissolvers are loaded with harsh chemicals, including suspected hormone disrupters and possible carcinogens. Depilatories can even cause second-degree burns if you're not careful. Best to stay away.

Threading: Perhaps the least product-heavy and most enterprising option of them all is threading. A plain cotton thread is wrapped around individual hairs in this process. It's a tad time-consuming for legs but is perfect for eyebrows. Best to see a professional for threading. Men are also having it done, so don't be shy to ask, boys.

Lasers/Electrolysis: Considering more permanent options? Lasers and electrolysis aren't always as lasting as you'd think, and both require electricity (and plenty of money) to power the process through several visits. If all goes well, though, you shouldn't have to pick up another razor or cry through another waxing session, which ultimately cuts your product consumption. Epilators are less permanent home versions that slowly reduce hair growth over time.

BODY ODOR CONTROL

Being social creatures often crammed into close quarters, we have a deep collective phobia of smelling bad. Advertisers tapped into that fear brilliantly back in the '80s. Raise your hand, they challenged us, but only if you're sure. God forbid your deodorant fails you on the treadmill, in a meeting, or on a date. So we diligently douse ourselves with whatever new stick on the market promises to protect us. The question is, what the hell is stopping us from smelling so foul?

Antiperspirants: Many of us swipe our underarms with antiperspirants every morning without really thinking about why our sticks keep us from sweating. The answer? Aluminum-based compounds. They close our pores and reduce the amount of perspiring we'd normally do. Although government bodies such as the FDA say there's nothing to worry about, the jury is still out on whether the mineral contributes to Alzheimer's, since aluminum is found in higher concentrations in the brain tissue of Alzheimer's patients. Some

We line pots and cans with materials that keep our food from coming into contact with ALUMINUM, yet we smear it FREELY against our skin.

researchers continue to study the link, including whether applying it to shaved underarms allows a more direct path into the bloodstream. So far, nothing conclusive has been found. Some say that until we know more, it's not a bad idea to avoid it. I mean, really, we line pots and cans with materials that keep our food from coming into contact with the metal, yet we smear it freely against our skin every day in the form of deodorant. Kind of contradictory, no?

The environmental impacts, however, aren't quite so fuzzy. As with all mining, digging up aluminum (or bauxite ore) has been tied to destructive practices around the globe, and vast amounts of energy go into processing the stuff.

Deodorants: Plain old odor-masking deodorants come with their own set of problems. Some—like Old Spice Classic, Revlon Hi & Dri, and fancier brands like Kenneth Cole

Reaction—replace aluminum with antibacterial triclosan, which is now being found in breast milk and is a hormone disrupter in frogs (see page 7 for more on triclosan).

Formaldehyde, an air-polluting, lung-irritating volatile organic compound (VOC) and probable human carcinogen, can be found in many deodorant preservatives. The VOCs may evaporate as roll-ons dry and offgas as sweat beads on your skin.

If you're a fan of spraying rather than rolling or rubbing on your odor fighter, don't think you're off the hook. That label might say CFC-free, but come on, all consumer products have had to be free of chlorofluorocarbons for a couple decades now. They still contain some smog-inducing VOCs (though less than in the past), and you're also misting yourself with fossil fuels—like butane (a.k.a. lighter fluid) and propane (a.k.a. barbecue grill fuel)—as well as phthalate-heavy fragrances.

Sprinkled on bodies nationwide (hell, Snoop Dogg has even woven the practice into his songs) is talc. Yet few people realize that powdering your privates has been linked to elevated uterine cancer rates (for info, see page 6). And while the health concerns of talc may be hotly debated, there's no question that talc mining can be devastating to local ecosystems. In 2003, it was discovered that talc was being illegally mined from an Indian wildlife sanctuary and tiger reserve. The UK's Environmental Investigation Agency and the *Observer* reported that trees were being chopped down, holes were being blasted in the earth, and water tables were being drained—all practices that threatened the habitat of the severely endangered creatures. And all for the sake of a little body powder. The mining company listed Unilever, Revlon, Avon, and Johnson & Johnson as its clients when the talc hit the fan in 2003. Talc is also commonly found in deodorants.

Natural Deodorants: Don't assume that buying your odor prevention stick from health stores means you're entirely wholesome. Many so-called natural deodorants still contain a lot of the same ingredients found in drugstore varieties. None of the alternative deodorants contain standard aluminum or triclosan (the antibacterial contaminant found in many mainstream brands). But over half of the sticks on health store shelves still contain petroleum-based propylene glycol (PG)—which, in 100% concentrations, is known as antifreeze and is extremely toxic to aquatic life. Many companies, such as Tom's of Maine, insist it's safe in small doses and point out that it's also found in fat-free ice creams (um, yuck!). Other companies have switched to PG-free formulas. Tom's says it tried to take the controversial ingredient out in 1993 but put it back in after customers complained that PG-free sticks were too mushy.

Besides propylene glycol, keep an eye out for suspicious synthetics, like the potentially carcinogenic preservative paraben, though most health store brands have phased it out. Check the ingredients to be sure. Some vitamin shops sell a deodorant cream made by Lavilin, which is said to prevent B.O. for up to a week (creepy). They call it an herbal deodorant, but it actually contains petrolatum and controversial BHT.

If you're shopping for a natural deodorant, look for those with the highest organic content to avoid any controversial chemicals. One award-winning alternative is **Dr. Mist**, a simple salt spray that can be used on armpits, feet—hell, even cold sores. I also have lots of friends that swear by scent-free **deodorizing crystals**, made with the natural rock salt alum. This relative of aluminum is less refined than the kind you find in drugstore antiperspirants and is said not to penetrate skin cells, but the science is, well, lacking. What I can tell you is that some municipalities, like Canada's capital city, Ottawa, use alum in their water filtration process, and some alum is even used by picklers (yes, picklers) along with dill and vinegar. If you're sold, keep in mind the trick is you have to swipe your underarms over a dozen times for this stuff to work. And start on clean skin.

Others swear by the powers of pure natural **baking soda** (yep, the stuff you put in your fridge). You can mix a tiny bit with a dab of water; use it dry with a powder puff; or make a bigger batch, cut with cornstarch and a few drops of essential oil, shake it, and then apply with a damp facecloth.

At the end of the day, keep in mind that body chemistries differ, so what works for some might not work so well for you. In completely unscientific observations, I've noted that natural brands may work for weeks or months and then suddenly conk out. Be prepared to switch things up. It's best to reframe your expectations of just how long an application can protect you. Translation: pack a spare stick in your purse, gym bag, or briefcase for emergency reapplication.

TOOTH CARE

Brush, rinse, spit. And maybe, if you listen to your dentist, floss. It's one of those rituals we do in a haze and don't think too much about (aside from you nutcases brushing to egg timers). But what exactly are we swishing and then spitting into our water system every morning?

Fluoride: Yes, scrubbing your teeth with fluoride helps prevent tooth decay, but so does general dental hygiene (regular brushing, flossing—you know the drill) and not consuming half your body weight in sugar. Swallowing fluoride in our tap water, however, has a mouthful of health and environmental implications that have even convinced the University of Toronto's head of preventive dentistry, once a vocal advocate of fluoridated water, to switch sides.

Fluoride in drinking water accumulates in your bones, for one thing, and drinking it has been linked to increasing bone cancer rates in young boys and to hip fractures. It's also building up in wildlife, leading, again, to fractures, lameness, and poor reproduction. If your municipality has you believing they're doing your teeth a favor by putting this stuff in your water, think again. Dozens of towns have dropped it—tell your town you think yours should too.

Toothpaste: Besides fluoride, you're spitting out eco-persistent triclosan (see page 7) every time you brush with toothpastes like Colgate Total. And with every tube you're squeezing out potentially carcinogenic saccharin and synthetic dyes. It's enough to make you let your teeth get furry.

Not that every "natural" toothpaste is all that natural. As with deodorant, many so-called natural toothpastes contain some of the same scorned ingredients as drugstore brands—ingredients such as propylene glycol and the sudsing irritant sodium lauryl sulfate (SLS). Read the label carefully if you'd rather avoid these. Tom's of Maine, Nature's Gate, and Auromère all argue that SLS isn't a big concern, but lots of brands are SLS-free. Tom's of Maine provides fluoride as an option, for those brushers who'd rather not skip on the cavity fighter.

MAKE YOUR OWN TOOTHPASTE

If you have about 2 minutes to spare in the kitchen, you can skip packaging woes altogether by making your own toothpaste from scratch. Just mix 3 tablespoons of baking soda (your whitener), 4 teaspoons of vegetable glycerin (your gel, found in health stores), and 15 drops of an organic essential oil such as wintergreen or spearmint for minty fresh flavor that comes from the earth, not the lab. Once in a while, you can mix in a little salt as an abrasive (based on a recipe from Pioneer Thinking, **pioneerthinking.com**).

Unfortunately, most toothpaste tubes aren't readily recyclable. The plus side of **Tom's of Maine** toothpaste is you can either mail your aluminum toothpaste tube back to Tom's or peel off the plastic thread around the opening and pop it in your recycling bin (though you might want to check with your city to see if they'll accept it).

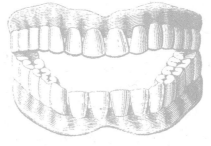

Whitener: Back when I was a tot, I used to brush two or three times in a row just to get my teeth Wonder Woman white. But besides obsessive oral hygiene and cutting out coffee, tea, and wine (we all know that's asking too much), how can you lighten your smile without putting poison on your pearls? Most whitening toothpastes contain sodium hydroxide (a.k.a. lye, a caustic drain cleaner considered a poison by the FDA) or potassium hydroxides (found in cuticle removal products and drain cleaners), as well as dozens of other chems.

Tom's of Maine makes a whitening paste that uses natural silica, but it has SLS. **Jason's PowerSmile** uses silica, calcium carbonate, and renewable bamboo powder, doesn't contain SLS, and does a good job brightening your fangs. You can also just add a little **baking soda** to your brush and scrub.

Mouthwash: Gargle much? You're basically swishing fake dyes and petrochemicals in your mouth every morning. A lot of drugstore mouthwashes, like Listerine, contain antiparasitic thymol, which used to come from thyme way back when but corporations now use a synthetic version. Since thymol is toxic to aquatic organisms, I wouldn't spit it out into a lake on your next camping trip.

Swish with something more in tune with nature, with tea tree oil, aloe vera, and witch hazel, like **Desert Essence** or **Jason's Healthy Mouth** mouthwash. Tom's of Maine makes a peppermint baking soda mouthwash, but it contains flavor-dispersant poloxamer 335, which is derived from natural gas and oil.

Homemade options are easy: put just a few drops of antibacterial **tea tree oil and peppermint oil** into a cup of warm water and swish. A straight **witch hazel** gargle can sooth sore gums or mouth sores.

Floss: Strange but true: a couple brands, like Crest Glide, are made with PTFE (a.k.a. Teflon). Sure, the floss won't stick between your chompers as easily, but it contains traces of PFOA, the persistent chemical used in the making of Teflon, which has been labeled a probable carcinogen. Oral care reps at Crest say you'd have to floss 365 times a day for 75 years to be exposed to 3 milligrams of the stuff. Still, is it totally necessary? Several floss makers have actually discontinued PTFE-containing versions. **Radius Silk Floss**, on the other hand, uses biodegradable silk threads coated with beeswax. Vegans might prefer the rice bran wax–veneered nylon in **Eco-DenT GentleFloss**. Nylon, however, is also a petroleum-based synthetic. At least Eco-DenT ditches unrecyclable plastic casing in favor of totally recyclable paper packaging. Whatever floss you choose, just don't flush it. It clogs up the sewers (not a pretty picture).

Toothbrushes: If we all listened to our dentists and ditched our toothbrushes four times a year, over 1 billion of them would be trashed in the US annually. Even if we changed our toothbrushes half as often, we'd still be scrapping 600 million of the petroleum sticks every year. And you can bet there's zero recycled content in the kind you pick up in your drugstore. In contrast, **Preserve** toothbrushes are made from old Stonyfield Farm yogurt cups and may

be recyclable in some municipalities. You can even return them to the company, and they'll turn the handle and the nylon bristles into plastic lumber. But Radius, a natural floss and toothbrush maker, has stopped taking toothbrushes back because they say it wasted more energy to truck all those brushes back and recycle them than it did to make new ones.

Better to just avoid tossing the whole handle out each time, when it's only the bristles that get mashed up. Look for toothbrushes with a replaceable head like **Eco-DenT**'s **TerrAdenT** brushes.

Getting a buzz off electronic toothbrushes? The UN's climate change tips actually ask people to give up their electric toothbrushes to save on power (thereby saving 48 grams of CO_2 a day). But if you're hooked on the vibe, make sure the battery in your plug-in rechargeable type is nickel metal hydride, not toxic nickel cadmium. As for the cheapie types that have flooded the market, just make sure to get one with replaceable heads and use rechargeable AAs instead of disposables.

Whichever brush you choose, remember that old bristles are great for precision cleaning, so don't toss 'em.

MAKEUP

How we've suffered for beauty (touch wrist to forehead and sigh dramatically). First there was the lead kohl eyeliner used by ancient Egyptians, then the white lead powder used to lighten the cheeks of the Greco-Romans, then more whitening lead face powder in the Renaissance. Unfortunately, we haven't yet let the lead thing die. Hell, it's still found in drugstore lipsticks! A whopping 60% of the 33 tubes tested by the Campaign for Safe Cosmetics in 2007 had detectable levels of the neurotoxin. Is it enough to dull your IQ? Unlikely. Do you still want to slap lead on your lips? I know I don't.

Even more shocking is the fact that deadly mercury (which accumulates in our bodies) is still legally allowed as a preservative in mascara and eyeliner. And although it may not be allowed in skin-lightening creams and soaps, the New York City Health Department found scary levels of the toxin in some imports after one woman got mercury poisoning from her lightening cream. Not that you'd ever spot mercury on any ingredient lists. At least Minnesota had the good sense to ban the poison from beauty products in 2008.

Of course, painting our faces hasn't been cruel only to humans—animals have also fallen victim to our beauty trends. Okay, so plastic/aluminum/glass-based glitter may have replaced shiny fish scale bits in adding sparkle to your eye shadow or lip gloss. And you won't find whale blubber in lipstick anymore. But you're still tinting your kisser with

> Lash-extending mascaras even contain polluting plastics like POLYURETHANE *(think floor varnish) and polyethylene (used in plastic bags).*

animal fats. Petroleum-based waxes, oils, and chemicals, as well as coal tar dyes and a host of carcinogens, are included in just about everything in your makeup kit. Lash-extending mascaras even contain polluting plastics like polyurethane (think floor varnish) and polyethylene (used in plastic bags). In addition, a whole slew of beauty enhancers (including pressed powders, mascaras, eye shadow, and antiaging creams) contain PTFE (a.k.a. Teflon), whose cancer-linked building block, PFOA, bioaccumulates in our tissues. It makes you wonder if the price of beauty is getting too high (and I don't mean the $60 price tag on that wrinkle cream).

Makeup Solutions: No one's asking you to put down your makeup brush and go bare. And luckily, going green doesn't mean giving up on good eye shadow. There are tons of trendy to classic shades made with certified organic cornstarch and natural mineral pigments on health store shelves these days. Lip shimmers, mascaras, and blush with certified organic ingredients are also available. For top-of-the-line foundation, lipstick, gloss, and mascara you'll want to check out **Dr. Hauschka**, **Suki**, **Sante**, and **Lavera**. (Lavera does contain talc, but the company insists it's totally asbestos-free.) The **Miessence** line of eye shadows, foundations, blushes, and cosmetics is also very clean, but you have to order it online (one option is **myorganicfamily.com**). **PeaceKeeper Cause-Metics**' line of lip glosses, lip sticks, and nail paints is pretty cool because all of the after-tax profits go to women's health and human rights issues. **Gabriel Cosmetics**' Zuzu line isn't considered quite as pure, but it is vegan-friendly. Ecco Bella still uses parabens in its foundations and mascaras.

Don't assume that all mineral makeup companies are as natural as they say they are. Check to make sure they don't contain parabens, irritating bismuth oxychloride, potentially dangerous nano particles, or fillers like talc. **Miessence** carries nano-free mineral blushes and powders, sans titanium dioxide even (**myorganicfamily.com**). **Earth's Beauty** also makes good nano- and cruelty-free mineral face powders and eye shadows with a base of organic/wild-crafted arrowroot powder (**earthsbeauty.com**).

By the way, **Organic Essentials** makes organic cotton balls, cosmetic rounds, and swabs to help you primp without pesticide-heavy cotton. Now go powder your nose in peace.

NAILS

Maybe it's the potent fumes that fill the room when you open a bottle or the harsh chemicals you need to remove it, but you can kind of guess that nail polish is one of the most toxic beauty products around. That smell comes from polluting VOCs like carcinogenic formaldehyde and the neurotoxin toluene. Inhaling a lot of this stuff can damage your kidneys, brain, and liver, and doing so day after day has made countless nail salon workers

Inhaling a lot of nail polish fumes can DAMAGE your kidneys, brain, and liver.

across the country seriously ill (then there are the sweatshop conditions many work in to get you an $8 manicure). Plus, most nail polish is made with the plastic softener dibutyl phthalate, a hormone disrupter that's been found in human blood and body tissues and is known to cause birth defects in animals.

As you might imagine, mainstream nail polish removers aren't much better than the polishes themselves. Liver, kidney, and neural damage can also result from long-term exposure to the acetone in your nail polish remover. Companies have tried to soften the image of harsh-smelling removers by marketing the presence of natural ingredients like vitamin E and aloe vera, but don't be fooled: there ain't nothin' natural about it.

The alternatives aren't always much better. Back in the mid '90s, a warning was issued that some nonacetone nail polish contained poisonous methanol, which is deadly to fish, birds, and wildlife. Check labels to make sure your acetone-free remover doesn't contain methanol.

Nail Polish Solutions: **No-Miss**, **Sante**, **Peacekeeper Cause-Metics**, and **Suncoat** are common health store nail polish brands that are free of the most contentious chems. Although that doesn't mean they're entirely natural, they do get their pigment from earthy minerals. FYI: more and more mainstream brands like **Revlon**, are also formaldehyde-, toluene-, and dibutyl phthalate–free now, but read the fine print to be sure.

For removers, **No-Miss Almost Natural Polish Remover** uses a fruit acid solvent, a lichen-derived solvent, water, and natural vanilla. **Suncoat**'s remover is 100% soy- and corn-based (though the stuff gives me a whopping headache). If you've used a Suncoat polish, you

MEANINGLESS TERMS

- **Hypoallergenic/Allergy-Tested/Dermatologist-Tested:** You'll find these labels all over beauty care products, and you probably assume they mean the product shouldn't irritate your eyes, skin, or whatnot. Somehow it must be purer—more natural even. Trouble is, these terms are fairly meaningless because they're not government regulated. Same goes for "fragrance-free" (ever notice how drugstore products labeled "fragrance-free" still smell perfumy—just not as strong as the next bottle over?). In fact, the FDA says there's no such thing as a nonallergenic cosmetic, since virtually any product can cause a reaction in someone somewhere.

- **Against Animal Testing:** This label became controversial when it was discovered that some companies just farm the testing out to outside labs, rather than testing the product on bunnies and mice themselves. Same goes for the use of "cruelty-free" or "not tested on animals." Sometimes the label should really say, "not currently tested on animals, since the ingredients were already tested on them 5 years ago." Of course, we prefer that to "still shoving chemicals in animals' eyes and making them sick to find out the lethal dose." Still, even though the labels are totally unregulated, what they say might be true—when you see one on an organic bottle of shampoo, for instance. Your best bet is to look for "no animal testing" logos certified by the Coalition for Consumer Information on Cosmetics (CCIC) or People for the Ethical Treatment of Animals (PETA). PETA's website offers a list of animal-testing policies and a cruelty-free pocket shopping guide (**peta.org**).

can remove it fairly easily by soaking your fingers in hot water for a few minutes, and then scratching the polish off with your nail.

SUNSCREEN

I have to admit I suck at the sunscreen thing. I take any shameless opportunity to connect with my Greek ancestry and get brown. But when I do slap some on, I make sure I get it right. The reigning kings of product research at the DC–based Environmental Working Group (EWG) investigated nearly 1000 name-brand sunscreens in 2008 and concluded that only one in five is both safe and effective.

Not only do a good number of these not block skin-damaging, wrinkle-inducing, cancer-causing UVA rays, but their chemical contents can be pretty frightening. Oxybenzone (found in over 400 products), for instance, is a weak hormone disrupter absorbed by the skin that's found in the urine of 95% of 6- to 8-year-old girls tested, as well as in waterways, soil, air, and gender-bending fish (that last part was confirmed by scientists at the University of California, Riverside). Wouldn't you know it, the list of freaky ingredients goes on: estrogenic octinoxate, the weak hormone disrupter homosalate, and the possible carcinogen enzulizole that can produce free radicals when exposed to sun.

Only **ONE IN FIVE** *sunscreens is both safe* **AND** *effective.*

Your safest bets are products whose active ingredients are **zinc oxide** or **titanium dioxide**. They're stable in the sun and provide good UVA and UVB protection. The problem is that zinc mines and titanium dioxide production are both pretty polluting. In addition,

HOW DO *YOUR* BEAUTY PRODUCTS RANK?

Punch in the name of any ingredient or personal-care product sitting in your bathroom and see how it scores. The Environmental Working Group did a hell of a job ranking over 40,000 personal-care products according to safety, breaking down the impact of each and every one. It's not a perfect system. For instance, it doesn't distinguish between regular lecithin and non-GMO, organic lecithin, and it says castor oil might be a developmental toxin but it ranks extremely low on the EWG toxicity scale. It's a little confusing that way, but the ranking does provide a strong idea of what's clean and green and what isn't (**ewg.org/reports/skindeep**).

sunscreens sometimes use nano versions of the ingredients (with freakishly minuscule particles). A good 15 studies found that nano-particle titanium dioxide doesn't penetrate unbroken skin. What about nano-particle sunscreens on damaged skin? No one's looked into that one, but I'd keep these away from cuts and scrapes.

Don't assume that health store sunscreens are always good picks. For one, many contain a PABA derivative called padimate O (a.k.a. PABA ester). It's safer than its older brother but can release free radicals and has been tied to DNA damage in some studies. Plus, some people are allergic to it.

Overall, the only natural products commonly available in health stores that make the cut for having the fewest risky ingredients and effectively blocking UVA and UVB rays are **Lavera Sun Block SPF 40 Neutral**, **Jason**'s **Sunbrellas SPF 30+ mineral-based sunblock**, **Badger SPF 30 Sunscreen**, **Soléo Organics All Natural Sunscreen**, **Mexitan sunscreen**, and all **California Baby** sunblocks. But don't take my word for it—search the database for yourself at **cosmeticsdatabase.com**. Or just fake that healthy glow with largely natural self-tanners and tinted moisturizers from **Dr. Hauschka**, **Lavera** or **Nature's Gate Organics**, available at any health store with a good beauty care aisle.

WHAT NOT TO WEAR

T alk about shopping 'til we drop. We're inundated with endless options for bundling our feet, draping our bodies, and adorning our earlobes. And the fact that we can now buy two pairs of pants, a few bangles, and hot boots for the price of a nice dinner makes us want to snag up even more of the stuff. I'm not saying I don't love discount pricing (or scoring a killer pair of jeans), but sale tags tell only half the story. The full cost of each item is paid every day by the planet and workers picking pesticide-laden cotton, digging for blood gems, and stitching up toxic shoes. But going naked isn't really going to help the situation (especially if it gets you arrested!). So let's find you some earth-friendly gear that rocks your socks off.

CLOTHING

Few of us question what we wrap around our bodies, unless the fit is off or the colors clash. It's just fabric, right? How much harm can a tank top do? You'd be surprised at the ecological implications of a single singlet, as those crazy Brits like to call them. Green fashionistas take note: from our pants to our underpants, our closets are stocked with environmental woes.

Cotton: Hard to believe, but the fabric industry is one of the most polluting on the planet. Cotton soaks up 10% of the world's pesticides and 25% of its insecticides, many of which

> ## MAD CLOTHING SCIENTISTS
>
> In the category of "what are those scientists on, anyway?" researchers are tinkering with genetic modification of bacteria to bring us clothing complete with sweat-digesting microbes. Nasty, really. But that's not all: others have developed sports gear that secretes vitamins and jeans that release anticellulite cream into your thighs as you wear them. It's enough to make that polyester shirt your dad wore in the '70s look natural.

are carcinogens and extremely toxic, causing major water pollution and making workers and wildlife sick. In fact, conventional cotton-farming methods require a third of a pound of chemicals to make one regular old T-shirt. Multiply that by what's in your closet (and drawers) and, presto, you're a major pesticide purchaser.

Genetically modified cotton is being touted as a solution, especially as high-tech crops such as Bt cotton are altered to produce naturally occurring insecticides. This approach might cut pesticide use at first. But one study revealed that Chinese users of the crop are finding that after several years, outbreaks of other bugs get so bad that farmers end up using

Conventional cotton-farming methods require a third of a pound of CHEMICALS to make ONE REGULAR OLD T-SHIRT.

20 times more pesticides than ever before. Farmers are also struggling with how to prevent original cotton strains from interbreeding with genetically modified types when their seeds are blown around by the wind.

Pesticide use isn't the only problem associated with the cotton industry. Human rights abuses are far too common in the fields and the factories, and child labor riddles the industry. According to Human Rights Watch, in Egypt alone, over a million children pick leaf worm from cotton plants every summer. Seasonal child labor in cotton fields is actually sanctioned by the government there, but only for 6 hours a day—not 11 hours a day, 7 days a week, as is common.

Synthetics: I don't know how they did it, but some folks figured out that you can take oily black goo pumped out of the earth (namely, petroleum) and spin it into a whole new category of fibers. It all started with panty hose (nylon was invented by researchers at DuPont in the '30s as a substitute for silk) and snowballed from there. Now, countless barrels of oil go into weaving billions of synthetic garments a year. Who knew the hunt for oil was being waged to supply your wardrobe (well, at least in part)?

Sweatshops: So you're sifting through a clothing rack and find a cool top for the price of a movie ticket. Do you (a) scan for defects, (b) think about the fact that you have enough tops already, or (c) mutter "Score!" and run to the cash register. The truth is, few of us would pick option (d): worry about the poor worker who had to sew the cheap thing. But come on, why else do you think you're dishing out only $18 for that shirt?

Don't assume that a high price tag means you're home free. Even pricy stores have been caught using sweatshops. And sweatshop workers aren't just toiling long hours with little pay in abusive conditions; they're also often working with toxic dyes to get your jeans that perfect shade of indigo—dyes that end up being dumped in streams, rivers, and waterways.

How do you know if your clothes were made under abusive conditions? Hard to say. You'll never see a dress that says "made in a sweatshop." Even buying clothes labeled "made in the USA" is no guarantee that workers were paid the legal minimum wage (terrible illegal sweatshops have been found in New York City and LA). And there's no real international

GORE-TEX'S GORY TIES

Whether you're trekking through the Himalayas, throwing yourself down a ski hill, or just staying dry through rain, snow, or sleet, you're probably well acquainted with this revolutionary high-tech fabric. But Gore-Tex is basically Teflon (PTFE) with micropores in it. And Teflon is made with the extremely persistent (and likely carcinogenic) chemical PFOA, which now thoroughly contaminates our air, water, wildlife, and bloodstreams. W. L. Gore & Associates (the maker of Gore-Tex fabric) says its PTFE is so "stable" that your coat's membrane won't offgas or leach in landfills. In fact, it won't even decompose. (Whether you see that as a good thing is another matter.) Sealed into your coat, I'm guessing, the PTFEs are probably safer for you (and your canary) than those in a burned nonstick pan.

So, should you toss your Gore-Tex jacket or boots as quickly as you should your nonstick pan (see page 163 for more on cookware)? All the suspicious findings to date have revolved around food-based products (like PFOA-coated burger wrappers), so I'd wait on the coat front. In the meantime, at least make good use of your garment.

Take note: some of the high-performance alternatives out there might be almost as bad. Polyurethane resin, used to make comparable—though cheaper—jackets and shells, creates all kinds of hazardous by-products during production and carcinogenic dioxins when incinerated. Look for outerwear made of recycled polymers—Patagonia makes a bunch.

certification system in place, although you can look for companies that tell you they're sweatshop-free or fair-trade. Or search for stuff that was union-made, like **No Sweat** (**nosweatapparel.com**). **American Apparel** (**americanapparel.net**) doesn't run a union shop, but it used to market its clothing as sweatshop-free. For some strange reason, the company decided to stop using this as a selling point, but it does sew all of its gear and weave all of its fabrics at a relatively respected factory in LA.

Clothing Solutions: In the quest for eco-friendly fabrics, designers have started to experiment with pretty much everything on the planet, and many plants—soy, bamboo flax, for example—can be spun into gorgeous material. The cool thing is, you can now get the stretch and suppleness of some synthetics without relying on oil-drenched clothes.

With a growing array of earth-loving textiles at their disposal, it's no wonder higher-end designers are getting in on the scene. **Linda Loudermilk** is about as patchouli as a pair of Manolos, but she uses soy, organic cotton, and bamboo blends in her luxury eco line (**lindaloudermilk.com**). Hollywood starlets also turn to funk machine **Deborah Lindquist** for vintage pieces and killer clothes made with recycled fabrics (**deborahlindquist**

Designers as patchouli as a pair of Manolos are now using soy, ORGANIC COTTON, and bamboo fabrics.

.com). Even rock stars are getting in on the action—Bono and his wife promote an ecologically sourced, fairly made line called **Edun** ("nude" backward) (**edunonline.com**). And while designer jeans may tax your wallet, they don't have to tax the planet if you buy a pair of certified organic butt huggers from **Loomstate** (**loomstate.org**) or **Del Forte Denim** (available at **thegreenloop.com**). Del Forte will also take your old jeans to make its Rejeaneration Denim line. More mainstream brands, like **Levi Strauss**, **Guess**, **Mavi**, and **Seven**, are all cranking out a few organic blues too. Of course, that doesn't mean those jeans were processed without chemicals. However, Levi, for instance, insists that its **Capital E 501s** were made with plant-based dyes and minimal chemical finishing agents. (FYI: dark jeans, as a general rule, have fewer chemical processes done to them.)

At the end of the day, whether you're looking for sassy weekend wear (**twice-shy.com**), sophisticated work gear (**earthspeaks.com**), or sizzling lingerie (**enamore.co.uk**) it's good to know you can stock your closet with green and still look hot. For kick-ass selection of all the coolest eco brands, check out **Greenloop** (**thegreenloop.com**), **Coco's Shoppe** (**cocosshoppe.com**), **BTC Elements** (**btcelements.com**), and **Pangaya** (**pangaya.com**).

But let's get back to basics and break down your general fabric options (keeping in mind that most green designers use a few different types).

Organic Cotton: Of all the alternative fabrics, **organic cotton** is the one you're most likely to see in stores. Activewear maker **Patagonia** long ago ditched conventionally grown cotton altogether, in favor of the pesticide-free type (plus, they use recycled polyester and fleeces made of old plastic pop bottles). **Levi**, **Nike**, and **Gap** are all buying organic cotton and blending it into their lines so that anywhere from 1% to 3% of their jeans, tees, and sport bras are made with pesticide-free fibers. It's a small percentage, but it represents a hell of a lot of organic threads. Nike buys over 7 million pounds of the stuff a year, making it one of the largest retail users of organic cotton in the world. American Apparel offers racy thongs, tight tanks, and tees in its line of organics. Looking for something a little more original and a little less, oh, corporate? **Eco-Ganik** makes gorgeous ethereal dresses and breezy tops with this fabric, among others (ecoganik.com). **Under the Canopy** also stitches funky basics and more with pesticide-free cotton (underthecanopy.com).

Bamboo: You can't get more baby soft than a slinky shirt made of **bamboo**—kind of like a cross between jersey and cashmere. The source is the fast-growing bamboo plant, which is super sustainable to grow in plantations (as long as natural forests weren't cleared to make way for them), but processing the green, treelike stalks can be very chemical-intensive. Look for companies like **Jonäno** that source bamboo with third-party certification, such as ISO 9000 or Oeko-Tex (jonano.com). They're not perfect, but they make an effort to green their production.

FYI: bamboo clothing is said to be naturally antibacterial and very breathable, so a slinky bamboo tank will never stick to your body and trap unwelcome odors the way synthetics do. **Beau Soleil** (shopbeausoleil.com) uses the fabric to stitch a lovely line of dresses, and **HTnaturals** makes clingy bamboo-blended basics (htnaturals.com).

Organic Wool: **Organic wool** can be more expensive than conventional types, but it's worth it when you consider that the sheep haven't been dipped in toxic pesticides to kill off lice (who knew?), nor have they had a square of their flesh near the tail cut away to prevent infection—a painful and strangely common process called "mulesing." (Mulesing is practiced in Australia and New Zealand to prevent blowfly infestation, though Australia has committed to phasing it out by 2010—see vegsoc.org/info/sheep.html for more info and woolisbest.

com/animal_welfare/mulesing for the industry's explanation, and decide for yourself.) SmartWool sells wool activewear from mulesing-free sheep (smartwool.com).

Organic wool is fairly hard to find, but **Patagonia** uses the sustainable fabric in its sweaters and cardigans (patagonia.com). **Stewart+Brown** makes luxury sweaters and knitwear from free-range, mulesing-free Merino wool, as well as other green fibers (stewartbrown.com).

Hemp: The classic stoner alternative, even nonorganic **hemp** is much gentler on the earth than mainstream cotton. It naturally uses much less pesticide and herbicide, and it grows faster than cotton without stripping the soil as it grows. Plus, an acre of hemp absorbs five times more carbon dioxide than an acre of forest, so it could play a role in curbing global warming (not that we want to knock down forests to plant hemp, but you get the point). Industrial hemp contains no psychoactive THC (tetrahydrocannabinol)— the trippy ingredient in weed. However, harsh chems may still be used to process it into softer fibers, especially if it's made in China, the world's biggest hemp fabric producer. Look

An acre of hemp absorbs FIVE TIMES MORE carbon dioxide than an acre of forest.

for ecologically processed (preferably organic) European- or North American–made hemp. Hemp can be blended with silk to make a gorgeous material now being used for eco wedding gowns. **Rawganique.com** and **The Hempest** (hempest.com) are both super comprehensive online sources for organic hemp clothing for both sexes.

Linen, Lyocell, and Lots More: Did you know that those **linen** pants in your closet are made from flax? It's probably the original eco-friendly fiber.

Speaking of textiles woven from surprising sources, supersoft **lyocell** (a.k.a. Tencel) is largely made from Forest Stewardship Council–certified wood pulp cellulose processed with nontoxic dissolving agents (sort of like rayon, but greener). **ParkVogel** (parkvogel .com) has a lot of the stuff. SeaCell is basically lyocell with a touch of seaweed (**Lululemon**

Yes, down-filled jackets are snug and toasty in blizzards, but they come with a heavy animal welfare conundrum. Down is either purchased as a by-product of the meat industry (with which you may not want to be associated) or plucked from living birds, causing them serious distress. If you'd prefer to go synthetic in solidarity with the birdies, look for polyester-based polyfill or hypoallergenic Primaloft. If you need a good, warm technical coat, **Patagonia** has developed its own environmentally friendly polyester-based version of Gore-Tex, made with used soda bottles, unusable second-quality fabrics, and worn-out garments. (In fact, Patagonia claims that by making its fleeces from recycled sources, it saves one barrel of oil for every 150 garments.) Some of its base layers and fleece gear are even recyclable through the company's Common Threads Garment Recycling Program (check **patagonia.com** for details). A truly dope coat option is made by **Hemp HoodLamb**. It's a hooded all-element jacket that's half hemp, half organic cotton, with smooth vegan "lamb fur" lining and funky features including a cell phone pocket (**hoodlamb.com**).

Athletica has **SeaCell** yogawear, but it got in trouble for making pretty grand health claims about wearing the fabric). **Ingeo** is corn-based, but Cargill, its maker, can't promise that it's free of genetically engineered ingredients. Supersupple **soy fiber** is woven from soy food industry leftovers, so it's what we might call "postindustrial recycled" (making it greener than bamboo, in my books). **Ramie** is an ancient fabric made from a plant native to Asia.

Vintage/Reconstructed Vintage: Mirror, mirror, on the wall, who's the greenest of them all? Why, that would be every fashionista's favorite form of reusing and recycling— **vintage clothing**! It's amazing what you can find with a little patience and a dream—and nothing new needs to be grown, sewn, shipped, and trucked. Plus, it's also the cheapest way to wear planet-friendly threads. I recommend shopping in opposite seasons. For instance, search for winter coats in the summer, when everyone's purging their closets of anything related to cold weather and the stores haven't been picked over.

VINTAGE CLOTHING *is the cheapest way to wear planet-friendly threads.*

If secondhand shops aren't your thing, many indie designers are sewing brand new

MEN'S SUITS AND DRESS CLOTHES

Boys, need to dress up for work, or just like to dress to impress? Sure, a beige organic tee is pretty easy to find, but will you wear it to an interview or your cousin's wedding? Probably not. Get fine organic dress shirts from **Boll Organic** (bollorganic.com). Need a proper suit? You can buy 100% certified organic hemp dress slacks and matching suit jackets at **Rawganique.com**. Add an Oxford shirt in one of seven funky hues to the mix, wrap a hemp tie around your neck, and you're set! If you're looking for something with sharper lines, check out **Bagir's EcoGIR** suits made of either recycled soda bottles that don't need dry-cleaning or organic cotton (bagir.com). When it comes to formal events, rent. Otherwise, look into getting some stylee vintage options tailored to your body.

dresses out of old raincoats and making funky patchwork sweaters with remnants of cardigans past. Ask for reconstructed vintage fashions at smaller boutique stores across the country, like AuH$_2$O (auh2odesigns.com); or hunt down stores that sell brands carried across the continent, like **Preloved** (preloved.ca) and **Deborah Lindquist**.

The piecemeal magic doesn't stop at clothing: many designers, such as **Ecoist**, are using old ad banners, newspapers, and candy wrappers to make funky bags, belts, and clutches (ecoist.com). Ask around at local boutiques or check out the accessories offered by Greenloop (thegreenloop.com).

Sew Your Own: Walk into any fabric store to ask for organic textiles and you'll probably be told that all cotton is natural. Sure, it technically comes from the earth, but is it pesticide-free? Fat chance. Manufacturers also tend to use all kinds of nasty dyes and potent chemicals to process the materials, including adding a wrinkle-resistant formaldehyde finish.

NearSea Naturals likely has the biggest and most inspiring collection of organic cotton prints, woven blends, wools, and knits by the yard (nearseanaturals.com). The company even sells organic thread, batting, and a really cool collection of buttons made of stuff like nuts and fallen antlers. **Organic Cotton Plus** is another source for organic fabrics (organiccottonplus.com). Look for bamboo jersey, fleece, and terry cloth by the yard, as well as bamboo yarns at the **Bamboo Fabric Store** (bamboofabricstore.com). And for one-of-a-kind vegan peace silk (you know, silk that moths weren't boiled alive to make), check out **Aurora Silk** (aurorasilk.com).

Fair Trade: Feeling guilty about that $18 shirt? Buying clothing that's fairly traded is one of the only ways to know for sure that the imported sweater you're wearing wasn't made in a sweatshop. The term "fair trade" applies only to goods purchased in the developing world and tells you they were sewn by worker co-ops or artisan groups that are paid a decent income, rather than starvation wages. Fair-trade producers are also supposed to avoid using toxic dyes and unsustainable resources that would end up damaging local ecosystems and the workers that live and breathe in them.

> *Buying clothing that's FAIRLY TRADED is one of the ONLY WAYS to know for sure that the IMPORTED SWEATER you're wearing wasn't made in a sweatshop.*

Most of the fair-trade stuff you find in local fair-trade shops, like **Ten Thousand Villages,** or from online sources such as **Global Mamas** (globalmamas.org) is pretty earthy (think large, bright floral prints and loose clothing). But the fashionistas are moving in. **Fair Indigo** is the first mainstream US-based fair-trade apparel line for men and women (fairindigo.com). Londoners are hugely into fairly traded fashions and have dozens of funky fair-trade clothing boutiques like **People Tree** (peopletree.co.uk). Luckily, Bono's eco-conscious Edun line is available at dozens of shops across the States. **Mercado Global** (**mercadoglobal.org**) offers fairly made scarves, wraps, and jewelry.

SHOES

Deciding what footwear is ecologically, socially, and politically correct is enough to make any eco-conscious consumer sweat. And with good reason. Even "all-natural" cotton canvas sneakers and sandals aren't so soft on nature when you consider that cotton accounts for some of the heaviest use of chemical insecticides on the planet. Plus, your rubber soles tend to be made from petroleum. Short of going barefoot, there are ways to put a little heart back into your soles. Just know that I can't promise that every company listed here is sweatshop-free—even workers' rights activists refuse to make those kinds of guarantees. So we'll just stick to what we know for sure: the ecological footprint of your shoes.

Toxic Manufacturing: In the shoemaking biz, sweatshops and harsh chemical use go hand in hand. In fact, the use of toxic chems in shoe factories has been decried in labor rights campaigns for the last decade or so. Part of what has historically made the factories so unbearable for workers is the use of adhesives containing nasty chemicals like toluene (the smog-inducing and neurotoxic oil- and coal-refining by-product). Public pressure got major sportswear giants to switch to toluene-free, low-VOC (volatile organic compound), water-based glues or solvents. But the rest of the shoe biz is still gluing your soles with the stuff, and it's contributing to higher cancer rates among shoe workers. Contact your favorite shoe companies to ask whether they have standards for using water-based glues. If they don't, tell them they should.

Tanneries were behind one of the WORST CASES of GROUNDWATER POLLUTION in India's history.

Leather: Leather may be the most popular material to wrap around our feet, but a hell of a lot of chemicals go into keeping those hides from decomposing on your toes. All sorts of nasty heavy metals are used in the tanning of leather. In fact, tanneries were behind one of the worst cases of groundwater pollution in India's history, in which alarming levels of arsenic, mercury, lead, and hexavalent chromium (the noxious chemical made famous in the movie *Erin Brockovich*) were found swimming in local water supplies. More and more leather makers are now using chrome-free processes, but that doesn't make them eco saviors.

Of course, the fact that leather producers tend to get their hides from the meat industry could be either a plus or a minus for you. Some say, "Well, at least the animal wasn't killed for this sexy suede boot alone; the leather would just go to waste otherwise." But others point to the horrors of meat-processing plants and the ecological burden of raising animals for dinner, and say they don't want anything to do with it on their feet. Especially since the meat biz makes a pretty penny selling these hides.

Fake Leather: Bad news, kids: just because your shoes are made without real animal hides doesn't mean you're in the clear. Sure, vegans love this imitation material, but most faux-leather footwear is made of what environmentalists consider the most noxious of plastics, PVC (vinyl). Just making the stuff creates vast quantities of chlorine-rich hazardous waste, as well as some of the most dangerous carcinogens in the world. Plus, vinyl is softened with hormone-disrupting phthalates that offgas into the air throughout their life. Jeez, who knew plastic could almost make leather look good? The last few years have seen a rise in the use of PU (that's polyurethane to you, mister) as a replacement for PVC in the faux-leather biz. Making this stuff is far from eco, but it's still considered moderately greener than PVC.

Running Shoes: When shopping for running shoes, it's impossible not to come toe to toe with the big brands on the market. You'll be happy to know that **Adidas**, **Asics**, **New Balance**, **Puma**, **Reebok**, and **Nike** have all started eliminating PVC and smoggy VOCs. Adidas and Puma gear, for instance, is nearly PVC-free. Adidas and Reebok are experimenting with using recycled rubber soles, and Nike is using what it calls "an environmentally preferred rubber" that reduces toxins by 96%. Looking to take the beef out of your bounce? New Balance (the celebrity-free "endorsed by no one" sneaker maker) manufactures many leather-free runners and walking shoes that are also free of PVC. Just know that the company doesn't guarantee that the glues are vegetarian.

Eco Sneakers: If you'd rather ditch big brands altogether, why not go for the most anticorporate street shoe in town? After years of biting attacks on mainstream shoe companies, big-biz-bashing **Adbusters** is now selling its own sneaks, called Blackspots (**adbusters.org**). The Converse-style union-made shoes are made of organic hemp, with a 70% biodegradable toe cap. Adbusters also makes a vegetarian Blackspot Unswoosher boot with recycled tire soles. **Converse** itself has revived its hemp sneaks (**converse.com**). In 2007, **Simple Shoes** developed a line of sneakers called ecoSNEAKS made with recycled car treads, recycled plastic bottle laces, hemp, certified organic cotton, and eco-certified leather (**simpleshoes.com**). Outdoorsy types should check out **Patagonia**'s sturdy hiking boots, as well as casual footwear made with Eco-Step outsoles (which are 30% recycled rubber), hemp laces, and 70% recycled-cork foot beds.

Earth-Friendly Footwear: All you fashionistas might be moaning at the prospect of wearing hemp on your feet, but relax, there *are* some über-cool footwear options for the green at heart. **Terra Plana** makes some hype toewear with vegetable-dyed leather and natural rubber soles (**terraplana.com**). Spain-based **El Naturalista** has equally funky collections for men and women, made with the same eco credibility (**elnaturalista .com**) that **Think!** has (**thinkshoesusa.com**).

> **H**emp-averse fashionistas take note: there ARE some ÜBER-COOL *footwear options for the green at heart.*

Wanna play Imelda Marcos without buying 5,000 pairs of shoes? **Mohop** makes sexy, sustainably sourced wooden sandals that come with five sets of adjustable ribbons that let you deck your foot out in an infinite number of styles (**mohop.com**).

If the thought of leather makes you gag and you're down with scoring stylee men's and women's dress shoes made of polyurethane, head to **MooShoes** (**mooshoes.com**). This adorable New York–based shop sells everything from hot high heels to classy guy gear and claims to get 70% of its stuff from unionized European factories. Italy's **Charmoné** makes sexy, sweatshop-free, vegan, PVC-free dress shoes and sandals for women with a mix of organic cotton, microsuede, recycled wood, and polyurethane (**charmone.com**). Actress Natalie Portman designed a vegan line of pumps, ballet slippers, and strappy heels for **Té Casan**, where all the proceeds go to the Nature Conservancy (**tecasan.com**).

Rather avoid plastic and animals altogether? One of the top skater shoe manufacturers, **Simple**, has exited the half-pipe zone to crank out loafers, sandals, and boots made with cool

> ## ONE, TWO, RECYCLE MY SHOE
>
> Though the recycling bin might not take your old shoes, secondhand shops do. Or you can send stinky sneaks (all brands accepted) to Nike's Reuse-A-Shoe program. They grind 'em up and turn them into basketball and tennis courts, as well as track and playground surfaces (**nikeorganics.com**).

natural stuff such as jute, wool, cork, bamboo, and natural latex. **Ecolution** has a line of basic organic hemp shoes, sandals, slippers, lace-up boots, and even kids' stuff (**ecolution.com**). Good old **Birkenstock** also makes some veggie sandals and clogs (**birkenstock.com**). And leather or not, all Birks are made with leftover cork from the wine industry, natural latex, and solvent-free glues, and they're fully repairable and resoleable. No wonder hippies love them!

For top-notch comfort and a little (okay, a lot) more money, nonvegans might consider slipping into **Mephisto** walking shoes (**mephistoshoes.com**). They're all about using vegetable dyes, toxin-free glues, natural rubber, and no plastics. And since the name sounds kind of green, I checked out **Ecco**, another line of extra-comfy shoes and boots (**ecco.com**). Turns out they, too, use vegetable dyes and a water-based finish and are Freon-free, though their soles and insole foam are synthetic.

Reconstructed Footwear: And now for something completely recycled: flip-flops made with used bicycle tire uppers, chipped-tire foot beds, and natural recycled hemp. Made by **Splaff Flopps**, the product is 100% waste-free and reused (**splaff.com**). In the kookier category, conscientious footwear designer **Terra Plana** has taken it up a notch, greenwise, with its Worn Again sneaks. These babies incorporate leather salvaged from old cars, old coffee bags, unwanted jeans, and surplus military jackets (**terraplana.com**). Brazil-based **Yellow Port** also makes kick-ass sneakers, saucy sandals, and platform boots with recycled canvas and tire foot beds (**yellowport.com.br**).

JEWELRY

I admit it. I have a jewelry fetish. I get weak when I see a good bangle or an oversized ring. But whether you're buying beads or browsing through Tiffany's, picking out the right ring or bracelet is not just about personal fashion when landscapes, communities, and even animal populations around the globe have been devastated to get them to you. Downer, I know, but it's time to face the dark side of bling.

Diamonds: Sorry ladies, Marilyn Monroe was lying: diamonds aren't a girl's best friend, but their environmental impacts *are* forever. Open-pit mining involves blasting a large area, stripping it of vegetation and trees, and leaving the land severely degraded. On average, a whopping 250 tons of ore has to be dug up and processed to carve up a single carat. And after all that digging, only 20% of the raw gems are considered good enough to wear! One in five diamonds is carved out of a riverbed (they're known as alluvial diamonds), and not surprisingly, vacuuming a river bottom tends to destroy its ecosystem. Another chunk is mined from the ocean floor.

Thanks to tree-hugging celebrity Leonardo DiCaprio, nearly everyone's heard the term "blood diamond" by now (if not, rent the 2006 movie by that name). Let's just say it ain't a reference to a new ruby-hued version of the stone, but rather a

On average, a whopping 250 TONS of ore has to be dug up and processed to carve up a SINGLE CARAT.

nod to the fact that part of the gem trade is run by gun-toting rebels financing vicious armed conflicts. It's the kind of scenario you can pretty much be guaranteed offers zero protection for the environment or for the poor people who have been caught in the crossfire over the years in places like Angola, Sierra Leone, Liberia, and, most recently, the Ivory Coast. The industry says only a small percentage of diamonds come from such countries, but Amnesty International estimated that, at its worst, an estimated 10% of the world's rough diamonds have been tied to groups engaged in all sorts of human rights abuses, from rape to child soldiering, as well as the forced relocation of millions.

Yes, certification schemes now say they can document the chain of custody between producers and you. In fact, the Kimberley Process, developed by industry and nongovernmental organizations (NGOs) in the last few years, is supposed to ensure that all diamonds that enter or exit the US and over 40 other countries are certified. But such certification tells you only that your diamond is conflict-free. The mine could still be ecologically damaging, pay its workers next to nothing, and employ children (70% of diamonds by weight are polished in India, often under appalling conditions, and at least 20,000 workers are children—although that might improve a little now that India is cracking down on child labor). Plus, Kimberley certificates aren't always obtained on the up-and-up. In fact, one group (Partnership Africa Canada) says that almost a quarter of Brazil's diamond exports in 2004 were shipped out on forged papers. Activists are gunning for a fair-trade diamond certification program so that you can know whether your rock came from a worker-run co-op.

Other Gems: Diamonds aren't the only friend you should keep an eye on. All gems have equally sordid pasts and are often traded in the same circles that run guns and drugs. Myanmar (a.k.a. Burma) supplies the world with 95% of its beautiful bloodred rubies, as well as jade, sapphire, and pearl, but you can bet these gems have a different sort of blood on them. Many countries, including the US, have banned or boycotted all Burmese goods, saying that buying them only validates and funds a brutal military dictatorship. But gem lovers *can* score fairly traded stones. **Columbia Gem House** is a fair-trade company that does its own mining, cutting, and marketing. Check **fairtradegems.com** to find American retailers that sell online.

ETHICAL DIAMONDS?

To avoid the whole ethical mess associated with diamonds from abroad, more and more conscientious gem shoppers are asking for Canadian diamonds. First the bright side: northern Canadian diamonds are blood-free, and tougher environmental regulations are in place, which is why you're seeing them marketed everywhere as the feel-good gem. But that's where the sheen ends. MiningWatch Canada published a report detailing the lake draining, wildlife disruption, and undermining of native peoples that happens when you dig up environmentally fragile ecosystems without sufficient government protection. For more dirt, check out the article "There Are No Clean Diamonds: What You Need to Know About Canadian Diamonds" at **miningwatch.ca**. If you're set on getting a new diamond, at least **Brilliant Earth** uses recycled gold and platinum for its Canadian gems and fair-trade diamonds mined by **Pride Diamonds** in Sierra Leone (the company also offers true-blue Australian sapphires). **Leber**'s **Earthwise collection** follows similar standards (**leberjeweler.com**).

Silver and Gold: What about all the shiny metals that fill our jewelry boxes? Did you know it takes 20 tons of waste rock and toxic tailings to produce 1 ounce of gold? Or that the mercury and cyanide used to separate gold and copper from rock have a nasty habit of ending up in groundwater, spurring the *New York Times* to equate some gold mines with nuclear waste dumps? The good news is that dozens of jewelry retailers have signed on to Oxfam and Earthworks' "Golden Rules," calling for mining reforms that protect communities and the environment from destructive practices (**nodirtygold.org**).

Even basic silver-mining communities are tarnished by groundwater pollution and toxic-waste dumping, as a large portion of mines are. And that cheap silver jewelry you find at street vendors and in many trendy shops could contain enough lead to poison a child— and they have been known to do just that.

In 2008 a swirl of controversy erupted around the most elite of metals, platinum. Nearly 90% of the world's platinum reserves are in southern Africa, where the BBC reports that huge open-pit mines are tearing up the land, thousands of villagers are being pushed off ancestral grounds, and more are being put at risk thanks to toxic mining runoff in drinking water. Not so shiny after all.

Animals: Jewelry made from animals should always get your back up. Although ivory is outlawed here, it is still smuggled into the US in record numbers. And if it isn't sliced from endangered elephants (100,000 elephants a year were slaughtered in Africa by poachers during the 1980s until bans came into effect), it's cut from hippos and walruses. You should also avoid trendy tortoiseshell, coral, conch, and peacock feather trinkets. Bones are another bad idea (though they are often meat industry leftovers).

Jewelry Solutions: Don't tear your pearls out! There are plenty of ways to adorn yourself in good conscience, especially if you're willing to shop online. **GreenKarat** says nuh-uh to "ethical" stones from Canada, offers a good selection of wedding bands made

FAKE IT, BABY:
LAB-GROWN DIAMONDS

All the most earth-conscious celebs are wearing fakes to avoid the human rights and environmental implications of traditional jewels. Why not join them and get your bling from lab-grown or cultured diamonds? These man-made high-pressure, high-heat creations are started from a real diamond "seed" and end up being optically and physically the same as the gems we so aggressively extract from nature. **Gemesis** cultured diamonds come in J-Lo colors like yellow and pink, and best of all, they're completely sustainable (**gemesis.com** or **diamondscultured. com**). Prefer a classic look? There are other types of high-quality synthetic diamonds besides the cultured kind. Moissanite stones will even cut glass, but it's hard to get a pure white one if you're picky. **Diamond Nexus** stones, said to be excellent diamond doppelgängers, also cut glass, and they're super cheap (**diamondnexuslabs.com**).

with recycled gold and platinum, and will custom-make rings with lab-grown diamonds, fair-trade or recycled stones, petrified wood, or even the lovely pebble you kept from the park where you first made out. Plus, you can send them a broken gold chain and they'll melt it down into a new ring! The company also ensures that the gold is refined at zero-discharge refineries. You can even offset the carbon emissions of your purchase (**greenkarat.com**).

Eco-Artware.com uses a selection of reused, recycled, and natural materials to make its Scrabble earrings and pottery shard necklaces. **Lucina Jewelry** (**lucinajewelry .com**), **Mercado Global** (**mercadoglobal.com**), **Wedge Worldwide** (**wedgeworldwide .coop**), **Ten Thousand Villages** (**tenthousandvillages.com**), and **Global Exchange** (**gxonlinestore .org**) are good online sources for

If you want to go TOTALLY FOOTPRINT-FREE, *antique markets and shops are the ultimate* JEWELRY RECYCLING CENTER.

fair-trade jewelry. **Moonrise Jewelry**'s focus is especially cool: not only does its work/training program promote the empowerment of women of all backgrounds, but its Premier Eco-Jewelry collection is made with fair-trade gems, ecologically mined materials, and recycled metals (**moonrisejewelry.com**).

Vintage: If you want to go totally footprint-free (no mining, no re-refining—just the two feet it takes for you to walk into the stores), antique markets and shops are the ultimate jewelry recycling centers, filled with loads of one-of-a-kind rings, bracelets, and brooches. Anyone wanting to score an engagement ring without contributing directly to the dirty mining biz should look here. Also keep an eye out for jewelry auctions in your town. You can score some incredible deals.

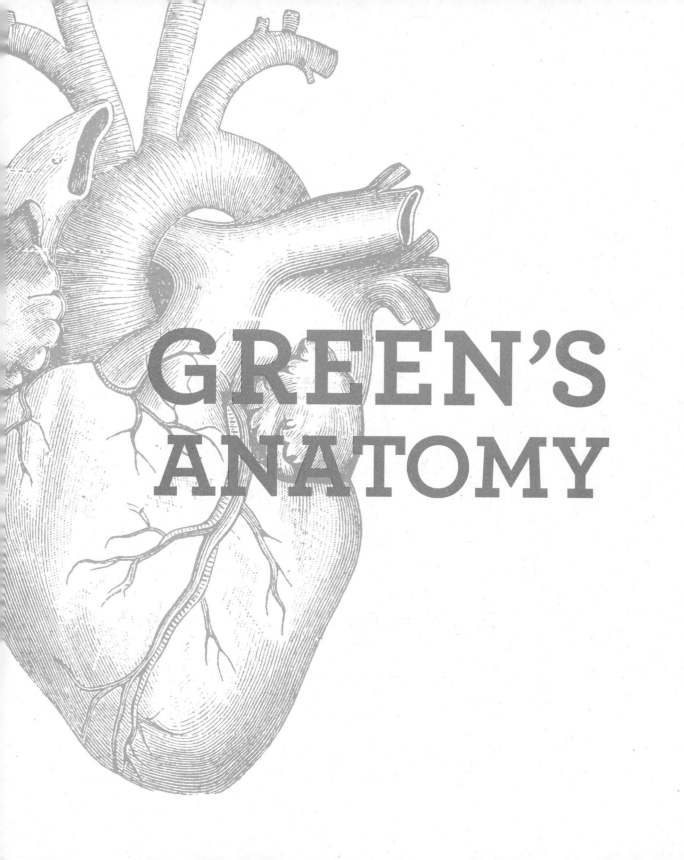

'll give you five bucks if you can think of a cliché that's less comforting in trying times than "at least you have your health." Still, the fear of losing that healthy status is a powerful force in North American society. Look at our obsession with popping pills, dieting, and weird ab machine infomercials (okay, so I did order a Pilates machine at 4:00 AM once). Just add up all the things you do in a day that have a potential impact, good or bad, on your body's well-being: swallowing supplements, taking a painkiller, smoking . . . Now, stop your navel gazing and spend a moment or two learning about what all that does to the planet.

PHARMACEUTICALS

You might pop a few echinacea pills after a co-worker sneezes on your keyboard, but when full-blown infection or illness hits, most of us run to our doctors for the most hard-core prescription we can get our hands on. Americans spend over $286 billion on prescription drugs a year, according to IMS Health (a pharmaceutical market research company), and that doesn't even include all the pills we buy over the counter. These powerful synthetic compounds are aggressively tested on animals and, alarmingly, the world's poorest (pick up Sonia Shah's startling book *The Body Hunters: Testing New Drugs on the World's Poorest Patients*). And though you might be on the lookout for weird side effects, few of us are tuned in to just what happens once those meds leave our bodies. Not to mention all the pollution involved in making the damn things in the first place. (Warning: you might need some antinausea tablets once you find out.)

Pharmaceutical Pollution: It churns out billions of synthetic pills a year, so it's no surprise that Big Pharma also pumps out vast amounts of pollutants. In 1990, the pharmaceutical industry released 266 million gallons of wastewater daily, according to Environmental Protection Agency (EPA) reports (did I mention that was each and every day?). Sure, the industry has taken on waste reduction and pollution prevention practices like any other, but harmful emissions continue to be pumped out of stacks. Many of the chemical solvents released can't be fully treated by wastewater treatment plants. Big Pharma manufacturers also emit plenty of hazardous particles into the atmosphere, including cyanide, smoggy volatile organic compounds (VOCs), and the neurotoxin toluene. In fact, in 2008 Pfizer forked out $975,000 worth of fines after violating the Clean Air Act. The pharmaceutical industry is now starting to open up to green (a.k.a. sustainable) chemistry, but the shift can't happen soon enough.

Sewage and Drinking Water: Swallow a pill, feel better. End of story, right? Wrong. Anywhere from 50% to 90% of the active ingredients found in our medications aren't broken down by our bodies. To put it bluntly, we basically pee and poop them out. Luckily, sewage treatment plants degrade most drug residues, but some—like antiseizure drugs, mood stabilizers, and more—basically pass through the sewage treatment process unscathed. Drug residues then end up flowing into our rivers, lakes, and oceans, and, yup, pouring back out of our taps. Plus, plenty of raw, untreated sewage gets into waterways, thanks to storm sewage overflows (the same overflows that toss condoms and tampons up on beaches), leaks, septic tank failures, and straight-piping. According

An investigation of drinking water in 24 major US towns turned up traces of EPILEPSY DRUGS, PAINKILLERS, AND PROZAC, to name just a few.

to an EPA report called "Green Pharmacy," it isn't known whether sewage treatment plants could be "cost-effectively modified" to eliminate or even reduce the problem.

So what *is* swimming in our water then? A 5-month long investigation of drinking water in 24 major US towns by the Associated Press turned up traces of epilepsy drugs,

THIS IS YOUR PLANET ON DRUGS

In the "damn, shouldn't we have been doing this all along?" category, European medical guidelines recommend that any new drug undergo long-term environmental toxicity testing to see how well it biodegrades, whether it's broken down by sewage treatment plants or disrupts the microorganisms that do all the dirty work in those plants, and just how it impacts fish, algae, and water fleas. But these new guidelines won't apply to drugs already on the market. For those, testing is happening out in the real world à la mass global experiment. Don't you just love being a guinea pig?

prescription and over-the-counter painkillers, Prozac, tranquilizers, and estrogen, to name just a few. Overall, roughly 100 pharmaceuticals have been found in the waters of the US and Europe.

Okay, so they tend to be in the parts per billion or trillion range (about a drop in an Olympic-size pool). How much impact can that have? So far, no pharmaceuticals originating from contaminated water have been discovered in humans, but that doesn't mean they won't be. And what about the poor fishies? If you've read up on the ABCs of eco-friendly sex (see page 63), you'll know that faint traces of birth control pills are feminizing fish out in the wild. Much of the Western world is gearing up to research all this, trying to figure out just what risks, if any, other drugs pose. In the meantime, the feds don't require any drug testing of drinking water and they've yet to set any safety limits. Gulp.

Proper Disposal: If expired or unused drugs are gathering dust in your medicine cabinet, do not—I repeat, do not—flush them. Health officials don't even want you to toss them in the trash. Medication can leach from landfills—a bad scene, especially when you consider how many meds, including nasal sprays, eye ointments, and hemorrhoid creams, contain traces of the known neurotoxin mercury. Instead, ask your pharmacy if they have a drug disposal program. (This is the one time where recycling is also a bad idea.) Your pharmacy makes sure they're disposed of in "an environmentally sound way." Your old meds are sent off to medical incinerators or chemical landfills fortified to take hazardous waste. Though burning and dumping them this way seems a little dodgy, it's certainly

> ## DO WE REALLY NEED SO MANY DRUGS?
>
> We've finally figured out that we're taking too many antibiotics. But we still run to our doctors in increasing numbers, asking for all kinds of meds, when we should be asking ourselves if we really need them. An ounce of prevention, people! Healthy eating and regular exercise could stop you from flushing a pound of cure down the toilet.

better than burning and dumping them in regular municipal facilities not designed to handle toxic waste. If your pharmacy can't help, call your municipality and ask if they have a drug take-back program. Many cities consider pharmaceuticals hazardous waste and ask that you drop them off at your local hazardous-waste depot.

NATURAL HEALTH REMEDIES

Back in the day before pink-coated painkillers and fizzy antacids, all our meds came straight from nature. Before Big Pharma started doctoring up synthetic formulas in sterilized labs, village doctors and tribal healers prescribed hundreds of plants from the wild to heal the worst of ailments. Of course, pharmaceutical companies know to look to nature too; otherwise, they'd never have found penicillin. Today, about 25% of all prescription drugs contain active ingredients that either originally came from plants or were designed to copy the effects of plants. Without a doubt, scientists are still picking over jungles for the next big drug. (Hey, you've seen Sean Connery in *Medicine Man*, right?) Given all that, I guess you could say it's only, um, natural (sorry, some puns are just unavoidable) that more of us are going back to our roots. Americans spend about $20 billion a year on herbal supplements. But just because something comes from the earth doesn't mean we extracted it in an earth-friendly way.

Collecting Wild Herbs: Lots of us down ginseng to liven our step, quicken our minds, and boost our immune systems. But the popular indigenous root is now scarce in North America, thanks to overharvesting. In fact, American ginseng is protected under CITES (the Convention on International Trade in Endangered Species of Wild Fauna and Flora), and in seven states you need a permit to harvest it. As you can imagine, policing forests for ginseng or other herb poachers can be a little difficult and is not, shall we say, a high priority. Lucky for poachers (who make five times more selling wild ginseng than the farmed kind), you're free and clear to pick the root if you spot it on private property.

Ginseng is far from alone on the list of missing herbs. Wild echinacea is endangered in the US, as is calming lady's slipper and the potent antiviral goldenseal. Sore throat soother licorice root has been depleted by about 60% in the wild.

You wouldn't know any of this by walking into a health store, where the term "wild-crafted" is not only common but revered as a sign the herb wasn't sprayed with pesticides and farmed on megaplantations. Indeed, according to the World Wildlife Fund's (WWF's) wildlife trade monitoring network, TRAFFIC, of the estimated 40,000 to 50,000 plants used by traditional and modern medicine around the world, the majority are snagged from the wild. Some herb companies insist that they practice ethical wild-crafting, but it's important to avoid buying any wild herb on the endangered or threatened list. For a full list of herbs at risk on US soil, as well as info on being part of the national Botanical Sanctuary Network, check out the United Plant Savers website (**unitedplantsavers.org**).

In contrast, some plants, such as yellow dock and Saint-John's-wort, are considered so widespread that you can pick to your heart's content and still be in the clear. FYI: megafarms growing medicinal herbs might take the heat off wild supplies, but in countries like China, herbs are pushing out food crops and big corporations are moving into what was once the territory of the local medical practitioner.

Endangered Wildlife: Where have all the wild things gone? The poaching of threatened and endangered animals has reached crisis proportions, in large part because of the rising popularity of traditional Chinese medicine (TCM), according to the WWF. Chinese medicine is also the number one threat to Asia's tiger, rhinoceros, and bear populations, even though these are supposedly protected. Poaching is so out of control in India, for instance, that not one Siberian tiger was left at the Sariska Tiger Reserve in 2005. We could laugh at the irony of it all if it weren't so bloody tragic.

And TCM-motivated hunting is in no way just an Asian problem. A lot of it happens right here in North America. Wild black bears are killed for their gallbladders and bile (in 2007, at least 30 were poached in the Lake Tahoe area of California alone), used in everything from hemorrhoid creams to hair

7 SOUND MOVES TO PROTECT YOUR HEALTH (AND THE PLANET'S)

Avoid toxic pesticides, as well as carcinogenic and hormone-disrupting chemicals, by buying organic food and natural personal-care products and cleaners.

Cut your smog emissions by making your home more energy-efficient. Every coal-fired watt you use makes it harder for you to breathe.

Clear your home of dodgy chemicals that build up in your tissues. Get rid of crumbling cushions (they're full of old-school toxic fire retardants; see page 182), toss your nonstick products (see page 163), and say no to chemical lawn pesticides (see page 254).

Reach for pharmaceutical drugs only when you really need them.

Boost your health with sustainable natural remedies that come from the earth.

Butt out. Cigarettes pollute you and the ecosystem.

Spend time in nature—it's actually good for you! It boosts serotonin levels, and just having trees outside hospital windows has been proven to speed recovery among the sick. Plus, it helps calm kids with ADHD (attention deficit/hyperactivity disorder).

tonics. Luckily, many American TCM practitioners won't prescribe such dodgy ingredients anymore, and the WWF is trying to promote the use of substitutes. But that doesn't mean you can't find any. Several products are still being imported illegally. Tell your TCM doc that you want to stay far away from anything suspicious.

Fish Oil: We're all talking about adding healthy oils to our diets, and popping fish pills seems to be one popular way to do so. The omega-3 fatty acids they contain are good for our hearts and our brains. But make sure your supplements are made with the smallest fish on the food chain—sardines, anchovies, herring, and the like—rather than cod or salmon. Why? Well, for one, they have lower levels

Make sure your supplements are made with the SMALLEST FISH on the food chain.

of heavy metals, mercury, and other pollutants. (FYI: ConsumerLab.com tested 41 fish oil brands and found none containing mercury or PCBs—the oils are supposedly distilled to filter out contaminants. Still, a British study found salmon and cod liver oil contaminated with flame retardants and pesticides. Make sure your brand of choice uses pharmaceutical-grade oil.) And most important for the fate of the seas, smaller fish are generally considered more sustainable than larger fish and get the thumbs-up from sustainable seafood guides like Monterey Bay Aquarium's Seafood Watch (**seafoodwatch.org**). American wild-caught sardines and Atlantic herring, for instance, are in the clear. Or better yet, skip the fish altogether and get your omega-3 from flaxseed oil or extra-rich chia seeds.

Natural Health Solutions: Ask your health store clerk about smaller local manufacturers with solid reputations. Their products may cost a little more, but the cheaper drugstore or big box brands often use lower-grade ingredients, artificial dyes, and hydrogenated oil fillers. **New Chapter** out of Vermont is considered a leader in eco sustainability and certified organic ingredients (**newchapter.com**). Also ask about food-sourced supplement made by the likes of **New Chapter**, **Botani Organics**, and **Source of Life**.

 *of the world's* VITAMIN C *comes from* LABS IN CHINA.

Source of Life, for instance, gives you vitamin C through camu berries and cherries instead of synthetic sources (80% of which come from labs in China).

Organic Herbs: Many herbalists recommend using organic herbs, so you can be sure your meds were harvested sustainably and without toxic inputs. Buying organic is thought to be especially important for your internal health if you're using tinctures or essential oils, since the herbs are so concentrated in these forms. Even if pesticides aren't showing up in your herbs, that doesn't mean they didn't have an impact on surrounding soil, waterways, and wildlife. As with food, it's a good idea to buy organic health supplements whenever possible, to make sure the planet stays as fit as you do. **Oregon's Wild Harvest** actually uses strictly certified organic herbs in all its herbal products, like silica made from organic horsetail and omega oils made with organic flaxseed (**oregonswildharvest.com**).

BUG REPELLENT

Can you hear that? That buzzing? That's the sound of mosquitoes making a beeline for your neck. You might as well call it the sound of summer because as the weather warms up, these bloodsucking creatures start looking to multiply, and the female can't lay her eggs without a little meal. That means you, and every exposed surface on your body, kiddo. But if you don't want to become a skeeter's breakfast, and West Nile phobia has got you nervous, what do you do?

DEET: As tempting as it is to douse yourself in a chemical that promises to confuse mosquitoes by biologically messing with their antennae so they can't find their target (namely, you), DEET is obviously not the greenest option. Have you seen what it can do to a pair of sunglasses? It's pretty potent stuff, and the US Agency for Toxic Substances and Disease Registry reports that, with daily use over several months (like, say, the length of the summer), a few people have developed shortness of breath, headaches, tremors, joint pain, and even seizures. Young kids are particularly at risk, and DEET should never be used on babies under 6 months. (For info on how much DEET kids can safely be exposed to, type in "toxfaqs DEET" at **atsdr.cdc.gov**.) DEET, by the way, is one of the top five contaminants found in US streams (there mostly as a result of being washed down shower drains and sent downstream from wastewater treatment plants), which isn't great news for aquatic life. It's also been found in low doses in Chicago's tap water.

Natural Repellents: Fear not, chemical-weary traveler, there are alternatives, and some of them do work. A much-touted study by the *New England Journal of Medicine* found that soy-based **Bite Blocker** rivaled DEET (**biteblocker.com**) in terms of effectiveness. *Consumer Reports* found **Repel's Lemon Eucalyptus spray** (**repel.com**) performed even better than DEET. According to the *New England Journal of Medicine* study, though, citronella products aren't all that effective and have to be reapplied as often as every 10 to 30 minutes. Seriously.

Bug Gadgets: Ultrasonic wristbands and devices are supposed to mimic bat sounds to keep bugs at bay, but mosquitoes don't seem the least bit bothered by them. Electric zappers are better at killing moths than insects that bite. Coils and candles work only if you're sitting right next to them and the wind is blowing your way. Traps that emit carbon dioxide and heat are growing in popularity, but some are said to be better than others. Pricy propane-run **Mosquito Magnet** traps (**mosquitomagnet.com**) are supposed to attract skeeters, sand flies, and blackflies by mimicking human exhalations, releasing a constant plume of carbon dioxide, octenol (a synthetic attractant), and heat into a vacuum trap. The company tells us that the amount of carbon dioxide emitted is minimal, equivalent to having a cow on your property. It's said to virtually eliminate the mosquito population in your yard within 3 to 6 weeks without harming non-bloodsuckers, and it's recommended by the US Army, the Centers for Disease Control and Prevention, and the Good Housekeeping Research Institute.

Bug Clothing: Campers who've suffered through northern blackfly and mosquito swarms have probably been tempted by the promise of insect-repelling clothes. Buzz Off Insect Shield makes gear for everyone from Tommy Hilfiger and L. L. Bean to lesser-known lines of baseball caps, fishing wear, and golf shirts. But while the company touts Buzz Off as a man-made version of chrysanthemum's naturally repelling properties, it's really just fabric embedded with permethrin. Too bad permethrin is really toxic to fish and tadpoles and can cause all sorts of physical reactions in humans, from nausea to asthma attacks, on top of being a suspected hormone disrupter and possible carcinogen. DC-based Beyond Pesticides says some of this stuff comes off on your skin, especially if you sweat.

The only anti-insect clothing I'd recommend is the old-fashioned bug shirt. These lightweight pullover hoodies with mesh over the face offer a personal refuge of sorts when you're in the deep woods. Think of it as the camper's burka. The **Original Bug Company** (**bugshirt.com**) offers shirts, pants, hoods, and something called gaiters (which are kind of like leg warmers, but aimed more at keeping your ankles bite-free than priming them for that *Flashdance* revival). Camping stores also tend to have ecological netting products for your outdoor pleasure.

TOBACCO

Among all the images of rotting gums and black, tumor-covered lungs, never once have you seen a pack of smokes with a warning about what cigarettes do to the earth. Perhaps that's because there's just too much to say.

Chemicals: Anyone who's read the side of a cigarette pack has seen the very partial list of chemicals and heavy metals lurking in these cancer sticks. Back in 1994, American cigarette manufacturers finally released a list of 599 additives they potentially toss into the tobacco mix for flavor enhancement. Some are as harmless as chocolate, but others (like the mosquito insecticide methoprene, which has been linked to frog deformities) are far more worrying. A few cigarette manufacturers say their sticks are additive-free, but don't fool yourself into thinking you're off the hook, folks. You're still sending a toxic cloud of up to 4,000 chemicals into the atmosphere when you light up—things like formaldehyde, benzene, and hydrogen cyanide, which are all air-polluting, smog-inducing VOCs. And in case you think your little ciggie won't make matters worse in a world saturated with chemicals, just multiply that smoke by the 45 million Americans who are also puffing.

Production: Meanwhile, back at the ranch, over 25 million pounds of pesticides are used on tobacco every year in the US alone, according to the US Geological Survey. But much of the production takes place in the developing world, where the protection of rivers and wildlife is about as high on the list of priorities as the risks to the workers who harvest it. Just drying the leaves out has led to serious deforestation in some parts of the planet. In southern Africa, about 500,000 acres of trees a year are chopped to fuel tobacco curing, according to *World Agriculture and the Environment*, by Jason Clay (put out by the WWF). In the '90s, tobacco curing and production were fingered as being responsible for nearly half of South Korea's deforestation.

> **Y**ou're sending a TOXIC CLOUD *of up to* 4,000 CHEMICALS *into the atmosphere when you light up.*

Litter: Finally, there are all those damn butts. With those 45 million American smokers tossing their filters onto sidewalks, streets, parks, and highways, we're talking a hell of a lot of litter. And they don't just disappear, people! Sure, cellulose acetate is a plastic that comes from wood pulp, so eventually it does break down, but it takes anywhere from 18 months to 12 full years to decompose. In the meantime, filters have been found in the stomachs of sick or deceased fish, birds, and other unsuspecting creatures that have mistaken them for food. Wherever they end up—whether beaches, parklands, or sewers—they inevitably leach out all the thousands of nasty chemicals they absorbed from your cigarette. So stop your illicit butting! Oh, and in case you needed more reasons to change your ways, dropped butts are responsible for a staggering 130,000 a year, according to the Center for Policy Alternatives. Cigarette-related fires kill up to 900 Americans a year and sear to a crisp thousands of acres of beautiful forest.

Herbal and Organic Cigarettes: What about herbal cigarettes, made of seemingly benign baking ingredients like cloves, basil, and cinnamon? What harm could they do? Turns out even these veggie sticks puff out plenty of tar and carbon monoxide (a greenhouse gas precursor that contributes to global warming). In fact, tests found that users of strawberry-flavored bidis (hand-rolled Indian cigarettes) exhaled even more carbon monoxide than those smoking regular brands. And just because these ciggies are herbal and sometimes come wrapped in pretty leaves instead of paper doesn't mean pesticides aren't used on their ingredients.

MENSTRUAL PRODUCTS

It's that time of the month and you're out of supplies. You run to the nearest pharmacy to stock up on whatever option has the widest wings, the driest weaving, and the biggest sale. And who can blame you? Most of what we know about what's on the shelves comes from cryptic TV ads in which girls release blue water from a vial once a month. And as much as we try to keep what happens on Aunt Flow's visits behind closed doors, we're creating a massive amount of waste that can't really be discreetly flushed down the toilet.

A woman uses about 16,800 sanitary pads or tampons in her lifetime.

Waste: A woman uses about 16,800 sanitary pads or tampons in her lifetime, according to a market research report by Packaged Facts. Multiply that by the 150 million women in the US (with 60 million or so of menstruation age at one time) and we're talking billions of pads and tampons a year in the US alone. That's a hell of a lot of landfill clogging, ladies! Even if you're a "light days" kind of girl and don't have long, heavy periods, you're still creating plenty of waste in your lifetime. And though companies tell us their tampon applicators are perfectly flushable, that doesn't mean sewer overflows won't wash 'em back up onto a shore or stream near you. (Horrifically, tampon applicators and other plastics have been found in the stomachs of birds like Hawaiian Laysan albatross chicks that had died in their nests.)

Production: Who knew so many materials go into keeping you dry and happy every month? (Wouldn't want that blue water to leak.) Superabsorbent rayon (often blended with pesticide-heavy cotton) forms the basis of most pads and tampons. Menstrual-product pushers are only too happy to tell you the stuff comes from trees. And yes, synthetic rayon is a wood pulp derivative, but it's not exactly natural. It's made extra absorbent in a fairly toxic chemical process. Companies do insist that they've ditched their old practice of bleaching the batting with chlorine gases, a process responsible for the carcinogenic and highly persistent by-product dioxin (which accumulates in fatty tissue). Instead, they say they use chlorine dioxide, oxygen, and/or hydrogen peroxide in a process called "elemental chlorine–free bleaching" to "significantly minimize the potential for dioxin formation." Tampax also says it tests its cotton fibers to ensure they don't contain detectable levels of pesticides, but though your private parts might be spared exposure, the cotton is still grown with toxic herbicides, fungicides, and the like, which ain't good for the planet.

And drugstore brands are chock-full of plastics: synthetic latex wings, polyethylene dry-weave layers in pads, and that "silky" coating on tampons. Not to mention all those damn applicators (bet you've never seen a little recycling symbol on those) and the nasty PVC wrapper that comes with pads.

Tampons and Pads: If you're going to buy drugstore tampons, cardboard applicators are better than plastic, and applicator-free types such as **O.B.** are another step up. But you really should be using tampons from **Natracare (natracare.com)** or **Organic Essentials** (**organicessentials.com**), made with 100% certified organic, non-chlorine-bleached cotton. They're free of synthetics and chemical additives, come with or without cardboard applicators, and work just as well as mainstream brands. These companies also make organic, chlorine-free pads and panty liners (with or without wings), as does **Seventh Generation** (**seventhgeneration.com**). Seventh Generation's pads and liners contain an absorbent gel derived from wheat but are not organic and do contain some plastic. Natracare, however, uses a biodegradable plant-based bioplastic in place of petroleum plastic as a barrier layer to keep the pads from leaking.

Recently, big sanitary-product brands have been pushing the idea of disposable wipes for gals on the rag. If you're keen on "freshening" your privates on the go, at least reach for an organic cotton wipe made with essential oils and healing calendula (**Natracare** makes some) instead of the chemical fragrances, petroleum-based ingredients such as propylene glycol, and even formaldehyde-releasing preservatives (namely, imidazolidinyl urea) in mainstream brands. A facecloth will do the same job without the landfill clogging.

Cloth Pads: If you're ready to take the plunge and go even greener, your next option is reusable cloth pads (which should last you about 5 years). Yes, it sounds a little icky, and it isn't for everyone, but if you can get past the minor psychological hurdle, give 'em a shot. **GladRags** (gladrags.com) and **Lunapads** (lunapads.com) make regular and unbleached organic cotton styles (FYI: dark colors stain less), as well as panty liners. Both offer styles with snap-on wings that stay on much better than the rest, which tend to slide off. Lunapads also do all-in-one padded organic "period panties," with or without a layer of nylon, in bikini, thong, or brief styles. They even offer ones with snap-on wings! **Many Moons** makes recycled pads using fabric ends from the clothing industry. To avoid all packaging problems, crafty girls can always sew their own (see **manymoonsalternatives.com/make_your_own_ pads.php**).

Sponge: If you're more of a tampon type, and bulky pads and period panties sound too cumbersome, you can use the ocean's best-known absorbent: **sea sponges**. Sure, stuffing a dried ocean critter (that's right, sponges are not flora) in your box might seem a little odd, but sponges work just as well as tampons, according to fans of the product, and you can wear them while swimming.

How do they work? (Warning: the following might not be suitable for squeamish readers.) Well, when it gets saturated, you just rinse, squeeze, and reinsert throughout the day. If you don't have a place to rinse it out, just pop a new one in (you're supposed to keep a film canister or a baggie in your purse to store used ones until you can rinse them). You can soak them in a tablespoon of apple cider vinegar or a few drops of tea tree oil and warm water overnight, but boiling them for 5 minutes is the only way to rid them of bacteria, and you should do this at the end of your cycle. Each sponge should last about six to eight cycles. Keep in mind that, as with anything from the sea, you have to make sure the sponges are harvested sustainably, as **Jade and Pearl**'s **Natural Sea Sponges** (a.k.a. Sea Pearls) are (jadeandpearl.com or gladrags .com). Sea Pearls are the only sea sponge legally available as a menstrual product in the US. They were exempt from a ban on sponges that took effect in the early '80s after the University of Iowa examined menstrual sponges and found them to contain bacteria, sand, grit, and other matter. Other researchers found some to be chemically contaminated (not surprising, when you think about how we treat the oceans as toxic dumping grounds). Plus, just as with regular and organic tampons, you might get toxic shock from sea sponges if you leave them in too long. But GladRags says it has never had a case of toxic shock among its sea sponge users.

Reusable Cup: Since you're experimenting, you can also try a reusable cup (literally a minicup you pop inside and empty two to four times a day). The **Keeper**, for instance, is made of natural gum rubber and lasts about a decade (keeper.com). If you're allergic to latex, you might want to use the silicone-based **DivaCup** (divacup.com). Trust me, women who try these swear by them. Just steer clear of drugstore posers like Instead Softcup, which looks like a reusable cup but has to be thrown out after one use. What's the point?

SEX

Let's cut the foreplay and get to the nub of our dilemma: sex is dirty. Just stop emptying the wastebasket in your bedroom for a year and see how much trash your love life produces—condoms, pill packs, massage oil bottles, broken-down vibrators, and, yes, those telling wads of crumpled virgin-forest tissue paper. To have an entirely eco-friendly sex life, you'd have to live alone in a hilltop monastery, but you don't have to be a monk to bring a little green to your boudoir.

Hormonal Birth Control: The pill has been wonderfully empowering for women (and a big step forward from the favored female contraceptive of the '30s and '40s—Lysol disinfectant!). But it means that over 100 million women worldwide are pissing out synthetic estrogen every day. American researchers found that adult trout exposed to a synthetic estrogen (estradiol) found in combination forms of birth control were half as fertile as fish kept in clean water. Shockingly, fertility was affected even when they were exposed to superlow doses—80 times lower than those turning up in the wild. In fact, researchers at Trent University found that low levels of estrogen hormones in water spawned hermaphrodite fish and lowered the number of males. Discharges from sewage treatment plants were fingered as the culprits.

Users of the patch, the implant, the shot, and any other form of hormonal birth control are all culpable here. The patch, in particular, has been embroiled in controversy because it releases much more hormone to the bloodstream than regular pills do (60% more, in fact). In 2006, the FDA started warning us about the potential impact of the patch on women. But few are talking about what flushing any of this down the toilet means for fish downstream, especially since about 4 million women ditch a patch a week (for 3 out of every 4 weeks). The manufacturer says women should instead fold the patches in half and then throw them in the wastebasket, but even then, hormones dumped in landfills could potentially leach into groundwater from leaky dumps. Activists want to see them returned to pharmacies for proper disposal.

If you think the patch sounds bad, vaginal rings (fairly new to the market) contain over a third more estrogen when you trash them than do a month's worth of discarded patches, and six times as many hormones as a month's worth of birth control pills, according to Women and Health Protection. Maybe that's why the manufacturer suggests that you reseal the ring in its triple-layered foil polyethylene and polyester pouch before you toss it.

Researchers found that LOW LEVELS OF ESTROGEN *in water discharged from sewers spawned hermaphrodite fish.*

FYI: **progestin-only pills** (which mimic the hormone progesterone and have fewer side effects but are somewhat less effective than progestin-estradiol combination pills) are also excreted in our pee, but their impact on aquatic life is less clear (although one study suggested that progesterone has a *de*feminizing impact on female minnows).

Condoms: Latex condoms are, of course, your best bet for preventing unwanted surprises, from babies to herpes. Yes, latex comes from the sap of the rubber tree, but undisclosed additives ensure that your safes, especially lubricated models, will not decompose. (Vegans should also be aware that most condoms are made with the milk protein casein.) And, gross but true, millions of condoms are said to slip into bodies of water every year, thanks to sewer overflows and all you boys who flush used ones down the toilet. (Betcha never thought about the fact that tying them off only helps them float to the water's surface.) Once in water, the latex doesn't biodegrade, so it's best to toss used condoms in the wastebasket.

Polyurethane-based condoms (male and female) and sponges are even worse. Although polyurethane might not cause reactions in people with latex allergies, it creates all kinds of nasty toxins in its manufacture and incineration, and it never breaks down.

MILLIONS OF CONDOMS *are said to slip into bodies of water every year, thanks to* SEWER OVERFLOWS *and all you boys who flush used ones down the toilet.*

If you're not vegetarian and aren't trying to prevent STDs, **lambskin condoms** are definitely biodegradable (and a little creepy). Unfortunately, the only biodegradable vegan latex condom—made by **Condomi**—comes from Germany and isn't readily available here.

IUDs: If you're with a trusted partner and your doctor thinks you're a good candidate, an **IUD** (intrauterine device) is probably the soundest eco option. A lot of women grew nervous about IUDs after one brand, recalled in the '70s, was linked to significant increases in pelvic inflammatory disease, but technology has improved and the risks are now much lower. One small, T-shaped copper thingy lasts up to 10 years! (The progestin-releasing versions last up to 5.) IUDs are about 99% effective, but be warned: they hurt like hell going in and out and are better suited to women who've already had children.

Sex Toys: I hate to take the fun out of your frolicking sessions, but be aware that the majority of jelly dildos and vibrators are made with that eco mood killer vinyl (PVC) and softened with high levels of potentially endocrine-disrupting, liver-damaging phthalates. In 2000, a German study found not only that sex toys offgas phthalates at pretty scary levels (up to 243,000 parts per million), but also that 10 other chemicals are offgassed from certain sex toys. In addition, lead and cadmium have been found in jelly and vinyl toys. Be wary of cheap metallic coatings, which might flake off in unwanted places.

Solid, high-quality **silicone** is much easier on the planet, as well as your body (though you'll want to stay away from products that claim to be made of silicone but come with a low price tag—they're likely faking it). Lovely **glass dildos** are the eco-friendliest—they can

9 NAUGHTY WAYS TO GREEN YOUR SEX LIFE*

1 Crack open a bottle of certified organic wine.

2 Pick out GMO- and pesticide-free strawberries to dip in fair-trade organic chocolate.

3 Ditch the petroleum wax candles and set the mood with long-lasting beeswax or soy versions. (Warning: never drip melted beeswax on skin—it's dangerously hot!)

4 Slip into something more comfortable—like, say, an ultrafeminine ensemble made of organic hemp or silk (enamore.co.uk) or a hot organic thong (americanapparel.net).

5 Reach for PVC-free toys.

6 Loosen things up with organic, petroleum-free lubricants and massage oils.

7 Save energy by doing it with the lights off.

8 Cut back on hot-water bills by soaping up together in the bath or shower.

9 Make love, not war.

* Thanks to Greenpeace Netherlands for some of these tips.

theoretically be recycled if you tire of them (especially clear glass ones). Plus, glass and silicone models last much longer than cheaper PVC types, which soon break, wear, and flake.

You'll be happy to know that **I Rub My Duckie**, as well as all other products from **Big Teaze Toys** (bigteazetoys.com), have been phthalate-free from the start, and **Vibratex**'s popular **Rabbit Habit** vibrator was reformulated sans PVC (vibratex.com).

Lubricants: Most of us are lookin' for lube in all the wrong places. Drugstore brands are loaded with petrochemicals, controversial preservatives, and sometimes animal-based glycerin or lactic acid (not to mention spermicides, which can trigger yeast infections).

Climatique makes flavored and unflavored **Sensua** lube with aloe and grapefruit seed extract to encourage healthy body chemistry (**sensua.com**). It's also 95% certified organic and latex-compatible. **Firefly Organics** is a totally natural lube made with ingredients like aloe, sesame seed extract, and cocoa butter (**organiclubricant.com**). It was also voted number one lube by *Playboy* magazine.

Massage Oil: With all that oil and bare flesh, is a massage ever really just a massage? The next time you whip out this handy seduction technique, skip the petroleum-derived oils laced with nauseating chemical scents and reach for something alluringly all-natural. **Body Candy Lickable Massage Balm** isn't organic, but its ingredients are pure, and its yummy flavors, like Orange Creamsicle and Cinnamon Hearts, are sweetened with herbal stevia. Health food stores often carry a variety of organic and all-natural massage oils. Even plain old almond oil would make for a nice rubdown.

FOOD FOR THOUGHT

You know you want to eat healthy. You know you'd rather eat food that's good for the health of the planet too. But let's face it, most of the time we reach for whatever we're in the mood for and what's on sale. The problem is, you can't tell by looking at a pear or a pepper just what it's been through to keep it looking firm and flawless even after traveling in a truck for a few days and then sitting on shelves for another week or two. Was it genetically engineered, sprayed with a flurry of chemicals, and zapped with gamma rays? Here's a breakdown of some of the major processes coming between you and your food, as well as solutions that will bring your appetite back.

INDUSTRIAL AGRICULTURE

Back in the day, people just called it food. Farmers couldn't even have dreamed of turning fossil fuels into fertilizers, and they relied on age-old techniques like crop rotation to rebuild the soil's nutrient level. No doubt it was hard work: weeds were pulled by hand, and crops didn't always survive insect infestations. But somewhere around the Second World War, things changed. Chemicals that had been developed for the war, like ammonium nitrate and DDT, made their way onto farmers' fields. The explosion of advanced mechanization, large-scale irrigation, and chemical inputs christened what was coined the "green revolution." Not because it was remotely eco-friendly. No no, the "green" part refers to the enormous jump in the sheer volume of food that could be produced on industrial-size farms.

It was a mixed blessing. Yes, the dramatic boost in yields meant a drop in food prices (and we suddenly had more wheat than the world would ever need), but the type of farming that the green revolution spawned was much more trying on the earth. And it's still with us today (it's one of the few '60s revolutions that actually stuck)—massive monoculture farms grow one lone crop, sucking up incredible amounts of water and demanding endless cycles of fossil fuel–based fertilizers to feed depleted soil and chemical pesticides that end up polluting local waterways and draining the soil of life. The irony, according to the David Suzuki Foundation, is that despite all the heavy spraying and newfangled machinery being used on fields, nearly a third of crops are still lost to weeds and pests. That's a rate, says the foundation, on par with crop losses before the era of chemical pesticides. Go figure.

Pesticides: Over 1,000 chemicals are available for use as pesticides in the US. That's kind of scary when you consider the hormone-mimicking, neurotoxic, reproduction-impairing properties of many of the chemicals being sprayed to keep fields free of weeds, fungus, and insects with relative ease and affordability. In fact, about 60% of pesticides currently being used (by weight) are hormone disrupters. Endosulfan, used on tomatoes, cotton,

> **N**early **A THIRD OF CROPS** *are still lost to weeds and pests. That's a rate on par with crop losses* **BEFORE** *the era of chemical pesticides.*

and other American crops, is one example. Low levels of exposure to this chemical in the womb are linked to autism, and it has the unfortunate habit of building up in the food chain.

Naturally, all pesticides are designed to kill one or more living things. Sure, you think, who cares about aphids? Well, it's not just pesky insects that are getting knocked off. There were over 86,000 accidental pesticide poisonings in the US in 2006. And countless animals die when they inadvertently, say, eat a grasshopper that's just been sprayed in a field. Fish, birds, and beneficial insects can also croak from exposure. Even when pesticides aren't the instant kiss of death, they might be weakening animals and creating weird birth defects (University of Florida researchers found that the closer male frogs live to farms the higher their chances are of being hermaphrodites). Wildlife services say that weakened birds may die more easily in bad weather or sing less, making them less likely to attract a mate and have little chicks of their own. Come on—you can't get much more heartbreaking than that.

Unfortunately, answers aren't the only thing blowing in the wind. Thanks to drifting air currents, less than 5% of pesticides are said to reach their intended target. Those winds carry many persistent chemicals halfway across the world, to accumulate in the fatty tissues of animals far from farmers' fields, like polar bears and whales. Even chemicals banned in the US 30 years ago are blowing over from developing countries where they're still in use. They also keep building up in the food chain long after they're out of fashion (which is why there's still a little DDT in all of us).

Oh, but all the pesticides used in North America are tested and safe, you say. Well, many older pesticides bypassed detailed safety reviews because they were already in widespread commercial use before stricter standards were mandated. In recent years, the feds have been retesting hundreds of these, though you might want to hold your applause. In the spring of 2006, union leaders representing EPA scientists admitted that researchers there are being pressured to gloss over testing and skip steps as they reevaluate the safety of commonly used old-generation pesticides. It's enough to make your skin crawl.

Sure, in isolation one pesticide might not affect us, but we eat more than one food item a day. Add up the three pesticides on your apple, the one on your potatoes, and the four on your salad, and you're ingesting a disturbing cocktail of chemical residues. Yes, the vast majority fall below EPA safety levels, but many of those maximums were set back in the '70s, before testing covered things like the effects on children's health or cumulative exposures. One study that tested pesticide combos found that an average of about 4% of tadpoles died when they were exposed to 0.1 part per billion of various pesticides when exposed to only one at a time, but a dramatic 35% of them died when they were exposed to the same low levels of nine different pesticides at once.

Add up the THREE PESTICIDES on your apple, the one on your potatoes, and the FOUR on your salad, and you're ingesting a DISTURBING COCKTAIL of chemical residues.

Just how often are you swallowing pesticides? A whopping 73% of the 93,000 fruits and veggies checked by the USDA tested positive for pesticide residues. The bottom line is that 90% to 100% of us can now brag about having pesticides in our tissues. Marvelous. And while you might be shaking your head and wondering why—for the health of our children, our wildlife, and ourselves—synthetic pesticide use hasn't been abandoned, you should know that there are ways you can avoid all those chems.

The Environmental Working Group ranked pesticide levels on 46 fruits and vegetables according to over 100,000 tests conducted by the FDA and the USDA. For a printable pocket-size guide identifying the 12 produce items with the highest residues and the 12 with the lowest, go to **foodnews.org**. You should think long and hard about buying nonorganic versions of the 12 worst offenders (like red peppers, celery, peaches, and apples).

Fertilizers: Pressure to squeeze every last dollar from farmers' fields means that crops are no longer rotated to let lands lie fallow so that the soil can rebuild itself. There's no real need when you pump the soil full of potent fossil fuel–based fertilizers. That's right—modern nitrogen-heavy fertilizers don't come from pigpens (manure) or compost, but from natural gas. In fact, 31% of all the fossil fuels used by North American farms go into fertilizers. And far too much of those fertilizers ends up seeping into rivers, lakes, and oceans, where too many nutrients can be a very bad thing. Overdoses of nitrogen and phosphorus from fertilizer runoff can create massive algae blooms that suffocate aquatic life, creating enormous dead zones. Think I'm kidding? There's one in the Gulf of Mexico that's now roughly 8,000 square miles and grows every time fertilizers start trickling down the Mississippi.

Water: Any kindergartner knows that crops need water to grow, but I bet you didn't realize that global agriculture sucks up roughly 70% of all the water we use on this planet. Yet US states that raise some of the most water-intensive crops (grains and cattle) are also being hit by serious water shortfalls—not good when you factor in expert predictions that the southwestern states could become barren dust bowls this century. Even "breadbasket" states like Nebraska, Kansas, and Oklahoma have been suffering through devastating droughts, like the record-breaking one of 2007. While experts predict that within 25 years there won't be enough water to grow the crops needed to feed the world's exploding population, researchers warn that we're squandering water every time we let our food go to waste. With up to 30% of American food ending up in the trash, the International Water Institute says we might as well be pouring 10 trillion gallons of water into the garbage can.

Transportation: Being a northerner in winter used to mean largely giving up fresh produce, other than carrots and turnips, and maybe a few oranges at Christmas. Now, of course, we snap our fingers and find pineapples in the produce aisle of a Wisconsin grocery store deep in the heart of blizzard season. Since we've yet to master the art of teleporting our fruit, that produce makes its way to kitchens on a circuit of planes, trains, ships, and diesel-spewing trucks. On average, our produce travels between 1,500 and 2,500 miles to get to us (and that's just the stuff from within the continent!). If you live in Detroit and you're buying grapes from Chile, those juicy clusters have come about 5,000 miles on smoggy ships (the shipping industry accounts for 27% of the world's smog-

Those juicy Chilean grapes had to TRAVEL 5,000 MILES on smoggy ships just to get to you.

inducing nitrogen oxide emissions, and that percentage is rising). But that's spitting distance compared to the 9,000 miles an apple has to trek to Vermont from New Zealand, even though perfectly delicious apples are sold locally. That's a hell of a lot of greenhouse gas emissions for something we take four bites out of and then toss in the trash because it's too mealy or bruised.

Land Use: As much as we try to sprout food in test tubes and labs, we still need land to grow it on. And as the globe's population explodes by over 90 million a year, the amount of topsoil on the planet dwindles by more than 25 billion tons in the same time frame, according to the United Nations Environment Programme. Fertile land, it seems, is running out. It doesn't help that our farming habits have a tendency to erode soil even further. And as our cities keep bloating and spreading out into dwindling farmlands, we're losing not only valuable sources of local food, but also vital watersheds, wilderness habitats, and carbon dioxide–absorbing green space. In fact, a study by American Farmland Trust says we're losing 2 acres of prime farmland to urban sprawl every minute!

Irradiation: Zapping our chicken or potatoes with gamma rays, X-rays, or electron beams to get rid of germs sounds like a sci-fi plot from the '50s, but food irradiation ain't fiction, honey. In fact, the US government allows the process on pork, chicken, wheat flour, oysters, spices, and produce like onions and potatoes. Why? Irradiation slows the sprouting, ripening, and molding processes so that products can sit

DO FRUIT SPRAYS WORK?

Who hasn't been intrigued by the promise of those fruit sprays in the produce aisle? **Fit**, for instance, says its natural product removes 98% more pesticides than washing with water alone because it lifts more of the waxes away (**tryfit.com**). So how does it stack up? A microbiologist at the University of Georgia reported that Fit did as well in lab tests at removing bacteria on lettuce, tomatoes, and apples as high levels of chlorine used by the industry to wash fresh-cut fruit. A 2008 study out of Washington State University and the University of Idaho found that Fit did even better than chlorine, getting rid of 99.99% of bacteria. But overall, the first researcher said most fruit sprays are about as good as washing with chlorinated municipal water.

As for the pesticides, it depends who you ask. Just rinsing produce thoroughly with tap water will remove many surface pesticides, say some. But the Pesticide Action Network UK will tell you that water has little effect on pesticides such as diphenylamine (used on apples) and chlorpropham (on potatoes). The group says that a product called **Veggie Wash** got rid of 93.4% of these two chems (compared to a 6.7% and 30% reduction, respectively, with water) (**veggie-wash.com**). Washing fruit with a mild natural detergent might help reduce some of the pesticide residues, but it won't get rid of all of them. Peeling also helps, but a good chunk of the nutrients are in the peel. It's a catch-22 for fruit and veggie lovers.

on shelves longer (if your strawberries last 3 weeks before rotting, that's a sign—untreated strawberries would spoil after 5 days). The feds will be allowing spinach and iceberg lettuce to get zapped in an effort to kill off microorganisms like *E. coli*, but activists say it's a cop-out. Not only does the process drain some of the vitamins out of food, but gamma radiation creates radioactive waste. Opponents also worry about nasty accidents with the nuclear materials at irradiation facilities (there are 30 in the US), as well as with trucks carrying the materials on public roads.

Irradiated foods are supposed to be clearly marked with an international symbol that tells you as much, but the FDA has proposed a rule change that would allow some irradiated foods to

We're losing 2 ACRES of prime farmland to urban sprawl EVERY MINUTE.

be labeled "pasteurized" instead—making the irradiation of foods virtually invisible. The FDA already lets manufacturers of processed foods made with irradiated ingredients or spices get away with not telling consumers. Weirdly enough, almost all irradiated packaged goods are irradiated *in* their packaging.

Genetic Engineering: GE foods. You know they make you uneasy, but you're not sure why. No doubt, it's freaky stuff: genetically modified organisms are developed in the lab when scientists take genes from one organism (say, a jellyfish) and insert them into unrelated species (say, a mouse), which is what researchers at Brown University did (don't ask). Okay, so you might not eat mice for dinner, but crops such as soybeans, corn, and tomatoes are commonly crossed with bacteria or viruses to improve hardiness, pesticide resistance, and drought resistance, or just to make ripe tomatoes less prone to squishing. It's a far cry from old-fashioned hybridization, in which gardeners and farmers crossbreed seeds from different varieties of a single crop to develop produce that is hardier or sweeter or smaller.

Just like the promise of a perfect, healthy child lures us to the idea of designer babies, genetic modification is pushed as the solution to the world's woes. Living in a country with high rates of vitamin A deficiency? No problem—rice can be crossbred with daffodils and bacteria so that it's packed with the vitamin. But earth advocates aren't biting. As thoroughly as the government says it tests genetically engineered crops before they're put on the market, critics say the testing is never thorough enough.

> *R*ice can be CROSSBRED *with daffodils and bacteria so that it's* PACKED WITH VITAMIN A, *but earth advocates aren't biting.*

And GE foods haven't been around long enough for long-term health effects to come to light. Back in 1999, a report came out that the pollen in Bt corn (the "Bt" part tells you a crop was crossed with a particular bacterium) wasn't just killing off intended pests; it was killing the larvae of pretty (and harmless!) monarch butterflies too. It turns out that the US Department of Agriculture (USDA) hadn't tested the impact on butterflies or moths that weren't considered a problem to farmers. Oops.

Lest we forget that nature is always up for a fight, and just as bacteria seem to get bigger and badder the more antibiotics we take, some herbicide-resistant GE crops are already proving ineffective against new strains of superweeds. Researchers are also on the lookout for outbreaks of superinsects that grow "stronger" in the face of pesticide-resistant plants.

And like a kid destined for a time-out, genetically tinkered organisms never stay put. Along with seeds, they're carried on the wind to neighboring fields, threatening to contaminate and crossbreed with natural and organic strains. Once you release one of these plants, it's virtually impossible to remove it entirely from the environment.

MONSANTO:
THE DARK PRINCE OF GE FOOD

You probably can't find a corporation much more maligned by food activists than Monsanto. It is, after all, the company that invented saccharin; was a major producer of aspartame, bovine growth hormone, and PCBs; and, along with Dow, manufactured the notoriously polluting and destructive herbicide Agent Orange, made famous during the Vietnam War. But perhaps most infamously of all, it's the king of genetically engineered crops.

Monsanto controls anywhere from 70% to 100% of the market share of several genetically modified food plants. And hey, since it produces Roundup (the most commonly used weed killer in the country, on both lawns and fields), its best-selling GMO crops are the Roundup Ready variety, which can basically be sprayed with tons of the potent herbicide without a blade of corn or a soybean being harmed.

I'd need a lawyer if I repeated all the names this company has been called over the years, especially after it sued the pants off many smaller American and Canadian farmers who either were unlucky enough to have fields downwind from Roundup farms and ended up sprouting Monsanto-patented plants in their fields, thanks to pollen and seed drifts, or dared to save their Roundup Ready seeds for reuse (an ancient farm practice that's against Monsanto rules).

The biotech giant also gained unwelcome acclaim for pushing terminator seeds, which are essentially sterile and can't be collected and reused. Environmentalists, farmers, and politicians around the world worry that the so-called suicide seeds will crossbreed with nearby plants and sterilize crops—an especially devastating possibility for poor farmers in developing countries. Luckily, there's an international moratorium against using and testing this technology in the field.

If you want to know which crackers and veggies were grown without genetic engineering, you're out of luck. The US decided against mandating the labeling of GE ingredients, so your guess is as good as mine. But about 75% of processed foods available on shelves and in freezer aisles contain at least one ingredient that's been genetically modified. The Center for Food Safety has put together a thorough guide on which foods are likely to contain genetically engineered ingredients and which are in the clear (**truefoodnow.org/ shoppersguide**). Other than that, buying organic is the only way to know for sure that your food was not grown with genetically modified ingredients.

PROCESSING—A CAN OF WORMS

When the first man boiled a corked bottle of food back in eighteenth-century Europe, essentially sterilizing it, do you think he had an inkling of the brave new world of processed foods he would eventually spawn? A few decades after the boiled-bottle development, the tin can was born, and soon people everywhere were eating foods that had been prepared months, or even years, earlier. Okay, so they weren't exactly tasty, but that's nothing artificial-flavoring specialists couldn't clear up.

Artificial Flavors and Colors: As a kid, I was vaguely aware that those yellow banana-shaped marshmallows they sold at the corner store had no connection to real bananas, but I loved them nonetheless. Ah, if only I knew then what I know now. A single artificial flavor, like the fake strawberry essence found in milkshakes, can contain well over 50 ingredients, and complex flavors such as roasted coffee or meat can involve thousands, according to Eric Schlosser's book *Fast Food Nation: The Dark Side of the All-American Meal*. Many of the ingredients are petroleum-derived and come with their own set of environmental ramifications. Even so-called natural flavors and colors can contain the same chemicals as, say, artificial banana flavoring—they just go through a different processing method, says Schlosser. And remember the hoopla about the natural flavoring in McDonald's french fries? Vegetarians were peeved to learn that the fries they'd been chowing down on for years were actually flavored with beef extract.

Over a dozen artificial colors have already been banned, but that doesn't mean the rest are entirely without controversy. Although many, such as FD&C Blue No. 1 and Green No. 3, are no longer coal tar–based, they still come from petroleum.  ("FD&C," by the way, means the colors are safe for use in *f*ood, *d*rugs, and *c*osmetics.) Some researchers have reported that artificial flavors and colors have a worrisome behavioral impact on kids. Scientists in the pediatric neurology department at Yale found that low doses of a mix of food colorings caused hyperactivity in rat pups and could potentially trigger attention deficit/hyperactivity disorder.

What happens when you eat a few different additives in one meal? When UK researchers combined monosodium

COLOR ME BAD

Think your store-bought blueberry pancakes get their blue hue from real fruit? What a knee-slapper! Try Red 40 and Blue 2. Seriously, why is it that the American versions of Oscar Mayer Lunchables, Skittles, and McDonald's strawberry sundae sauce all come loaded with fake coloring while the British versions use natural ones? Well, the Brits are already phasing out the dodgiest food dyes linked to behavior problems in kids, and it's about time we do the same. The Center for Science in the Public Interest has petitioned the Food and Drug Administration to put a warning label on foods containing any of eight artificial food dyes. Until they're banished from shelves, here's a list of which ones to avoid:

- Yellow 5 (tartrazine)
- Red 40 (allura red)
- Blue 1 (brilliant blue)
- Blue 2 (indigotine)

- Green 3 (fast green)
- Red 3
- Yellow 6 (sunset yellow)
- Orange B

glutamate (MSG) and brilliant blue, or aspartame and quinoline yellow, in the lab, the additives stopped nerve cell growth and messed with nerve signaling. The effects were anywhere from four to seven times more pronounced when the additives were combined than when they were consumed on their own. It's enough to make you spit up your Twinkies.

Preservatives: This family of synthetics keeps a loaf of bread mysteriously fresh, moist, and mold-free for weeks. But though they might be hailed as a great way to cut back on food waste, they're not always entirely benign. There are, of course, genuinely natural preservatives, like salt, vinegar, lemon, and sugar, but a quick glance at an ingredient list tells you that companies who make processed foods rely on much more. The preservatives that keep packaged meats looking perfectly pink and pathogen-free (nitrites or nitrates) can react with the amino acids in protein to form highly carcinogenic nitrosamines. Sulfites have been linked to hives, nausea, and difficulty breathing (note that sulfur dioxide, sodium and potassium bisulfite, and sodium and potassium metabisulfite are all sulfites). And BHT and BHA may keep fats and oils from going rancid, but they might also contribute to tumors. Is it really worth making yourself sick just to eat 6-month-old cookies?

Just having a swig of cola can be a tainted experience. When sodium benzoate (used to kill microorganisms in fruit juices and soft drinks) is mixed with ascorbic acid (vitamin C), as it is in many drinks, low levels of cancer-causing benzene may be created—the same pollutant that comes coughing out your car's tailpipe. In 2006 the FDA reopened an investigation into the problem preservative that had been closed 15 years earlier. New tests found the carcinogen in soft drinks at levels two and a half to five times higher than safety standards. The FDA then tested 200 soft drinks and juices and found that 10 of them failed to meet those standards (including SunnyD, Kool-Aid Jammers, and the kids' juice BellyWashers, whose 2006 scores were off the charts). All the major offenders have been reformulated to eliminate the problem. Notably, some didn't test high enough to get the reformulation request but still tested positive.

Packaging: What goes into a Ding Dong or frozen dinner is one thing; what's wrapped around it is a whole other ball of plastic. There's the sheer volume of waste involved in packaging food in largely nonrecyclable plastics, and the fact that it tends to come double- and triple-wrapped in various shrink wraps, boxes, and trays doesn't help matters much. Not when nearly a third of all the garbage Americans toss per year is packaging.

Nearly A THIRD OF ALL THE GARBAGE Americans toss per year is PACKAGING.

The situation is even more disastrous when you consider that a good deal of our processed foods come encased in polyvinyl chloride (PVC), which is considered by environmentalists to be the most toxic plastic on the planet, thanks to nasty pollutants like dioxin that are created in the making and incinerating of the plastic. So why is it so popular? Maybe because it's just so damn versatile that you can shape it into hard shells and clear plastic clams, or you can add softeners to it and call it shrink-wrap. Problem is, those softeners, called phthalates, have been known to migrate into food. In the late '90s, *Consumer Reports* tested supermarket cheeses wrapped in PVC plastic wrap and found them to have high levels of the plasticizer DEHA, which has been linked to developmental problems and birth defects in rats. Delish.

Can Linings: From beer to beans to Beefaroni, it all comes in a can. And whether it's steel or aluminum, that can has been lined with the controversial hormone disrupter bisphenol A (the same stuff used to make baby bottles). Bisphenol A has not only been found to leach

7 SIMPLE PACKAGING TIPS

Buy products that don't come with any!

Know your numbers. If you're buying something that comes in plastic, check the bottom for numbers (like 1 and 2) that tell you the plastics are recyclable in your area.

Renewable and recyclable glass is at the head of the class because it's renewable and you're guaranteed it won't leach into your food or drinks.

Buy dry. If you're picking up an ingredient like chicken broth, the powdered kind goes a lot further than a can of water-filled broth, which gets used up in one meal.

Buy in bulk. Even consider bringing your own container for filling. Many bulk stores will be happy to weigh your containers empty and deduct that weight from the cost of whatever you're buying.

Good things come in small packages. For instance, cereals that come in smaller boxes often contain the same amount of, say, muesli, as the bigger boxes, which are just full of air. Compare product weights to be sure.

Keep an eye out for biodegradable food packaging (but remember that most biodegradable plastics should never be put in the recycling or compost bin!).

---

into foods like tomato sauce, apple juice, creamed corn, and, yes, Chef Boyardee; it's also been tied to birth defects and reproductive damage, as well as breast and prostate cancer. Even though the FDA stands by the bisphenol A industry on this one, of the 160 or so studies conducted on the compound, 90% have found cause for worry. Naturally, industry points to the other 10% to back its ongoing use of the chem, and government regulators say that adults have nothing to worry about (babies are another matter; see page 133). But less than half a cup of some canned chicken soup or tomato sauce tested would contain doses of bisphenol A exceeding those found to affect animals. It's also one of the top 10 contaminants found in streams tested by the US Geological Survey.

Want to avoid the whole mess? **Eden Organic** foods come in bisphenol A–free cans (**edenfoods.com**). Or buy **dry beans**, **bottled beer**, **jarred sauces and soups**, and **fresh or frozen veggies** instead.

Nonstick Surfaces (From Pans to Popcorn Bags): You may have thrown out your nonstick pan by now because of health concerns about PFOA (see page 163), but did you know that PFOA also turns up in your food packaging? The nonstick, grease-repellent surface and widespread environmental contaminant is used in products like microwave popcorn bags and candy wrappers, and it's especially popular at fast-food joints, where it's used in french fry containers, cardboard pizza trays, and burger wraps. That may help explain why, even if you've never sautéed a thing in your life, the chemical can be found in 95% of us, according to research by the US Centers for Disease Control and Prevention (in fact, FDA studies show that greaseproof wrapper chems can leach into food at levels several hundred times safety standards). Many companies—including Burger King, Frito-Lay, Kellogg's, Kraft, and most recently McDonald's—have told Ohio Citizen Action that they don't use or have phased out the use of PFOA-coated

Palm oil isn't just taxing your heart; it's also giving parts of the PLANET a coronary.

packaging. The EPA has asked that companies voluntarily phase this stuff out, and it should be mostly gone by 2010 but can still be around until 2015.

Palm Oil: Cookies, chocolate bars, crackers, pie crust—if it's processed, it probably contains palm oil, the world's second-largest oil crop after soy. Thanks to their high melting point and cheap price tag, palm oil and palm kernel oil have replaced partially hydrogenated trans fats in many foods. The shortening's popularity has exploded in North America since the government started mandating the labeling of trans fats at the start of 2006. Ironic, really, considering that many companies moved from palm oil to trans fats in the '60s because of the saturated-fat scare. Palm oil is also poured into soaps, creams, detergents, lipstick, gum, candles, animal feed—hell, it's even used as a plasticizer in ultratoxic PVC (vinyl) and can be found in health store dish detergents. Now Asian utilities are eyeing the oil for use in "cleaner, greener" biodiesel.

CURBING TAKEOUT TRASH

Feeling guilty about all the packaging that comes with your takeout? Why not bring your own reusable plastic food containers with you next time? You'd be surprised how supportive (or at the very least ambivalent) restaurants are about using them. Most fast-food chain workers barely even flinch at the request, and some groovier places might even cut you a discount. And if you're addicted to takeout coffee, there's no excuse not to get a handy reusable mug so you can lug your latte around. Stainless steel mugs are the safest.

The problem is, palm oil isn't just taxing your heart (controversy remains about whether it's actually all that healthy); it's also giving parts of the planet a coronary. Most of it (83%, to be exact) comes from Malaysia and Indonesia, which have over 25,000 square miles of palm plantations between them, according to the Center for Science in the Public Interest's 2005 report. One study found that almost 12,000 square miles of rainforest was lost to oil palm plantations between 1973 and 2003 in Indonesia alone.

On the somewhat brighter side, some companies, including Unilever, have joined up with nongovernmental organizations (NGOs) such as the WWF to form the Roundtable on Sustainable Palm Oil (RSPO). The group is developing environmental standards for palm oil production and is establishing a certification system. The Rainforest Action Network, however, says that, so far, the RSPO principles aren't well enforced and don't prevent rainforest destruction.

In the meantime, organic palm oil is available. **Spectrum** makes it (**spectrumorganics. com**), but it's hard to find. It's easier just to avoid palm oil altogether. Most of the processed foods in health stores don't include it, but you will spot it in some health store cookies or carob chips.

FOOD SOLUTIONS

Okay, so all that doom and gloom has made you want to boycott food. Don't pull a Nicole Richie on us and stop eating! There's plenty of hope in the world for people who love a good meal or three a day.

Organic: Some farmers never stopped plowing the land the way their grandparents did. Others have come to it as escapees from mainstream agriculture. And still others are city slickers looking to get their hands dirty and give back to the earth. But organics are now big business, and so are sales of organics—they're jumping about 20% every year, amounting to $20 billion in 2007. Back in the day, crunchy granola types had to hunt down pesticide-free produce and packaged foods in select health stores. Today, Wal-Mart is the single largest distributor of organic milk (although it was accused, in 2007, of mislabeling products as organic that weren't—Wal-Mart claims these were isolated incidents).

But what does "organic" mean exactly? It goes way beyond simply being pesticide-free. Sure, an organic tomato will have been grown in soil in which no chemical fertilizers or pesticides have been used for at least 3 years, but there's more to the story. Special attention is paid to fostering the soil's nutrients. No sewage sludge can be spread on crops (unlike regular

Well, big organic farms are less likely to have as much biological diversity and are more often mechanized. Still, some say they have bigger budgets that make meeting stringent organic standards easier than it might be for smaller farms. Depends whom you ask.

Local vs. Organic: For years, earth lovers have been telling us, "Buy organic, buy organic." But recently the message has become a little more muddled. The community's been divided over whether you should really buy organic berries from Mexico over nonorganic stuff grown 30 miles away. Come winter, northerners don't have much choice, but what about the rest of the year? Buying locally means that

Eating food that was grown **CLOSE TO HOME** *is one way to make sure you get the* **MOST NUTRIENTS** *out of every bite.*

fewer dirty fossil fuels went into trucking the food. It also means you're helping to preserve local green space and threatened farmlands close to home. Plus, did you know that the vitamin content in your fruits and veggies diminishes with each passing day after they were

---

I ♥ COMMUNITY-SUPPORTED AGRICULTURE

Feeling like your relationship with food has grown distant? Aloof even? Revive that romance by connecting to a local farmer in your area through community-supported agriculture (CSA). How does it work? Organic farming can be insecure work, so if you show the farmer you're ready to commit by paying for a summer's worth of fresh, seasonal, organic produce in advance (or, in some cases, with postdated checks), then presto, you're a shareholder. You'll be showered with bountiful food baskets that surprise and delight once a week (some farms even offer eggs, milk, and flowers too), and suddenly that feeling of disconnection from the food chain vanishes. Some CSAs will invite you to work a few hours on the farm (giving you a direct hand in the food you're soon to eat). Most deliver to a drop point in your neighborhood, and some deliver straight to your door. There are over 1,000 CSAs across the US today. Go to **localharvest.org/csa** and punch in your zip code to find one near you.

TOP 10 REASONS TO EAT ORGANIC

You don't have to worry about biting into chemicals with every mouthful. **1**

Growing organic food doesn't involve poisoning wildlife, workers, and waterways. **2**

There's never been a reported case of mad cow disease in organic cattle. **3**

Your meat and eggs are drug-free. **4**

It's the only guarantee that you're not eating genetically engineered ingredients. **5**

Your food hasn't been zapped or irradiated. **6**

Organic farms are hotbeds of life, fostering vibrant biodiversity, not sterile fields. **7**

Organic produce is higher in vitamin C and contains 30% more antioxidants. **8**

Eating an organic diet may reduce the levels of pesticides coursing through your body. **9**

Organic farmers can actually make a decent living, unlike most conventional farmers, whose income is in the red and dropping every year. **10**

picked? Eating food that was grown close to home is one way to make sure you get the most out of every bite.

Unfortunately, nonorganic local farmers also spread fossil fuel–based fertilizers to boost yields and spray chemical pesticides to keep bugs and weeds at bay. Ideally, you could get both local and organic in one, but lots of major grocery chains buy cheaper California

WHICH CORPORATIONS ARE HIDING BEHIND YOUR FAVORITE ORGANIC/NATURAL BRANDS?

- **Kellogg's:** Kashi; Morningstar Farms; Gardenburger; Bear Naked

- **Kraft:** Back to Nature; Boca

- **Coca-Cola:** Odwalla

- **Cadbury:** Green & Black's

- **Mars:** Seeds of Change

- **Hershey:** Dagoba Organic Chocolate

- **ConAgra:** Lightlife, Alexia

100-MILE DIET

Ah, the cross-country road trip. Who hasn't dreamed about packing up and heading out across the continent in search of new sights and sounds? Well, most of our food travels more than we ever do—at least 1,500 miles. Factor in all the emissions created by dirty diesel trucks, smoggy ships, and cargo planes, and we're talking a hell of a lot of climate-changing pollution. On the first day of spring 2005, Vancouverites Alisa Smith and James MacKinnon moved beyond feeling guilty about their food choices and decided they were going to break the long-distance grub cycle once and for all. For one whole year, they ate and drank only what was grown within 100 miles of their apartment. And the ground rules were tough. Chicken would have to be raised locally, which is easy enough, but it would also have to be fed local feed. The same was true for every ingredient in every loaf of bread and every slice of pie.

Smith and MacKinnon quickly realized that items like sugar ain't a local resource. Okay, so at the beginning meals were kind of boring (it took some time to find truly regional sources) and involved a lot of potatoes (since wheat was nearly impossible to find within their radius), but they eventually discovered mouthwatering delicacies like warm Salt Spring Island brie with ground hazelnuts and frozen wild blueberries, and spring salmon with organic sage butter (being West Coasters, they were pushed off their vegan diet by the proximity of the ocean, full of local seafood). Yes, they found it a little time-consuming to do their own canning and preserving so that they'd have enough local supplies come winter. Just getting through the cold season was a feat in itself. But they did it, proving to us all that eating strawberries in January is just plain overrated. If you're interested in giving the diet a go yourself, if only for a day or a week, head to **100milediet.org** (launched by Smith and MacKinnon). Punch in your zip code, and it'll spit out a map of what your 100-mile borders are. The starter guide will give you plenty of useful tips on how to tackle the diet, like freezing local produce in season and planting winter gardens.

organic produce all year long, rather than supporting, say, Michigan-grown organics when they're in season. Some argue that local farms are just not big enough, and they'd rather buy from one large farm in the southern states than from six midsize farms near Kalamazoo. But that's starting to change. Whole Foods health food chain says it's going to make an effort to support local *and* organic; so is Wal-Mart. And you should too.

MEAT

Whether your incisors glisten at the sight of a sizzling steak or the thought of a lean roasted chicken breast gets you peckish, there's little question that Americans love their meat. They're swallowing nearly 200 pounds of meat a year (including chicken and fish). That's up a hefty 50 pounds per person from 50 years ago. And those animals aren't exactly running around the farmyard like they used to.

Factory farms, a.k.a. Concentrated (or Confined) Animal Feeding Operations (CAFOs), are now the main producers of meat in this country, crowding staggering numbers of animals into much fewer farms. Since 1985, the number of hog farms, for instance, has plummeted by nearly 75%, yet the total number of hogs squeezed onto those farms remained steady, according to the Natural Resources Defense Council (NRDC). The intense concentration of ownership in the pig biz brings new meaning to "hogging the market." Same goes for chicken production: 10 large companies produce more than 90% of the nation's poultry.

So what's the problem? We need to feed ourselves, don't we? Well, the meat industry is vacuum-packed with environmental woes. Warning: you may want to put that burger down while you read this.

SLOW FOOD

Tired of rushing through meals that take 30 seconds to prepare, a minute to swallow, and aren't even healthy to begin with? About 20 years ago, a small group of gourmets in Italy got together to stand up for real food as McDonald's prepared to move into an old Roman plaza in their city. They issued the Slow Food Manifesto. The gourmets wanted a return to home-cooked meals and 2-hour lunches, to food as art and a source of sensual pleasure. In the mid '90s, followers were encouraged to eat locally grown organic foods and to buy from small-scale artisans and food producers. The movement fostered a return to heritage fruits and vegetables that you won't find in the supermarket and ancient family recipes in which everything is prepared from scratch. Now, over 80,000 people around the globe—fed up with the feeding frenzies we call meals—have signed on to the eat-slowly-with-friends philosophy. There are 170 Slow Food groups, or "convivia," across the US that invite members to "taste, celebrate, and champion the foods and food traditions important to their communities." To learn more, check out **slowfoodusa.org**.

Manure Pollution: Time to take a mental walk around the lagoons of poop stored on factory farms. But don't inhale. You'll be breathing in toxic gases like ammonia, hydrogen sulfide, and the potent greenhouse gas methane—a stew of fumes that can trigger headaches, wheezing, even diarrhea. When the holding tubs break, flood, or just plain seep, we're talking serious pathogenic waterway and groundwater contamination that can make both local residents and aquatic life sick. In New York State, 3 million gallons of liquid manure spilled from a dairy farm into a nearby river, killing millions of fish in 2005. In North Carolina 10 years earlier, an 8-acre hog poop lagoon burst and spilled 25 million gallons of manure into a nearby river, killing 10 million fish and closing over 364,000 acres of coastal wetlands to shellfish farming, according to the NRDC. Combine that with pesticide runoff from produce and grain farms, and it's no wonder the Environmental Protection Agency has said that agriculture is behind nearly three-fourths of the water quality concerns in American rivers and streams.

This Is Your Meat on Drugs: It's estimated that two-thirds of the over 30 million cattle slaughtered for burgers and steaks every year in the US are pumped up with growth hormones (including natural sex hormones like progesterone and testosterone, as well as several synthetics). The practice has been at the heart of a European ban on laced American meat since the '80s, and EU scientists have linked American consumption of hormone-treated meat to the high rate of hormone-related cancers like colon, breast, and prostate cancer in the US, as well as immune system damage in children.

Regardless of the cross-border politics, growth hormones are turning up downstream from factory farms and, disturbingly, have been found to alter sex-related traits of fish and turtles. Speaking of sex, a University of Rochester Medical Center study found that men whose moms had eaten red meat 7 days a week while pregnant had a sperm count 25% below normal and were three times as likely to have visited fertility clinics. And where do you suppose researchers pointed the blame? You guessed it: growth hormone–laced meat.

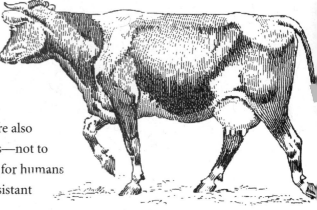

The mass dosing isn't limited to hormones. Livestock are also commonly given a daily injection of low levels of antibiotics—not to treat illness, but to boost growth by up to 3%. The problem for humans arises when the bacteria living inside those animals grow resistant to the antiobiotic. Swallow the resistant bacteria through undercooked meat and you might get a dangerously drug-resistant bug. In 1999 alone, the FDA estimates that over 11,000 people contracted a strain of food poisoning resistant to the Cipro family of drugs, thanks to antibiotic-fed chicken.

Drugged meat or not, over 90% of our exposure to the dangerous pollutant dioxin comes from our food, especially animal fats such as meat, fish, dairy, and eggs. The feds say you can limit your exposure by trimming away the fat, or by baking instead of frying, but come on, is anyone else freaked out that there are toxic environmental pollutants in our meat to begin with?

Processing Plants: Once animals are trucked to slaughter, a whole other set of problems arises. Meat-processing plants are notorious for emitting foul odors, but their pollution problems go way beyond a bad smell. Vast quantities of water are used, not only to rinse down the plant and the carcasses, but also to scald chickens in energy-intensive hot water before their feathers are plucked. Some water can be reused, but most of it is just plain nasty—full of blood, manure, fat, feathers, hair, and bones. A great deal of water is also used in cooking and canning the meat, and a lot of energy goes into refrigerating the stuff.

Four half-pound steaks create as much **POLLUTION** *as driving 155 miles.*

Greenhouse Gases: Yes, it's true—gassy livestock account for 18% of the world's greenhouse gases—more than cars, trains, and planes together! Combine that with the carbon dioxide spewed in the transport of animals to slaughter, from slaughter to supermarket, and finally to your dinner table, and four half-pound steaks create as much pollution as jumping in your car and driving 155 miles, according to Japan's National Institute of Livestock and Grassland Science. Just reducing our meat intake by 20% would have the same impact as forcing every sedan driver in the US to switch to a Prius, say University of Chicago researchers. Beans and vegetables suck up eight times less fossil fuel than meat does, according to research by Cornell University's College of Agriculture and Life Sciences prof David Pimental.

Feed: Livestock need to eat. Trouble is, they eat a lot. In fact, for every pound of meat, animals are fed up to 8 pounds of grain. And the growing global demand for meat (as well as biofuel) is partly to blame for skyrocketing grain prices. But what else goes into that meat? Pimental says that grain-fed beef production sucks back about 12,000 gallons of water for every pound of beef (if you factor in the H_2O needed to grow the grain, feed the cow, and process its parts in the packing plant). That means your burger is dripping with waste.

And after all that, are we even giving these animals a decent diet? Corn fattens cows up nicely, giving them a good marbled cut, but their digestive tracts aren't designed to process it, so they get sick more often (too much corn can lead to ulcers and bacteria associated with sudden death, says research reported in the journal *Science*) and need more antibiotics. (Plus, they burp and fart up more methane.) USDA scientists have found that grain-fed cattle have more *E. coli* in their intestines than do grass-fed cows, and that *E. coli* has a nasty way of contaminating cuts of meat and ground beef (not to mention neighboring spinach farms) when the poor cow gets picked apart at the processing plant.

Of course, that's nothing compared to what happens when you mix a little dead cow into cattle feed. Hello! Did anyone ever consider that cows are vegetarian? You'd go crazy, too, if you were forced to eat your brother for lunch. Sure, the FDA may have banned cow brains and spinal tissue—and any other parts at high risk of spreading mad cow disease— from cattle feed in 1997 (although they could still be fed dried cow blood, as well as dead chicken and hog bits), but sloppy enforcement and cross-contamination from other livestock feed mean that America's mad cow problem ain't going away just yet. (Speaking of which, high-risk cattle parts are finally slated to be removed from all animal feed and pet food by April 2009.)

Organic and Grass-Fed Meat: If you're not into giving up meat entirely, try cutting back on your servings, and buy local organic meat whenever you can. Organic meat is drug-free, and the animals are given organic feed, access to the outdoors, and more room to roam on pesticide-free land. Grass-fed animals that are free to munch in farmers' fields are not just happier, they're healthier—and not just in terms of their own sickness rate; they're also more nutritious for us humans to eat. They're lower in saturated fats and higher in omega-3 fatty acids. If your meat is labeled "natural," make sure to ask your butcher and the grower what that means. (For more on meat labels, see page 112.)

VEGETARIANISM

The Union of Concerned Scientists says that being a vegetarian is one of the top things you can do for the environment. Not that vegetarians should presume their own eco righteousness. Beans, the veg-head protein of choice, aren't necessarily all that holy. Brazil, the second-largest soy producer after the US, has been tearing down rainforests not only for beef but for, gasp, soy. Large soy farms there have been linked to poor working conditions, slave labor, and high levels of pesticide use. And it's not just rainforests that are losing ground. Half of Brazil's soy comes from savannas once teeming with 90,000 insect species, 550 birds, and 150 mammals (including jaguars) that are now being pushed out by soy monoculture, according to the WWF. But, tofu lovers—and this is a big but—the vast majority of soy is grown for cattle feed, not human feed. So you're generally off the hook for rainforest destruction. More good news? A moratorium on growing soy in freshly cleared rainforest seems to have curbed deforestation for soy, but we'll see if that trend holds as commodity prices go through the roof.

Being a VEGETARIAN is one of the top things you can do for the ENVIRONMENT.

If you're as uncomfortable with the unknown impacts of playing god with crops, as, oh, all of Europe is, you'll be perturbed to learn that 85% of American soy (and over half the world's) is genetically modified—patented by Monsanto (the notorious biotech company and manufacturer of Agent Orange; see page 77 for more on Monsanto). To add to the

TOP 6 REASONS TO GO VEGETARIAN

It's a gas, gas, gas. Animals raised to feed our hunger for meat burp and, um, fart out more greenhouse gases than cars, trucks, and planes combined.

Tanking up. The average meat-centered diet essentially burns a gallon of fuel a day, twice what it takes to feed a vegan (according to Cornell's David Pimental).

Rainforest crunch. An area of rainforest larger than New York State is estimated to be destroyed every year for grazing land, says the WWF. In the last 5 months of 2007 alone,

1,250 square miles have vanished from Brazil's rainforest, according to the *New York Times*.

Saving Nemo. Over three-quarters of the world's fish stocks are on the verge of collapse, according to the UN Food and Agriculture Organization.

Dodging Dolly. You'll be steering clear of controversial cloned livestock recently okayed by the FDA.

Tainted love. You won't be munching on antibiotics, hormones, and dioxin-laced fats.

corporate soya plot, chemical giant DuPont owns Solae, which makes the heavily processed soy protein isolate found in Yves, SoLean, El Burrito, and Gardenburger products. Solae makes both GE-free and genetically engineered soy, so be sure to check with the brands (El Burrito admits it uses both; Yves says it's GE-free; SoLean and Gardenburger both say they're not GE-free). (For a full list of Solae products, check out the cobranded products in the media room at **solae.com**.)

Don't freak—the planet is still better off for your being a veggie lover! To mediate any sins affiliated with the veg diet, always buy certified organic when you can. You can feel good knowing that your protein source, whether chickpeas or tempeh, was grown on a sustainable farm without chemical inputs or genetically modified seeds. Buying from local organic companies is even better, since less fuel is needed for transport. Health stores are loaded with organic meat alternatives.

Beans are the original vegetable protein of choice, and ambitious boys and girls can even get the dried kind in bulk. Those of us without the foresight to soak stuff overnight can get organic canned beans by brands like **Eden** in any health store (and Eden doesn't use bisphenol A linings in its cans). **Organic tofu** and flavored **organic tempeh** can be had almost everywhere. If you're one of those veg-heads who think eating anything that emulates meat is nasty, try **nut burgers** instead. For quick, protein-rich meals, look for frozen tofu vegetable lasagnas, veggie loaves, burritos, and the like in the freezer section (though frozen, packaged foods have a higher carbon footprint).

SEAFOOD

Anyone who's been dumped has probably heard the old consolation, "There's plenty more fish in the sea." Ah, if only this were still the case. We eat over 130 million tons of the poor creatures a year (95 million of those tons are wild-caught), and that figure keeps climbing as docs tell us to cut back on red meat and stock up on omega-3 fatty acids. Our fish stocks, however, can't keep up.

Wild Fish Stocks: The stats are pretty dismal. According to a report in *Nature* journal, only 10% of large, open-ocean fish are left in the sea. The Food and Agriculture Organization of the United Nations (FAO) says a whopping three-quarters of fish stocks are on the brink of collapse, being fished at or beyond sustainable levels. That collapse, warn scientists, is coming midcentury (apocalypse-style) if we don't get our act together.

What have we been doing wrong? Well, besides treating the ocean as a giant toilet, we basically vacuum the ocean floor by laying down massive weighted nets that scrape up everything in their path, including 1,000-year-old coral and vast quantities of unwanted fish. The undersized, unmarketable, or simply accidental bycatch (including dolphins, seals, whales, and sea turtles) is tossed overboard, often dead. The FAO says that one in four animals caught as bycatch in fishing equipment dies (about 27 million tons each year).

A *whopping* **THREE-QUARTERS** *of fish stocks are on the* **BRINK OF COLLAPSE.**

The UN is calling for a ban on bottom trawling in international waters (64% of the planet's oceans fall outside national jurisdictions), saying that an immediate moratorium needs to happen if we're going to prevent "irreversible destruction on the high seas." But the global community has yet to bite.

Fish Farming: If catching wild fish is draining the oceans, farmed fish must be the right choice, no? Well, it depends on how it's farmed. Gone are the days when buying farmed salmon was automatically seen as the best way to protect wild breeds from overfishing. Unfortunately, that fatty pink flesh is loaded with much more than just omega-3's. We're talking distressing levels of dioxins, DDT, flame retardants, and seven times the amount of hormone-disrupting PCBs found in wild salmon. (Farmed salmon's diet of ground-up fish meal is concentrated with toxins.) Oh yeah, and that juicy pink flesh? It's fake. Since farmed

NOT SO WILD ON SALMON

Buyer beware: a *Consumer Reports* investigation found that 13 of 23 salmon fillets labeled "wild" were actually farmed.

salmon is gray and not the lovely hue of wild salmon, artificial coloring is added to their feed.

The salmon farms themselves are ticking off a lot of environmental observers. Just feeding the carnivorous fish involves trawling the seas for enormous quantities of small fish, such as anchovies. In fact, according to the Coastal Alliance for Aquaculture Reform's report "Farmed and Dangerous," it takes roughly 3 pounds of wild fish to grow 1 pound of farmed salmon. At the end of the day, over 2 million tons of fish meal is fed to carnivorous farmed fish, including salmon, grouper, and sea bream.

Overcrowded ocean pens are essentially feces factories and harboring grounds for diseases like sea lice. So, not only are caged fish pumped full of antibiotics, but 95% of young wild salmon that swim past infected farms while migrating out to sea die, according to a recent University of Alberta study. Escapees also introduce diseases abroad and throw off ecosystems by crowding wild habitat. And watch out for the genetically modified, disease-resistant, fast-growing fish being developed by some aquaculture farms. Who knows what would happen if GE escapees were to mix with wild breeds?

On the other hand, contained systems for farming **tilapia**, **catfish**, and even **trout** on land, rather than in water, are seen as an excellent option, ecowise. Holistic aquaponic methods combine fish and veggie farming through a highly efficient chemical-free indoor system that recycles nutrient-rich fish poop to feed hydroponic veggies.

It takes roughly **3 POUNDS** *of wild fish to grow* **1 POUND** *of farmed salmon.*

Tuna: All this bad news about salmon came down the pipe right about the time another favorite was swimming out of favor: tuna. Findings of high mercury content meant lunchtime would never be the same. If you're eating fresh tuna in, say, sushi or steak form, and you're a woman of childbearing age, even conservative sources say once a month is plenty. However, if you're eating a sandwich with canned light tuna (which is often skipjack tuna), you can have it weekly (though environmentalists suggest monthly is safer). You need to be especially cautious about eating white, or albacore, tuna, which has three times the mercury level of the light stuff. Then again, an investigation by the *Chicago Tribune* found that American tuna companies sometimes use high-mercury yellowfin, not lower-mercury skipjack, to make light tuna (6% of the time, according to FDA tests), so light cans aren't always safer either. Confused? Who isn't! In 2006, *Consumer Reports* magazine warned pregnant women to stay away from canned tuna altogether.

And you know those reassuring little "dolphin safe" labels you look for on cans of tuna? Sad to say, the federal standard doesn't require certification for all tuna labeled "dolphin safe." Tuna boats outside the eastern tropical Pacific aren't inspected but can still use the logo. **RainCoast Trading–**brand canned tuna catches younger northern tuna using hooks and lines, not dolphin-snaring nets. Plus, it tests all its fish for mercury and PCBs and uses bisphenol A–free cans (**raincoasttrading.com**). **Whole Foods 365** canned tuna isn't as local (it comes from the Indian and South China seas) but it is regularly tested for mercury and is also dolphin-free.

Tuna isn't the only fish drowning in NEUROTOXIC MERCURY.

Toxins in Other Fish: Of course, tuna isn't the only fish drowning in neurotoxic mercury. Thanks to our polluting tendencies, our oceans are full of the stuff, and high levels can be found in Atlantic halibut, sea bass, shark, swordfish, and Gulf Coast oysters. Mercury

SHOULD MOMS IGNORE FISH WARNINGS?

In late 2007, the *Washington Post* ran a front-page piece titled "Mothers Again Urged to Eat Fish." According to the article, pregnant and breast-feeding women should ignore government warnings about mercury in fish and eat more than three servings of the swimmers a week if they don't want babes being born too small and too early and flunking IQ tests later in life. The finding came from a group called the National Healthy Mothers, Healthy Babies Coalition, a nonprofit org with a long and impressive list of members, including the American Academy of Pediatrics.

But as mothers across the country started upping their consumption to safeguard their growing babies, the fish really started to hit the fan. Turns out the coalition leaders hadn't actually consulted the 150 medical and government groups in their membership circle. In fact, the chair of the American Academy of Pediatrics claimed to be "appalled" by the findings, saying that they weren't backed up by real science. Several other weighty bodies—like the Centers for Disease Control and Prevention, and the National Institute of Child Health and Human Development— called the findings bogus. The Food and Drug Administration basically told the *New York Times*, "Dude, we've seen pretty much every study out there on this topic and we haven't seen squat that would make us change our recommendations." Well, not in those words, but you get the point.

I PROMISE NEVER TO EAT

- X Bluefin tuna
- X Chilean sea bass
- X Shark
- X Orange roughy
- X Hoki
- X Atlantic halibut
- X Any other endangered/threatened fish

levels are so high in shark, swordfish, king mackerel, and tilefish that the FDA says women of childbearing age and children shouldn't eat them at all. And *Consumer Reports* advises pregnant women to steer clear of Chilean sea bass, halibut, American lobster, and Spanish mackerel.

Overfished: Flagrant disregard for fishing regulations and pitiful levels of enforcement are serious problems for many stocks, including Russian king crab and the oh-so-tasty but oh-so-overfished Chilean sea bass. Turns out policing is hard to carry out in the remote Antarctic waters where the late-breeding bass are caught. Pirate fishermen are netting 10 times what's permitted and are considered totally out of control. (**Alaskan king crab**, **European sea bass**, and **wild-caught Pacific black cod** from British Columbia or Alaska are a much greener substitute for the sea bass lovers.) Atlantic cod, Atlantic sole, and imported shrimp (both trawled and farmed) are other big no-no's.

Sustainable Seafood: Turn that frown upside down, seafood fans. The Marine Stewardship Council (MSC) has set up an internationally recognized standard that assesses whether a fishery is well managed and, you guessed it, sustainable. Interestingly enough, the entire commercial stock of **wild Alaskan salmon** has been certified since 2000, and over 25 other fisheries have been certified to date (there's even a small amount of certified Chilean sea bass now!). Even more surprising, **Wal-Mart** announced in 2006 that it plans to source all its wild-caught fresh and frozen fish from the MSC.

SHRIMP'S MUDDY RECORD

How much shrimp cocktail can you stomach? Americans eat about 3 to 5 pounds of shrimp each in a year. About half the shrimp we eat come from the ocean, where giant weighted nets bring up 4 to 20 pounds of unwanted bycatch for every pound of shrimp. According to the UN's Food and Agriculture Organization, we're talking nearly 2 million tons a year of discarded sea turtles, sharks, and fish—a mix of commercially useless species, undersized juvenile fish, and seabed debris that get pulled to the surface so quickly that anything still living ends up dead.

So the farmed stuff should be safer, right? Well, the bulk of farmed shrimp comes from Asia, where a recent report from the AFL-CIO–affiliated Solidarity Center revealed the kind of workers' rights abuses that make you want to cry "vegetarian." The 3-year-long investigation yielded a report documenting physical and sexual abuse, child labor, human trafficking, and debt bondage. Not all crustaceans from the two countries investigated (Thailand and Bangladesh) are sweatshop shrimp, but we do know that Costco, IGA, Wal-Mart, and Sam's Club were selling shrimp from farms fingered in the report. Funny, when just last year Wal-Mart got credit for greening shrimp with its demands that all its shrimp meet sustainability standards. Now Wal-Mart and the Thai government are both talking about cracking down on abusers.

Labor abuses aren't the only thing that's fishy about shrimp farms. Remember the tsunami of 2004? Blame the brunt of its brutality on the rampant mangrove deforestation tied to shrimp farming. Same goes for the horrific cyclone that hit Burma. In addition, noncertified shrimp get daily doses of antibiotics, including human-grade drugs like Cipro, and chemical pesticides banned in North America are commonly used to kill parasites, fungi, and insects in shrimp ponds.

American shrimp from the Gulf of Mexico are considered a tiny bit better because the industry is more strictly regulated and the nets are supposedly designed to let sea turtles and other fish escape (though they still ensnare far too many threatened snapper). The top eco-conscious choices are **British Columbian wild-caught shrimp**, **California coonstripe shrimp**, and **Oregon pink shrimp** (the fishery has been certified sustainable by the respected Marine Stewardship Council). Though the USDA has yet to officially iron out its organic seafood program (until it does, California refuses to allow the label "organic" on seafood), a number of southern US farms are raising organic shrimp certified by European orgs.

Keeping track of which sea creatures from which coast caught by which methods get the green light can be nearly impossible. For a good pocket-size (and printable) guide, check out "Seafood Watch" at seafoodwatch.org. It focuses mainly on environmental sustainability and identifies fish heavy in mercury or PCBs. The Environmental Defense Fund has a website called "Oceans Alive" (**oceansalive.org**), which focuses on the health concerns associated with each fish and even has a handy chart that tells you how many meals a month of, say, yellowfin tuna or mahi mahi you should eat if you're a man, woman, older child, or young child, with big check marks down the side letting you know if it's in the "eco-worst" or "eco-best" category. The site also has consumption advisories, recipes, and a downloadable pocket seafood selector.

Organic Seafood: If you're looking for organic seafood, good luck. Very few countries certify it. Organic farms have been seen as a bit of a mixed bag: the number of salmon (or cod or trout) per pen is cut in half, they're fed human-grade fish meal, the fake pink dye is banned, but pesticides used to treat sea lice are still allowed (though restricted) and a carcinogenic chlorine-based disinfectant may also be permitted. It's better than conventionally farmed salmon, but far from perfect. If you see the "organic" label on North American fish, note that no standards are yet in place to control the use of

> **F**armed oysters, clams, and mussels get the THUMBS-UP *from environmentalists.*

the term, so there are no guarantees that what you're eating is actually organic. Still, you can find farmed East Coast antibiotic-free salmon fed organic feed at **Whole Foods** stores (**wholefoodsmarket.com**). (Organic salmon farmers, by the way, often use a natural algae-based pigment to make the flesh pink.) The chain also tries harder than most retailers to ensure that the fruits of the sea it sells are sustainable, though in a 2008 Greenpeace report, Whole Foods was fingered for selling some fish that shouldn't be on shelves. It's since been buttressing its sustainable seafood sourcing policies.

Shellfish: Shellfish lovers of the world, rejoice! **Farmed oysters**, **clams**, and **mussels** get the thumbs-up from environmentalists, so eat away. What makes them so ecologically sound to farm is that they basically feed themselves by filtering plankton out of the water, cleaning as they go. In fact, they even filter pollutants from surrounding water as they munch.

DAIRY

Ads tell us milk does a body good, but does it do much for the planet? Beyond the lagoons of manure and greenhouse gases, each dairy cow burps up nearly 20 pounds of smog-forming volatile organic compounds a year, helping dairy lands like the San Joaquin Valley flunk federal smog standards again and again. Many cows are also injected with bovine growth hormones (rBGH or rBST), designed to boost milk production by 15%. The hormones have been clinically linked to increases in mastitis (inflamed udders), infertility, and lameness in animals. And use of the milk boosters goes hand in hand with upping levels of antibiotics, since overworked teats are often swollen with infection (yes, that means pus in your milk). Luckily, the storm of controversy that has dogged hormone-heavy milk finally got **Wal-Mart**,

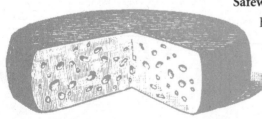

Safeway, and others to go rBGH-free for their in-house brands. **Starbucks** lattes are now totally free of the dodgy synthetics too (though organic milk was dropped from the menu). For a list of hormone-free dairies in your state, go to **sustainabletable.org**.

Organic Milk: Even organic milk has not been immune to controversy. As cartons of organic milk are flying off the shelves, organic dairy farmers have been accused of watering down standards to keep prices low and quantities flowing. The biggest scuffle has been the debate over how much time organic dairy cows should graze outside. Thanks to the vagueness of organic standards and lax enforcement, many dairy farms have been certified as organic when they provide little to no grazing time and look more like factory feedlots. The Organic Consumers Association even started a national boycott of half a dozen dairy companies in 2006. The USDA (which regulates organic standards) finally started moving to close the offending loophole in late 2008.

SUGAR

They say humans are composed mostly of water, but by now we must be about 40% sugar, given the amount of the white stuff we down. No joke—some of us eat our own body weight a year in hidden and not-so-hidden sugars. Just drinking one can of soda a day means downing half a large mason jar of sugar every week. And many fruit juices and fruity waters contain just as much of the sweetener, despite their healthy image. We all know sugar's bad for us, and we spend more and more time talking about what it's doing to our kids

SUGARCANE has probably contributed more to the LOSS OF BIODIVERSITY worldwide than any other single crop.

(elevated rates of obesity), ourselves (kidney stones, type 2 diabetes, heart disease), and our teeth (hello, cavities). But where do these powdery crystals come from? And what kind of environmental footprint does sugar leave?

Sugarcane: Tall stalks of tropical sugarcane are the sweet source behind up to 70% of the world's sugar. According to a WWF report, sugarcane has probably contributed more to the loss of biodiversity worldwide than any other single crop, because so many rainforests have been felled and important wetland habitats destroyed to plant it. Some countries devote half of their landmass to sugarcane. Pretty astounding. Beyond habitat loss, great quantities of unwanted leafy foliage growing on cane stalks are burned off in fires that release vast amounts of greenhouse gases into the atmosphere. Even the polluted wastewater discharged from the annual cleaning of sugar mills can have a deadly impact. In the 1995 mill cleanup in one region of Bolivia, millions of fish were killed in neighboring waterways, according to the WWF.

Efforts are under way to green up production in spots around the globe. Brazil, the world's leading grower of sugarcane (for both sugar and ethanol), has started taking action to improve the sustainability of its crop. It says it has drastically cut back on the need for water irrigation and uses 50% less fertilizer than Australia's sugarcane growers use. Brazil is also looking at ways to generate energy from sugarcane waste and has pledged to ban cane field burning by 2014 to limit polluting emissions. The country is also ditching 80% of its 500,000 sugarcane cutters in favor of mechanization, purportedly to reduce the workers' rights abuses giving it bad press in Europe. Of course, buying **organic sugar** is the greenest option. And fair-trade certified organic sugar? Now that's sweet.

Chemical Sweeteners: But I don't even eat sugar, you say—I sweeten my coffee with little yellow and pink packets. Well, take a seat and stay awhile. We need to have a little chat. Saccharin was the original artificial sweetener, discovered by accident in the late 1800s. Thanks to related bladder cancer findings in lab rats, the FDA tried to ban it in the '70s, but Congress placed a moratorium on the saccharin ban after serious consumer backlash from dieters (and industry players) across the country. You can still buy saccharin, but it's required to have

Researchers have found that SUCRALOSE (a.k.a. Splenda) lasts up to **7 YEARS IN WATERWAYS.**

a label warning that continued saccharin use can be "hazardous" to your health. Why some still insist on buying it, I don't know.

After years of speculation about aspartame's shadowy health impacts, including ties to cancer, lymphoma, and leukemia in rats, a recent US study won a lot of good press for concluding that there's no link between cancer and aspartame use among the half-million consumers interviewed. But diet cola junkies shouldn't celebrate just yet. In July 2005, a 7-year study by the European Ramazzini Foundation of Oncology and Environmental Sciences concluded that, for a 150-pound person, ingesting four to five 20-ounce diet drinks a day could spike your chances of leukemia, lymphoma, and other cancers. The study was brushed aside by regulators, but I'd think twice before downing that much cola on a regular basis, for more than one reason.

Even if that's enough to make you sleep peacefully at night, you might want to note that NutraSweet's aspartame factory south of the border is ranked up there with some of the most polluting facilities in the US. It released nearly 329,595 pounds of polluting methanol into Georgia's wastewater system in 2004 and pumped over 13,000 pounds of methanol into the air, according to EPA files. And scientists from the Norwegian Institute for Air Research have found that sucralose (a.k.a. Splenda, a chlorinated compound) is actually persistent in the environment, lasting up to 7 years in the waterways. They're still trying to figure out just what impact that might have on aquatic life. In the meantime, just google "Splenda" and you'll see that health and animal rights activists aren't short on beefs with the sweetener.

High-Fructose Corn Syrup (HFCS): You want to talk hidden calories? This is the culprit right here. Since this corn-based sweetener is up to 20% cheaper than other sugars and helps extend a product's shelf life, it's no wonder that cornstarch-derived syrup is in just about everything we eat, from burger buns to salad dressings. Though it technically comes from corn (a highly sprayed and commonly genetically engineered crop), HFCS is considered synthetic because of all the lab processing required to produce it. That doesn't stop the folks at Dr. Pepper Snapple from labeling 7UP "100% natural," a claim that ruffled a lot of feathers. Of course, with no one policing the widespread abuses of the term "natural," what's to stop them? Not only are we packing on the pounds because of the sheer volumes of HFCS we eat, but some researchers say that because of the way the sweetener is processed, our bodies don't feel full as easily and also pump more fat into our bloodstreams. Keep in mind that low-fat foods like yogurt can have up to 10 teaspoons of fructose sweeteners to keep our taste buds happy. How's that for a tricky treat?

Sustainable Sugar Alternatives: Looking for alternatives to destructively farmed sugar or chemical sweeteners that won't leave a bad taste in your mouth? For one, try fair-trade **organic sugar** (the fair trade part's important to avoid sugar cane's nasty labor record). And since sugar can be found in pretty much every fruit,

Low-fat foods like yogurt can have up to 10 TEASPOONS of FRUCTOSE sweeteners to keep our taste buds happy.

vegetable, and grain, there are dozens of plant-based sweeteners out there, including **barley malt**, **brown rice syrup**, and **agave nectar** (which is supposed to be lower on the glycemic index).

If you're looking for a natural sweetener that's calorie free, try **stevia**. It comes from the leaves of a Paraguayan and Brazilian shrub and has been used for ages in South America. I

Sugar derived from beets might sound "alternative," but it's actually the source of 55% of American sugar, and a good 1.3 million acres of sugar beets are grown in 12 US states—hardly a mom-'n'-pop crop. In fact, sugar beets are a heavy recipient of dodgy chemical pesticides like Monsanto's Roundup. So much so that Monsanto has now developed genetically engineered Roundup Ready sugar beets that are set to hit the market in 2008. The Center for Food Safety and the Sierra Club have filed a lawsuit against the USDA for deregulating the new frankenbeets, arguing they'll cross-pollinate and contaminate conventional sugar beets, organic chard, and table beet crops. They're pushing for Hershey, Mars, and American Crystal Sugar to take the same stance against GE beet sugar that they took in 2001. By the way, since sugar beets and sugarcane are used interchangeably to make a single sack of refined sugar, it would be impossible to tell if your bag of conventional sugar was GE beet-free.

won't lie, the ultraconcentrated sweetener takes a little time to get used to (I've yet to convince anyone it tastes good in my cookies), but it's nice in tea and doesn't cause tooth decay or affect blood sugar levels. Though it's commonly used in Japan, as well as Asia and South America, in the US the FDA has been giving the herbal sugar a hard time. Some say the FDA is just protecting the chemical sweetener industry. Either way, you can buy stevia as a dietary supplement in health stores (and weirdly, Coca-Cola is now trying to patent the stuff).

Products like **NuStevia** and **OnlySweet** eliminate some of the bitterness of stevia by cutting it with corn-based maltodextrin. **Xylitol**, which traditionally comes from birch tree bark, though is often made with Chinese corn, is much better for baking. It's also said to fend off cavities and is suitable for diabetics. Just note that it's toxic to dogs. **Smart Sweet** makes xylitol from American birch (xylitolworks.com). The natural sugar alcohol **erythritol** is another baking option and comes in organic form from **Organic Zero** (wholesomesweeteners.com) and **Smart Sweet**.

CHOCOLATE

Why is it that we often hurt the things we love the most? Oh, sweet chocolate, can you forgive us? You gave us your delicious beans and grew peacefully in the cool shade of the rainforest canopy, surrounded by teams of flittering birds, insects, and friendly mammals. Then, sometime between the Aztecs' christening you the food of the gods and today, our relationship turned bitter.

Sun-Grown Cocoa: In the '70s we began moving cocoa trees out of the shelter of the rainforest and onto single-crop farms in the blazing sun. Yields were certainly higher, helping us keep up with growing demand, but the trees grew stressed and prone to disease. Only hybrid cocoa plants fed high levels of chemical fertilizers and pesticides can survive the heat and dryness of open fields. And the shift often involved felling any rainforest in the way—destroying wild habitats and increasing soil erosion and runoff—all to make room for the popular cash crop.

Pesticides: The pesticides used on cocoa plants are often extremely hazardous and antiquated (see the sidebar on dirty pesticides on page 108), and they inevitably end up contaminating local groundwater and air. Think none of this affects you? Lindane, a persistent organic pollutant banned in many countries, turned up in every sample of chocolate tested in the late '90s by the UK's Pesticide Action Network.

Child Slavery: Slavery is part of chocolate's dark history, just as it is in the coffee and sugar biz. But in this case slavery isn't just a blemish of the past. Media exposés a few years ago revealed that forced labor is still very much alive on the cocoa plantations off West Africa,

CAROB

Can't stomach the eco consequences of chocolate? Or maybe, like me, you're just allergic to the stuff? The carob tree is a hardy, drought-resistant crop native to the Mediterranean that produces what some say is a cocoalike pod. Okay, so it doesn't really taste much like real chocolate, but it looks like it. Just as with chocolate, organic carob is best.

where 70% of the world's chocolate comes from. According to Save the Children, roughly 200,000 of the 600,000 children working in Ivory Coast cocoa fields work in dangerous conditions with machetes and pesticides. Many work on family farms, but an estimated 15,000 have been kidnapped or sold into slavery.

Hershey says an International Institute for Tropical Agriculture survey of 2002 found no slaves on the 4,500 farms checked, but the chocolate bar giant acknowledges that conditions need to improve. Kraft's assessment of the survey isn't quite so clear-cut: "while the investigation was inconclusive about the extent of child slavery, it did find that as many as 300,000 children were exposed to hazardous working conditions."

About a year earlier, the chocolate industry had signed on to the Harkin-Engel  Protocol—a voluntary action plan for monitoring the industry and certifying slave-free chocolate by 2005. Activists say the deadline has come and gone and little progress has been made. But the cocoa biz says it just needs more time and hopes to have half of Ghana and the Ivory Coast up to the standards of the protocol by 2008. Chocolate manufacturers like Hershey, Mars, and Cadbury have also joined with government groups, NGOs, researchers, and local farmers to develop the Sustainable Tree Crops Program (for coffee, cocoa, and cashews). The program is hoping to reduce pesticide use and improve overall farming practices and income levels for growers.

Organic Chocolate: All this dark talk about cocoa can upset earth-loving chocoholics. Well, get a hankie and dry those tears. Organic cocoa is grown without toxic chemicals, so noshing on **fair-trade organic chocolate** is virtually guilt-free. Also look for organic chocolate chips and fair-trade organic cocoa powder for baking and sipping.

COFFEE AND TEA

Can you tell by the Starbucks on every corner that Americans like their hot beverages? All right, so we drink only about 8 gallons of tea each a year, but we're swigging a good 25 gallons of coffee. It's no wonder caffeine has been detected in drinking water in cities big and

STARBUCKS' BIG GIVE (SORT OF)

Labor orgs have been pressuring major coffee companies to start selling fair-trade java for years now, saying the industry is making mountains off the backs of underpaid farm workers. Starbucks gave in (somewhat) and started selling fair-trade coffee in 2002, and these beans accounted for 6% of its sales in 2006 (about 18 million pounds). By 2007, over 55% of its beans had passed through the company's Coffee and Farmer Equity Practices program, in which farmers are paid a better price if they meet certain enviro and social standards. Great, except that two-thirds of qualified farms hadn't met most of the standards. Fair-trade activists want to see certified fair-trade purchases climb. And can someone please tell me why Starbucks can't sell beans that are both organic *and* fair-trade? The two should go hand in hand, or cup in cup.

small. Sure, it might be good to the last drop, but that's a hell of a lot of liquid, with some pretty heavy ecological ramifications.

Coffee: People say there's nothing quite as American as a cup of joe and some apple pie. Maybe they're right about the apple pie, but the red berry–covered coffee bush originated in Ethiopia, not New England. Leave it to seventeenth- and eighteenth-century Europeans to turn coffee into a common colonial crop, complete with slave labor and low-paid workers. And wouldn't you know it, the legacy lives on. Up to 25 million families in developing countries worldwide spend long hours each day trimming, weeding, and handpicking coffee beans for about the price of a cup of Dunkin' Donuts coffee. It would take them 3 days

WHAT'S THAT IN YOUR DECAF?

If you've managed to wean yourself off your caffeine addiction but still like to savor the flavor of a good brew, you're probably well acquainted with the world of decaf. What you might not realize is that, unless otherwise indicated, chemical solvents are used to extract caffeine from the bean. These chemicals include ethyl acetate (found in nail polish remover) and the probable carcinogen methylene chloride (which doesn't break down well in water and can be found in drinking water—gee, wonder why). If the package says "Swiss Water decaf," that means water was used to squeeze out the caffeine rather than chems. And if it says naturally decaffeinated, it means the caffeine was extracted either through the Swiss Water method or using carbon dioxide and water.

DIRTY PESTICIDES IN THE DEVELOPING WORLD

You think we have problems with pesticides in the US? Consider this: the UN warns that about 30% of the pesticides available in developing countries pose "a serious threat to human health and the environment" and don't meet international standards. Many, like DDT, have been banned in the developed world, but we're still making them and selling them to farmers in poor countries with shaky enviro regulations. To make matters worse, they're often poorly labeled, lacking warnings, safety info, or any mention of the highly hazardous ingredient. A disturbing study by the Institute of Development Policy Analysis found that internationally banned pesticides are being aggressively imported, peddled, and marketed in places like Bangladesh (even though they're illegal in that country), to the point that, by the late '90s, sales of outlawed pesticides were triple what they had been a decade earlier.

just to afford a Starbucks grande latte! It's no wonder Global Exchange calls coffee farms "sweatshops in the fields."

Like cocoa plants, coffee bushes are no longer grown under shaded rainforest canopies; rather, mass deforestation makes way for monoculture coffee plantations in the blazing sun. Sure, these farms produce higher yields, but they do so at a bitter cost. Out of their moist, cool element, the plants need large amounts of chemical fertilizers to get their nutrients. Sun-grown coffee attracts far fewer birds (a natural pest control), so chemical pesticides come into play. Planting coffee bushes in the sun also leads to greater soil erosion, which makes the farms more vulnerable to flooding. Pretty heavy consequences, all for a cup of java.

It would take coffee pickers 3 DAYS OF WORK just to afford a Starbucks grande latte.

Tea: The story is very similar on tea plantations. Working conditions are abysmal, and workers make very little money. Indian tea pickers, for example, average less than two bucks a day. Monoculture tea farms in places like India have been found to support nearly 50% fewer birds than rainforest-grown tea. Pesticides banned in the West, like DDT, are still being sprayed on tea leaves in developing countries. One French study found that dozens of green teas from China and Japan contained high levels not just of pesticides, but also of lead. Try reading that in your tea leaves.

KNOW YOUR COFFEE/ CHOCOLATE LABELS

Before you start fretting about your next coffee break or chocolate treat, rest assured that you can get your fix without endangering the earth. You just have to learn how to navigate all the mumbo jumbo that comes with your mochaccino.

- **Certified Organic:** No chemicals used in growing or processing; composting done, and weeds pulled by hand; shade cover maintained over coffee and companion plants; GMO-free. No criteria for protecting labor standards, even though organic farming is more labor-intensive. Best in combination with the "fair-trade" label.

- **Certified Fair-Trade:** Grown by small-scale farmers who are fairly paid and are part of an independent, democratic co-op; ecologically sensitive practices should be in place to ensure the product is sustainable and conservation-oriented (most bushes are shade-grown), but not guaranteed to be organic. (Over 500,000 farmers now produce certified fair-trade coffee.)

- **Shade-Grown:** Planted the traditional way, under the forest canopy, which attracts migratory birds.

- **Bird-Friendly:** Shade-grown and certified organic. (The criteria for certification have been developed by the Smithsonian Migratory Bird Center of the National Zoo. For each bag of coffee you buy at health stores, 25 cents goes to the Smithsonian's research and conservation programs.)

- **Rainforest Alliance-Certified:** Shade-grown by family farmers using integrated pest management (IPM) practices (not organic, but reduced pesticide use); trees and native plants planted in any areas not suitable for crops and as buffer zones along rivers and springs; farms hire locally, pay fair wages, and ensure access to clean drinking water and facilities.

- **Green Coffee:** Not necessarily eco-friendly—this term just means you roast it yourself. But many companies offer up green beans with heart (fair-trade, bird-friendly, and organic) and sell home roasting equipment.

- **Biodynamic Coffee:** Take organic production, fold in the cycles of the moon and stars, sprinkle in some crystals and complicated rituals, and you've got yourself a cup of ultraholistic biodynamic joe.

FOOD LABELS

You'd think shopping for earth-, body-, and critter-friendly foods would be simple—buy organic. But even conscientious shoppers can be confused by all the green labels that crowd the aisles. From "cage-free" and "naturally raised" to "sustainably harvested" and "pesticide-free," the options for responsible eating are seemingly endless. It's important to know which terms are government-regulated, which are enforced, and which tags can be whipped up by anyone with a brick of tofu and a dream.

Natural: Think this label is regulated? Take a wild guess. Sure, references to "nature," "Mother Nature," "nature's way," or "natural" should mean that a product comes straight from the earth, that the addition of manipulated ingredients like hydrogenated oils and synthetic preservatives would be unheard of. But alas, everywhere you look, someone's using and abusing the word "nature" because no one's watching. Although the USDA does regulate the term "natural" when it comes to meat (natural meat can't have artificial flavoring or coloring, chemical preservatives, or synthetics), it's not policing it.

> *Everywhere you look, someone's* **USING AND ABUSING** *the word "nature" because no one's watching.*

Organic: It may be organic, and then again it may not—if it's not certified, it's impossible to know. Some small farmers rebel against all the pricy red tape of certification and say their standards are higher anyway. This is an easier sell to trusted customers at, say, local farmers' markets. But again, it's strictly a trust system.

USDA Organic: This stamp reflects the fact that the US (namely, the Department of Agriculture) finally implemented a national organic system in 2002. Trouble is, it created a ceiling, not a floor, and certifiers that might have been more stringent were forced to "harmonize" or drop their standards to get in line with the national program. Several attempts to significantly water down USDA regulations have been bucked, though criticisms remain about organic chickens not getting genuine outdoor access.

In general, to qualify for organic certification, farms have to be pesticide-free for 3 years and must avoid synthetic inputs such as pesticides and antibiotics, as well as the deliberate use of GMOs, while emphasizing soil building. Certifiers also tend to have basic stipulations about animal welfare—except for that chicken thing, although European programs are better than those in the US on this front. They're also ahead in including labor and social equity clauses.

100% Certified Organic: You might pay a little more for it, but that's the price of purity, baby. No synthetic inputs can be snuck in.

Certified Pesticide Residue–Free: This NutriClean label doesn't mean that no pesticides were used; it just tells you that the pesticide residues on that piece of fruit fall below the limits set by the program for each pesticide. The certifier (Scientific Certification Systems) says those standards are *up to* 1,000 times tougher than legally permitted pesticide levels (though many are the same as the EPA standard) and that they encourage farmers to use pesticides that "decay before harvest."

Fair-Trade: The certified fair-trade logo ensures that any coffee, chocolate, sugar, or whatnot you get from the developing world is produced under strong labor standards. The logo often implies that ecologically sensitive practices are encouraged, but it doesn't guarantee it. Your best bet is "certified organic" *and* "fair-trade," but these are two expensive labels and not every farm can afford them, which means that not everyone thinks things are so fair. Still, it's the only way to know for sure that what you're buying hasn't been made in the equivalent of a sweatshop.

The fair-trade logo often implies that ECOLOGICALLY SENSITIVE *practices are encouraged, but it* DOESN'T GUARANTEE IT. *Your best bet is also* "CERTIFIED ORGANIC."

Biodynamic: Certification standards for this label are similar to those for "organic" but go one step further by requiring farmers to be in sync with the rhythms of nature and the cosmos and to use specially prepared herbs and minerals in compost and field sprays. Biodynamic farming embraces a philosophy focused on healing the earth; certifiers include Demeter USA.

GE-Free (or GMO-Free): Sorry, but so far there's no law mandating the labeling of genetically engineered/biotech foods. But you can help make it happen by firing off an e-mail asking your US representative to cosponsor the "Genetically Engineered Food Right to Know Act."

Heirloom or Heritage: Did you know that three-quarters of the world's edible crops have disappeared over the last century? Yep, that's according to the UN's Food and Agriculture Organization (FAO), which also says we used to eat about 10,000 different species of food plants and now 90% of the world's diet is down to 120. It seems the food biz didn't like all that variety and whittled it down to a few hardy, easily harvested types with a uniform appearance that could be patented and sold. Heirloom or heritage fruits, vegetables, herbs, and even turkeys are those that have been revived from our history. These strains have been around for at least 50 years, and their seeds are pollinated by nature, not man. These terms are not regulated.

> We *used to eat about 10,000* DIFFERENT SPECIES *of food plants, and now 90% of the world's diet is down to 120.*

Grass-Fed (or Pastured) Meat: Grass-fed cows are said to be much healthier (the animals get sick less and their meat is more nutritious for the end consumer) than a typical grain-fed cow. In fact, USDA researchers have found that hay- or grass-fed cows are less likely to have *E. coli* in their digestive tracts than are grain-fed types (and that's a good thing, since *E. coli* might otherwise contaminate your burger). But there are no federal standards or enforcement mechanisms in place for this label.

Naturally Raised Meat: This label generally means that your steak or pork was raised without hormones, antibiotics, or animal by-products. It could be free-range too, though animal lovers are upset that the USDA isn't making access to the outdoors mandatory now that the government is looking to step in and regulate this label.

Interestingly enough, **Chipotle** has committed itself to serving humane 100% naturally raised pork, and about 80% of its restaurants serve naturally raised chicken, with half offering naturally raised beef (chipotle.com). The private label **"Certified Naturally Grown"** is aimed at small farmers who can't afford organic certification and does have strong standards for grazing time.

Omega-3 Eggs: Sure, these eggs are better for your heart, thanks to flax- and vitamin E–infused diets, but are the hens happy? Omega-3 omelets are just as likely to come from hens kept in laying cages as regular old eggs are, and they're just as nonorganic.

Cage-Free (or Free-Run) Chicken: These cluckers don't have access to the outdoors, but they should be allowed to run around open-concept barns equipped with wire-grid floors. The United Poultry Concerns says, though, that cage-free hens are just crammed into massive sheds. By the way, this is an industry-devised term; no feds oversee the label or inspect the farms.

Free-Range (or Free-Roaming) Chicken: These hens get to see the light of day and snack off the land, but for how long? Hard to say, when the USDA hasn't created a minimum time. Also the term is regulated only for chickens, not for eggs, beef, or pork.

Hormone- or Antibiotic-Free: The USDA says that *no* poultry or pork may be injected with hormones in this country, so the "hormone-free" part of the claim is kind of useless (beef cattle are the only animals that are allowed to be treated with growth hormones in the US). Even on beef the approved label is "no hormones administered," since all animals have natural hormones coursing through their bodies. "No antibiotics administered" or "raised without antibiotics" means what it says but, as with the hormone labels, a company can use the label at will. Though the USDA holds producers responsible for accurate use, no one's really watching.

Certified Humane Raised and Handled: Though this SPCA-approved label doesn't mandate access to the outdoors, it does tell you that your chicken was not caged, your pig was not shoved in gestation stalls unable to turn around, and your dairy was not pumped full of growth hormones. Antibiotics may be given if, and only if, the animal's sick. All farms are inspected.

United Egg Producers Certified (Formerly Animal Care Certified): This label appears on about 80% of egg cartons sold in US supermarkets that meet the United Egg

TOP 5 EATING HABITS TO HEAL THE WORLD

Support local growers, whether through farmers' markets, farm-fresh food box deliveries (like CSAs; see page 85), or just keeping your eye out for "local" labels at the grocery store.

Go vegetarian or reduce meat/dairy intake—eating 20% less meat is like switching from a sedan to a Prius.

Choose fair-trade coffee, sugar, chocolate, and anything else you can find so you can be sure you're not supporting "sweatshops in the fields."

Buy certified organic products to avoid pesticide panic and spare waterways, wildlife, and workers from encounters with toxic pesticides.

Avoid resource-intensive, packaging-heavy fast food and heavily processed junk.

Producers' voluntary guidelines, but animal advocacy orgs say that these birds are still subject to laying cages, beak trimming, and forced molting (underfeeding birds to prolong egg laying). In fact, the Federal Trade Commission forced United Egg Producers to drop its misleading Animal Care Certified logo in 2005.

WATER

In terms of popularity, bottled water is the fastest-growing beverage in the world. Despite the fact that water flows freely from our taps, Americans are gulping back 8.8 billion gallons of the bottled stuff annually. Yes, from a health perspective we should be happy the bottled-water biz is taking sales away from sugar- and caffeine-laden colas. But from an environmental perspective, that's a hell of a lot of plastic for a liquid that once didn't come in anything.

Why are we sucking back so much bottled agua anyway, when sometimes it's little more than municipal water cleansed of off-putting odors and the taste of chlorine? Take Dasani, for instance. Coca-Cola, its maker, made the shocking admission that the designer water is actually just filtered tap water. Same goes for Aquafina and a quarter of all bottled waters out there. Why, then, you may ask, am I paying $1.50 for a mere 12 ounces of the stuff, especially when bottled water is less regulated than tap water? Well, people, we're suckers for a pretty package and good marketing. And many of us are willing to pay for portability and for the privilege of not having to use water fountains, which are harder and harder to come by.

By buying bottled water, you're encouraging the industry to commodify a priceless public resource, draining underground aquifers and disrupting ecosystems. Sadly, many places let companies set up shop and take as much water as they want without restriction or proper fees.

Bottles: Thin, light, clear—how bad can hitting the bottle be? Well, every year, 1.5 million tons of plastic go into supplying our bottled-water habit; and all sorts of nasty toxins, like benzene and ethylene oxide, are emitted during the manufacturing process. And let's not forget that plastic comes from petroleum, and a good 1.5 million barrels of oil a year goes to manufacturing those bottles, according to the Sierra Club. Another disturbing fact is that more water goes into making those bottles than you'll find inside the bottle itself!

"But water bottles are recyclable," you say. "What's the problem?" Well, for one thing, not all people are doing their part. Only 23% of the bottles are being recycled—that means 38 million bottles end up in dumps every year. Plus, even if you recycle yours, it doesn't go into making new water bottles. It gets "down-cycled" into hoodies and carpets instead—a dead-end solution.

Refilling your disposable bottle, thinking it's better for the environment? That may be true, but unfortunately, it's not so good for your health. Researchers say that without careful and regular cleansing, refilling plastic water bottles is a bad idea: bacteria buildup inside those bottles could trigger gastrointestinal illness or even pneumonia. Something about the type of plastic used for water bottles makes them more susceptible.

Even if you're not refilling it and your bottle came "fresh" from the store, there are other dangers to be concerned about. In the fall of 2008, the Environmental Working Group found traces of Tylenol, degreasing chemicals, and fertilizer residues, as well as high levels of carcinogenic trihalomethanes, a by-product of chlorination. A few years prior, the Natural Resources Defense Council (NRDC) tested 1,000 bottles of 103 brands and concluded that a third of them tested positive for arsenic or *E. coli*. In an earlier study by the NRDC, six brands tested positive for harmful chlorination by-products and for the ultratoxic solvent toluene. A study by the Institute of Environmental Geochemistry at the University of Heidelberg, Germany, found that disposable PET water bottles (PET, or polyethylene terephthalate, also goes by the "#1" recycling designation) leach a metallic element called antimony into your water. The longer the water sits in the bottle, the more antimony it

A quarter of all bottled waters are actually just FILTERED TAP WATER.

has. You and the planet would be far better off if you got yourself a reusable stainless steel canister (as described next) and refilled it at the sink.

Polycarbonate Plastic Bottles: These clear, hard, refillable bottles have long been fixtures of the hiker/biker/earthy/sporty set, touted for their ability to keep water tasting clean and plastic-free. Then, in 2008, the other bottle dropped. Though concerns have been raised about polycarbonate's leaching potential since the '90s, outrage began mounting around the plastic's key ingredient (the hormone disrupter bisphenol A). Even at low levels, scientists were linking bisphenol A to early puberty, breast and prostate cancer, obesity, and more. The FDA was attacked for giving the dodgy chemical a clean bill of health after being outed for basing those conclusions on only two industry-funded studies. By the time the National Toxicology Program raised serious concerns in April 2008 and 2 days later Canada announced that bisphenol A was going to be deemed a "dangerous substance," retailers had started dumping their inventory. Wal-Mart, Toys"R"Us, and REI announced that they were yanking the bottles from shelves. Even Nalgene, the

If your polycarbonate bottle looks worn, TOSS IT. Or better yet, turn it into a pencil holder, DECOUPAGE VASE, or waterproof first-aid kit.

brand that made the bottles famous, dropped polycarbonate like a hot potato. And still, to date of publication, the FDA has stood by the plastic.

Plenty of you are still using your old bottles thinking you're in the clear—that, at worst, it only affects babies. Although it's true that babies are most vulnerable, 93% of us have bisphenol A coursing through our bloodstreams, and a 2008 study linked higher levels of bisphenol A in adults to heart disease and type 2 diabetes. Do you really want to add more of the chemical to your diet? If your polycarbonate bottle looks worn, toss it. Or better yet, turn it into a pencil holder, decoupage vase, or waterproof first-aid kit. And reach for nonleaching water canisters made of unlined, high-grade stainless steel like **Klean Kanteen** (**kleankanteen.com**). Swiss-based **SIGG** makes aluminum canisters lined with a food-grade coating said to be free of bisphenol A (**sigg.ch**).

FYI: water cooler containers—the kind you find in offices and kitchens around the country—are also made of polycarbonate, though some companies are now offering glass.

Water Filters: If you're concerned about lead in your pipes or pesticide runoff from nearby farms, or you just hate the taste of chlorine, filters can be an excellent alternative to

MUST-READ BOOKS

- *In Defense of Food: An Eater's Manifesto*
  by Michael Pollan

- *Animal, Vegetable, Miracle: A Year of Food Life*
  by Barbara Kingsolver, with Steven L. Hopp and Camille Kingsolver

- *Fast Food Nation: The Dark Side of the All-American Meal*
  by Eric Schlosser

- *Slow Food Nation: Why Our Food Should Be Good, Clean and Fair*
  by Carlo Petrini

- *Bottomfeeder: How to Eat Ethically in a World of Vanishing Seafood*
  by Taras Grescoe

buying bottled water. (For portability, just fill up a reusable mug or bottle before you leave the house.) The question is, are you buying the right filter? Carbon filters vary in price range and quality (generally the more you spend, the more they'll filter out). Basic carbon filters like those made by Brita are great for taking that nasty chlorine flavor out of the water and will reduce but not eliminate lead, mercury, copper, cadmium, and benzene levels. In the "isn't it ironic?" category, Brita was bought out by, of all companies, Clorox, the maker of cleaning products laden with the very compound a Brita filter filters out! Some people have raised questions about whether Brita's styrene-methylmethacrylate copolymer plastic container leaches anything into the water. So far, no real dirt has floated to the surface, and third-party tests by the National Sanitation Foundation and the FDA found them to be safe.

There are, of course, plenty of alternatives. You just have to be willing to spend a lot more cash. **Reverse osmosis** filters out fluoride, minerals, and heavy metals but costs a mint and typically wastes 4 to 9 gallons of water for every gallon filtered. Pollution Probe's water report says that **distillers** are best at removing "the largest number of chemicals," plus they work on bacteria, viruses, fluoride, arsenic, heavy metals like lead, and even VOCs. The only thing is that they're pretty pricy, slow, and energy-intensive, and the machines need to be cleaned often.

There are three main certifying bodies to look for on filter labels: CSA International, the Underwriters Laboratories, and—best known of the three—the National Sanitation Foundation (NSF). Not all certified filters are of equal quality, but these bodies do make sure that any claims made by a filter are accurate, and NSF-certified filters have to meet particularly stringent standards. Before you settle on any particular brand, head to the NSF website (**nsf.org**) and look up the products you've been eyeing. You'll be able to see exactly what each filter is certified to remove. If you want them to work at all, make sure to give them lots of TLC; in other words, change them or clean them regularly, depending on the model.

ALCOHOL

What would summer be like without a nice cold beer to air-condition our insides, or winter without a glass of red to ward off the cold? And just imagine how glum office parties and frat houses would be without embarrassing quantities of the social lubricant. Even environmentalists get a thirst for the happy juice, though any earthy considerations tend to get checked at the bar door. Sure, you might support your local microbrewery or winery, but does that guarantee you a chemical-free drink? Well, fortunately for all you greenies out there, new options keep pouring in.

Wine: Back in the days when grapes were crushed between busy little toes, you didn't have to worry about pesticides in your wine. Alas, the chemical industry got to wine growers, as it did most other farmers on the planet. Pesticides, herbicides, and fungicides are the order of the day, sprayed over vineyards to keep bugs, weeds, and molds at bay (call me the green Dr. Seuss). The Pesticide Action Network (PAN) keeps a database of the top 50 pesticides used on wine grapes, several of which are on its bad-actor list because they're acutely toxic, groundwater contaminants, carcinogenic, or all of the above. PAN's European branch found that all 34 bottles of wine it tested contained at least one pesticide residue. The traces left in your glass aren't supposed to be harmful, but they're there.

A few growers have even turned to genetically engineered fruit. The Center for Grapevine Biotechnology is trying to breed a fungus-resistant grape that would need less chemical input, and scientists in Florida have spliced fluorescent jellyfish genes into the mix in the search for a cure for a vine-withering disease. Others are just trying to engineer the tastiest wine. Either way, consumers aren't likely to embrace frankenbooze, if they know what they're drinking.

But don't worry, dear winos. Pesticide use has come down at vineyards all across California in recent years. Nearly half of the 3 billion bottles made in California now follow the state's Code of Sustainable Winegrowing Practices. All right, so it's voluntary, but still it's a start. Luckily the state's brimming with certified organic wineries, like Napa Valley's **Frog's Leap** (frogsleap.com) or Mendocino's **Bonterra** (see the sidebar on Fetzer). You can even score certified organic bubbles from **Domaine Carneros** (domainecarneros.com), though only its estate brands are made with its organic grapes.

Or venture beyond organic (yes, it gets greener!). You'll find a few **biodynamic wines** that ensure genuine biodiversity on farms and align their practices with the cycles of the moon. **Frey**

> All 34 BOTTLES *of wine tested by European activists had at least one* PESTICIDE RESIDUE *in it.*

Vineyards (freywine.com) is a good source. One foot on Benziger's rolling biodynamic farm and you know you've found a piece of pesticide-free heaven (though, again, unless it's an estate wine made with Benziger's own grapes, it's not necessarily biodynamic).

Keep in mind that American wines can't call themselves "certified organic" unless they're

FETZER'S SUSTAINABLE GRAPES

It's always nice to see a big grower go green, especially when it means you can drink a glass or two of vino without an eco hangover. California-based **Fetzer** first pledged to shift all of its vineyards to organic agriculture practices in 1985, and since then it has become one of the largest certified organic wineries in the world (fetzer.com). Its **Bonterra** brand is 100% organic. Even Fetzer's nonorganic wines contain about 10% organic grapes (the rest are purchased from other vineyards), and the company is an industry leader in sustainable practices.

Fetzer was the first major winery to buy 100% renewable energy to power its facilities. Its tractors and trucks run on biodiesel blends. Grapes are irrigated only in very dry, hot weather to keep them from burning. Stems and seeds are composted and then spread as natural fertilizer. Fetzer's bottles are made of recycled glass (and are now 16% thinner to reduce their footprint). The labels on its Bonterra line are printed with soy-based inks. Plus, Fetzer pleases vegans by steering clear of (gulp) bull's blood, egg whites, and gelatin in its wine, even though the FDA has okayed all of those ingredients as wine additives. I'm feeling warm and fuzzy already, and I haven't even had a glass.

totally free of sulfites (that's tough when totally sulfite-free products go skunky fast), so most organic wines just say "made from organic grapes" and use only trace amounts of sulfites. In certified vineyards, grapes are fertilized with compost—not fossil fuel–derived fertilizers—and cover crops like clover and Queen Anne's lace are grown to attract beneficial bugs. Note that some European wines don't tell you they're organic on the front label, like **Château Chavrignac**, which has been fully organic since 1964 (**chateau-chavrignac.fr**). Others might not be organic but, like Australia's **Banrock Station**, give back to the earth (**banrockstation .com**). Through its wetlands foundation, Banrock funds wildlife and wetland projects in pretty much every country it's sold.

Do-it-yourself winos will be happy to hear that the greenest strategy of all is to make your own inebriant. You get to refill your glass bottles, and some do-it-yourself places offer organic grapes and try to minimize their use of sulfites—be sure to ask around in your area.

Natural Corks vs. Plastic: When plastic corks started popping up on the scene, there were rumors that the end of natural cork was near. Getting over our disdain for plastic stoppers, the story went, was all part of giving overharvested, slow-growing cork trees a break.

The rumors were only partly right. Yes, cork harvesting is a slow process (cork trees live to be about 500 years old, and it takes a good 40 years to grow a solid layer of harvestable cork). And yes, the end of cork is near, but only, insist environmentalists, if we stop buying cork! What? How could this be? Well, the WWF says harvesting cork bark is a sustainable ancient

> The GREENEST STRATEGY *of all is to* MAKE YOUR OWN *inebriant.*

practice that actually keeps the few cork forests in this world (mainly in the Mediterranean) alive and thriving. Turning to plastic makes these forests more vulnerable to encroachment by developers. Ad campaigns across Europe are now encouraging wine lovers to say no to plastic stoppers and put a cork in it.

Beer: If the thought of an ice-cold beer gets you hot but pesticides don't, you've got to find yourself a nice organic brew. Otherwise your hops will be heavily doused in synthetic fungicides, your barley will be sopping up pesticides, and any corn syrup used in the fermentation process could come from genetically engineered stalks.

Certified organic labels distributed across the country include **Wolaver's** (**wolavers .com**), **Butte Creek** (**buttecreek.com**), **Eel River** (**eelriverbrewing.com**), and **Goose Island** (gooseisland.com). Even the big boys are stealthily pushing organic brands now. Miller owns **Henry Weinhard's Organic Amber** labels (**henryweinhards.com**). Anheuser-Busch owns **Green Valley's Organic Wild Hop Lager** (**wildhoplager.com**) and **Crooked Creek's Stone Mill Organic Pale Ale** (**stonemillpaleale.com**).

Many microbreweries say their beer's better for you and the world because it's made with all-natural ingredients, as well as being unpasteurized and preservative- and additive-free. Some avoid killing trees by steering clear of labels. Is it important to support the local little guy over behemoth beer giants trucking their brew across the country? No doubt about it. Are microbrewers using organic or GM-free ingredients? Don't assume so unless it's written on the label (although you might have to call for clarification on their GMO policy). One thing is clear: supporting brews made close to home cuts back on the amount of fossil fuels used to get that cold one into your fridge. If that local beer is also organic, pour yourself a second glass.

The END OF CORK is near, but only if we stop buying cork.

Hard Liquor: Time for a toast—organic booze is finally flowing into American stores. Keep your eyes peeled for award-winning **Juniper Green Organic Gin** (**junipergreen.org**), made with organic juniper berries, coriander, angelica, and savory and distilled from organic grain; **Square One Organic Vodka** (**squareonevodka.com**); **Prairie Organic Vodka** (**prairievodka .com**); **4 Copas Tequila** (**4copas.com**); and **Papagayo Organic Spiced Rum**. **360 Vodka** isn't organic, but the grain is US grown, and the booze is filtered through coconut shells at an energy-efficient distillery and bottled in 85% recycled-content glass. If your local liquor stores don't carry any conscience-soothing booze, ask them to start. And don't forget to green your mix—look for certified organic juices and nectars when you're breaking out the cocktail shaker. And skip the straws and mini-umbrellas.

Supporting brews made CLOSE TO HOME cuts back on the amount of fossil fuels used to get that cold one into your fridge.

NO KIDDING
AROUND

Wee little creatures enter our lives, and we do all we can to care for them and shelter them from the world. We put caustic cleaners out of reach, we install carbon monoxide detectors to pick up on poisons in the air, and we buy tamper-proof lids to keep them from swallowing what they shouldn't. But new reports tell us our children's bodies are being inundated with chemicals we didn't even realize were lurking in our homes and in the goods we give them. What's a worried parent to do?

ENVIRONMENTAL TOXINS

We might picture pollutants in the air and in lakes, but never in our worst nightmares do we imagine them lodged in our children's tissues. Well, the CDC (Centers for Disease Control and Prevention) has been testing the urine, blood, and saliva of thousands of Americans, including kids, for the presence of toxic chemicals and the results aren't exactly cheery. Many children have higher levels than adults of stuff like heavy metals and phthalates (the potentially hormone-disrupting chem found in some soft plastics, fragrances, and beauty products). Kids were also found to have higher amounts of nonstick chemicals (found in furniture, carpets, clothing, popcorn bags, fast-food wrappers, and frying-pan coatings), brominated flame retardants (found in mattresses, clothing, furniture, and carpets), and some insecticides. What's more, the children tested positive for substances like PCB and DDT that had been banned before they were even born!

More jaw-dropping news came from the Environmental Working Group's (EWG's) tests on 10 umbilical cords (collected by the Red Cross) in 2004. What they found was beyond disturbing: an alarming average of 200 industrial chemicals and pollutants in each cord. Overall, they detected a grand total of 287 chemicals, of which

Overall, a grand total of 287 CHEMICALS—stuff like fire retardants, pesticides, and stain-resistant chemicals—have been detected in UMBILICAL CORDS.

180 are carcinogens, 217 are neurotoxins, and 208 cause birth defects in animals—stuff like mercury, fire retardants, pesticides, stain-resistant chemicals, trash incinerator and coal plant emissions, as well as car exhaust pollutants.

Many of these chemicals keep accumulating in the environment and our bodies, so perhaps it's not surprising that childhood cancers are up 21%, asthma rates are four times higher than they were in the '80s, and birth defects are on the rise. But it is, without a doubt, enough to make a parent mad as hell.

PHASING OUT CHEMICALS MAKES A DIFFERENCE!

Hearing that your child's body is burdened with chemicals we phased out years ago can be incredibly depressing for a parent. Part of the problem is that mothers inadvertently pass part of their toxic load on to their sons and daughters in the womb. Hard to control, but that doesn't mean we should give up the fight. Studies from around the world prove that banning chemicals does lower the level of toxins floating through our bodies over time. The last CDC biomonitoring study confirmed that removing lead from gasoline, paint, and other consumer products has made a huge difference—just 10 years ago, almost one in 25 children had worrisome levels of lead in their blood. By 2002, the number had dropped to one in 60! And in Sweden, high levels of flame retardants in mother's milk (levels that doubled every 5 years from 1972 to 1997) quickly dropped after manufacturers voluntarily pulled the nasty family of chemicals from products in the late '90s. For more info on getting the toxins out of your family, pick up *Raising Healthy Children in a Toxic World: 101 Smart Solutions for Every Family*, by Philip J. Landrigan, Herbert L. Needleman, and Mary M. Landrigan.

We've been unwittingly swaddling our children in fire-retardant PJs and feeding them persistent pollutant–tainted food—and where has the government been through all this? The EPA's Voluntary Children's Chemical Evaluation Program actually relies on companies to tell *it* if a product is especially dangerous to kids, not the other way around. Either way, funding ran dry for the program in 2007. While we wait for the feds to get off their fannies, here are some practical and easy ways to green your child's world and stop your blood pressure from hitting the roof at the same time.

PERSONAL-CARE PRODUCTS

Babies are tiny little things and far more vulnerable to the effects of chemicals than big people are. Yet nearly every cream, oil, and powder we dab on their bodies is loaded with dodgy chemicals and fragrances. By the way, those artificial scents that make your bundle of joy smell so sweet are crammed with potentially hormone-disrupting phthalates. In fact, a study published in the journal *Pediatrics* measured levels of nine different phthalates in the urine of 163 infants aged 2 to 28 months, and they all tested positive (most for seven or more phthalates). The more baby lotion, shampoo, and powder used on them, the higher their levels. Too bad several phthalates have recently been banned from kids' toys but are still okayed to be slathered on toddler skin (see page 141 for more on toys).

Plus, don't ask me why nearly every conventional baby product out there, including baby oil, jellies, and diaper ointments, is a petroleum industry by-product. As the old saying goes, what's good for the car must be good for the . . . baby? It makes even less sense when you consider that petroleum-based mineral oil and petroleum jelly actually block pores and can irritate rashes. Add ammonia and other skin irritants like sodium lauryl sulfate, and

TROUBLESOME TALC

We all had our butts powdered with talcum powder when we were kids, but now it's time to break with tradition. Talc may trigger respiratory problems and is linked to ovarian cancer in women who dust their underwear with it. Talc can be tainted with asbestos, but all cosmetics-grade talc is supposed to be asbestos-free. The National Institutes of Health (NIH) wanted even noncontaminated talc to be officially categorized as a probable carcinogen, but that was vetoed. Skip the controversy and try plain old cornstarch, rice starch, or arrowroot powder instead. The bonus is, you can buy these in bulk. Or look for them in the baby aisle of your local health store.

HEALING CALENDULA

Those pretty marigolds in your garden are hiding a powerful secret. The flowers, also known as calendula, hold potent healing abilities you'll learn to love if you've got a kid in your house or on the way. Creams containing this naturally anti-inflammatory, antifungal, antiviral plant work wonders on your baby's diaper rash (which is why it's so common in health store infant lotions). Calendula creams are also great for rubbing on scraped knees after a Little League game or when a bed-jumping session goes wrong.

you have yourself a bottle of baby lotion or cleansing gel. Check out the EWG's incredibly extensive report on every brand of baby cream, oil, and wash for details on which products you may want to avoid and why, and which choices are safer (cosmeticsdatabase.com/special/parentsguide).

Personal-Care Product Solutions: All this info can bring on postpartum depression, but cheer up—truly natural options are out there. You just have to read the labels to make sure products are as pure as they seem. Look for healing lotions with ingredients like calendula, chamomile, comfrey, shea butter, natural oils, and little else to help relieve diaper rash, cradle cap, and dry skin patches; **Badger** (badgerbalm.com) and **Babybearshop** (babybearshop.com) make some of the purest. Keep an eye out for alternatives to conventional no-tears shampoo free of synthetic fragrances and petrochemicals like PEGs and ceteareth; **Earth Tribe Kids Pure Botanical Baby Shampoo** (earth-tribe .com) or **Organic Blessings Little Angel shampoo** (organicblessings.com) are two good ones. **California Baby**'s **Sunblock Stick** (californiababy.com) is one of the most natural and effective sunblocks for your kids.

CLOTHING

Kids' clothes are so damn adorable it's hard to imagine they can be doing much harm. Truth be told, though, those PJs your little one's wearing probably contain flame-retardant chemicals in one shape or form. Synthetic fibers like polyester simply melt at high temps, so they have fire retardants built into the fabric. Only

1% of children's sleepwear is treated after the fact (that is, only if it's blended with nylon or acetate).

Best to avoid synthetics altogether and look for snug **cotton** brands instead, though you also want to minimize swaddling your kids in conventional pesticide-heavy cotton, especially if it's decorated with offgassing PVC plastic cartoons. (It can be hard to tell whether an article is made with PVC that's been softened with potentially hormone-disrupting phthalates, but if it's squishy plastic and has a strong plastic smell you might want to stay away. Or call the company directly if you're unsure.) And remember to wash all new clothing before you dress your kids in it, because it could have a sheen of wrinkle-resistant formaldehyde. Little ones don't need the exposure to a lung-irritating carcinogen.

Clothing Solutions: You don't have to dress your babe in a hemp sack to be earth-friendly. In fact, green kids' designers are sprouting up everywhere and stitching funky little outfits out of organic cotton, soy, and bamboo.

Sprout makes colorful bamboo/organic cotton kimonos, hoodies, and onesies for kids up to 24 months old (**sproutkidsclothing.com**). **Babysoy** designs supersupple two-tone tees, bodysuits, hats, and more (**babysoyusa.com**). **Kate Quinn Organics** sews the sassiest organic cotton dresses, velour jackets, jumpers, and hipster tuxedo shirts for kids as old as 8 (**katequinnorganics.com**). Julia Roberts' kids have been snapped in fun 'n' funky **Fig Organic Kids Fashion**, which makes stylee, colorful clothes with pretty screen printing on

WASH *all new clothing before you dress your kids in it, because it could have a sheen of wrinkle-resistant* FORMALDEHYDE.

organic cotton (**figkids.com**). Girls who love a good pirouette will absolutely adore **Twirls & Twigs**' whimsical collection made with a crafty mix of sustainable fibers, designer leftovers, and recycled cotton (**twirlsandtwigs.net**). Easy one-stop online shops like **Green Edge Kids** (**greenedgekids.com**) sell many of these labels and more under one (virtual) roof, though hand-me-downs and secondhand shops are the greenest.

DIAPERS

How do you look a baby in the eye and coo, "You're a little environmental menace, aren't you, shnookums?" It's really parents, though, who should be guilt-tripped, considering they're the ones who buy, and then toss, 5,000 to 8,000 diapers per child. That's about 18 billion disposable diapers a year in the US alone. I know, I know—they're oh so convenient; but all that plastic uses 3.5 billion gallons of oil, and about 250,000 trees go into making the cellulose filling in American diapers every year (with the average American baby pooping on 20 to 25 mature trees' worth of cellulose during the diaper years, according to the National Audubon Society).

They're then bleached a blinding shade of white—a process that emits nasty toxins like carcinogenic dioxins. (More controversy bubbles to the surface in alternative circles when you start chatting about the superabsorbent polyacrylates [SAPs] in diapers. SAPs were associated with toxic shock syndrome in tampon users in the '80s, but seriously, babies won't suffer from toxic shock as a result of having a little of this stuff near their bums. Still, some parents will tell you it gives their babies rashes.) Add it all up and you've got yourself one screaming headache.

Greener Disposables: If you can't kick your addiction to disposables, at least switch to greener brands. **Seventh Generation** and **Tushies** are chemical-, fragrance-, and chlorine-free and are made with unbleached cotton and cellulose. But they still use mostly regular petroleum-based plastic, and trees are axed for the pulp. Both brands insist they stay away from old-growth forests, and Tushies says its pulp comes from sustainable, Scandinavian, family-owned forests. Unlike their sister product, TenderCare—as well as Seventh Generation—Tushies are SAP-free.

> *Every year, 3.5 billion* GALLONS OF OIL *and about 250,000 trees go into making the* PLASTIC AND CELLULOSE *filling for American diapers.*

By far the greenest of the disposables is Swedish-made Nature Babycare (**naty.com**), which makes disposable diapers with biodegradable GE-free, corn-based plastic with a mix of SAP and totally chlorine-free wood pulp certified by the Forest Stewardship Council (FSC) and OK Compost. You can pick up one or more of these brands at your local health store or order them online from **tushies.com, seventhgeneration.com,** or **tendercarediapers.com**. Diapers.com and Target carry Nature Babycare.

Reusable Diapers: Truthfully, cloth-pushing parents aren't necessarily holier than thou if they're running their washer (full of hot, bleach-heavy water) and dryer (one of the most energy-intensive appliances) day and night. Only air-drying parents come out clean—especially if they use sustainable materials and wash them with natural soaps and an Energy Star washing machine or a portable pressure washer (see "Cleaning Cloth Diapers" for more info).

You don't have to go for the old-fashioned pinned, folded, cotton types (though those are the cheapest). New reusables come with elastic bands and snazzy Velcro tabs. Some

DIAPER WARS

The first throwaways were pretty poorly designed and didn't really catch on with moms and dads until the late '60s and '70s. Then, as environmental concerns started peaking in the late '80s ('twas the era of the *Exxon Valdez* oil spill and acid rain, after all), eco activists started pooping on plastic diapers' landfill-clogging record. By the time Earth Day 1990 rolled around, half the states were looking into either taxing or all-out banning the tossable bum wraps, and diaper service sales started taking off.

That's when mainstream diaper corporations launched an aggressive campaign against reusables, attacking cloth types for everything from the pesticides needed to grow cotton to the water pollution involved in washing poop-filled diapers. The cloth biz and environmental orgs fought back with studies of their own proving that cloth diapers use fewer resources than disposable types, but we all know who won the final battle for our wallets.

Well, get your rattles out—the battle of the nappies is heating up again. A 4-year-long British study recently concluded that cloth diapers are as damaging to the environment as the plastic type. The whole thing is giving environmentalists a bad case of diaper rash—and with good reason. Yes, the government-funded report did look at the life cycle costs of three options: home-laundered cloth, commercially laundered cloth, and disposables. And yes, the hefty 200-page paper weighed everything from the dirty oil extraction process involved in making plastic diapers and the water and pesticides used in growing cotton to the electricity needed to iron fold-'n'-pin types. In the end, the study concluded that all three are neck and neck.

But the report hinges on a few old-fashioned assumptions. The UK's Women's Environmental Network says that warm-water washes in A-rated (Energy Star) machines, for example, reduce climate-changing pollutants by 17% (not to mention all the water savings). The report also factored in a good chunk of tumble drying when parents should be air-drying their diapers—not just to save a lot of power but also to make them last longer. Investing in diapers made with unbleached, pesticide-free fibers like organic cotton, hemp, or bamboo puts you even further ahead, especially if they're stitched locally and used on more than one kid. Thanks to the outcry, the British government has supposedly promised to reassess the cloth diaper issue. Keep your eyes peeled for yet another report weighing in on the diaper wars at some point in the future.

are made of terry cloth, others of flannel. Even big chain stores sell brands like **Kushies** cotton flannel diapers (kushiesonline.com) and **Bumkins** polyester-cotton blends (bumkins.com).

Only a few brands of reusable diapers are made with organic fabrics, and they can be a little harder to find in stores but are readily available online. **Firefly Diapers** makes trim Quick Dry diapers with organic cotton fleece and low-impact dyes (fireflydiapers .com). **ChildOrganics** sells a variety of hemp and organic cotton diapers (childorganics .com). **New & Green** also carries supersoft bamboo (newandgreen.com). **Better for Babies** (betterforbabies.com) and **Loveybums** (loveybums.com) are other good sources of cloth diapers in eco fibers as well as organic wool diaper covers with elasticized legs and more. To find out where you can buy **Bamboozle** diapers made with renewable bamboo, head to bummis.com.

For pails of useful info on cloth diapers, including reviews and tips on overnight diapering, washing, and deciding which cloth diaper system is right for you, check out cutofcloth.com.

Cleaning Cloth Diapers: So you've got your first dirty diaper. Start by (1) shaking any solid poop into the toilet or (2) dunking the diaper in the toilet water (icky) or (3) investing in a handy diaper sprayer that attaches to the toilet. Beyond that, there are two ways to clean cloth diapers. Both involve tossing used diapers in a pail (one with a good lid on it to keep odors locked up) until you're ready to wash them, but the wet route means throwing them in a sealable pail that's half-filled with water plus ¼ cup baking soda, ¼ cup vinegar, a few drops of tea tree oil, and ideally a few squirts of **Bi-O-Kleen**'s **Bac-Out Stain**

> *Bleach will* BREAK DOWN CLOTH DIAPERS *faster, and the wrong detergent will give your babe a rash.*

& Odor Eliminator (bi-o-kleen.com). The second, more popular option is the dry route: you sprinkle a little odor-eating baking soda in the bottom of your pail, pretreat stains with a little Bac-Out, toss the diaper into the pail, and wash a whole pile at once every 3 days.

By the way, bleach will break down cloth diapers faster and the use of Ivory Snow in cold, hard-water washes could lead to product buildup. The wrong detergent will give your babe a rash. A good laundry product for diapers is **Bi-O-Kleen** laundry liquid or powder (not the Premium Plus one), **Ecover** liquid (ecover.com), **Ecos Free & Clear** laundry detergent (ecos.com), or **Seventh Generation Delicate Care** (seventhgeneration.com).

KEEPING CLOTH DIAPERS GREEN

- Wash in cold or warm water.
- Skip the dryer and hang to dry.
- Avoid chemical detergents.
- Flush only poop-filled liners.
- Buy enough diapers to wash full loads.

For a detailed breakdown of which laundry soaps are compatible with cloth diapers, check out pinstripesandpolkadots.com/detergentchoices.htm.

Diapers and diaper covers shouldn't be washed with other clothes, which is where things can start getting wasteful. But cloth lovers will kick ass on the green front if they've got one of those cheap, portable, hand-cranked washing machines that do a 5-pound diaper load using 90% less water and very little power (see **Wonder Wash** at laundry-alternative.com/washing.htm or **Wonder Clean** at lehmans.com).

Open-air drying is always best (plus the sun helps bleach the fabric), but if you must

gDIAPERS

gDiapers are the bum wrap for breeders who want their babes to be well dressed and light treaders in one ministep. They're basically a flushable diaper system with an adorable reusable outer pant and an inner lining made of wood pulp from farmed trees. (No old-growth trees are axed, the company insists, but trees are chopped to make the cellulose.) They're free of nasty bleaches, perfumes, and dyes, and are made extra absorbent by SAPs (described earlier). The good news is that you can actually put pee-soaked gDiaper liners in your backyard compost bin, and they should degrade within 150 days. Otherwise, gDiapers' flushable feature comes into play. The company says you'll need to flush twice to get them down without clogs. You'll have to do your own calculating to compare how much water your toilet uses per flush with how much water your washer would need to do a load of dirty diapers. Ultimately, they're not dirt-free, but gDiapers are a greener compromise for parents who aren't keen on cloth but don't want to toss plastic with every poop.

use a dryer once in a while, skip the chem-filled fabric softener and add ¾ cup vinegar in the final rinse. It's easier on the earth and reduces diaper rash.

If you're too busy or pooped to clean your own reusables, consider a diaper service. Check your phone book for listings in your area. Just note that it can be impossible to find a service that doesn't use harsh bleach. Be sure to ask.

Wipes: Many moms would smack me if I tried to take away their disposable baby wipes, so let's compromise. While you're at home, why not try the old damp-cloth method? When you're out and about, take along some unscented, alcohol- and chlorine-free **Seventh Generation** or **Tushies** baby wipes with you. Like everything else mentioned here, you can pick them up at most health stores and green general stores. They're moistened with things like aloe vera and vitamin E and, unlike other wipes, aren't chlorine-bleached, so the manufacturing process didn't create supertoxic dioxins. You can also buy reusable organic cotton or hemp wipes from **New & Green** (**newandgreen.com**) or **Hankettes** (**hankettes .com**).

BABY BOTTLES

As far back as 1999, *Consumer Reports* found that polycarbonate baby bottles leach small amounts of estrogen-mimicking bisphenol A when heated or after prolonged use, but the FDA insisted we were safe. Since then, critics have charged that investigations into the products' safety have been marred by conflicts of interest. The *LA Times* reported that government studies were being conducted by a private consulting company with close ties to the chemical industry. And still the FDA stuck by the compound.

By the winter of 2008, two more organizations had tested Avent, Dr. Brown's, Evenflo, Gerber, and Playtex baby bottles and found that all five brands leached bisphenol A, and

RUBBER VS. SILICONE NIPPLES

If you can't use nature's best nursing device—the female breast—then you should know that standard amber-colored rubber nipples may be contaminated with low levels of carcinogenic nitrosamines. Best to replace them with clear, safe, silicone nipples, which also last longer.

BISPHENOL A-FREE BABY BOTTLES AND SIPPY CUPS

- **BornFree:** bisphenol A-, phthalate-, lead-, and PVC-free plastic baby bottles, training cups (6–12 months), and drinking cups (12+ months) (all made of safer PES), as well as vented glass bottles (newbornfree.com)

- **Evenflo:** glass bottles with rubber nipples and a bisphenol A–free plastic Comfort line (evenflo.com)

- **Dr. Brown's:** glass bottles with silicone nipples (handi-craft.com)

- **Klean Kanteen:** stainless steel kids' bottles with sippy cup lids (kleankanteen.com)

- **Thermos Foogo:** line of sippy cups and pop-up silicone straw cups; stainless steel inside and out (thermos.com)

- **Green to Grow:** bisphenol A- and phthalate-free PES plastic baby bottles (greentogrow.com)

- **MAM:** line of baby bottles and training bottles in nonleaching, bisphenol A–free polypropylene plastic (mambabyusa.com)

what's more, leaching increased dramatically when the bottles were heated (one zap in the microwave caused as much leaching as 60 to 100 rounds in the dishwasher). It didn't help matters that the FDA admitted its green-light approval of bisphenol A in baby products rested on two industry-funded studies. Congress wisely called on the FDA to reassess matters. But the clock was ticking on the plastic. By the spring of 2008, when the National Toxicology Program raised concerns of its own and Canada announced in the same week that it was declaring the plastic dangerous, the market shook. Playtex said it was shifting to bisphenol A–free bottles and Toys"R"Us, Wal-Mart, and others announced they were phasing the plastic out. Almost overnight, safer plastics started popping up everywhere, with every company offering bisphenol A–free alternatives (made with #4, #5, and PES [polyethersulfone] plastics).

For those who would rather stay away from the politics of plastic altogether, (even if, to date of publication, the FDA has stood by industry) old-fashioned glass bottles are making a big comeback. While you're shopping for your tiny tot, don't forget your older babes could still be slurping on bisphenol A in their clear, hard sippy cups. And young'uns could be sucking back phthalates through soft plastic bottle liners.

FOOD

What we put in our babies' bellies is even more important than what we slather on their bottoms. Young children tend to eat a lot of only a few types of food, even after they move beyond their milk habit, so it's important to pay close attention to what we spoon into their mouths.

Baby Food: If your child is in the mushy fruit and veg stage, you should know that many conventional baby foods have tested positive for several different pesticides that are considered probable human carcinogens, neurotoxins, and endocrine disrupters (punch in "baby food" at **ewg.org** for more info). The fact that babies tend to eat much more of a small number of foods doesn't help. To add insult to

All the nutrients in most jarred foods have been BOILED AND PASTEURIZED AWAY.

injury, all the nutrients in most jarred foods have been boiled and pasteurized away.

What's the point, when it's so easy to make your own? Just steam some peeled apples, peas, yams, or whatnot (ripe bananas and pears don't need steaming) and toss them in the food processor or blender. You can even make a huge batch and pour extras into ice cube

TAINTED FORMULA

Just like baby bottles, baby formula has been rocked by controversy. In fact the metal cans are lined with the same dodgy bisphenol A and have been found to leach, particularly into liquid formula. If you can't breast-feed, always look for powdered formula or for liquid formula in nonleaching polypropylene plastic (#5). Breast pumps, tubes, and jars should also be bisphenol A-free, like **Medela**'s (**medelabreastfeedingus.com**).

FYI: even though trace pollutants are turning up in mother's milk, the medical and environmental communities agree that it's still more nutritious and provides more immune-building antibodies for your child than formula does.

KIDS' FOODS WORTH SPENDING MONEY ON GOING ORGANIC

- All bottled baby food (purees may contain trace pesticides).

- High-pesticide fruits—like apples, peaches, pears, nectarines, imported grapes, cherries, and berries.

- High-pesticide veggies—like spinach, potatoes, bell peppers, and celery.

- Meat, eggs, and dairy products (which could otherwise be heavy in hormones and antibiotics).

- Anything else you can afford to buy. (Conventional broccoli and cereal might not have much pesticide residue on them, but that doesn't mean wildlife, waterways, and workers didn't suffer from being doused in chemicals used in their production.)

trays for freezing. Toss the frozen cubes into large phthalate-free baggies (all **Ziploc** and **Glad** products are phthalate-free), and then defrost them in the fridge or on the counter. If you're worried about the plastic used for ice cube trays, check out **Fresh Baby** PVC-free freezer trays (Fresh Baby also carries natural baby cookbooks) (freshbaby.com). Homemade baby food is much cheaper than store-bought stuff, and it's far healthier, especially if the foods you use are local and organic. If your produce is not organic, be sure to clean it well with a natural fruit wash like **Fit** before you cook it (for more info on cleaning fruits and vegetables, see page 75).

If you don't have time to make your own baby food, health stores and even grocery stores are stocked with certified organic bottled brands such as Earth's Best (earthsbest.com), BoBoBaby (bobobaby.com), and Healthy Times (healthytimes.com). They also make wheat-free organic teething biscuits, cereal, applesauce, and cookies—pretty much everything your kids like to eat, although they can be fairly high in sugar, even if it's in the form of organic cane juice. Wouldn't you know it, big brands like **Gerber** make organic baby food now too.

Big-Kid Food: It would be great if you could afford to feed your family nothing but organic food, but hey, it's not cheap or always locally available. Still, buy as much of it as you can, as often as you can. Many of the persistent chemicals used on crops 30 years ago are still in our bodies—and our children's bodies—to this day. It's best to remove as many potential sources as soon as possible—especially in light of one study by researchers from the Centers for Disease Control and Prevention and Emory University, which concluded that "organic diets provide a protective mechanism against organophospurus pesticide exposure in young

PREPPING FOR PREGNANCY: GETTING THE TOXINS OUT EARLY

Moms can pass hundreds of chemicals on to their unborn babies, so it's a good idea to start phasing out the hidden toxins lurking in your life when you're planning a pregnancy, or at the very least when you find out you're pregnant. Here are a few tips for giving your unborn baby a head start in life:

- **Say goodbye to tuna.** Canned albacore, fresh tuna, and swordfish are high in neurotoxic mercury, which can be harmful to your babe-to-be.

- **Avoid pesticides.** Home pesticide use on lawns and indoor bugs is one of the main reasons that biomonitoring studies are finding pesticides in our bodies and newborn babies.

- **Eat lean.** Animal fats store persistent chemicals such as PCBs and dioxins, so it's best to cut them out and choose fat-free milk and lean cuts of meat.

- **Embrace stains.** Stain-resistant coatings on older furniture and carpets are full of persistent PFOS (perfluorooctanesulfonate) that is building up in our bodies (see page 230 for more info).

- **Work clean.** Any woman working with powerful chemicals at her job should consider asking for a position change while she's pregnant. Hairstylists, for instance, should say no to chemically dyeing and perming. The children of hairdressers in a large, 20-year-long Swedish study were found to have higher rates of birth defects, cleft palates, and spina bifida. Even heavy use of hairspray was linked to lower birth weights.

children whose diets regularly consist of fresh fruits and vegetables, fruit juices, and wheat-containing items. Such protection is dramatic and immediate."

Look at what your kids eat and drink the most of—like milk and apples—and consider switching to organic for those first. Organic milk isn't much more expensive than regular. Dry organic goods like cereal and produce like bananas and carrots are also quite affordable. It's the organic red peppers that'll kill your budget, but you can build up to those. Signing up for a food box via community-supported agriculture is a great way to get organic produce at a good price (see page 85 for more on CSAs). FYI: buying organic is the only way to be sure that what you're eating doesn't contain genetically engineered, irradiated ingredients.

Whether you yourself are vegetarian or not, keep in mind that 94% to 99% of our exposure to persistent organic pollutants like PCBs and dioxins comes from our food, especially fatty stuff like dairy, fish, fatty meat, and even breast milk. You might want to limit your child's intake of red meat, fatty fish like farmed salmon (which has also been found to have brominated fire retardants), tuna (especially canned white albacore and fresh tuna, which are high in mercury), and other fatty meats and dairy products. (See the "Food for Thought" chapter.)

Look at what your kids eat and drink the most of and consider SWITCHING TO ORGANIC for those first.

BABY'S ROOM

Besides Lamaze classes and diaper shopping, one of the first things parents work on when they find out they're pregnant is the baby's room. The main concern tends to be whether to paint it blue or pink, or go Switzerland-neutral with yellow. But as we put all that blood, sweat, and panic into fixing up the nursery, we don't really think about the chemicals we're carting in.

Cribs, Car Seats, and Children's Furniture: This is where we rest our babes so they can be safe and snuggly through the night, so we tend to look for cribs that meet basic safety standards and, well, that's about it. The question is, what's the stuff made of? Composite woods are bound together with carcinogenic formaldehyde, which offgasses smog- and asthma-inducing volatile organic compounds (VOCs) long after we assemble the furniture.

Same goes for all the other pressed-wood furniture we buy. In fact, a 2008 report by Environment California found that 12 of 21 composite cribs and changing tables (including products from Child Craft, StorkCraft, Delta Enterprises, and Jardine) emitted formaldehyde at levels known to encourage allergies and respiratory problems in kids. Even a solid oak crib with one composite-wood drawer was enough to spoil air quality in a nursery. In fact, in the fall of 2008, California's attorney general sued Child Craft, Delta, StorkCraft, South Shore Industries, and Jardine for failing to warn consumers (under California's Proposition 65) about the carcinogenic formaldehyde emissions coming from their products. It's best to get unfinished solid wood that you can finish yourself with natural hemp oil, a beeswax polish, or some sort of VOC-free wood finish.

Be leery of anything stuffed with polyurethane foam. According to a 2008 report by Friends of the Earth, 56% of all infant carriers, 44% of all car seats, 40% of all strollers, and 19% of all portable cribs were found to have high levels of persistent fire retardants that build up in our bodies. An organic cotton or hemp sling can help you cart your babe anywhere without worry—available at any eco baby shop, like **Best Baby Organics** (**bestbabyorganics.com**), or specialized retailers like **Pretty Momma Sling** (**prettymommasling.com**)—but you still need a car seat if you're going to pop your child in a vehicle.

The Ecology Center rates car seats for toxicity, but you'll notice that even within one brand, like Britax, one model might get the green light while another fails miserably. Best to check the guide yourself (**healthycar.org**). Friends of the Earth says it found the same inconsistency even within the same models of Graco Pack 'n Play portable cribs that they tested. One crib might have high levels; another might have none. It can be impossible to tell, so call whoever made your product and demand clarification, as well as a move away from brominated fire retardants altogether.

Specialty furniture designers like **Argington Modern Children's Furniture** use only sustainable Forest Stewardship Council–certified woods and nontoxic finishes for their adjustable cribs, high chairs, changing tables, and beds (**argington.com**). **Totally Organic** carries more traditional and whimsically painted FSC-certified cribs, trundle beds, youth beds, and more (**totallyorganic.us**). **Q Collection Junior**, endorsed by Gwyneth Paltrow, crafts the first cribs, chests, and changing tables certified for indoor air quality by Greenguard (**qcollectionjunior.com**).

At the big-brand level, **IKEA** makes brominated fire retardant–free cribs, cabinets, changing tables, and high chairs from farmed trees, rather than pillaging from natural forests. And all of IKEA's pressed woods are essentially formaldehyde-free (ikea.com).

The cool thing with both IKEA and Argington is that a lot of their baby furniture is multifunctional, adding to the longevity of the products. Cribs can be converted into junior beds, and changing tables can turn into big people's tables or shelves. For a large selection of sustainable cribs, toddler beds, changing tables, and cute kids' furnishings, check out the **Dax** online eco department store (daxstores.com).

Mattresses: Knowing what's in your baby's mattress is enough to give any parent bad dreams. Conventional mattresses are stuffed with offgassing polyurethane foam that might have been treated with dodgy fire-retardant chemicals (though some of the most dangerous brominated fire retardants have been phased out, that doesn't mean many other persistent formulations aren't still on the market), as well as antibacterial and stain-repelling chems. Rip open the plastic wrapping when you get it home and you can just smell the fumes coming off it. Be sure to air it out for several weeks before you plop your baby down on it. You might even want to put a tightly woven dust mite–proof cotton barrier cloth between your baby and the mattress.

And invest in organic bedding made with natural fibers such as cotton and naturally fire- and water-resistant wool. **Naturepedic**'s **No-Compromise crib mattress** is made with organic cotton, has a nonleaching polyethylene surface, and comes with a dust mite barrier cloth. It's wool- and latex-free for children with allergies (naturepedic.com). **Natura** makes mattresses with breathable natural latex innards instead of springs, though not all its mattresses are organic cotton, so ask. Natura also carries organic cotton sheets, crib skirts, bumper pads, and organic cotton/wool comforters (naturaworld.com). Online shops like **EcoBedroom** (ecobedroom.com) and **Good Night Naturals** (goodnightnaturals.com) sell a variety of earth- and body-friendly mattresses for your child, including more affordable chem-free options for parents planning on only one child or for those who want more durable beds for longer-term use.

If you're worried about your kid peeing on the mattress every night, don't—I repeat, do not—get a vinyl mattress cover (though it's probably already built-in). Vinyl offgasses potentially hormone-disrupting phthalates now found in babies' urine. If you can't find a vinyl-free crib cover, just buy clear plastic polypropylene sheeting used for house painting and wrap that like a flat sheet around the mattress. Better yet, buy a wool puddle pad from a company like Natura. (See page 177 for more on mattresses and bedrooms.)

Paint: Renovating parents take note: the EPA has issued new rules to protect children from lead-based paint hazards when contractors are repairing pre-1978 houses. Limit exposure to lead dust by dusting with a damp cloth regularly and getting kids to wash their hands frequently. If you're worried, talk to your doctor about testing young children for lead. Be sure to slap **VOC-free latex**, **clay**, or **milk paints** on your nursery walls to avoid nasty fumes. (See page 231 for more info on paint.)

Carpeting: In kid-friendly households, the natural choice for flooring seems to be soft, cushy carpeting that your rug rats won't scrape their knees on, but wall-to-wall types are made with petrochemicals, and although the industry has greatly greened itself over the years, VOCs still offgas from new carpets. Carpets have also been known to trap allergens such as dust mites.

Cushy **cork**, fast-growing **bamboo**, and **local wood** flooring certified by the Forest Stewardship Council are all sustainable options (though you want to make sure that bamboo flooring is formaldehyde-free). If you want to soften up the room, throw down a vegetable-dyed **organic hemp rug** in sage green or Oregon grape (**rawganique.com**). (See pages 223 and 227 for more info on flooring and carpeting.)

> *Cushy cork, FORMALDEHYDE-FREE bamboo, and local wood flooring certified by the Forest Stewardship Council are all SUSTAINABLE OPTIONS.*

TOYS

We all love to find that perfect gift for the tots in our lives—the kind that secures you the title of "cool aunt" or "hip dad." Trouble is, most of the items on their wish lists are loaded with the types of toxins you don't want them playing with. And after the recall of millions of mainstream toys like Thomas & Friends trains and Barbie in 2007, toy shopping became downright nerve-racking. Especially once we learned there was only one toy inspector at the Consumer Product Safety Commission. Luckily, regulators are starting to wake up and smell the toxins.

Plastics: Action figures and dolls are often molded from that eco villain PVC, considered the worst of all plastics. In the late '90s, Greenpeace warned the public that 20% of PVC toys

it had tested contained lead. At the time, health agencies said that although that might be true, the vast majority did not have "extractable lead that exceeded the international standard." Translation: not a lot of lead could be chewed or sucked out by young ones. Of course, all that changed once alarming levels of lead started being detected in toys on a mass scale a couple years back. The good news is that a new consumer protection law that kicks in starting 2009 should seriously reduce (though not eliminate) the amount of lead in toys.

Now, if it's a soft, squishy toy destined to be drooled on and chewed by the youngest ones in your circle, the PVC was likely softened with potentially hormone-disrupting or carcinogenic phthalates, which have a nasty habit of offgassing into the air. Even plain old modeling clay can be made with PVC and has left phthalates on the hands of kids who played with it, according to the Vermont Public Interest Research Group. No wonder phthalates are turning up in the urine of every baby tested! Lucky for us, Congress came to its senses and voted to force six phthalates out of children's products starting in 2009 (three will be banned permanently, and the other three will be kept off shelves unless manufacturers can prove they're safe).

For updates on toy safety, as well as a searchable database of toxic toys, check out **toysafety.net**.

Stuffed Animals: It ain't just plastics that can spoil playtime. Teddy bears are stuffed with either synthetic petroleum-based fills or pesticide-heavy cottons. Many toys, including teddy, are sprayed with brominated fire retardants, the very kind turning up in breast milk. Yeesh! Better to get all-natural kinds made with organic fibers, wool batting, recycled sweaters, or tofu—yes, tofu. **Tofu Bear** and his buddies **SOYnia Bunny** and **SOYphia Goat** are ultrasoft snugglers made with patented Soysilk. These cashmerelike plushies are woven from the waste created in the manufacture of tofu and are petroleum-free (**tofubear.com**).

Kenana Critter Knitters offers wonderfully unique fair-trade, vegetable-dyed, knit elephants, monkeys, tigers, and more (**kenanausa.com**). **MiYim** makes an adorable collection of huggable organic cotton bears, bunnies, hippos, and monkeys in regular and puppet form (**miyim.com**). **Eco-artware.com** has the cutest little piglets, penguins, ducklings, and elephants, which they call **sweater critters**. They're made of old wool sweaters and stuffed with shredded secondhand polyester. Too cute.

Wood: Wooden toys look so old-fashioned, you just assume they must be good for the planet. But even a carved choo-choo train can be made with varnishes and paints high in air-polluting VOCs and lead (Thomas the Tank Engine's maker ended up paying a $30 million settlement over lead paint woes). Plus, you wouldn't want your kids' playhouse to be chopped from old-growth trees that provide habitat for other kids (like baby bears or baby baboons), now would you? Look for wooden toys and games crafted from sustainably harvested woods like **rubber**, **bamboo**, and **FSC-certified sources** (especially American grown ones) and sealed with nontoxic finishes like beeswax.

Packaging: Don't even get me started on all the freakin' packaging that quadruples the size of the actual toy and ends up in landfills—a serious problem when you realize that Americans spend about $22.5 billion on toys annually.

Keep an eye out for toys with minimal packaging. Who needs a giant, oversized box for a toy half its size? These toys only take up more room on the truck, so more emission-spewing trips are needed to haul them to you. By making the packaging a touch smaller on a private-label brand of toys, Wal-Mart says it'll need 497 fewer freight containers and will save $2.4 million per year in freight costs, 3,800 trees, and over 1,000 barrels of oil. Not bad. No word yet, though, on whether Wal-Mart is working to improve labor conditions in its supply factories around the world.

Look for toys with MINIMAL PACKAGING. Who needs a giant, oversized box for a toy HALF ITS SIZE?

Eco-friendly Toys: Though earth-conscious toys aren't exactly taking the malls by storm, there is a decent selection out there if you know where to look. Many smaller toy stores carry all sorts of cool products, and even large corporations like **Toys"R"Us** are stocking organic and FSC-certified wooden toys. **Plan Toys** makes great dollhouses, boats, instruments, and whole cities with wood from trees that no longer produce rubber (**plantoys.com**). And they're coated with a nontoxic finish. **HaPe** makes a cool line of memory, strategy, and creative games from sustainable bamboo: young tots can balance monkeys in a tree, while older kids can fiddle with trapezoids (**hapetoys.com/bamboo.asp**). California-based **Tree Blocks** crafts unique tree houses and dollhouses from reclaimed wood (**treeblocks.com**).

If you're willing to shop online, you'll find all kinds of cool stuff. **EcoToyTown** has a fun collection of earth-friendly toys, including a crate of stuffed vegetable teddies made of organic cotton, hemp Frisbees, garden flower and leaf presses, and nifty cooperative board games (**ecotoytown.com**). These are feel-good games based on saving the earth cooperatively, rather than stealing property, sinking battleships, and generally beating the crap out of your competitor.

Magic Cabin has an amazing website that makes me want to be a kid again

ARSENIC IN OUTDOOR PLAY SETS

If you've got a wooden outdoor play set that's more than a few years old (made in 2003 or before), chances are it's heavy in arsenic. Same goes for our gazebos, fences, and decks. In fact, over 90% of all outdoor wooden structures in the US were made with arsenic-treated lumber (pressure-treated chromated copper arsenate [CCA] wood). Sure, the wood is weather-resistant, but that arsenic leaches into the soil over time, and CCA wood has now been banned for anything residential, including play sets, picnic tables, and boardwalks. The Environmental Protection Agency isn't telling us to rip out our old backyard sets, but they are warning parents to make sure their little ones wash their hands thoroughly when they're done playing on CCA wood sets and in surrounding soil.

Even though arsenic is really, really bad for us (it's a known human carcinogen), the EPA said CCA wood doesn't pose any "unreasonable risks to public health" and anyone who's worried should just paint the play set with an oil-based semitransparent coating once a year. But the Environmental Working Group tested 263 decks, play sets, picnic tables, and sandboxes across 45 states and found that arsenic levels on wood surfaces remain high for 20 years, even if they were resealed just 6 months prior. And in nearly two of five backyards and parks, the soil tested had enough arsenic to qualify as a hazardous EPA Superfund site. Many municipalities across North America have since torn arsenic-laced playgrounds down.

If you get rid of yours, whatever you do, don't toss the dismantled wood in a fire—you don't want to be inhaling that stuff. Treat it as toxic waste and take it to your municipal hazardous waste depot. And if you choose to keep your set up, be sure to reseal it every 6 months. For more info, see **ewg.org/reports/allhandsondeck**. By the way, wood with a greenish tinge is almost definitely CCA. For an arsenic home testing kit, head to **ewg.org/reports/poisonwoodrivals/orderform.php**.

(**magiccabin.com**). It has all sorts of whimsical eco-friendly toys made with natural or recycled materials, like a recycled-tire horse swing, jungle safari play sets made of rubber wood, silk dress-up costumes, nature study kits, organic stuffed blossom babies with musical leaf beds, build-your-own birdhouse kits, travel toys, outdoor toys, beach toys, instruments—you name it. Note: not everything on this site is earth-friendly, so read product details carefully.

Vermont-based **Nova Natural** is another solid source for a broad range of imaginative toys (**novanatural.com**). And **Planet Happy** has a huge selection of fun organic/fair trade/recycled/phthalate-free stuff to keep your kids busy and happy for days (**planethappykids.com**).

Greener Electronics and Gizmos for Big Kids: Looking to keep older kids entertained? Forget electronics that are filled with dodgy heavy metals and run on polluting single-use batteries (see page 185). Reach for toys that run on alternative fuels instead.

Arbor Scientific makes a way cool hydrogen fuel cell car that uses a real fuel cell. All you need to do is add water to make it run (**arborsci.com**). The **Solar Powered Shop** carries tons of solar-powered toys, including a monkey that travels across rope hand after hand, a Viking

---

GREAT GREEN KIDS' BOOKS

Spark lifelong interest in the powers of Mother Nature with books like *Does It Always Rain in the Rainforest?* (by Melvin and Gilda Berger). Bright, big, colorful books on bugs, birds, or bears are great for younger children. And no budding environmentalist's library is complete without Dr. Seuss's *The Lorax*—it's a moving tale about the regretful Once-ler, who long ago chopped down all the beautiful Truffula Trees in the land for profit. Don't worry: it's got a hopeful twist.

For more hands-on inspiration, *Earth Book for Kids: Activities to Help Heal the Environment* (by Linda Schwartz) outlines activities like testing your detergent for phosphates and checking the impact of oil pollution in water, and it has info on pesticides, endangered wildlife, water conservation, and more. In the creative realm, *EcoArt! Earth-Friendly Art & Craft Experiences for 3- to 9-Year-Olds* (by Laurie Carlson) suggests projects for twigs, weeds, and pebbles, and gives info on recycling and composting. Want to teach your kids about climate change? Pick up *The Down-to-Earth Guide to Global Warming* (by Laurie David and Cambria Gordon).

5

ship that moves its own oars through water, a cable car, and racers that all run on the sun's rays (**solarpoweredshop .com**). **Amazon.com**'s got build-your-own solar-powered helicopter or windmill kits, as well as an awesome all-in-one Physics Solar Workshop with 12 models and 30 experiments designed by Greenpeace.

If you do need batteries, invest in rechargeable ones and a charger to cut back on all that unnecessary waste (see page 191 for recommendations). Millions of batteries go into powering our tots' toys each year—and that means just as many are chucked in landfills when those robots and talking dolls stop running.

If you can't tear your children away from the computer, try downloading **Adventure Ecology** (**game.adventureecology.com**) or buying **SIMPark** (where you create your own state park), **SIMAnt**, **SIMSafari**, or any other earth-focused SIM games by the folks who brought you SIMCity (**amazon.com**).

Sweatshops plague the toy biz as much as the clothing biz. Buy from a trusted local source or BUY FAIR-TRADE.

Sweatshop-Free: Sweatshops plague the toy biz as much as the clothing biz. To be sure your gifts aren't bringing misery to others or to the earth, you have two options: buy from a trusted local source or buy fair-trade products. If you don't have a fair-trade shop near you, head online to **Ten Thousand Villages** (**tenthousandvillages.com**) or **Global Exchange** (**gxonlinestore.org**) for things like fair-trade soccer balls, lead-free wooden puzzles made by disadvantaged Sri Lankan youth, a lovely cloth vegetable-dyed Peruvian doll, a cheery stuffed cotton fish mobile to hang over your baby's crib, ornate kites, chess sets, and more.

PRELOVED GIFTS

If your kids have already grown bored with last year's toys, don't just toss them. Donate them to charity. Many needy children would be all too happy to "recycle" them! But please don't pawn off any toys that were included in a recall.

TOP 10 ENVIRONMENTALLY FRIENDLY THINGS YOU CAN DO FOR YOUR CHILDREN

Walk or bike your kids to school (can you believe the number of kids doing so has dropped by a whopping 75% within a generation?). If that's not feasible, ride your bikes on weekends—a family that bikes together saves the planet together!

1

Keep the kids inside on smog-alert days (going for a car ride when there's a smog alert on is a big no-no!). And be honest: explain how pollution from cars, smokestacks, and leaving the lights on makes it hard to breathe!

2

Get leaching plastics like PVC and polycarbonate out of their lives.

3

Show them that less is more: try not to always reward good behavior with toys—the planet doesn't need the resource extraction, chemical pollution, and landfill clogging that comes with making and eventually trashing toys. Committing to a fun activity is a much more fulfilling reward for the whole family.

4

Feed them organic foods whenever you can afford it so they get a pesticide-, hormone-, and antibiotic-free diet.

5

Say no to high-fat, high-sugar, chemical-laden processed foods—there are plenty of natural alternatives, even for packaged kids' snacks.

6

Use natural shampoos, creams, and soaps. What you put on your tot's body is just as important as what you put in it.

7

Create a nontoxic nursery or kids' room, full of earth-loving children's books.

8

Resist the urge to swaddle your babe in landfill-clogging disposable diapers. If cloth is out of the question, get unbleached, chlorine-free throw-away diapers or hybrids like the gDiaper (see page 132 for more on gDiapers).

9

Teach them to love nature. Take them to the park, on little hikes, or for picnics in conservation centers, where there are often all sorts of earth-friendly educational activities for young'uns.

10

You can also troll through local guild shops, craft stores, and galleries for handcrafted toys made by artisans in your area. Of course, if you buy local, less fossil fuel is used in transport, and craftspeople often have an eye toward using less toxic sealants and natural materials. But ask questions to make sure materials were sourced sustainably!

SCHOOL

You'd think our institutions of learning would be exemplary role models for the thousands of kids who pass through their hallowed corridors. And yes, they might preach about the three *R*s and the perils facing endangered critters, but the reality is, when it comes to green issues, most schools need to be sent to detention. Sure, they talk about nourishing young minds, but then they poison them by spraying deadly pesticides on the grounds and mopping hormone-disrupting chemicals on the floors.

Whether you're a college kid trying to turn your campus on to solar power, a high schooler hoping to get your team into organic shorts, a parent lobbying to get the poisons out of your tot's play area, or a concerned teacher, you *can* convince your school to go green. You just need to get organized.

Pesticides: Toddlers crawl on them, teenagers are tackled face first onto them, and college kids sit on them cross-legged as they gossip about their cute TAs. Grassy school yards see a lot of activity, so no matter how old the students (and teachers!) are, toxic pesticides shouldn't be sprayed on school grounds. Many are linked to cancer, neurological damage, and developmental problems. The youngest kids are the most vulnerable because their organs can't easily eliminate toxins from their systems and their brains and nervous systems are still developing. Whether used outside to keep grass bug-free or inside to keep ants and roaches under control, chemical pesticides are a bad idea.

After several incidents of toxic pesticides like Roundup wafting into school vents, kids swallowing insecticide granules, and fumigants making students sick, the federal government was kicking around a bill (the School Environment Protection Act) that would force schools to notify parents when pesticides were used on school property, but the bill didn't get enough votes to pass.

You'll have to contact your school and/or your school board directly. Ask about the pesticide policy, demand that students and parents be notified before bug-killing chems are used, and press school leaders to establish an integrated pest management (IPM) policy that looks at minimizing toxic chemicals or cutting them out entirely.

Recycling and Waste: No doubt, kids are messy, but if you're a teacher or a high school or middle school student and want to figure out how much waste your classroom's churning out, just pull out some gloves and a scale and go digging through the trash. Figure out what your school is tossing unnecessarily and change it. University kids could try this tactic, but it might take a while to canvass a whole campus.

If your college isn't recycling, start a campuswide campaign to instigate change. Try to ban hard-to-recycle plastics, like polystyrene, from your cafeteria. Set up a swap room where students can take old computers, desks, and pretty much anything they want to unload that other budget-crunched students would be all too happy to have.

Waste-Free Lunch: If you're packing a lunch for yourself or your kids, be sure to toss it into a reusable lunch bag or box (but not the vinyl/PVC kind, which could be tainted with lead and offgas phthalates). A typical American school kid trashes nearly 70 pounds of lunch packaging every school year. Instead of buying prepackaged snacks, which tend to come in nonrecyclable landfill-clogging wrapping, purchase things like crackers, trail mix, or carrots in bulk and throw a handful into a small plastic food container. If every student packed a zero-waste lunch, we'd save 1.2 billion pounds from landfill a year!

If every student packed a ZERO-WASTE lunch, we'd save 1.2 billion pounds from landfill a year!

IS YOUR SCHOOL MAKING TOO MUCH WASTE?

- **Is the cafeteria handing out disposable cutlery and plates?** Make sure reusable forks and dishes are promoted.

- **Are there recycling bins in every class and hallway?** The easier they are to find, the more likely they are to be used.

- **Is your school composting?** Organize food scrap bins in the cafeteria and build a composter outside. You can spread all the highly nutritious soil it generates on school grounds. Teachers can even work with their classes to build a composter from scratch, as described at **bluegrassgardens.com/how-to-build-a-compost-bin.htm**.

- **Are printers and photocopiers loaded with 100% recycled paper** high in postconsumer content? Institute a paper-saving policy for teachers and students.

CAFETERIA FOOD

Does your school cafeteria use fresh, local ingredients? Fat chance, right? It probably serves more frozen fries and greasy burgers than anything else. You might have trouble convincing your school to spend more cash on organic stuff, but you may be able to persuade the powers that be to cook with local ingredients. A fresh salad bar (sourced locally whenever possible) could be a good way to get students to eat more veggies. Look into setting up a farm-to-school program and an organic food garden on school property. For tools and tips, download the Center for Ecoliteracy's "Rethinking School Lunch" guide from **ecoliteracy.org**.

Get your whole school on waste-free lunches with tips from **wastefreelunches.org**. And check out **Laptop Lunches**' reusable bento box–style lunch made of nonleaching plastics (**laptoplunches.com**).

Energy Use: In the spring of 2006, England's education secretary announced that all UK schools must become more carbon-neutral by 2020 and should be "models of energy efficiency and renewable energy." On top of that, the secretary asked that schools serve up healthy, local, and sustainable food and drinks, prepared on-site. Wow. If only we had a national mandate for that here!

But why wait around, when you can take action now to make sure your own school is cutting back on excess energy use? It'll save your school money: one out of every four dollars that schools spend on electricity is needlessly wasted on inefficient boilers and leaving lights on, according to the US Department of Energy.

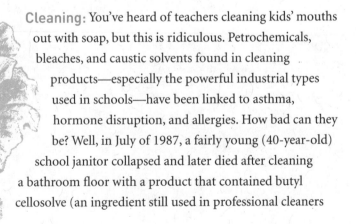

Cleaning: You've heard of teachers cleaning kids' mouths out with soap, but this is ridiculous. Petrochemicals, bleaches, and caustic solvents found in cleaning products—especially the powerful industrial types used in schools—have been linked to asthma, hormone disruption, and allergies. How bad can they be? Well, in July of 1987, a fairly young (40-year-old) school janitor collapsed and later died after cleaning a bathroom floor with a product that contained butyl cellosolve (an ingredient still used in professional cleaners today) without any ventilation. The school fought it, but workers' comp ruled that it was indeed the chemicals that killed him, according to *Art Hazards News*.

But let's get real: your school's not likely to switch to baking soda and vinegar, and buying small consumer-sized cleaners from health stores isn't really an option for large schools with high-volume demands. Instead, give school officials a list of eco-friendly institutional cleaning products approved by third-party certifiers like Green Seal (**greenseal.org**).

E-Groups: Getting your school to embrace the greener way can be about as easy as getting a class full of 5-year-olds to sit still. It's even harder when you're just one person, so join forces with a group of like-principled people. If you're in college, look into whether an environmental group is already up and running on campus. With so many colleges and universities going green, there's bound to be at least one.

National groups like the Sierra Student Coalition (**ssc.org**) and the Student Environmental Action Coalition (**seac.org**) have chapters in every region of the country to unite students who care about climate change, campus sustainability, and other big-picture issues. High schoolers and middle schoolers can form an environmental club with the help of a geography or earth sciences teacher. Start by assessing your school's impact on the earth by measuring its ecological footprint (learn how at **globalfootprints.org**). Then pick an area in which you think your school is slacking off. Do your homework on the issue before meeting with school staff and making your pitch. Just because you're young doesn't mean they won't listen to you.

Green PTA: If the local PTA isn't interested, concerned parents can start their own coalitions with other green moms and dads who want "idling-free" zones outside, Energy Star computers in classrooms, and organic milk in the cafeteria. Some school boards already

SCHOOL OF GREENER LEARNING

Looking for a greener future at an eco-conscious college or university but confused about what's out there? Get your hands on "Making a Difference Colleges," the authoritative guide to green, socially responsible, progressive, and alternative colleges (**sageworks.net**). Which school owns a 13-acre organic farm? Which school went carbon-neutral first? For a list of the earth-friendliest, punch in "greenest schools" at **grist.org**. Hint: they're as diverse as Costa Rica's Earth University and Harvard.

> ## TIPS TO HELP YOUR SCHOOL SAVE
> ## ON ELECTRICITY COSTS
>
> • **Make sure programmable thermostats** are set no lower than 75°F in the summer and no higher than 70°F in the winter.
>
> • **Be light-bright:** switch to ultraefficient compact fluorescent, T8 bulbs. Install motion sensors and timers to save even more.
>
> • **Post signs above monitors** and switches reminding students to switch off computers and lights at lunch and recess. Consider installing motion sensors or timers on lights.
>
> • **Get schooled on the benefits** of upgrading computers: Energy Star models can save up to $55 a year in energy. For more tips, see the US Department of Energy's website: **eere.energy.gov/buildings/energysmartschools**.

have parent environmental networks—be sure to ask. Just like the kids, you need to do your homework before you talk to school staff. Draft a policy you'd like to see in place, and once you've met, work together on coming up with a written action plan.

School Supplies: Whether you're in your last year of high school or plugging away at your PhD, you can bet that millions of students across the country just like you are buying copious amounts of correction fluid, plastic binders, and lily-white ancient forest–filled notebooks every August and September. And I'd wager that few have considered the ecological ramifications of losing yet another pencil. More than 14 billion of the damn things are manufactured every year, not to mention all the

If you're a slave to highlighters, look for the **REFILLABLE WATER-BASED** *type so you're not tossing out a* **NONRECYCLABLE** *plastic marker every 2 weeks.*

highlighters, pens, and crayons that students go through on an annual basis. Refillable pens or pencils are generally better than single-use ones, and even Paper Mate makes **Earthwrite**-branded pencils using 100% recycled content (**papermate.com**). Dixon sells **Prang crayons** made from soy oil instead of petroleum (**dixonusa.com**). For paper, look for 100%

postconsumer, acid- and chlorine-free lined notebooks. If your local store doesn't carry it, request it. And be sure to store that paper in vinyl-free binders made of recycled cardboard.

As for markers and highlighters, I'd tell you to give them up cold turkey, but I have to concede that I was a highlighter junky as an undergrad. If you're a slave to the yellow wand, at least look for the refillable water-based type so you're not tossing out a nonrecyclable plastic marker every 2 weeks.

Last but not least, you need something for carrying your gear to class. **Green Earth Office Supply** sells 100% postconsumer recycled-rubber school bags and messenger bags, as well as every green school supply item you could dream of, including a cool binder made of unused or defective circuit boards, Green Disk rewritable CDs made with 80% recycled content, and biodegradable pens (**greenearthofficesupply.com**).

LICE

A lice alert's been issued, and your little ones have started scratching. Now what? Once the bugs strike, most people run to the drugstore for a bottle of any louse-killing drops or shampoo they can find, but beware: those are dripping with nasty chemical pesticides. Three types of over-the-counter topical treatments are common. One contains pyrethrins, derived from chrysanthemum blossoms, which aren't *as* bad, though they are neurotoxins (interfering with nerve function) and are very toxic to aquatic life. If you're allergic to ragweed, you could very well have a reaction to them.

The second kind, permethrin, isn't even allowed on bug-repellent clothing for campers in Canada (don't ask me why it's okay in the US). So why are we rubbing this possible carcinogen and suspected hormone disrupter on our children's heads? Permethrin-based treatments might have formaldehyde in them, and patients with asthma might experience trouble breathing.

If you think that's bad, open door number three. Lindane, a neurotoxin from the same family of chemical pesticides as DDT, has been banned for agricultural use in over 50 countries! The US Environmental Protection Agency recently banned lindane, except as a treatment for head lice, which has pissed off both children's advocates and environmentalists. The warning label on lindane shampoo and lotion talks about seizures and death and warns that anyone under 110 pounds is at risk of serious neurotoxicity!

To make matters worse, lice attacks are a bit like bad horror movie sequels: they keep coming back, even when you use the strong stuff. Some lice are reported to be resistant to all three products. Instead of committing yourself to chemical bath after chemical bath, douse your house with an all-natural enzyme-based solution like **Natural Ginesis**'s **Nit Free** mousse (**naturalginesis.com**). Its **Kleen Green** enzyme cleaner works on fleas, bedbugs, and scabies, as well as lice.

Some home remedies recommend covering your head in a thick layer of petroleum jelly, olive oil, or mayonnaise overnight. Unfortunately, these treatments won't do much but make you never want to eat mayonnaise again. Tea tree oil is often prescribed in alternative circles, but the astringent can be pretty drying and hard on the skin with prolonged use.

No matter what, you'll never completely get rid of lice unless you remove the nits (lice eggs) near the scalp, so you'll need a good nit comb and a lot of patience. To prevent spread or recontamination, be sure to wash all your clothing, bedding, and towels in hot water.

PETS

We cuddle and, yes, even clothe them like they're our furry children, but in the process we're turning the poor things into nature's outlaws. With all the plastic bags used for poop-and-scoop and kitty litter that we toss, along with flea control chems and not-so-earth-conscious edibles, our pets are becoming little eco monsters. Luckily, there are many ways to get Mittens back to her natural roots.

Litter: Let's start with the back end. Whether in a box, cage, or backyard, all animals do it. Many of us fill our feline "powder rooms" with chemically scented, nonbiodegradable clays that hog landfill space. Unless, of course, your municipality accepts kitty litter in its municipal composting program—and very few do. If you flush it because the label says you can, don't be fooled into thinking it just disappears. It ends up being filtered out at the water treatment plant and sent to landfills.

Need another reason to stop flushing? The parasites carried without symptoms in cat poop are being flushed out to sea and killing sea otters off the Pacific coast. Seriously. Cat poop is responsible for 17% of sea otter deaths off California.

As convenient as it seems, the clumping kind is the worst for your dear Fluffy. (If it clumps in the box, it can clump in his belly and make him sick, an especially dangerous scenario for kittens.) Most clay litters, clumping or not, kick up silica dust, which can cause respiratory problems in both cats and humans. (FYI: to avoid potential exposure to parasites, pregnant women shouldn't change litter at all.) Silica gel crystals (a.k.a. sodium silicate, a high-temperature mix of sand and soda ash) are probably the most odor-absorbing litter on the market, but unless your city accepts litter in its municipal composting program, you should bypass this one. It's not biodegradable and shouldn't be added to backyard composters.

There are ways to bring balance back to your litter box. **Good Mews** (stutzman-environmental.com/goodmews.htm) and **Yesterday's News** (yesterdaysnews.com) are made of recycled paper pellets, but not every cat will like it and lazy scoopers could find it stinky. For the scoopable variety, you have a few popular choices. Corn-based **World's Best Cat Litter** (worldsbestcatlitter.com) and wheat-based **Swheat Scoop** (swheatscoop .com) are both flushable and biodegradable, as well

The PARASITES *in cat poop that are being flushed out to sea are killing sea otters.* SERIOUSLY.

as clay-, chemical- and fragrance-free, and can even be added to home composters once fully scooped of poop. (Swheat Scoop is made of non–food-grade GE-free American wheat; World's Best couldn't tell me if its corn was GE-free.) But it's the pine-based litters that probably neutralize ammonia odors best. Pick one that's made with chem-free by-products of the lumber industry, like **Feline Pine** (naturesearth.com), so you know that no new trees needed to be axed to make it.

Hamster and bunny owners should look for cage liners made of recycled wood, like reclaimed cellulose-based **Carefresh**. **Swheat Scoop** also makes litter for small critters.

Poop-and-Scoop: Dog lovers go through a lot of plastic bags in their lifetime. If you're walking your pooch twice daily and he poops both times, you're going through more than 10,000 plastic bags worth over a 14-year life span! Now, doesn't it seem silly to put perfectly biodegradable dog poop into a bag that takes over 100 years to break down? Make scooping more earth-friendly with compostable bags. **BioBag**'s dog bags take only 45 days to break down in a good compost environment (biobagusa.com). Speaking of pet-waste composting, find out how to do this safely in your own yard at cityfarmer.org/petwaste.html. If you've got a few hundred bucks to spare, you can also get an automated indoor food composter that accepts pet waste, through naturemill.com.

Cleaning: Need to clean up an accident without resorting to noxious chemicals? **Only Natural Pet Store** (onlynaturalpet.com) carries a selection of natural pet odor and stain remover sprays, as does **de Botanica** (debotanica.com). If Maggie got herself a little dirty in the process and needs a bath, look for an all-natural pet shampoo made without unpronounceable chemicals and synthetic fragrances. **Halo** carries herbal grooming supplies for your little muffinhead (halopets.com), as do de Botanica and several human body care companies, like **Aubrey Organics** (aubrey-organics.com). Or just use a mild natural baby shampoo.

Food: Of course, our loyal friends need to eat. Mine reminds me of this within hours of his last meal. Trouble is, most conventional pet food brands are loaded with additives and preservatives and support the bottom (read "rancid") end of the not-so-earth- or animal-friendly meat industry. The word "by-product" in the ingredient list is basically telling you that your pet is getting all those bits that humans wouldn't touch.

The food could even include 4-D animals—dead, diseased, dying, or disabled—as well as restaurant grease.

Sadly, euthanized shelter pets can also make the cut. In fact, the National Animal Control Association has a policy that states, "Dead animal disposal can include cremation facilities, landfill burial, or rendering" (as in meat-rendering plants). Ick. "Meat meal" is basically mysterious odds and ends that have been stripped of their fat and water content, but if a specific animal is identified (as in lamb meal or chicken meal), *National Geographic*'s Green Guide pet product report says it's not quite as bad.

Pet lovers might be a little disturbed to know that pet food is often tested on animals. And that doesn't mean it's given to a few happy free-roaming pets to see if they like the flavor—no, we're talking about dogs confined to cages in research labs. PETA maintains a list of companies that steer clear of such testing. If you're curious, call up some pet food companies and ask if they test their products on animals; if they say they don't, ask if their policy against testing applies to subcontracted labs.

Several mainstream pet food makers are hopping on the alternative-health bandwagon and marketing their lack of dyes or the addition of antioxidants. It's a good start, but there are better options. In fact, there are too many to name! But here are a few. **Karma** is at the top with its 95% organic pet food (it even has organic free-range chicken and organic kamut!). Find a local source at **karmaorganic.com**. **Wellness** is loaded with veggies and human-grade meat (**wellnesspetfood.com**). **Wysong** (**wysong.net**) and **Solid Gold** (**solidgoldhealth.com**) are other good brands.

Natural pet food is so hot right now that even celebrities have infiltrated the world of kibble. (See Paul Newman's **Newman's Own Organics** [**newmansownorganics.com**] and Dick Van Patten's **Natural Balance Pet Foods** [**naturalbalanceinc.com**], both of which have respectable ingredient lists.) Even the bigger pet store chains carry a slew of premium alternative foods now. Just be sure to read labels carefully and look for the purest ingredient lists.

Remember that cats, in particular, don't need carbs (in fact, high-carb diets are linked to the epidemic of diabetes in felines). So look for high-protein options (wet food often has fewer carbs and more protein than dry) or frozen raw-food brands like **Steve's Real Food** in specialty pet stores (**stevesrealfood.com**). Raw pet food is controversial in some circles (the same circles that thought wheat gluten–heavy mainstream brands were safe), but what do you think animals eat in the wild? They ain't boiling beef. Word is that many pets thrive on raw food.

If you have the time, you can design your pet's menu from scratch. My brothers have been doing this for our family dogs for years. It's the best way to know what's actually in your dog's or cat's food bowl and can be exceptionally nutritious if you do it right. You'll need a good cookbook to get started, but don't reach for just any old one filled with cute pet photos and unhealthy or excessively elaborate recipes (I mean, really, are dogs meant to eat macaroni and cheese?). *Dr. Pitcairn's Complete Guide to Natural Health for Dogs and Cats* has some great homemade-diet suggestions for pets, as well as tips on tending to your pet naturally. For raw-feeding tips, check out **rawmeatybones.com.**

Fleas: As soon as you see your pet scratching hard, you know you're done for. But you don't want to reach for commercial flea collars and powders, because they're loaded with potent pesticides that actually poison many animals and can be toxic to your kids. Take organophosphates, for instance. This old-school family of pesticides (which includes chlorpyrifos, malathion, and diazinon) is designed to mess with insect nervous systems, and—wouldn't you know it—these pesticides also have the potential to damage the nervous systems of our pets, triggering seizures, twitching, and sometimes death.

Even more common are collars, sprays, dips, spot treatments, and shampoos containing pyrethrins, which can be especially toxic for cats. Yes, some may be derived from chrysanthemum blossoms, but synthetic versions called pyrethroids (including permethrin) ain't natural; and synthetic or not, they're all neurotoxins (see page 153 for more info). Note: a 2008 study linked the use of pyrethrin-based flea shampoos by pregnant moms with autism.

It's no surprise, then, that most vets have moved away from both types of flea control systems. They now tend to focus on newer-generation products such as Advantage and Revolution. Veterinarians and the product manufacturers swear by the safety of these products and insist they won't harm a hair on your pet's head. But even though they're considered less toxic, you'll still find pet owners who insist their dog's or cat's sudden vomiting and shaking came on right after such flea treatments. Something to keep in mind.

So what's a flea-infested owner to do? First, bathe your pet in mild soapy water to drown any existing fleas. You can also sprinkle Muffy or Buster with all-natural **diatomaceous earth** (fine white powdery fossilized algae that grinds away at the fleas' exoskeleton) every few days, but this is quite drying and the fine powder can be irritating to inhale. Instead, try dipping your pet's comb in **Natural Genesis**'s **Kleen Green** enzyme-based solution as you brush your pet. You can even use the diluted product to clean your home and bathe your pet. Vacuum your house thoroughly and often, even daily, to remove eggs, larvae, and adults—

making sure to vacuum furniture (both under and over), baseboards, cracks, and crevices. Throw some diatomaceous earth or borax in the vacuum bag to kill any eggs and sprinkle some around your house as well, under rugs and furniture.

But don't stop at your pet and your living room. Those fleas are coming in from somewhere, and you might as well fend them off the best you can in your backyard. Sprinkle diatomaceous earth everywhere and release microscopic nematodes, which prey on flea larvae and pupae (you can pick up nematodes at garden supply stores).

Natural flea-repelling shampoos, diatomaceous earth powder, and other remedies are available from **onlynaturalpet.com** if you can't find any at your local pet store.

Natural Health: Watching our pets struggle with illness or injury is painful for puppy lovers and feline fiends alike. But there are alternatives to conventional vets and their high-potency pharma treatments. A growing list of practitioners are dedicated to holistic animal care. You can use the **herbal home remedies** that keep our own bodies humming to nurse furry companions back to health. Boost weakened immune systems by adding fresh crushed garlic (for dogs, *not* cats), echinacea, and powdered vitamin C to your pet's food. For older animals, stir in other antioxidants, such as liquid vitamin E and grape seed extract. Stave off digestive difficulties and boost nutrient absorption by sprinkling probiotics on their dinner. Squeezing in capsules of salmon or herring oil can soothe itchy skin and dandruff.

When more complicated illness arises, **alternative vets** can prescribe homeopathic and herbal remedies and offer chiropractic adjustments. Some even provide animal-friendly acupuncture to treat sore hips, stubborn urinary tract trouble, and seizures. To fill a pet's prescription, you can find a slew of natural remedies specially formulated for animals at some pet stores. But beware: they're often merely marked-up versions of human herbs. If you opt to treat your tabby with self-prescribed human health store goods, be sure to contact your vet first to find out which dosage is best.

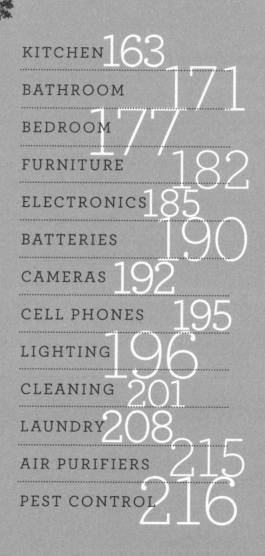

HOMEWARD
BOUND

There's no place like home. The damn cliché is such a truism we even weave it into doormats and cowboy songs. It is, after all, where your family is (even if it's just you and the cat), along with your cushy couch and the remote. Too bad home is also where the toxins are. Yes, lurking in your cozy abode are some serious pollutants that can make the indoor air quality in a house worse than a smog-alert day. They're hiding in your cookware, cleaning products, coffee table, and candles. They're even building up in household dust (which is a problem when you dust as infrequently as I've been known to) and settling into your tissues. Now, stop thinking about how our houses affect us and consider how what we do inside those four walls weighs on the world. Those long showers, the loads of warm-water laundry, the blazing lights left on at all hours of the day—they all consume gobs of polluting electricity and precious water resources we can't afford to waste. Let's not forget that the planet is also our home. You don't want me to have to use another tired catchphrase—you know, the one about how you can never go home again.

KITCHEN

Some sort of instinctual pull must draw us close to our food source—hence, the tendency for house parties to turn into kitchen parties (I've conducted my own scientific studies on this one) and for kitchens to trump comfy family rooms as the center of activity in many homes. Even if you can't cook to save your life, and toast and fried eggs are as creative as you get, you need to know how to get sizzling, get clean, and get out with the least damage to your stomach and the planet.

Cookware: Ever charred the bottom of your nonstick pan? Who hasn't! The problem is, you're not just offending your taste buds: burned nonstick-coated pans can release toxic fumes that'll literally kill a canary if you have one in your kitchen. Teflon says such high-temperature burning doesn't happen under normal circumstances, and the stuff is perfectly safe otherwise. Nonetheless, 95% of humans have the chemical that is used to make nonstick surfaces like Teflon in our bloodstreams (as do 100% of umbilical cords, according to Johns Hopkins University).

It turns out PFOA, the compound used to manufacture the coatings, beats out nasty pesticides like DDT when it comes to

> **95%** *of humans have the CHEMICAL that is used to make nonstick surfaces like TEFLON in our bloodstreams.*

indestructibility in the ecosystem (what an honor). Quite disconcerting, when you consider that nearly a dozen studies have tied it to thyroid damage and a scientific advisory panel to the Environmental Protection Agency (EPA) concluded in January 2006 that PFOA is a "likely human carcinogen." Sadly, we've surrounded ourselves with it, in cookware, burger wrappers, popcorn bags, french-fry cartons, and candy packaging. And even though polar bears have never popped corn, the chemical is turning up in their systems—and in most other wildlife—at alarming levels. The EPA has sweetly asked major corporate manufacturers of the substance to voluntarily phase out 95% of their usage by 2010 and to ditch the compound entirely by 2015.

So, although the government hasn't told us to ditch our nonstick woks, whisks, colanders, and waffle irons, environmentalists are saying there's no better time than the present to remove the chemical from your life, since any molecule you get in your system could be with you for life.

Cookware Solutions: If you're not up to the role of human guinea pig, you might want to switch to **stainless steel**. It's a little stickier, but much safer (those with nickel allergies may want to look for nickel-free versions, however). **Cast-iron skillets** (made, in part, of recycled scrap iron filtered of contaminants) are another sound choice—plus, a little iron in your diet is actually good for you! Keep it rust-free by seasoning it with coconut oil or another oil high in saturated fat.

If you're longing for nonstick surfaces, check out ceramic-coated aluminum pans. They're totally nonleaching, chemical-free, and as slippery as any Teflon pan, without the worry. The **Eco-Chef pan** is available from Kroger (**kroger.com**) and its subsidiary Fred Meyer, or directly from the manufacturer, Starfrit (**starfrit.com**). **Cuisinart** is getting in on the act with its ceramic GreenGourmet line. Another brand, GreenPan, makes a PTFE-free nonstick pan coated with something called Thermolon, made of oxygen, silicon, carbon, aluminum, and titanium (the company assures us that there's no free aluminum in the coating). My main reservation about this one is that it's nanotechnology-based, and questions remain about nanotech's safety.

If you've got a wallet full of cash, **lightweight titanium** is another option. You'll find some woks and thin camping cookware that are solid titanium, but solid titanium isn't the best heat conductor, so most are titanium-coated aluminum with nonstick titanium dioxide surfaces; these are considered nontoxic. Many surfaces are made of safe, nonleaching titanium-ceramic blends. Beware that some titanium pans out there get their nonstick surface from the same chemicals used in Teflon, a.k.a. PFOAs. Talk about sneaky! Be sure to read the fine print and the FAQ (frequently asked questions) section of corporate websites.

Copper and aluminum are great heat conductors, so they warm up quickly and save energy, but because of health concerns, aluminum and copper pots should always be coated with stainless steel (a little copper isn't bad for you, but too much of it can be poisonous, and safe daily exposure doses haven't really been determined). Hard anodized aluminum cookware is said to seal in the aluminum and create another nonstick surface that can handle acids like tomato sauces with minimal leaching (we'll talk more about aluminum shortly).

Glass is a great renewable source and is valued by natural medical practitioners and people with enviro sensitivities because it's inert and is perfect for stove-top cooking or baking.

Bakeware Solutions: Glass and cast iron aren't exactly on the table for anyone with a penchant for muffin-mixing. And most of the stuff on the market is coated with nonstick chemicals. Those little paper muffin cup liners might create a barrier between your cranberry muffin and the tin, but they tend to be made with bleached virgin paper, and they're disposable—tsk-tsk. So what is an eco-conscious baker to do?

Well, you have a few options. **Ceramics** are popular for bakeware, although you have to make sure the glaze is lead-free (see the sidebar on lead for more info). Big spenders can fork out the money for top-notch enamel-coated, cast-iron cookware from companies like **Le Creuset** (lecreuset.com). **Stainless steel** cake molds and tart dishes do exist, but they can be hard to find unless you head online. And **silicone** isn't just for *Baywatch* babes. Nope, this nontoxic, man-made fusion of silicon (basically sand) and oxygen is now being molded into muffin trays, sheets, bread pans, and even oven mitts. It looks kind of freaky, as manufacturers tend to add bright dyes to it, but I've yet to dig up any dirt on this stuff other than the fact that sand mining can be bad for the environment—but so is digging for steel, iron, and clay. It's available pretty much anywhere that sells bakeware. Silicone/fiberglass-blended baking sheets such as **Silpat** are also safe.

Perhaps the earthiest option for the oven is **stone bakeware**. Stone bakeware is a lot like your ceramic mug, but the clay is cooked at a higher temperature, making it stronger, chip-resistant, watertight, and oven-safe. The good stuff is unglazed and has the same color as terra-cotta. But like anything that's mined, clay isn't without environmental repercussions, especially in developing countries such as India, where clay mining has been accused of draining water tables and polluting the air.

The **Pampered Chef**'s line of high-quality stoneware is made with more sustainable American clay, and it comes with a 3-year unconditional guarantee, so even if you drop and crack it, they'll give you a new one (pamperedchef.com). Plus, after you cook on its porous surface a few times with a fatty food, it becomes naturally nonstick for life.

Aluminum Foil, Baking Trays, and Cans: We put everything from beans to beer in aluminum cans, and traces of aluminum can be found in items such as baking powder, antacids, buffered aspirin, and hemorrhoid meds. We consume about 10 milligrams of the metal a day, and most of that comes from food. Pots and pans give us 1 or 2 milligrams daily (versus the 50 milligrams that you get from swallowing one antacid). Foil, I imagine, accounts for much less, unless you're baking off it at every meal and sucking on the stuff.

Aluminum has been tied inconclusively to Alzheimer's, Lou Gehrig's, and Parkinson's diseases, as well as anemia and glucose intolerance. So, should you stop using aluminum foil and trays? I wouldn't panic. Any leaching is negligible, though leafy foods and acidic ones like citrus and tomatoes absorb the most. And the longer food is stored or simmered in aluminum, the more of the metal it'll suck up.

The good news is that ALUMINUM FOIL sheets and containers are 100% RECYCLABLE. The bad news? Not every municipality accepts them, so ask.

As for the planet's health, well, as you'd predict, mining aluminum (or bauxite ore) ain't pretty: vegetation is stripped, habitat lost, soil eroded. Because aluminum smelting is so damn energy-intensive, smelters are often situated near cheap and dirty power sources—coal and destructive dam projects.

LEAD IN THE KITCHEN

Think crappy baking skills are behind your lead-heavy muffins? Check your bakeware: the glaze on most ceramic bakeware and cookware can contain lead, as does old china and—surprise, surprise—lead crystal (which most of us know as just crystal—you know, the sparkly stuff you're afraid to break). Regulations limit lead content in glassware and glazes on ceramics used in preparing, serving, or storing food, but it's still in there. You might want to ditch dishes that are heavily scratched or chipped. Acidic foods such as fruit juice, wine, and pickles boost lead leaching. Come on, doesn't everyone use their crystal glassware for wine?

To be fair, the amount of lead that leaches into your wine over the course of a dinner still falls under maximum limits, but if you kept it in a crystal decanter for a few weeks, you'd be sucking back over 100 times the accepted levels—not to mention rancid wine. Older china and imported ceramics have been a source of lead poisoning, so beware. To be cautious, don't serve up any food on lead tableware to children or pregnant women, say health agencies, and soak new crystal in vinegar for a day and rinse before using. Don't store food in ceramics purchased from Mexico or South American countries, where lead levels can be quite high, though fair-trade, lead-free dishes are available at Ten Thousand Villages locations (tenthousandvillages.com). **Emile Henry**'s bakeware and cool Flame Top cookware (emilehenryusa.com), as well as **Le Creuset** products (lecreuset.com) are also lead-free. If you're uncertain about your brand, call the consumer hotline.

And aluminum production gives as much as it takes, emitting about 95 million tons of greenhouse gases industry-wide in 2005 and dumping massive amounts of caustic waste.

Aluminum Solutions: The good news is that aluminum foil sheets and containers are 100% recyclable. The bad news? Not every municipality accepts them, so ask. Most accept foil trays, though. Aluminum is actually the most recycled metal on earth, and the industry says a third of all aluminum in use comes from recycled sources. Overall, you're better off with tinfoil than plastic wrap any day. But you can boost your green factor by getting 100% recycled foil, called **If You Care** (**ifyoucare.com**), at some health stores or from online shops like Greenfeet (**greenfeet.com**). The Scandinavian import requires 95% less energy to make than nonrecycled foil needs. That's true for all recycled aluminum products, so all you urban myth circulators trashing the recycling of aluminum cans and saying it takes more energy to recycle them than it does to make new ones are flat-out wrong.

Plastic Wrap: Can you imagine the excitement in 1950s homes when Dow first introduced the ultraclingy polyvinylidene chloride (PVDC) film Saran Wrap? It stuck to everything: bowls, pots, and especially itself. The stuff even had patriotic roots, having first been sprayed on fighter planes during the war to protect them against salty sea spray. For years, most plastic wrap was either PVDC or PVC. And, as I've said before, PVC is considered the dodgiest of plastics. It can emit dangerous dioxins when being made and during incineration. On its own, it's quite rigid, so softening chemicals called phthalates are added to make it nice and pliable so you can stretch it across your bowl of leftover pancake batter. As much as a third of PVC and 10% of PVDC wrap can be made up of the potentially hormone-disrupting plasticizers, which have been found to drift into food. In the late '90s, in fact, *Consumer Reports* tested various grocery store cheeses and found that those that came in manufacturer's plastic wrapping or individually wrapped slices tested negative, but those wrapped in PVC cling wrap had very high levels of the hormone-disrupting phthalate DEHA (found to cause developmental problems in rats).

Plastic-Wrap Solutions: You can't tell from the packaging, but major manufacturers such as **Glad** and **Saran** have switched to much less controversial low-density polyethylene (LDPE), which is less clingy but phthalate-free. If you're unsure about your brand of choice, call the company info line. **Saran Premium Wrap** is now also chlorine-free as part of "the company's commitment to use more environmentally responsible ingredients in our products." But even if you're using less environmentally damaging plastics such as LDPE, note that all plastics have eco ramifications (they all come from petroleum, for starters). Plus, they don't biodegrade, and plastic wrap isn't recyclable (see page 347 for more on plastics).

So try to find alternatives whenever possible. Plates can be used to cover bowls or other dishes. **Tupperware, GladWare, and Ziploc containers**, which are phthalate- and PVC-free, are better than plastic wrap, since they can be washed and reused (look for reusable storage containers with the number 5 on the bottom; it's the safest). **Pyrex**, **IKEA**, and **Crate and Barrel** carry all kinds of glass storage containers in different shapes and sizes, so there's no excuse.

Consumer Reports found that cheeses wrapped in PVC CLING WRAP had very high levels of HORMONE-DISRUPTING PHTHALATES.

Refrigerators: No one wants to dole out cash for new appliances, but older models can really hold your energy bills hostage. If you're in the market for a new fridge, the **Energy Star** label (though not perfect) is an easy indicator that what you're buying is more energy-efficient. A fridge with this label uses 40% less energy than conventional models sold in 2001 do—a good thing, considering that up to 15% of your energy bills go to keeping your milk cold and your ice frozen.

A third of us also have a second fridge that's about 20 years old tucked away in the basement or garage. These babies are serious power leachers and should be turned in to the conservation police. Some municipalities will even pay you money to do so. Oh, and if you're going off the grid, you'll want a superinsulated **Sun Frost DC fridge** that uses less energy than a 40-watt bulb and is said to last 25 to 50 years (they also make AC versions for all us on-the-gridders) (**sunfrost.com**).

Ovens: Like to slave over a hot stove? When it comes to ovens, gas ranges are more efficient than electric, but neither come with Energy Star ratings. Certainly the use of natural gas is cleaner, in terms of greenhouse gases, than getting your electric power from a coal plant. High-tech electric ovens without

> ## MICROWAVING YOGURT TUBS AND TAKEOUT CONTAINERS
>
> **Y**ou think you're doing a good thing by saving your old yogurt and margarine tubs and using them to store food, and you are. But whatever you do, do not heat leftovers stored in old plastic tubs in the microwave. The plastics will leach into your grub! Same goes for takeout containers. Transfer the food to a microwave-safe dish, or better yet, throw it in the toaster oven or a frying pan to get it sizzling again.

coils are generally more efficient than the old-fashioned type, but they can take longer to heat up. Spending a little more on self-cleaning ovens (because of their extra insulation) and/or convection ovens (because they cook foods faster) will save you money in the long run, thanks to energy saving.

Microwave Ovens: No matter how often we use these things, many of us will never be totally comfortable with them (you can tell by the way people take four paces back after they press "start"). Despite their omnipresence in North American kitchens, controversy still clings to microwaves. The official line is that the radiation is non-ionizing (which means it's not related to the cancer-causing ionizing radiation used in X-rays), but a tiny amount of radiation is indeed emitted from these machines. The level falls below national safety standards, but it still freaks some people out. To avoid leaks, make sure the door's seal and hinges aren't damaged or dirty. And keep anyone with an older-generation pacemaker away from old microwaves. The electromagnetic field emitted could trip them up. No joke. The shielded design of modern pacemakers and microwaves is said to prevent this startling side effect.

Government websites insist that microwaving doesn't affect the nutrient content of food, and many studies concur; but a handful of others demonstrate

Modern dishwashers actually use HALF THE ENERGY and ONE-SIXTH THE WATER *that hand-washing dishes requires.*

just the opposite. A study out of Stanford University found that microwaving frozen breast milk drastically diminishes the amount of infection-fighting agents naturally present in mother's milk. Another out of Japan in the late '90s concluded that microwaving zaps the vitamin B_{12} content of food. A more recent study, published in the *Journal of the Science of*

Food and Agriculture in 2003, found that microwaves nuke out 97% of the flavonoids in broccoli. So even though microwaving your food is more energy-efficient than cooking it in the oven (50% to 75% more, in fact), that's not enough to convince most environmentalists and health nuts that using the contraption is a wise idea.

10 WAYS TO FIRE UP YOUR TASTE BUDS WITHOUT COOKING THE PLANET

Baking in ceramic or glass? Reduce your oven temperature by 25°F and cook your food in the same amount of time, since these materials conduct and retain heat better than metal.

Who says pasta needs to cook at a raging boil for 12 straight minutes? Try cooking it for 1 or 2 minutes in boiling water, then turn off the stove and cover the pot for 20 minutes. It takes only a few minutes longer and saves energy. You can do this with basically any pasta—just test it periodically until you figure out the timing for your particular brand of penne or linguine.

Keep a lid on it (your cooking, that is). Otherwise you're just letting all that heat escape—unless, of course, it's integral to the recipe, as for a reduction sauce.

Smaller is always better: Think toaster oven over electric oven and handheld mixer over food processor.

Human power obviously burns much more cleanly than electricity, so consider a manual coffee grinder, a hand beater, a food mill, a mortar and pestle, and a plain old knife over fancy plug-in gadgets. The Amish have even developed cool hand-cranked blenders and food processors (**lehmans.com**).

Be sure to match pan size to the element you're cooking on. A small pot on a large burner is just wasting energy. And small burners use less energy.

Keep your metal burners clean so they reflect heat better. (Same goes for your refrigerator coils and cooling your food, by the by.)

Rice cookers and slow cookers (Crock-Pots), are much more efficient at whipping up your dinner than are stove-top methods. Just make sure you stick to Teflon-free models and look for those with stainless steel interiors.

If you're cooking with frozen food, be sure to thaw it first (unless otherwise indicated); it'll take longer to cook that fish or whatnot if it's still half frozen.

Curiosity kills your electric bills. Keep your oven door closed as much as possible while you're cooking. Peeking inside causes at least 20% of the heat to escape, and the poor oven has to waste energy warming itself up again.

DISHWASHER TIPS

- **Sure, scrape food off your dish** before you toss it in the dishwasher, but there's no need for all this crazy double-washing business. If your dishwasher can't clean a layer of gravy off your plate, you need a new dishwasher.

- **If you have an air-dry button, use it;** your dishes will dry just as well without a blast of heat (and you'll use 20% less energy overall). It just takes a little longer. If your machine doesn't have an air-dry option, no biggie—just open the door after the final rinse.

- **Don't start your dishwasher until it's full.** No wasteful half loads!

Dishwashers: Ever wondered what's more water-intensive—hand-washing your dishes or using a dishwasher? Most of us would guess that anything done by hand (and is so damn time-consuming) would win this battle, but researchers at the University of Bonn in Germany decided to settle the bet once and for all with cold, hard science. And guess what—modern dishwashers prevailed, using half the energy, one-sixth the water, and less soap to boot. Not sure who the winner would be if they compared hand-washing to using an old dishwasher from the '80s, though. Or whether the hand washers in their study were very frugal with water. New Energy Star–qualified types, by the way, use at least 25% less energy and a third less water than basic models use.

No matter how you wash your dishes, get low-flow aerators for your taps. And if you are your own dishwasher, turn the water off while you lather up or, if you've got a whole slew of dishes to catch up on, fill one sink for washing and one sink for rinsing. Might as well save water anywhere you can, especially knowing that about 20% of the water used in your house is used in the kitchen, and most of it goes toward washing dishes.

BATHROOM

Ever had the water cut off to your bathroom? Panic tends to set in fairly quickly. No showers, no flushing, no washing your hands. Did I mention no flushing? We're in there many times a day and take all that free-flowing water for granted. And that water might come cheap to homeowners (Americans pay some of the lowest water bills in the world, which is partly why we're so wasteful with it, using 100 gallons of it per person per day), but filtering it

H₂O DIET

To calculate how much water your house is wasting, both indoors and out, and for tips on putting your household on a water diet, visit **h2ouse.net**.

and piping it to you costs our municipalities billions of dollars and uses up a hell of a lot of electricity. Can someone tell me why we need to wash our hair and flush our toilets with water pure enough to drink?

Showers: I'm not about to ask major water hogs to go cold turkey and shower with the water off right out of the gates; but if you're taking 20, 30, 40 minutes or more in there, you need to reassess. Every minute you stand there, you're spraying yourself with up to 10 gallons of water. A 5-minute shower is ideal, but I'd even take 15 from you 1-hour shower junkies. Set an egg timer to keep yourself on track.

If your shower can fill a 1-gallon jug with water in under 10 seconds, **YOU NEED A NEW HEAD.**

No matter how long you're in there, a handy dandy **low-flow shower head** will decrease the amount of water you use. If your shower can fill a 1-gallon jug with water in under 10 seconds, you need a new head. Look for one that uses no more than 2.5 gallons per minute. **Real Goods** sells a $12 shower head that uses as little as 1 gallon per minute (**realgoods .com**)! You'll save money not only on your water bill, but on your electricity bill too—that water doesn't just heat itself. And if you're up for turning off the water as you lather up, install a shower adapter that you flick on and off without having to reset the water pressure and temperature.

Shower Curtains: Of course, the longer you're in the shower, the longer you're exposed to your shower curtain, and if your curtain or liner is vinyl, it may be offgassing potentially hormone-disrupting phthalates. Vinyl (or PVC) is a nasty polluter from birth right through to its final resting place in a municipal incinerator, so it's something you definitely want to avoid. In fact, a 2008 report by the Center for Health, Environment and Justice found that one of the curtains it tested released as many as 108 volatile organic compounds (including the neurotoxin toluene), some of which persisted in the air for nearly a month. To make matters worse, chemical fungicides are often added to make shower curtains more mildew-resistant. And still they get gross, and since they're hard to clean we just toss 'em and buy new ones. Even fabric curtains can be coated with water-repellent nonstick coating, made with persistent contaminants that have been found in most of our bloodstreams and in a shocking amount of wildlife.

So what's an eco-sensitive bather to do? Well, you can find **hemp shower curtains** online. And really, if hemp was good enough for most of the world's sails for centuries, it should be good enough to withstand a measly shower. Rawganique.com sells naturally fungus-resistant organic hemp shower curtains from $69. If you're crafty, you can buy hemp fabric by the meter at hemp shops and sew one yourself. Just pop them in the wash now and then.

On the cheaper side, **IKEA**'s **plastic shower curtains** look like the vinyl types you find everywhere, but they're actually made of polyethylene vinyl acetate (PEVA). Target and Kmart are also shifting over to PEVA. It's still vinyl, but without the chlorine, which is the part that creates dangerous dioxins during manufacturing and incineration. You can also install a **shower door** or **sliding enclosure**. They last forever, you can clean 'em to your heart's content, and they won't let water spill all over your bathroom floor.

If you're ADDICTED TO A DAILY SOAK, *wash your sins away by filling the tub only* ONE-QUARTER FULL.

Baths: A typical bath uses up to 40 gallons of hot water (double that if you've got one of those big tubs). A 5-minute shower with an efficient shower head uses about a quarter of that. I'm not saying you shouldn't bathe. Just make it a special treat, as opposed to an everyday event. If you're addicted to a daily soak, wash your sins away by filling the tub only one-quarter full.

SHOWER FILTERS

All that chlorinated water is enough to make your skin itch. If you've got dry skin, eczema, or anything of the sort, chlorine will often make it worse. You could also be inhaling harmful trihalomethanes (a dodgy by-product of using chlorine in water). And of course there's the lead. Best to get a good carbon shower filter to make you breathe easy.

THAT DRIPPING FAUCET

This ain't no drop in the bucket. A dripping tap can fill 110 water bottles a day. If you let it go unattended, you could be wasting over 3,000 gallons a year! Can't seem to tighten it yourself? Call a plumber or professional handy-man or -woman to do the job. While you're at it, install a new water-saving aerator on your faucet. Every drop counts.

Heavy soakers should note that tub time can be toxin-drenched. It's not just that you might fall asleep in there—if your tub is old, there's a good chance you're soaking in lead. For over a century, the neurotoxin has been added to porcelain enamel, and both new and old bathroom fixtures (from sinks to tubs) may leach the substance, but older bathtubs that have been scrubbed with abrasive cleansers for years leach the most. According to one sample, 62% of porcelain tubs were leaching the stuff! This is a serious problem if you've got little ones lapping up bathwater.

If you're nervous about potential exposure, some hardware stores carry household lead-testing kits, or you can get one online at **leadinspector.com**. If your tub tests positive, resurfacing it should eliminate your exposure to the neurotoxin. You can do it yourself with a tub refinishing kit, available at hardware stores, or call in a pro. Just look in the phone book under "bathtub refinishing." If you have a newer acrylic bathtub or acrylic tub liner to cover an old porcelain tub, you should be safe. Whatever you do, get rid of any vinyl slip mats lining your tub and switch to **all-natural rubber** instead. Anyone with latex allergies should check out the **polypropylene** options at IKEA (**ikea.com**).

Towels: Next time you're in the market for new towels, skip the pesticide-heavy cotton type tied to child labor abuses in Egypt and invest in unbleached, undyed cotton or 100% organic towels, dyed with low-impact vegetable dyes. If you're looking for something other than beige, California-based **Native Organic Cotton** (**nativeorganic.com**) sells towels and bathrobes made of 100% certified organic US-grown cotton, woven in earth tones created with color-grown fiber ("color-grown" means they use a cotton plant that naturally grows in sage or brown hues, with no added dyes). Green home web stores like **Earthsake** carry a wide range of towel brands and fabrics, from ultrasoft bamboo to even softer luxury Italian Legna towels made of sustainably harvested trees (**earthsake.com**).

Toilets: Up to 65% of indoor water use happens in the bathroom, and about a third of that water goes right down the toilet with every flush—as much as 7 gallons per flush with old toilets. Not sure what your toilet's sucking back with each round? Just check the back of the bowl, in front of the tank: there should be a label there telling you how many gallons per flush it uses. If your house was built after 1992, it should have a **low-flow unit** built in; otherwise, you're shit out of luck (couldn't resist that one). Of course, you can wander over to your neighborhood hardware store and buy a good one for a couple hundred bucks. These units use less than 1.6 gallons of water per flush (your municipality might even have a rebate program in place, so ask). You'll save at least 14,000 gallons a year. Better yet, get a fancy **dual-flush toilet**, which uses more water to swallow up solid waste than it does mellow yellow.

If you're renting or don't have the cash for a new toilet just yet, pick up a cheap toilet tank dam or water-saving bag from the hardware store for a buck or two. Even a weighted plastic bottle in the tank will do. But no bricks, please—they break down and can screw up your plumbing.

Toilet Paper: We all buy it, and sure, most of us prefer the feel of extra-cushy three-ply— the kind that's "cottony" soft—but is it really worth flushing bleached-out ancient forests down the toilet on a daily basis? "How much damage can a little square of tissue really do?" you ask. Well, Americans use 26 billion rolls of TP a year, feeding the $12 billion

LEAKY TOILET?

Water bills suspiciously higher than usual? You've probably sprung a leak without knowing it. So how do you know if your toilet's tanking? Well, do you have to jiggle the handle to make it stop running? Does it sound like a creek is babbling in your bathroom? Ever seem like there's a phantom flusher in your house? Even if it's doing none of the above, you could still have a silent leak. Find out by putting a small amount of food coloring in the tank, then wait 20 minutes. If you see color in the bowl, you're leakin', darlin'. Time to call a plumber. You're wasting about 200 gallons a day!

disposable-tissue market. And every time you flush a wad of Kimberly-Clark toilet paper, a chunk of old-growth Canadian forest goes down with it. Americans import a good 300,000 tons of tossable tissue products from their northern neighbors ever year, and most of that is coming from the oldest ancient forest in North America: the Canadian boreal. For more on Kimberly-Clark and the Greenpeace campaign against it, check out kleercut.net. (FYI: the company's also been accused of some pretty bad mercury and dioxin pollution from its US plants over the years.)

And wouldn't you know it, the same chemical that's causing so much controversy in the world of reusable water bottles and ceramic dental fillers is turning up in toilet paper. Yep, bisphenol A and three other chemical compounds that mimic female sex hormones are used

in paper production. Researchers in the department of waste management at a university in Dresden, Germany, found that not only did both recycled and nonrecycled bathroom tissues test positive for the chems, but they're a significant source of estrogenic emissions to wastewater. The investigators concluded that tainted toilet paper could contaminate the sewage sludge that many municipalities treat and spread on farmers' fields (yes, American municipalities too).

For those of you wondering who the worst offenders are when it comes to chopping down old-growth forests, Charmin and Cottenelle toilet paper, Kleenex and Puffs facial tissue, and Bounty, Scott, and Viva paper towels all top the Natural Resources Defense Council's list of products to avoid. Kimberly-Clark (maker of Kleenex, Scott, and Cottonelle) says in its 2007 sustainability report, "We believe there is no environmental preference between using recycled or virgin fiber in the manufacture of our products." To appease customers, however, Kimberly-Clark has come out with Scott Naturals and Kleenex Naturals, which contain some recycled content. The company claims that its practices are sustainable, and that it has indeed worked to protect old-growth forests. Greenpeace, of course, has its own thoughts on that. For the he said–she said, check out kleercut.net/en/ResponsetoKC.

Toilet Paper Solutions: Wanna hear the good news? If each household in the US switched just one roll of the virgin bleached stuff with one roll of the recycled kind, we'd save 423,000 trees—bam, just like that. One roll. Just imagine what would happen if we replaced a dozen rolls, or shifted over to recycled tissue altogether. Several brands contain some degree of recycled material, but read the fine print and look for a high level of postconsumer content (minimum 80%).

Some good choices are **Seventh Generation** (seventhgeneration.com, available at health stores) and **Whole Foods' 365** brand (wholefoodsmarket.com). None of these use chemical bleaches in their whitening process, which is another key feature to look for. The label "elemental chlorine-free," by the way, tells you the paper was made without chlorine gas in a process that creates fewer emissions but could still release dioxins into the environment. Look for products labeled "process chlorine-free," like the ones just listed.

When it comes to paper towels and facial tissue, there are even fewer eco options. But if we all switched one box of tissue and one roll of paper towel over, we'd save another 700,000 trees. Even Kleenex's website admits that the only thing recycled about its facial tissue is the cardboard carton. **Seventh Generation** is the main brand that churns out

If each household in the US switched just one roll of VIRGIN BLEACHED TP *with one roll of the recycled kind, we'd* SAVE 423,000 TREES.

100% recycled, chlorine-free–processed facial tissues, napkins, and paper towels. It turns out that few of us are willing to part with the extra softness that comes from blowing your schnozz with virgin forest. And though it's nice that Bounty is marketing its half-sized paper towels as "future friendly," it would be nicer to see a major disposable-paper product brand be genuinely future-friendly and go the recycled route.

BEDROOM

Ah, the bedroom [cue Isaac Hayes music]. It's a corner of the home full of pleasurable possibilities, and at the top of our list is getting good, sound sleep. Most of us spend about a third of our lives nestled in bed. (I'm a mess without my 9 hours. I never could figure out you kooky people who survive on 4.) But all that time sandwiched between blankets and mattresses can get you tossing and turning when you consider what they're made of.

Pillows and Comforters: We all need a place to rest our heads, but our pillows and comforters are likely to be stuffed with either petroleum-based polyester fillers (who knew a night's rest could contribute to our dependence on fossil fuels?) or down. With down, we tend to imagine fluffy feathers falling naturally from plump, happy birds as they waddle around sunny barns, shedding their winter insulation. I hate to burst any bubbles, but you should know that down feathers are forcefully plucked from geese, chicken, or ducks either before or after they're slaughtered. The feathers are then sterilized with formaldehyde, bleached, and sprayed with chemical antiallergens. Not so idyllic after all. Note: plucking birds while they're alive causes them considerable pain and distress.

Pillow and Comforter Solutions: If you're sticking to mainstream shops, IKEA makes a point of not using down and feathers from living birds; instead, its pillows and comforters are made with by-products from the poultry biz. A greener sleep would include 100% **organic cotton fill pillows**, which are slightly heavier and firmer; or fluffier and more breathable **organic wool fill**. Wool is naturally resistant to dust mites and mildew, so it's great for anyone with allergies (FYI: wool labeled "Pure Grow" comes from farmers in Sonoma County, California, who follow sustainable, humane sheep-ranching practices).

    Natural rubber (either shredded or molded) is another excellent option for those with asthma or nonlatex allergies, as it's naturally dust-resistant and hypoallergenic. Others swear by pillows stuffed with **buckwheat husks**, but they're not exactly cushy. If you're looking for the feel of down without the animal cruelty and allergens, you might want to check out pillows stuffed with **kapok pod fibers**. The seeds on this majestic tropical tree produce silky threads and are hand-harvested without the tree itself being axed. You can pick up any of these pillows from online shops like **EcoBedroom** (ecobedroom.com) and **Earthsake** (earthsake.com). Rawganique.com even has 100% hemp pillows to complete its hemp bedding sets.

    For comforters, the same stores carry toasty and breathable wool in an organic cotton casing. Note that many companies sell wool comforters cased in conventionally grown cotton, sometimes for a better price. If that cotton is unbleached and undyed, it's generally called natural bedding, rather than organic. **Euphoria**'s organic wool comforters or duvets, available from AllergyBuyersClub.com, are handmade in North America with organic cotton outer shells and lightweight certified organic lamb's wool on the inside. **AllergyBuyersClub. com** also offers some stuffed with alpaca wool; and **Cleanbedroom.com** sells llama, alpaca, and organic merino wool options. Vegans might prefer comforters stuffed entirely with organic cotton or hemp (see **Rawganique.com**).

Sheets: We all dream of silky sheets with a high thread count, but no one wants to be wrapped in a pesticide-drenched crop. Sure, cotton is natural, but this water-hogging plant is also the proud recipient of 25% of the world's insecticides—chemicals that inevitably end up contaminating local groundwater and making both workers and wildlife sick. And over half of all American cotton is grown from genetically engineered seeds. Then it's bleached with chlorine, soaked in chemical dyes, and sprayed with a wrinkle-resistant permanent-press chemical finish, likely carcinogenic formaldehyde. Washing your sheets before you use them will eliminate about 60% of that formaldehyde, according to one study. But even a few visits to the washing machine won't get rid of it completely. It's best to skip on iron-free promises—a little crinkling won't kill anyone.

Sheet Solutions: Pesticides, chemicals, and human rights abuses (see the sidebar on Egyptian sheets) not something you want to get twisted up in each night? I don't blame you. Wrap yourself in 100% **organic cotton bed linens,** free of bleaches and dyes. **Indika Organics** sells a high-end environmental bedding line of duvet covers and shams made of vegetable-dyed Peruvian cotton, beautiful hemp, and bamboo, but it doesn't come cheap (**indikaorganics.com**). **Anna Sova** also sells luxury organic bedding (**annasova.com**).

Over half of all American cotton is grown from GENETICALLY ENGINEERED SEEDS.

Coyuchi's bedding gets its hues in part from naturally colored cotton strains from Latin

THE DARK SIDE OF EGYPTIAN SHEETS

We fawn over luxurious Egyptian cotton sheets and pay a mint for them. Unfortunately, the 1 million children working Egyptian cotton fields don't get to see much of that money. Human Rights Watch says that young cotton pickers, hired seasonally to remove leaf worm infestations from leaves because they're just the right height, work 11-hour days, 7 days a week, in 100°F heat. And all the children surveyed reported being beaten by their foreman. Egypt developed child labor laws in 1996, but Human Rights Watch says the laws aren't being enforced. On a positive note, Egypt has been successful at reducing the amount of pesticides it uses on cotton and has banned a few really bad ones. Still, that doesn't really wash away its sins, now does it?

America (**coyuchiorganic.com**). And one-stop green shops like **Gaiam** sell a good selection of sheets from organic jersey to bamboo–organic cotton blends (**gaiam.com**). Organic hemp sheets (said to be surprisingly soft), organic flax linen, and organic cotton bedding are available from **Rawganique.com** for a pretty penny. The budget-crunched can get full sets for a better price at **Native Organic Cotton**, which uses low-impact dyes (**nativeorganic.com**).

While you're dreaming away, your POLYURETHANE *stuffed mattress is offgassing air-polluting* VOLATILE ORGANIC COMPOUNDS.

Your best bet, pricewise, might be 100% fast-growing bamboo sheet sets from **Bed Bath & Beyond**, or better still, organic cotton sheet sets from **West Elm** for under $100 (**westelm.com**). But be leery of cheaper bamboo sets at stores like Target and JCPenney that are blended with conventional cotton. And there's no promise that harsh chemicals weren't used in the dyes, processing, and finishes.

Mattresses: Now for what hugs your frame night after night, even when your love life fails you. We tend to choose a mattress based on whether we prefer firmness or deep, cushiony comfort. But while you're dreaming away, your polyurethane foam–stuffed padding is offgassing air-polluting volatile organic compounds (VOCs). And something's got to be sprayed on that ultraflammable foam to keep it from bursting into flames every time a fool smokes in bed, but does it have to be superpersistent fire-retardant chemicals? The worst offenders (part of the PBDE family, see page 352) have been phased out, but troublesome fire retardants (including harmful chlorinated tris) might still be used.

Salespeople also try to sell you on stain-resistant finishes, but note that these can be made with chemicals from the same dodgy family behind nonstick frying pans. But 3M, the maker of Scotchgard, phased out its most persistent ingredient (PFOS) by the end of 2002 and insists that its modified recipe has a "low risk" of accumulating in the food chain.

Although modern furniture designers are making it impossible for us to use traditional box spring frames, many of us are still partial to them. But less expensive frames made of plywood or particleboard often contain offgassing formaldehyde. And whether it's solid wood or particleboard, fat chance that wood was sustainably harvested.

Mattress Solutions: Bypass the monsters under your bed and invest in a traditional spring-based mattress with organic cotton and wool batting (wool, by the way is naturally fire-retardant) and, preferably, FSC-certified wood slats. Or you can skip the box and coil thing altogether and opt for natural rubber (latex is also naturally fire-safe). It's a nice springy, supportive base for organic cotton and wool mattresses, and you can choose the level of firmness you prefer. The **Organic Mattress Store** (theorganicmattressstore.com), **Abundant Earth** (abundantearth.com), **EcoBedroom** (ecobedroom.com), and **A Happy Planet** (ahappyplanet.com) are just some of the many shops that have a good selection of alternative mattresses.

If spending a few thousand on a mattress system is totally out of the question, then you'll be happy to hear that **IKEA** has been brominated fire retardant–free since 2002, and it has pretty decent forestry policies. Plus, IKEA's particleboard is virtually formaldehyde-free. It's still stuffed with synthetics but it's a decent start.

DONATING OLD MATTRESSES

Got an old mattress you want to kick to the curb? Most retailers will snag it from you when you're buying a new one, but you need to make sure they're not landfilling it. These clunkers take up a hell of a lot of room at the dump. Look for companies that either donate mattresses to charity or recycle them for parts. Or call your local homeless shelter or women's shelter and ask if they'd like it. You can sleep soundly, knowing you're giving your mattress a second life and giving someone else a much-needed place to rest.

If you're shopping in a run-of-the-mill mattress store, **Sealy** says it stays away from chemical flame retardants and uses new fiber-based flame-retardant barriers instead. And though its mattresses are still polyurethane foam–based, they're also free of Teflon-based stain-resistant treatments.

FURNITURE

Nomads must not have had much furniture. I mean, really, worrying about shelves and dining-room tables would have seriously slowed them down as they chased antelope and buffalo across the countryside. Of course, to this day, furniture still weighs us down (anyone who has moved a pullout couch knows they weren't designed to be lifted up five flights of stairs). But we all accumulate it, and that collection of coffee tables, couches, and ottomans somehow makes our home what it is: ours. Too bad all that stuff isn't just creating atmosphere—it's poisoning it with fumes and deforesting the planet.

Foam: Let's start with that pillowy couch you're parked on. The soft, cushy part tends to come from foam—polyurethane foam, to be exact. Polyurethane itself isn't the greenest thing on the planet. Making the petroleum-based plastic creates toxic by-products such as toluene diisocyanates and the probable carcinogen methylene chloride. But it's hard to find a sofa that isn't stuffed with this stuff.

An additive that is more avoidable, however, is the flame-retardants. That fluffy foam is quick to catch fire, so for decades furniture makers have been turning to brominated fire retardants to put a stop to that. The thing is, those chemicals don't just stay put in our couches. They're in the dust from decaying foam that fills our homes (the Environmental Working Group found them in every home it sampled), and environmental agencies say they're turning up virtually everywhere they test (air, water, land, arctic seals). These chemicals (tied to thyroid and developmental problems in lab animals) are considered persistent, bioaccumulating toxins—which means they build up in our fatty tissues and stay there. Perhaps scariest of all is that they're turning up in human breast milk—an upsetting fact, considering that babies exposed in the womb and through breast-feeding are most at risk from the troubling health effects.

The worst of the worst (known as pentaBDE and octaBDE) have already been banned by 11 states, but most furniture makers are just using other types of brominated fire retardants (mainly decaBDE, deemed toxic by Canada's health agency) or harmful chlorinated tris. In fact, according to a 2008 report by Friends of the Earth, which tested 350 pieces of furniture for the presence of bromine, 52% of all furniture tested in domestic residences contained high levels. Yowsers.

Better to stay away from foam if you can afford to go the natural route. Back in the day, couches used to be stuffed with natural latex, and green furniture makers are turning to the tree-tapped substance once again to fill their sofas. They're also turning to organic cotton and wool batting, as well as recycled fabrics, to stuff their designs. A couple are reducing the amount of petroleum-based stuffing in your couch by using foam that's part soy- or corn-based. Really, there are plenty of green surfaces for you to park your derriere on these days. Just know that you'll need to pad your wallet a little more to get them (see page 184).

Wood: Sure, wood is natural and renewable, but that doesn't make your bookcase soft on the earth. Wood furniture is generally teeming with toxins. It's coated in toxic varnishes, glues, waxes, and paints that release smog-inducing, lung-irritating VOCs. Pressed woods such as particleboard, fiberboard, and even some plywoods are often major culprits because they're bound with formaldehyde. Although the industry has reduced emissions by 80% over the last couple of decades, VOCs like formaldehyde are still out there causing headaches, allergic reactions, and nausea in unsuspecting home dwellers. Worse yet, furniture can offgas noxious vapors for years!

That lovely COFFEE TABLE *in your living room might be the last incarnation of a* 200-YEAR-OLD TREE.

When hunting for wooden furniture, beware of particleboard posing as the real thing. Increasingly convincing veneers might dupe you into thinking you're buying maple when you're actually buying sawdust and resin glued together. These are okay only if you find stuff that's formaldehyde-free and made from nonvirgin wood sources. When in doubt, ask.

Then there's the whole deforestation factor. That lovely coffee table in your living room might be the last incarnation of a 200-year-old tree. If it's tropical wood, that's an especially bad thing. Rainforests are the world's lungs and don't deserve to end up as a TV stand. What can you do to avoid this? Look for wood products that are old growth–free. The Forest Stewardship Council (FSC) label is considered the strongest on the market, though it doesn't guarantee that tropical furniture is old growth–free. Best to stick with nontropical FSC woods, and the more local the better.

At least the list of furniture makers emphasizing both FSC and nontropical woods, like San Francisco's worker-owned co-op **Woodshanti** (**woodshanti.com**) and Portland's **Joinery** (thejoinery.com), is always growing. There's a database of manufacturers at fsc-info.org, but it's not all that consumer-friendly. You can also check the site of SmartWood, which both certifies FSC products and runs the Rainforest Alliance's SmartWood Rediscovered Wood Program for certification of reused, reclaimed, recycled, and salvaged wood products (ra-smartwood.org). If you spot a Sustainable Forestry Initiative (SFI) label on wood products, know that the industry-run program doesn't get much respect from enviros.

Green Furniture: **Green Culture** has perhaps the biggest selection of enlightened furniture online (including bedroom, dining-room, and kids' room sets) but they're not 100% eco-friendly or certified. Be sure to read the fine print (greenculture.com). Seattle-based **Greener Lifestyles** has slickly designed fair-trade couches, armchairs, dinner tables, and more made with FSC-certified, low-VOC finishes and natural latex fill (greenerlifestyles.com). Brooklyn-based **Vivavi** has a gorgeous selection of eco

> *f* **GREEN FURNITURE** *is out of your price range, shop for secondhand options on sites like* **CRAIGSLIST.COM.**

designers doing everything from patio furniture made with water hyacinths to armoires made with reclaimed stalks of sorghum plants and FSC-certified birch wood (vivavi .com). **Dax**'s virtual eco department store also has a ton of earth-friendly furniture options (daxstores.com), and **Furnature** offers couches, chairs, futons, and bed frames for the chemically sensitive (furnature.com). For the home office, **Legaré** offers FSC-certified modular and easily assembled pieces (legarefurniture.com). (For green patio furniture, see page 264.)

Reclaimed and Recycled Furniture: You can't get much greener than furniture that uses **reclaimed wood** (from old barns, homes, or naturally felled trees) or **postconsumer recycled waste** (like cork, wheat straw, or sunflower husks). You can score beautiful reclaimed wood stuff from Berkeley's **Wooden Duck** (thewoodenduck.com), Washington State's **Alan Vogel**'s **Time Warped Furniture** (alanvogelfurniture .com), and Seattle's **Urban Hardwoods** (urbanhardwoods.com). For more reclaimed furniture stores across the country, see ecobusinesslinks.com/ recycled_green_furniture_manufacturers.htm.

Let's not forget about **antiques**. Not only are they fun to hunt, this is furniture recycling at its finest! Don't think you're doomed to doilies and your grandmother's tacky side tables. There are lots of eras and styles to pick from, including American primitive, art deco, and Victorian. If exotics are more your thing, you can get stunning antique cabinets, armoires, and tables from the Far East and South Asia that will make your place pop. Sure, they've traveled a ways on a cargo ship to get here, but it's better than buying a brand-new teak table. Also keep in mind that many antique dealers sell refurbished stuff and even make new furniture with reclaimed barn doors or whatnot.

If both antiques and modern green furniture are out of your price range, look through the classified ads or go to **Furnituretrader.com** or **Recycledfurniture.com** to outfit every room in your house. **Craigslist (craigslist.com)** and **Freecycle (freecycle.org)** are other must-visit sites for secondhand furnishings.

ELECTRONICS

Not to romanticize the past, but back in the day, electronics were made to last several years—decades, even! Sure, they're cheaper now, but they might as well be disposable at the rate you have to replace them. Over 85% of the 2 million tons of used or unwanted electronics make their way to landfills every year, according to the EPA. To make matters worse, all those gadgets are teeming with toxic heavy metals and chemicals, like the nasty endocrine-disrupting fire retardants found in outer plastic casings and circuit boards, the superpotent greenhouse gas (nitrogen trifluoride) used in flat screens, and the up to 8 pounds of lead in traditional cathode ray tube TVs. In fact about 40% of the heavy metals in landfills come from electronics.

Electronic gadgets are teeming with TOXIC HEAVY METALS *and chemicals—and 85% make their way to* LANDFILLS *every year.*

What's wrong with having toxic trash at the dump? Leaching. That's the problem. Not good, when you consider that millions of old TVs will become obsolete in June 2009, thanks to a mandatory switch to digital signals. That means an estimated 23 million *American Idol* and Maury Povich lovers either will have to get a new set or will score a digital converter box. Bottom line: it's time to think twice about how you purge your place of used gear.

Recycling: If you've squeezed the last drop of life from your gadgets, or you just can't get by without a bigger and badder computer, there are many places you can bring your old electronics for recycling. First of all, if you have an old laptop or PC you want to get rid of, get in touch with an organization like the National Cristina Foundation (**cristina.org**), which targets its donations to schools and nonprofit orgs that use the equipment for training, job development, educational programs, or programs to improve the lives of people with disabilities, students at risk, and economically disadvantaged people.

More and more companies, like **Sony**, **Motorola**, **Hewlett-Packard**, and **Dell**, have take-back programs of their own. Dell will take your old one even if you don't buy a new one from them. Plus, the company will recycle other computer-related stuff. For instance, you can send Dell your keyboard, mouse, monitors, and printers. Hewlett-Packard picks up printers, scanners, fax machines, desktop servers, monitors, and handheld devices, as well as cables, mice, and keyboards. Check with the company first. Or call your municipality to ask whether it takes back old tech. Many do or will put you in touch with local companies or organizations that do.

Ideally, mandatory national "extended producer responsibility" regulations would be in place (meaning that manufacturers would take responsibility for the full life cycle of their products by, for instance, funding national recycling programs). While we hold our breath, several states have taken the lead. Roughly a dozen states, including Oregon, Maine, Texas, and New Jersey, now force manufacturers of computers and other high-tech stuff to fund take-back programs. Another dozen are considering it. Others are hoping to model their system after California's, where consumers cough up a $6 to $10 recycling fee on TVs, computers, and portable DVD players. For more info on legislation and policies, head to **computertakeback.com**.

Warning: recycling e-waste can be a dodgy business. Dismantling all those toxins is dangerous, so the dirty work is often done by prison workers or exported overseas (an estimated 50% to 80% of American electronic waste is being shipped overseas, according to the Worldwatch Institute). Workers in India, China, and Africa often use their bare hands to extract recyclables, with no protective gear to safeguard them from hazardous innards. Toxic fumes, acid spills, and contaminated groundwater are common. No wonder China tried to ban imports of e-waste in 2000, but the nightmare is only worsening.

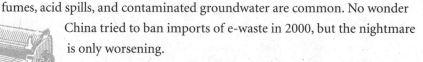

Make sure that whoever is taking your old computer isn't just dumping it on poorer countries with weak environmental and worker safety laws. To locate responsible recyclers in your area, check out the Basel Action Network's list of e-Stewards at **ban.org**. Oh, and you should harass your federal representative about the fact that the US is the only developed country that has refused to ratify the 1994 Basel Convention banning the export of hazardous waste from rich countries to poor.

Buying New: In the market for new tech? Who isn't? One problem with most household electronics is that they act like unwanted houseguests, using power even when you're not home. Yes, even when you've turned your gadgets off, they're actually still on, in standby mode, wasting a surprising amount of electricity to power all those little lights, timers, and clocks. All that phantom power-sucking adds up to a startling 10% of your home's energy bill. You're actually spending more money to power your DVD player when it's off than when you're watching the latest Will Smith flick! TVs, VCRs, and cable boxes are the worst culprits, but stereo systems are almost as bad.

To help usher those unwanted ghosts out of your home, look for the Energy Star label on everything from DVD players and TVs to computers and major appliances. To earn the government logo, electronics must use a minimal amount of energy when off, so, for instance, an Energy Star DVD player must consume 75% less than conventional models. Starting in 2009, you'll find Energy Star set-top cable/satellite/Internet boxes that are at least 30% more efficient than the energy waster you have now. According to the Natural Resources Defense Council, if the two TVs, one DVD player, and three phones in the average American home were replaced with Energy Star models, we'd save over 25 billion pounds of greenhouse gas emissions, which is tantamount to taking 2 million cars off the road.

> *All that* PHANTOM POWER-SUCKING *adds up to a startling 10% of your home's energy bill.*

FYI: the Energy Star seal of approval hasn't historically told you anything about how efficient your set is when it's on. It's been a little disappointing, since most power is consumed when these electronics are in active mode, not standby mode. But the EPA is

FLICKING OFF PHANTOM POWER

To curb all that power leaking from your electronics when they're off, the answer is simple. Just unplug them all when you're not using them. That includes your microwave and coffee maker. To make things easier, put your entertainment center on one power strip that you can readily flick off.

starting to rectify this problem, and Energy Star sets made after November 2008 will be up to 30% more efficient than conventional models and will actually save energy while they're on *and* off.

How do products match up when they're actually in use? In general, VHS players—even the newer ones (yes, some people still use these)—consume more energy than DVD players. And since your computer uses less power than your TV, watching films or downloaded television shows on your desktop or laptop is a greener choice, especially compared to jumbo-screen TV sets. Of course getting your guy to watch the game on anything but his big screen might be a losing battle.

TVs: Generally, the bigger and sharper the image, the more juice your set needs to deliver it. A Samsung 32-inch LCD model might use only 1.9 watts on standby and 116.8 when actually on, whereas a 40-incher by the same company uses 16.3 watts on standby and 209.1 when on. Is seeing the pores on your favorite starlet's nose really worth all that extra power use? Philips' 42-inch Eco TV creams them all by using less power than a 100-watt bulb when on (as little as 75 watts). And in standby mode? A teeny 0.15 watt. Plus, it might not advertise it well, but it's virtually free of six major heavy metals. As a rule of thumb, plasmas are the biggest energy vampire and rear-projection systems are low power users. For a full breakdown of how much power HDTVs suck back, check out CNET's handy dandy quick guide to the power consumption of nearly 100 sets (**cnet.com**).

POWER-SAVING TV TIPS

- **No quickies, please.** Turn off the quick-start button (it makes your TV use up to 50% more power in standby mode).

- **Dim it down over there.** The brighter your settings, the more juice gets used.

- **Bigger ain't better.** Smaller screens use less power (duh).

- **Pass on the plasma.** These bad boys use the most power of all the flat screens.

- **You have the power.** Put all your electronics on a power strip and switch it off.

- **Turn me off.** The best reality shows happen when the TV's not on.

Computers: As for computers, laptops aren't just lighter; they use much less power than desktop models. Yep, the typical laptop draws anywhere from 15 to 30 watts of electricity, depending on how old it is, while bulkier desktop models use anywhere from 80 to 160 watts. Flat-screen LCD monitors for desktop computers will lessen your energy consumption. **Hewlett-Packard** was the one of the first companies to work with consumers and government to take back aging gear and deal with it in an environmentally friendly way. But HP slipped in the ranking when it was discovered that an HP laptop contained a type of fire retardant (deca) that it claimed to have stopped using years before. Very sneaky. HP, by the way, has vowed to remove the last of its troubling fire retardants and PVC components by 2009.

Dell has made the same commitment. The company climbed in the ranks when it stopped using American prison labor several years ago, initiated a free recycling program, and began publicly supporting producer take-back regulations, unlike most of the electronics industry, which has been vocally against them.

> Laptops aren't just lighter; they use much **LESS POWER** *than bulkier desktop models.*

Both companies, however, have been overtaken in Greenpeace's quarterly electronics report. For all the latest details on how electronic makers stack up, head to **greenpeace.org**. Note: the electronics guide is updated every 3 months.

E-TUNES: THE GREENEST WAY TO GROOVE OUT

Clunky eight-tracks and toxic vinyl might be history, but are we any better off today with all the digital music devices we own now? Tapes (yes, some people still have these) and CDs just tend to collect dust in our basements when we're tired of them. Trash those unwanted or scratched CDs (and DVDs), and you can bet the polycarbonate plastic (heavy in hormone-disrupting bisphenol A) and aluminum coating don't biodegrade. Plus, they'll release nasty fumes if they're incinerated by your municipality. MP3 players and iPods, on the other hand, can hold thousands of songs in the palm of your hand, so they create a lot less waste. The problem is that they contain all the same toxic crap that every other electronic item on the market does, but they tend to die even faster, meaning that kids are chucking and buying new iPods and MP3 players way too often. Ask about corporate take-back recycling policies before you buy. Apple has one in place for its iPod, and Dell has one for its Pocket DJ, so be sure to use them. Unless you're listening to tunes on a CD made of old straw, the digital route just might squeak out as the greener option.

Other Electronics: Nokia has edged its way to the top of the class. It was an early pioneer in wiping out harmful chemicals from its product line, having gone PVC-free by 2005 and totally PBDE-free by 2007, with the rest of the brominated fire retardant family projected to be gone soon. **Sony**'s got a good take-back program and has promised to phase out PVC and brominated fire retardants (BRFs) in some video cameras, laptops, and digital cameras by 2010, but unfortunately it hasn't agreed to clean up all its products. **Samsung**'s and **Toshiba**'s recycling systems aren't perfect, but they were offering models free of the worst chemicals by 2008. The prize for most improved has got to go to **Apple**. The hipster company had been heavily criticized for being an eco laggard, but it's finally starting to clean up its act and should be PVC- and BRF-free by the end of 2008. Keep your eyes peeled. By the way, the biggest slackers at the time this book was written were Panasonic, Microsoft, and Philips, with Nintendo trailing at the very back of the pack. Check back with Greenpeace for updates.

BATTERIES

If you have a dusty battery drawer somewhere in your home, good for you—you've taken an important step toward keeping a good chunk of household hazardous waste out of the landfill. Still, many of the 3 billion alkaline and rechargeable batteries purchased every year in the US end up in the dump. Thankfully, mercury (used to prevent corrosion and increase shelf life) was largely phased out of the mini power logs back in 1996, but there could still be some in there. So just because manufacturers might say you can simply trash alkaline batteries at will, that doesn't mean you should. Instead, bring your old batteries to your hazardous-waste depot or search for a local drop spot at **earth911.org**.

Recycling Rechargeables: Now, what to do with those rechargeables that just won't charge any more, no matter how hard you try? Thanks to an industry-sponsored program that was originally designed to keep nickel cadmium out of the waste stream (it's a cumulative toxin to plants, animals, and humans alike, as well as a known human carcinogen), there are thousands of locations where you can take your old rechargeable batteries (nickel cadmium or not) from cellular or cordless phones, power tools, laptops, camcorders—you name it. Just stop by your neighborhood RadioShack, Target, Sears, Office Depot, Home Depot, Lowe's, or other stores, including any cell phone store. Or call 1-800-8-BATTERY for the collection site nearest you (you can also visit **rbrc.org**). Warning: the drop boxes are quite small and hard to spot in big stores, so ask.

Once you're rid of your old ones, might I be so bold as to suggest that you never buy single-use batteries again? That's right, never—or as close to never as you can get. There's really no need to buy the disposable type when there are plenty of excellent rechargeable alternatives to choose from. And one rechargeable can replace anywhere from 300 to 700 single-use batteries!

Buying Rechargeables: Yes, it's true—a battery is a battery, and the metal extraction process used to make the bloody things involves everything from habitat destruction to air and water pollution. Stay away from nickel cadmium batteries. They're bad news for the planet. Most consumer rechargeables now run on nickel metal hydride (NiMH) anyway, which is much more benign. You can even score rechargeable alkalines, but they don't last as long. In terms of performance, the top-rated nickel metal hydrides in 2006 were **Powerex**, **Sanyo**, and **Energizer**. **Rayovac** was number 5 of the 10.

One RECHARGEABLE can replace anywhere from 300 to 700 single-use batteries.

The higher the mAh (milliamp hours) number on the side of the nickel metal hydride battery (for example, 2,000 or 2,700), the longer it will last per charge (and the longer it generally takes to charge up). Ready-to-use models that come fully charged are a little less powerful, but they're perfect for consumer electronics that aren't heavy drainers or gadgets you use only here and there. They avoid the "self-discharge" problem of regular NiMH batteries that slowly lose their charge over time. That makes ready-to-use—a.k.a. precharged—batteries great for remote controls or anything you don't want to be constantly fiddling with. If you need big power in shorter bursts, stick with regular, higher-capacity options.

Solar and Crank Battery Chargers: Why bother at all with the dirty coal needed to charge your gadgets when you can run your batteries on the sun's rays? The **Soldius1 universal solar charger** will power up your cell, MP3 player, or PDA in 2 or 3 hours on your windowsill—a little longer on cloudy but bright days (**soldius.com**). Soldius even makes a solar backpack that can charge your gizmos while you're walking or biking around town. **Freeplay** makes a great little hand-cranked FreeCharge charger for times when your cell dies in an emergency and there's no socket or sunlight around. Looking for more oomph? Freeplay also has a nonspill, lead-acid gel battery capable of jump-starting engines, as well as powering your GPS or cell. All you've got to do is step on the foot pedal to get it going (**freeplayenergy.com**). Talk about portable power!

CAMERAS

Weighing in at over 100 pounds, the first daguerreotype camera was not for the masses. Now everyone and their kid has one (you can even buy a SpongeBob SquarePants version). But that doesn't mean their insides have fewer antiquated toxins. Both digital and traditional point-and-shoots can contain dangerous components, including lead, cadmium, and mercury, in their lenses, sensors, and displays.

Most companies have switched to lead-free solder in recent years and are moving to phase out harmful heavy metals. But detailed reports of emissions reductions and eco initiatives don't always give you the full picture. Film and digital camera maker Kodak, for instance, has long been embroiled in a battle with eco activists regarding methylene chloride and toxic dioxin pollution around its industrial park in Albany, New York. As for who's the greenest of them all—digital or traditional film—it's time to assess.

Film: Conventional camera users may have cursed the mounds of film wasted over the years because of low light, blinking kids, or severed heads (yes, Mom, I know you didn't mean to photograph us from the nose down). But what about the eco implications of processing all those shots? Fortunately, the volume of chemicals needed to print Grandma's birthday party pics has dropped from 2 quarts to 3 ounces since 1968—a whopping 96% reduction, according to *E* magazine's EarthTalk. Nonetheless, those chemicals still add up.

Of most concern to municipal water treatment folks is silver. As nice as it looks around your neck, it's actually a pollutant when in water. Silver is found in the film itself and then is transferred to photo-processing water. Most commercial minilabs have silver recovery machines. The metal is refined and recycled into things like jewelry (back to the pretty type of silver). The rest of the chems in the processing stew are said to be nontoxic and largely biodegradable in municipal water treatment plants (although sewer overflows might mean that some end up in lakes and streams—a very bad thing).

If you're one of those dinosaurs with a home darkroom, don't think you can just dump your chemicals down the drain (though most of you do—

The volume of CHEMICALS *needed to print Grandma's birthday party pics has dropped a* WHOPPING 96% *since 1968.*

shame on you!). You should be keeping your used chemicals in jugs and calling up a silver recovery company for proper disposal. Just look up "silver recovery" in the Yellow Pages.

All you tofu-heads out there might be grossed out to learn that film is made using a gelatin base (the collagen in cow or pig bones, hooves, and connective tissue). If you're a hard-core vegan, this might be enough to make you drop your old camera and switch to digital.

Digital: Beyond being hoof-free, how does digital measure up? Well, traditionally these cams have been serious battery hogs. But technology has been advancing in leaps and bounds, so almost all new digies use rechargeable batteries and chew through them much less quickly than models from 3 or 4 years ago do. At this moment, **Sony Cyber-shots** and **Canon PowerShots** are generally much more efficient than most brands on the market, but at the rate of camera tech evolution, this info might already be obsolete. (Just kidding. Er, maybe not.)

Although printing digital images doesn't involve the same chemical bath as film processing does, inks are still used to print those pics. Most are water-based, but some pigments contain toxic heavy metals and polluting VOCs (unfortunately, it's tough to tell which are low-VOC at this point). At the very least, your pics should be printed on Energy Star–certified ink-jet printers, available at camera stores or pretty much anywhere you'd buy cameras. Be sure to refill or recycle your old ink cartridges, depending on the make.

But let's get real. Digital cams have the upper hand ecologically because most people don't bother printing 95% of their pictures. "Sure," some would say, "but you're sucking up computer power to look at those images." The truth is, though, we all have computers

There's something about photographs that makes us feel guilty for wanting to toss them. But hey, maybe you have valid reasons to destroy all proof that your ex ever existed, or perhaps you're hoping to erase any hard-copy images of you with a mullet. Either way, I don't judge. Just know that your prints can't be tossed in your recycling bin, thanks to the chemical coating on the paper. That's not to say you can't run them through a shredder or throw darts at them before you junk them.

anyway, and few of us bought them just to upload digital shots of our dogs rolling in the neighbor's flower beds. The main downside to digital is partly our own fault: people keep buying new cameras all the damn time when it's really not necessary.

Don't be lured by promos telling you to trade in your old digie within the year for discounts on a jazzier model. Buy only what you need. If you're shooting primarily family pics and printing standard 4-by-6 images, you don't need more than 6 megapixels. The more pixels and added features your camera has, the more batteries it sucks up. And you'll save power by turning off the flash when you don't need it, as well as shutting off the digital screen that lets you see what you're shooting. I know, I know, that's half the reason you like digital—I'm just saying. It's also good to have an old-fashioned viewfinder option in case you drop your camera and crack the digital screen.

Disposable: Oddly enough, single-use cameras are considered the greenest option of all (although the image quality is pretty low-grade). Yes, it's counterintuitive, but despite being called "disposable," they're actually returned to the manufacturer and their parts are either ground down and remolded or simply reused about 10 times. In fact, they have the highest recycling rate of any consumer product. **Fujifilm** says it has a recycling rate of 110% (the extra 10% comes from the return of cameras that people bought on vacation in other countries). And **Kodak** says 90% of the camera, by weight, is reused.

> *Oddly enough,* SINGLE-USE CAMERAS *are considered the* GREENEST OPTION *of all.*

CELL PHONES

Let's take a quiet moment to look within. Now, ask yourself just how many cell phones you've owned in your lifetime. Go ahead, count 'em. Don't forget that time when you accidentally dropped one in the toilet, or when one fell out of your bag who knows where. Some of us can go back to the time before camera phones and BlackBerries, back to when they called them "car phones" and you needed a briefcase just to hold the battery. Man, were we ever cool.

No matter what the reason, most cell users get a new one every year and a half or so. That's a hell of a lot of waste, considering that nearly 85% of Americans have them. Sure, they're small, but they pack a punch: they're full of lead, brominated fire retardants, nickel, cadmium—all kinds of fun stuff that accumulates in our tissues. Then there's the whole brain cancer controversy tied to the frequencies that these babies give off. Various studies have found that rat brain cells have died and gene expressions

Most cell users get a NEW PHONE *every year and a half, creating a hell of a lot of* WASTE.

have been altered when exposed to cell phone radiation. And though short-term risks are low, an hour of cell use a day over 10 years is linked to increased risk of a rare brain tumor. Interestingly, independent studies have been much more likely to find physiological impacts than industry-funded ones (doesn't take Sherlock Holmes to decode *that* mystery!). In the meantime, the Food and Drug Administration says you can minimize any potential risk by using hands-free sets and reducing the amount of time you yap on them. At this point we spend a whopping 2 trillion minutes on mobiles a year.

Going back to the toxins lurking in the hardware, many companies are starting to remove the most persistent chemicals from their phones. All new **Sony Ericsson** phones are free of PVC and brominated fire retardants; the same goes for **Nokia** and **Samsung**. Most, but not all, LG products are PVC-free as of 2008 and will be BRF-free by 2010. Many of Motorola's cells are BRF-free, but the company has refused to phase out PVC entirely. **Toshiba** phones will be totally free of both nasties by 2009. Keep your ear to the ground for **Samsung**'s **water-cell battery** expected for 2010. (For alternative ways to charge your phone, see page 192.)

Get over your fear of commitment and cozy into a long-term relationship with the phone you already have. Don't just ditch it when a younger, slimmer, sexier model tempts you (that means you, iPhone users). And if you do move on, or your phone dies, be sure to give it away. The nonprofit Rechargeable Battery Recycling Corporation's Call2Recycle program has cell phone recycling drop boxes at many cell phone stores, as well as at Home Depot, Sears, Circuit City, and countless other locales (for locations near you, check out **rbrc. org/call2recycle**).

LIGHTING

Afraid of the shadows? You'd have to assume our whole nation is, considering our obsession with lighting every corner of our homes, offices, and malls as brightly as possible. In fact, 25% of our household energy bills are spent on keeping those bulbs lit. The question is, if you're leaving a room for 5 minutes, is it better to leave a light on or turn if off? Regular bulbs should always be turned off as soon as they're not needed, as they're superwasteful and inefficient. On the other hand, if we're talking regular fluorescent tube lights, many agree it's worth turning them off only if you're leaving the room for more than 15 minutes, since they take more energy to start up. For compact fluorescents, though, that number drops to 5 minutes.

Bottom line: for every kilowatt-hour of electricity you waste (a single 100-watt bulb left on for 10 hours uses 1 kilowatt), power plants release about a pound and a half of climate-changing CO_2 into the air on average. Not to mention all the other pollutants spewing out of the stacks. If that fact doesn't convince your family to be responsible with its light usage, tape pictures of coal plants billowing toxic clouds next to the light switch. Maybe that'll work.

Of course, there comes a time when we all need light in our life. So which ones should you get?

Incandescent: Regular incandescent lights haven't changed much since Edison's time— they're still incredibly inefficient. In fact, only 5% to 10% of the electricity they consume is emitted as light; the rest is wasted as heat. So-called long-lasting incandescent bulbs are just lights that put out less output, or lumens. They'd lose against compact fluorescent lights (we'll discuss those shortly) any day.

Halogen: Halogen lighting was hailed as top of the line in the '80s and '90s. These fancy incandescents still rock if you want sleek, modern ambience and high-quality light, but the coolest part is that they use up to 40% less energy than their plain incandescent cousins. Plus, they last a long time (about 3,000 hours). The downside is that these babies are fire hazards (you can fry an egg on the tall torchiere types found in student apartments everywhere), and they're not as efficient as compact fluorescents. Get a pro to install in-ceiling types.

LED: This superefficient, power-saving technology still hasn't broken through to mainstream hardware stores, but it is making its mark in the world of accent lighting (see **progresslighting.com, brillialed.com, cooperlighting.com,** and **allpurposeleds.com**). They'll cost you up to eight times more than halogens, but they last 20 to 25 times longer and use 90% less energy.

Compact Fluorescent: **Compact fluorescent lightbulbs (CFLs)** are definitely the greenest way to go. If every house in the US switched just one lightbulb to the compact fluorescent kind, we'd save enough energy to light over 3 million homes for a year and more than $600 million in annual energy costs. In terms of greenhouse gas savings, it would be like taking a good 800,000 cars off the road. Sure, they've got the word "fluorescent" in their name, but they're nothing like the nasty office lighting you've seen that flickers overhead, giving you headaches. In fact, the light they give off is fairly comparable to that of regular bulbs if you buy the right ones (see the sidebar "Feeling Blue about Your Hue?"). Yes, they cost more up front, but

> **I**f *every house in the US switched just* ONE *lightbulb to the* COMPACT FLUORESCENT *kind, we'd save enough energy to light over* 3 MILLION HOMES FOR A YEAR *and more than $600 million in annual energy costs.*

the price has come down, and they use two-thirds less energy and last 10 times longer than incandescents. And with all the energy you'll save, you can expect to cut the lighting portion of your bill in half.

CFLs aren't angels—they contain a millimeter-wide pinch of mercury—or about 4 milligrams' worth (compared to the 25 milligrams in watch batteries and 500 in silver dental fillings). It's the nature of fluorescents. But before you get freaked out and swear off them forever, consider this: your super-energy-efficient CFLs contain much less mercury than what's spewing out of the coal-fired power plants that power your regular, inefficient bulbs (nearly five times less mercury actually). Manufacturers keep dropping the amount of mercury their bulbs use, and some have gotten it down to 1.4 to 2.5 milligrams per lightbulb.

Neolite has by far the lowest levels, with only 1 milligram of mercury. But while other companies do have slightly higher mercury levels, they're not considered high enough to be dangerous. By the way, if you've got traditional tube-shaped fluorescents in your ceiling, you should stock up on **Philips' Alto lights**. They're the only fluorescent lamp granted nonhazardous status by the state of California. The Alto Energy Advantage bulb should save you nearly 40 bucks in energy savings over its lifetime.

Be sure to read labels, as each light promises to last a different amount of time. Overall, an easy rule is to look for the Energy Star symbol, which points the way to most of the best CFLs and guarantees that your light uses 75% less power than regular bulbs. And if your Energy Star bulb doesn't last as long as advertised on the box, call the company for a refund or replacement (that means you need to save your receipts).

Full-spectrum lights are either CFLs or incandescents that are said to emit all colors in the visible spectrum. They've also been credited with fighting everything from tooth decay to cancer. Yes, that's a little far-fetched, and some call them full-on fakes, but many people insist that they help with seasonal affective disorder (SAD).

Natural-spectrum lights are supposed to most resemble sunlight. They filter out the yellows and greens that regular lighting has (so they tend to look bluish, which never feels all that natural to me). Note: natural-spectrum lights aren't always compact fluorescents; those that aren't don't save any more energy than regular lights, but they can last a good long time. Check the label.

Ambient Lighting: If you've got some fixtures in which CFLs just won't work, at least use the minimum wattage possible. If you're trying to create ambience over, say, a dining-room table, it's better to have six 15-watt bulbs in your chandelier than six 60-watters (though they do make chandelier-sized CFLs now). And make sure you have a dimmer switch. Dimming a light by just 10% doubles the bulb's life.

It's important to note, though, that you can't use dimmer switches with many CFL bulbs. Put a regular CFL on a dimmer switch and it'll flicker or hum and shorten its life, but you shouldn't have a problem if you buy high-quality CFLs labeled as dimmable. Chandelier owners take note: dimmable chandelier-sized CFLs are now available (yay!). The other option is to pick up three-way CFL bulbs with low, medium, and

Dimming a light by just 10% DOUBLES the bulb's life.

high settings. Of course, you'll need three-way lamp fixtures for them to work. They even sell CFLs in saucy party colors like red and blue, as well as smaller globe-shaped bulbs. For higher-end ambient lighting, see the discussion of LEDs.

Disposing of Compact Fluorescents: No matter how long they last, they eventually end up in the trash. But because of their mercury content, do not—I repeat, do not—throw your CFLs or any fluorescent lights out with your regular garbage. When they burn out (and trust me, it doesn't happen very often—these babies can last 5 years or more), take them to a household hazardous-waste depot for safe disposal or recycling (they can even reuse the mercury) or punch in your zip code at **earth911.com** for local drop points. You don't want that toxin leaching out in landfills and contaminating groundwater.

If a fluorescent bulb happens to break in your home, don't panic: the tiny amount of mercury shouldn't make you sick. Just open some windows and turn off duct heating or cooling for a while. Carefully scoop any chunks into a sealable plastic bag, use sticky tape to pick up smaller pieces, and wipe the area with a damp paper towel; then put it all in the plastic bag and take it to your hazmat waste depot, just as you would your burned-out CFLs. If you're dealing with a carpet, skip the paper towels and go straight to duct tape to clean up smaller shards. If you need to vacuum after all the other steps have been followed, be sure to replace your vacuum bag immediately and seal it in a plastic bag. Wash your hands and you're good to go.

LIGHTING TIPS

- **Get motion sensors** for outdoor lights. Even if one is triggered 10 times a night for 5 minutes, that's much better than leaving it on from nightfall to sunrise.

- **Use targeted lighting** (like a desk lamp) when you're reading or doing the crossword.

- **Some lamp shades and fixtures are light leeches:** they soak up all the bulb's rays and leave you in the dark, wasting precious wattage. Choose lighter-colored lamp shades.

- **Dimming a light by just 10%** doubles the bulb's life.

- **One 100-watt bulb gives off more light** than do four 25-watt bulbs (it's actually closer to that of six 25-watters). Better to use one stronger bulb than six weak ones.

Candles: Light up a few candles, take a couple of deep breaths, and let a day's worth of stress melt away while you're saving a little on electricity, right? Well, I wouldn't inhale too deeply, knowing those candles are emitting nasty pollutants like benzene, formaldehyde, soot, and lead. Indeed, most candles are made of paraffin, a totally unromantic waste product of the petroleum industry. Some candles can actually emit black soot made up of polluting polyaromatic hydrocarbons, according to the EPA. That soot is created during incomplete combustion of carbon-containing fuel. You can tell whether your candle is creating excess amounts of this indoor air pollution, known as ghosting or fogging, by checking for dark, oily deposits that are impossible to wash off around electric outlets, appliances, vertical blinds, and walls.

As yummy as they can smell, highly scented candles or candles that are soft to the touch are frequent culprits. That includes aromatic candles billed as "aromatherapy." (A quality candle containing high-grade aromatherapy oils will give off scent for only a few moments.)

Keeping wicks trimmed (yes, there's a reason why candle labels tell us to do this!) and away from drafts helps reduce soot emissions. Obviously, staying away from scented and gelatinous petroleum candles is a good idea too. (And if oily black soot isn't enough of a reason for you, artificially scented candles can also give off potentially hormone-disrupting phthalates.)

Even if a black cloud hasn't descended on your pad, there's still a chance that your favorite candles are made with dangerously high levels of lead, especially if they were purchased from a discount store or made in China. The toxic compound is placed in paper or cotton wicks because it's thought to make candles burn more slowly and evenly. A recent study found that one leaded candle-burning session a week can send enough lead into your home's atmosphere to raise a child's blood lead count above federally accepted levels and increase chances of behavioral and learning problems. Eek!

Lead wicks were banned in the US in 2003, but some leaded imports are still being allowed in. Consider chucking any candles that puff black soot when you snuff them. You can test your wick by peeling apart any fiber in the wick and seeing if it has a metallic core. If it does, rub it on white paper—if you see a gray smudge, it's probably lead. If it tests positive, toss it.

Alternative Candles: Set the mood without filling the air with noxious fumes. Long-lasting **beeswax** is said to actually clean the air by releasing calming negative ions that cling to dust, making particles heavy so that they fall (of course, you kick them up again when you walk around, but still, kind of a cool thing). They might be pricier, but be sure to buy 100% beeswax candles—there are lots of watered-downed versions on the market that are mixed with paraffin or bleached.

The other alternative is **soy-based veggie wax**. These candles burn clean, long, and bright, and their manufacturers say that, dollar per hour, they're actually cheaper than paraffin.

CLEANING

Decades of marketing have taught us that your house ain't clean unless you can see a bald man reflected in your floors and your children can eat off your garbage can lid. And, of course, those grimy dishes, tubs, and toilets have to sparkle with one easy stroke. As a result, we've got cupboards stocked with toxic soups, full of chemical whiteners, colorants, perfumes, smog-making VOCs, and harmful petroleum-based chemicals. They're major contributors to indoor air pollution (which can, shockingly, be anywhere from 2 to 100 times higher than pollution in outdoor air). Anyone with asthma or chemical sensitivities can tell you just how harmful these products can be to your health, but what about the ecosystem's health?

Chemical Cleansers: Hidden behind claims of streak-free floors and whiter whites are some of the worst chemicals in your home. Sure, many of the ingredients in cleaning products wash down your drain harmlessly, but many others make it through sewage treatment processes to wreak havoc on our waterways. Some surfactants (the stuff that makes things sudsy and easily spreadable) used in degreasers, disinfectants, and general cleaners break down into hormone-disrupting agents that have been gender-bending fish. And 61% of American streams tested positive for this stuff in 2002! The Environmental Protection Agency politely asked manufacturers to stop using the estrogen-mimicking nonylphenol ethoxylates (and at least Proctor & Gamble and Unilever were supportive), but so far not everyone's agreed and the battle of the mops rages on as enviros and fishermen's groups demand a full-on ban.

Several states have recently canned phosphates from dishwasher detergent. The ingredient was phased out of laundry soap way back in Duran Duran's heyday, but for some reason dish detergents slipped under the radar. Why the big fuss? Phosphates feed blooms of toxic blue-green algae that have invaded lakes and rivers across the country, causing serious health scares. Drinking water contaminated with these algae, known as cyanobacteria (a.k.a. pond scum), will make you nauseated, headachy, and feverish; it also builds up in fish and can kill your dog if the dog drinks from an affected lake.

Of course, no discussion of modern cleaning agents is complete unless we face up to our addiction to antibacterial … er, everything. If I were Dr. Phil, I'd give all you antibacterial addicts a good whoopin'. Exposure to household germs isn't a bad thing. In fact, it bolsters our immunity to them. But it is bad when those bug-fighting ingredients, like triclosan, make their way into 58% of our streams, as well as into breast milk. (See page 9 for more on antibacterial chemicals.)

And what's up with using a mop once and then throwing it away? Yes, the other ecological nightmare on my pet peeve list is all those disposable cleaning wipes, mops, and dusters

If I were Dr. Phil, I'd give all you ANTIBACTERIAL ADDICTS a good whoopin'.

hidden in our broom closets. They're clogging our landfills for no good reason, and even if they claim to be biodegradable, it doesn't mean they actually break down in the dark, airless heap that is your municipal dump. Our moms didn't need these before and we don't need

HOW GREEN IS YOUR CLEANER?
METHOD AND CLOROX GREEN WORK

Walk into any Target or crack open the eco issue of any magazine and you'll see Method. Its products are slick 'n' sexy, and their main claim to green fame is that they're "biodegradable" and "naturally derived." And although Method is far greener than conventional brands (it stays away from all the worst offenders—like triclosan, bleach, phosphates, and parabens), Method comes clean about a few iffy ingredients in its extensive online FAQ section (something you always want to check on corporate sites). It fesses up to some petroleum-based ingredients and sudsy sodium lauryl sulfate, an irritant that many crunchy granolas try to avoid. Not to mention synthetic fragrances (that explains why I get a headache just sitting near an open bottle of Method stuff). Method's dish and hand soaps also tested positive for fairly high levels of 1,4-dioxane, but the company says it has since reformulated its hand soap but has yet to find a suitable ingredient replacement for its dish soap. Method does have a purer fragrance- and dye-free line called **Go Naked**, which will be welcomed by the scent-sensitive.

Clorox Green Works offers a pretty specific list of ingredients that tells you the surfactant in most products is alkyl polyglucoside (you wouldn't want to squirt this in your eye, but it is considered more biodegradable than other agents). The brand passed the Organic Consumers Association's 1,4-dioxane testing and gets a thumbs-up from the US Sierra Club (which, admittedly, Sierra has gotten some flak for)—although OCA hadn't tested Green Works' dish soap (which contains sodium lauryl sulfate). Some say you should stay away from a cleaner made by a company that's responsible for so many caustic chems being poured down drains nationwide; others say that buying **Clorox**'s **Green Works** line encourages big companies to offer cleaner products. Strictly scrubwise, I have to admit this line does a really top-notch job and gives off only very mild citrus scents.

them now. Also, don't be a sucker. It may smell like green apples or have an orange on the label, but that doesn't mean it's any more natural. In fact, some citrus-containing degreasers were also found to have the nasty surfactants mentioned earlier.

Keep in mind that even cleaners advertised as organic have been found to contain troubling levels of the known carcinogenic contaminant 1,4-dioxane. It's not on ingredient lists because it's not added intentionally. However, it's the by-product of a process called ethoxylation used to make certain sudsers (including plant oils) milder. Dish soaps are the worst offender (see the section on dish detergents).

Sorry to say, it's hard to tell which bottle is better or worse, since ingredient lists aren't mandatory. But there are some clues. "Caution" means slightly toxic. Products labeled with the word "warning" are moderately toxic and could make you really sick but won't kill you, unless the label also says "may be fatal if swallowed." Stay away from any products labeled "danger," "poison," or "corrosive"—they're the most toxic.

Finally ready to toss your old chem-heavy cleaners? Don't just dump them down the toilet. Take them to your local hazardous-waste depot. Then you can clean green in peace, knowing you're not wiping out the planet or your lungs.

WHAT DO YOU MEAN, IT'S "BIODEGRADABLE"?

If there's one term that companies toss around to get a little eco credibility for their products, it's this one. The word "biodegradable" is about as abused as the term "natural." The insinuation is that whatever you purchased will fully break down and return to nature after you chuck it. Back in 1989, seven US states sued the maker of Hefty garbage bags for saying that some of its bags would biodegrade, when in fact they only partially degraded (into plastic bits) in direct sunlight, and not at all in landfills. The Federal Trade Commission issued guidelines for how the term should be used and took action against several companies that made misleading or flat-out false biodegradability claims a couple decades ago. Little has happened since, and basically the label isn't policed.

Be your own sheriff. Read labels carefully. Look for certification symbols and details about biodegradability testing standards, and do your research. If a product sports the word "biodegradable," call the company and ask what it means. Has the product passed any particular tests? Under what conditions does the product degrade (only in full sun or also in dark, airless landfill piles)? And just how long does it take to return to Mother Nature's warm embrace?

Don't be duped by tricky wording. Many mainstream cleaning products say they contain "biodegradable surfactants" (surfactants make things sudsy and rinse "clean"). But what about the rest of the ingredients? And keep in mind that being biodegradable doesn't necessarily make an ingredient eco-friendly. DDT, for instance, can break down into two compounds that, according to *Consumer Reports*' Greener Choices eco-labels center (**greenerchoices.org/eco-labels**), are more toxic than DDT itself. You want to look for products that are certified biodegradable by Scientific Certification Systems or certified to meet the standards of the Organisation for Economic Co-operation and Development (OECD), but that still doesn't tell you that a product is 100% biodegradable. Even superbiodegradable products such as Campsuds should never be used directly in rivers or lakes, where they could harm fish. (In that case, soap up at least 200 feet away from freshwater and bury your wash and rinse water in a hole 6 inches deep. According to Campsuds maker Sierra Dawn, the soil's bacteria will completely and safely biodegrade the detergent.)

All-Purpose Cleaning: If you're looking for a good, all-natural, truly eco-friendly all-purpose cleaner, that's easy: just combine one part vinegar and one part water in a spray bottle. You can add a few drops of essential oil if you want to mask the vinegar scent. In tandem, a vinegar-dampened sponge and a sprinkle of baking soda or salt make a good all-purpose grease-cutting scouring agent.

Want the ease of the ready-to-spray types? Health stores are stocked with a variety of largely natural cleaners by companies like **Seventh Generation** (**seventhgeneration.com**), **Ecover** (**ecover.com**), and **Earth Friendly** (**ecos.com**). But which ones work best? I have to admit I found Seventh Generation's Kitchen Cleaner to be good only for lightweight jobs, like walls and counters. **Citra Solv**'s (**citra-solv.com**) cleaner and degreaser is much better at cutting through postmeal messes left on stove tops and sinks (note, though, that the orange peel oil, a.k.a. d-limonene, that makes it a good grease cutter is also a VOC that can irritate asthmatics). Creamy cleansers, like the ones that **Ecover** and **Earth Friendly** offer, score strong points for slicing through kitchen grease and tub scum well, though they can leave a powdery finish if not rinsed well.

If you must banish bacteria, try **Benefect**'s products—they're 100% plant-based, with no added dyes or fragrances. They kill 99% of germs naturally with thyme oil. In fact, Benefect makes the only botanical hospital disinfectant and fungicide registered with the EPA and used everywhere from hospitals to eco-conscious hotel chains like the Fairmont, on everything from ducts to kitchen cupboards (**sensiblelifeproducts.com**).

Or bypass cleaning products altogether with the special microfiber cleaning cloths like those made by **Blue Wonder**. Its patented microfiber knit (half polyester, half nylon) is ultra-absorbent and antibacterial, and it magically enables you to clean windows, sinks, stoves, pots, TVs, and pretty much any surface you can think of without cleaners (**bluewondercloth .com**). Lots of people who have to avoid mainstream cleaning products because of chemical sensitivities swear by it.

Windows: You might not want birds crashing into them, but you do want your windows to look barely there. Just be aware that you're inhaling a fine mist of the lung irritant ammonia with every squeeze of the nozzle. Windex's Vinegar Multi-Surface cleaning fluid and its outdoor version don't actually contain ammonia, but all conventional window cleaners contain chemical detergents, surfactants, and perfumes. (Don't be fooled by newer pseudo-natural lavender and orange types.) Some window cleaners even contain nerve-damaging butyl cellosolve. And really this is one area where the homemade option (see the window

RECIPE FOR WINDOW CLEANER

In a spray bottle, combine ¼ cup vinegar, ½ teaspoon natural dish detergent, and 2 cups water, and start squirting.

cleaner recipe in the sidebar) works as well as or better than almost anything you can find in stores, though **Ecover**'s glass cleaner does dry much more quickly.

Toilet and Bathroom Cleaners: Freud would say our culture has some serious potty-shame issues. We keep whatever it is we do in there behind locked doors, and then regularly douse the room in enough bleach, artificial fragrances, and harsh disinfectants to throw any CSI off the trail. It's important to keep your bathroom clean, but do you really need to eat off your toilet? Yes, you say, my 2-year-old niece just might lick the bowl. Well, do you want her licking highly caustic chemicals?

Pretty much every bathroom product comes with the "cleaning power" of chlorine bleach. Too bad chlorine bleach can produce carcinogenic, bioaccumulative dioxins as well as trihalomethanes, including carcinogenic chloroform, when it mixes with organic matter like dirt and poop in our sewer systems. Not to mention that the caustic cleaning fluid triggers headaches in many (including me). Combine that with sodium hydroxide (which nearly every bathroom cleaning product has in various concentrations), and you're misting your shower stalls and squirting your toilets with chemicals that can burn your skin and irritate your eyes, nose, throat, and lungs.

You definitely don't need to be flushing nonstick coatings into our waterways that end up accumulating in the bodies of wild animals and humans, so stay away from toilet cleaners with Teflon. And did I mention the smog-inducing and asthma-triggering VOCs that come from the whole toxic soup of cleaners we use? To add insult to injury, we're now buying landfill-clogging disposable toilet wands, prefilled with bleach, to do our dirty work.

Even for tough jobs, you can pour in 1 cup borax and ¼ cup vinegar, let it sit a few hours, and then scrub. Calcium stains will come off if you drop two or three easily dissolvable vitamin C tablets (yes, the kind you take for a cold) into the bowl and let it sit overnight. The stains should easily wipe away with your scrub brush. If you want a ready-made toilet cleaner and are stuck on the blue dye type, at least reach for an otherwise green version, such as the one made by **Seventh Generation** (seventhgeneration.com). It even smells like fresh peppermint. **Ecover** (**ecover.com**) makes a potent pine-scented version.

As for the rest of the bathroom, there are two kinds of people in this world: spray shooters and cream users. Fans of a good lathery spray will, hands down, attest to **Clorox Green Works** bathroom cleaner (see the sidebar "How Green Is Your Cleaner?"), but **Biokleen**'s **Soy Cream Cleaner** (**biokleen .com**) and **Earth Friendly**'s **Creamy Cleanser** (**ecos.com**)

> **T**o get rid of tough, built-up soap scum, just rub on **STRAIGHT VINEGAR** that's been warmed up.

are great for anyone who prefers nonspritz products. For areas where you don't want a lot of bubbles, such as countertops and toilet seats, **Seventh Generation** and **TerraCycle Natural Bathroom Cleaner** (**terracycle.net**) sprays are a hit.

IS THERE A GREEN VERSION OF DRANO?

Stuck with a little lagoon full of hair and debris that just won't drain properly? It's enough to make any eco-head entertain the idea of pouring that blue skull-and-crossbones stuff down the sink. But wait—before you turn to acids and industrial lye, which can seriously harm your health, the wastewater stream, and PVC pipes, there are alternatives.

For less serious jams, it's always worth trying the old combo of baking soda and vinegar. Pour some baking soda and 1 cup vinegar into the drain, wait 15 minutes while it fizzles and pops, and then pour in a kettle of boiling water. Do this several times, until the clog clears. For tougher situations, try 1 cup washing soda (a stronger relative of baking soda that you can find in the laundry section of your grocery store or any health store), followed by 3 cups boiling water. Again, repeat until you break on through to the other side. Just don't overdo it if you have PVC pipes.

All-natural enzyme- and bacteria-based cleaners, like **Citra Drain** and **TerraCycle Natural Drain Cleaner and Maintainer**, also eat away at milder clogs (though they won't necessarily break down drains jammed with hair, in my experience). Let the cleaner sit for several hours, and then flush with water (and, possibly, repeat a few days in a row).

Simple plungers can also work well. Another good chem-free option is **Drain King**, available at hardware stores. It attaches to your garden hose and creates a hard-core water flush. Could be messy if you're not careful. FYI: One Second Plumber is not actually enviro-friendly as it claims to be; it contains acetone and tetrafluoroethane, a potent ozone-depleting chemical.

For the most hard-core jobs, you'll need to snake out the drain. If you're not comfortable trying it yourself, call a plumber. To avoid future sink jams, get yourself a metal strainer that fits over your drain and do monthly, even weekly, baking soda sessions.

Instead of buying a scouring powder for your tub, try sprinkling on **baking powder** or **straight borax powder** and rubbing with a damp sponge. **Plain vinegar** is a good basic bath cleaner. To get rid of tough, built-up soap scum, just rub straight vinegar (heating it up first really helps) on your shower door or tub, wait 5 minutes, and then rinse. Got mildew problems? Pull out an old toothbrush, dip it in a paste of borax and water, and go to town. You can also try putting two teaspoons of antifungal **tea tree oil** in two cups of water, spray, and walk away without wiping.

Dish Detergents: No one likes washing dishes, but a sink full of bubbles seems to make the whole thing more pleasant. Too bad the petrochemical process used to make some plant-based sudsers (as well as chemical ones) creates carcinogenic 1,4-dioxane. Citrus Magic dish soap's level was off the charts when the Organic Consumers Association tested dozens of products in 2008. **Life Tree** had the lowest levels (**lifetreeproducts.com**), followed by **Seventh Generation**, **Whole Foods**' 365 brand, and then **Ecover**, which all had trace amounts. Check out **organicconsumers.org/bodycare** for more details. Note that some original poor scorers, like **Earth Friendly**'s **Dishmate**, have since been reformulated.

As for which worked best, one small, completely unscientific study found that **Ecover**'s suds cut through grease the best and is a fave among green converts, but it does contain sodium lauryl sulphate. Powders in general seemed more effective than gels at getting the grime off. Feel free to add a tablespoon or two of white vinegar as a rinse aid.

Wood Polish: Furniture-polishing sprays might not have the same notorious ozone-destroying CFCs they used to back in the day, but they still contain air pollutants that fill your home with fumes. And lots of them have ingredients, like phenols, that have ties to cancer. Why risk it, when you can buy all-natural furniture polish from the health store or make your own with a simple mix of 1 cup oil and ½ cup vinegar? Or if you find that too oily, flip it: ¼ cup vinegar with a few drops of olive oil makes for a good wood cleaner/polish.

LAUNDRY

Let's be honest. Laundry is one of those chores few of us like to do—especially if you have to schlep bags of dirty socks to a gritty old Laundromat every week. But you can make the experience much less irritating for the earth and your skin if you dump those mainstream cleansers at the curb.

Laundry Detergents: If you believe advertisers, the hills are alive with the smell of laundry. In fact, they've somehow bottled the scent of spring, sunshine, and tropical breezes. In truth, your laundry detergent is probably the farthest thing from nature in your pantry. Most of the laundry products at mainstream shops are filled with artificial dyes, clingy perfumes, and petroleum-based chemicals that can build up in our bodies and our water systems.

It's impossible to know many specifics of what's in mainstream brands, since they don't tell you, but you can look for hints on the label. If it says it contains optical brighteners, you might want to pass. These don't easily break down in nature, and many are toxic to fish. Not good, considering we add this stuff to water. If it's artificially scented, you can bet that "summer meadow" or "spring rain" is heavy in phthalates, a hormone-disrupting family of chemicals that also offgas from vinyl. And the stain-fighting power of bleach might seem like a bright idea (buh-doom boom) until you realize it's pretty caustic, poisons thousands of children a year, and can end up forming deadly dioxins when it mixes with other elements in the environment (in fact, bleach-heavy detergents have been blamed for high levels of dioxins in San Francisco Bay).

Some of the stain-digesting enzymes added to laundry powder since the '60s are essentially the same proteins you buy from the health store to help digest your food. Pretty harmless. There used to be problems with workers at detergent plants inhaling the stuff, but they say it's all been corrected and home exposure to enzyme dust would be minute. Still, many newer synthetic antibacterial enzymes are more troubling and aren't readily biodegradable.

Laundry Detergent Solutions: Thankfully, there's a slew of legitimately nontoxic, cruelty- and chemical-free products out there. Just beware of greenwashing. Even the big boys offer perfume-free lines these days, which are indeed better for the scent-sensitive, but they don't make your suds chem-free. And note that "phosphate-free" labels are pretty meaningless here, considering that all major manufacturers eliminated the ecology-disrupting mineral from their powdered products a decade or two ago. "Cold water" brands are a soft step up because they encourage consumers to wash without energy-wasting hot water, but that doesn't mean they're made with natural ingredients in any way.

But there are lots of genuinely green laundry soaps out there, and your local health store should carry a wide variety. **Seventh Generation**'s and

Biokleen's laundry detergents are good solid workhorses. **Ecover** makes a good all-around laundry soap with lightly scented and unscented options. **Soap nuts**, a.k.a. soap berries (literally nuts you toss in a sack and into your washer), get good reviews when it comes to washing clothes that aren't supersoiled, but they don't do so well in cold water. Bad news, since warm-water loads use much more energy.

HANGING CLOTHES TO DRY *in sunlight is the cheapest whitener on the market.*

Want to whiten your whites without resorting to toxic bleach? You've probably spotted all the **oxygen bleaches** on shelves these days. They're made with either hydrogen peroxide or sodium percarbonate (which is a mix of washing soda and hydrogen peroxide). Note that although they're considered safer for the environment than bleach and don't give off harsh fumes, both can still be corrosive in stronger concentrations, which is why you might spot a skull and crossbones on more potent brands. Of course, hanging clothes to dry in **sunlight** is the cheapest whitener on the market. You can also try adding **baking soda** or **lemon juice** to your wash.

Eco adventurers willing to try something a little off the beaten path might pick up those

WASHER EFFICIENCY

Did you know that washing machines are at their most energy-efficient when they're packed with a full load? Front-loading machines use about 40% to 60% less water and 30% to 50% less energy than top loaders. And, according to the Environmental Protection Agency, an Energy Star clothes washer can save you $550 in operating costs over its lifetime (not to mention 7,000 gallons of water a year), compared to other washers on the market. Plus, these guys spin out more water than others during the spin cycle, so you can reduce your drying time. Save even more power by washing in cold water and do your part to prevent global warming while getting the stink out of your football socks.

mysterious **laundry balls or discs** available at health stores. These electrically charged or magnetized pucks are said to soften water, dramatically reducing the need for soap. Plus, they claim to work for up to 700 loads. But beware: the Federal Trade Commission says they're bogus.

Stain Removers: It's amazing how frantic we get about stains. A little Shiraz or salsa hits your shirt, and the party stops. Suddenly, everyone acts like an expert and starts yelling out random tips on how to get that giant splotch off your favorite top. That's if you catch it quickly. Even worse are those mystery stains you notice only when you do your laundry a week after you wore the damn thing. And if you're as klutzy as I am, you wonder how you can make oil stains fashionable, since they appear on nearly everything you own. Stay away from oh-so-handy disposable stain-removing laundry wipes and pens. The world doesn't need the extra trash. Also keep in mind that do-it-yourself solutions aren't automatically earth-friendly. My god, Martha Stewart's website recommends pouring lighter fluid on mustard and grass stains. What's the point, when there are perfectly natural, ecologically sound solutions?

Natural stain-removing gels by companies like **Ecover** are pretty good overall, and eco-safe bleaches (made of hydrogen peroxide) do a decent job on wine stains. Though, if you really want to get tough stains out of everything from diapers to carpets, you'll need some of **Biokleen**'s enzyme-based **Bac-Out Stain and Odor Eliminator**. The other no-fail stain buster is a tub of seaweed enzyme–based **Pink Solution** (pinksolution.ca). It's tougher to find, but if you see it at Costco snag it. You can use this Canadian-made product for all your household cleaning needs, from 5-year-old carpet stains to rusty toilets. (I put the stuff on a beet stain, washed the soiled, white hoodie a week later, and like magic it was gone.) Or dilute it for lighter cleaning jobs.

Dryers: Let's clear the air and get one thing straight: first and foremost, hang-dry what you can. Your clothes dryer is the second biggest electricity-using appliance—after your refrigerator. But if you need your undies dry in a hurry, or your municipality has banned clotheslines (yes, this really happens; see the "Right to Dry" sidebar), there are ways to green up your drying habits. For one, you could get a new clothes dryer if yours is over 12 years old. Energy Star doesn't certify dryers because none are all that efficient. New clothes dryers generally use 15% less energy than clothes dryers built before 1990 because they have more efficient motors and controls.

New clothes dryers generally use 15% LESS ENERGY than clothes dryers built before 1990.

If you've got a moisture sensor built into your dryer, be sure to use it so you don't keep tumbling long after your shorts have been baked. Otherwise, set your dryer on its lowest

HOMEMADE FABRIC SOFTENER

U p to trying a home brew? Add some baking soda to your water-filled washing machine (before filling it with clothes), and then pour in 1 cup vinegar during the rinse cycle. Missed that oh-so-brief window? Just pour some vinegar on a damp cloth and toss it in the dryer. Don't worry, you won't smell like salt and vinegar chips, and it'll keep static cling at bay. "But I don't want to give up my spring-fresh scent," you say. Not to worry—you can create your own aromatic blend by adding 10 drops of an essential oil to your green liquid softener (if you bought the unscented type) or that damp cloth destined for the dryer.

ATTACK OF THE STATIC CLING

Everyone's been there. You're wearing a cute skirt or a kicky pair of pants, thinking, "Damn, I look good," and then suddenly you feel it coming on—the cling. Panic sets in as you realize that within minutes your Sunday best will be hugging your body like bad plastic wrap. In such moments, we all dream of having a can of Static Guard in our purse, but what's in that stuff anyway? Turns out it's got humidity-loving chemicals such as dimethyl ditallow ammonium chloride (talk about a mouthful!), which is toxic to fish and algae and isn't readily biodegradable. It also has chloromethane (which breaks down very slowly in air) and lots of petroleum-based ingredients, such as butane, propane, and isopropanol.

When you're being menaced by the cling, reach up under your outfit and brush the inside of the fabric with a metal hanger. Sounds bizarre, but it just might get you out of a staticky situation. Remember, you can also avoid static by pulling your clothes out of the dryer before they're fully cooked or using nature's clothes dryer—the clothesline. A reusable chem-free dryer cloth like the **Static Eliminator** is another cool option. It combats static remarkably well and lasts for up to 500 loads (**staticeliminator.us**).

setting. And don't automatically turn the dial to 60 minutes. Your clothes can often dry in much less time. Start with 30 or 40 minutes and remove your clothes before they're bone-dry. Synthetics often dry after 10 minutes and really shouldn't even go in the dryer.

Fabric Softeners: Next on the list: toss your fabric softeners—both liquids and dryer sheets. Sure, the fruity scent clings to your jeans long after you've washed them, but so do all the other chemicals. Not good, when you're talking about chems like chloroform, a probable human carcinogen, and benzyl acetate, a suspected kidney, liver, and respiratory toxicant. One study even found that fabric softeners gave off the hazardous air pollutant toluene. Plus, dryer sheets aren't recyclable, no matter what they say on the box, and using them will void warranties on many new dryers because they clog lint traps and vents. Fabric softener solvents are especially harmful if exposed to heat (um, isn't that what dryers are all about?). A study published in *Consumer Reports* found that using a liquid softener on terry cloth, fleece, and velour made the fabrics seven times more flammable! Pretty scary.

Turn to all-natural options like **Ecover** or **Seventh Generation** instead. If you're a total disposable–dryer sheet junky and refuse to abandon your ways, then at least shift to a more natural product, like **Method**'s dryer sheets (though I'm not sure why they have to package them in plastic). Just note that even their Go Naked sheets have a fragrance oil added to them. And beware of reusable spiky laundry balls you pop in the dryer to soften your shirts—most are made with that problematic plastic PVC and could be offgassing harmful plastic softeners onto your clothes. (For info on static-busting dryer cloths, see the sidebar on static cling.)

Dry Cleaning: Nearly 28,000 dry cleaners across the country use the supertoxic chemical perchloroethylene, a.k.a. perc, to clean your clothes. Sure, perc is a great dissolver of dirt and oil. It's just a shame that it's so damn bad for us. In fact, the chem is classified as a possible carcinogen and is considered acutely toxic to wildlife and fish. This is particularly worrisome because perc is now a major groundwater contaminant, thanks to improper disposal procedures. No wonder California and New Jersey are phasing out the chem altogether and in 2006 the EPA banned any new perc operations in residential buildings (it also tightened regulations for all perc cleaners). Need more disturbing info to turn you off your dry-cleaning habit? Turns out food that spends one hour in a car with dry-cleaned clothes (like, say, a bag full of groceries) absorbs elevated levels of perc. Not so appetizing, is it?

Don't believe the hype. Many clothes tags say "dry clean" or "dry clean only," but most of these garments can be HAND-WASHED in cool water with GENTLE, NATURAL SOAP.

"But what about my closet full of 'dry clean only' tags?" you cry. Well, for one, don't believe the hype. Many clothes tags say "dry clean" or "dry clean only," but most of these garments can be hand-washed in cool water with gentle, natural soap—especially most synthetics, blends, and wool. Silk is tricky because it might shrink, and rayon can shrivel up; best to test a small swatch.

If you have to hire a pro for suits and whatnot, and you're looking for greener options, note that cleaners who hang "organic" signs in the window aren't organic in the crunchy granola sense of the word. The petroleum-based hydrocarbons they use are commonly made by the grandest of eco villains—ExxonMobil. Sure, hydrocarbon solvents are a little better than perc for your health and the planet, but they're still hazardous air pollutants and smog-inducing VOCs.

A silicone-based process developed by GreenEarth Cleaning is also somewhat controversial. The EPA considers GreenEarth's process a sound alternative to other ozone-depleting chems, but one study tied extremely high exposures of the solvent to cancer in lab rats. In 2008, Canada's health agency declared the silicone used by such dry cleaners (known as D5) to be bioaccumulative and persistent in the environment, meaning that it can build up in the food chain and "may cause long-term adverse effects on sediment-dwelling organisms." The silicone lobby argues that the product is perfectly safe. If you're curious and want to track down GreenEarth dry cleaners, go to **greenearthcleaning.com**.

Really, your best bets are either **wet cleaning** or **carbon dioxide–based cleaners**, though they're definitely harder to find. Wet cleaners use specially formulated detergents, water, and often computer-controlled machines, and can accommodate most "dry clean only" garments. Supposedly, that includes wedding gowns, wool suits, silks, leather, comforters, and rayon. Of course, wet cleaning is not entirely holy, since the process can release soap surfactants and bleaches into the sewers, though the solutions used are purportedly biodegradable.

CO_2-based cleaners using liquid carbon dioxide have also gotten the green thumbs-up. Although they do add a little CO_2 to the air, proponents say they're still ahead of the curve because they originally removed CO_2 pollution from stacks to get their solvent, making them carbon-neutral. Both wet cleaners and CO_2 cleaners are starting to pop up in more and more towns. To find one near you, punch in **departments.oxy.edu/uepi/ppc/cleaner_ near_you.htm**.

AIR PURIFIERS

Forget televised outdoor air quality alerts. Your nose and your lungs will tell you when the air in your home just ain't cutting it. Whether winter's got your windows shut tight (and the air in your pad is about as fresh as your woolly socks after a heavy round of shoveling), or summer's pollen- and smog-heavy winds leave you gasping, most of us are breathing in all sorts of irritating indoor air pollutants, including animal dander, dust, and mold. That's no surprise. But when Clean Production Action got seven US environmental groups to test the vacuum cleaner dust in 70 homes, they found endocrine-disrupting compounds, carcinogens, and bioaccumulating toxins like brominated fire retardants, phthalates, and pesticides (even DDT) in the dust of pretty much every home tested (for the "Sick of Dust" report, see **cleanproduction.org/Safer.Dust.php**).

It can be impossible to rid your home of this stuff entirely, especially if the sources of those pollutants (your furniture, your electronics, your lead blinds) remain, but you can get rid of a sizable amount of dust by, yes, simply dusting your home with a damp cloth and vacuuming regularly. In fact, anyone with serious allergies should be doing this daily. You can even get vacuum cleaners with HEPA filters built in (see **allergyconsumerreview.com** for suggestions). For most people, that should be good enough. But if you have allergies, are chemically sensitive, or just want the air in your home to be as pure as possible, you might consider getting a room or whole-house air filter. Before you panic and run out to buy one, you need to know what you're doing. Consult Allergy Consumer Review (**allergyconsumerreview.com**) and Air Purifiers America (**air-purifiers-america.com**) to see what would work best for you: **HEPA filters** or **carbon filters**.

Negative ionizers, by the way, are generally bad news. The American Lung Association says harmful particulates that have been ionized by these electronic air filters have a better chance of sticking to your lungs.

For those of you with forced air, *Consumer Reports* says a cheapie furnace filter such as the **3M Filtrete allergen air filters** should do just fine to control airborne dust, pet hair, and dander. Be sure to change these every few months.

PEST CONTROL

We're not the only creatures that like to scurry inside when the air gets brisk or the sun starts roasting. October through February is peak time for rodent infestations, not to mention all those squirrels, raccoons, and birds that like to nest under our roofs. And warmer months open up doors to ants and all kinds of creepy crawlies. Though it may be tempting to reach for that can of bug killer or rat poison, remember that's a definite ecological no-no that can make everyone in your home ill, not just the invaders. So what's a bug-weary, beleaguered homemaker to do?

Any breach in your fort is an **INVITATION TO MINIATURE OUTSIDERS** *looking for a warm place to call home.*

Physical Fortifications: No matter what the pest, you've gotta start by battening down the hatches. Any breach in your fort is an invitation to miniature outsiders looking for a warm place to call home. Seal up any cracks or gaps around baseboards, cupboards, vents, electric outlets, and pipes (mice can squeeze through a hole the size of a dime). Perforated and sheet metal, concrete, and wire-mesh hardware cloth are all rodent-resistant. A good caulking job should help keep ants out. Weather stripping under doors is another must. Leaky taps and toilets are like rivers of freshwater for all sorts of pests—get them fixed! Food in your cupboards should be kept in airtight plastic or metal containers or sealed bags. Casually folding the cellophane down over your crackers ain't good enough, people. Vacuum often, clean your kitchen daily, and be sure to sweep under, around, and, yes, even behind your appliances frequently. (I know this is tough if you're usually as nonchalant about cleaning as I am, but you're at war, kids—take it seriously!)

Animals: If you're already stuck with unwanted furry guests, stay away from poison powders and sprays, which kill the mouse over either days or minutes by making it bleed to death internally, attacking its nervous system or inflicting an equally horrific death. Plus, these can and do make your pets and curious young kids sick too.

    Traps are your best bet, but be sure to get the cruelty-free kind. Glue traps are just plain evil, since they tear a strip off the poor thing's skin as it tries to escape. Instead, use food to lure the whiskered scramblers to live traps. But you'll be defeating the point of these if you let a little mouse die of dehydration in your basement. Check the traps often, and release any captives several miles from your home or they'll be back. The reusable **Victor Tin Cat Repeating Mouse Trap** (available at hardware stores or from **victorpest.com**) can hold up to about 30 mice, but the more traps you have going, the better.

Kitchen Bugs: Some mainstream bug killers list benign boric acid (borax) as their active ingredient, but they don't tell you that the (unlisted) so-called passive or inert ingredients, which make up 95% of the product, can actually be quite toxic. The group Beyond Pesticides says that more than 200 "inert" chemicals are actually hazardous air and water pollutants. Warnings have been issued in the past against buying the two products Miraculous

Insecticide Chalk and Cockroach Sweeper, thanks to illegal pesticides and traces of lead.

If roaches have taken over your kitchen New York–style, a powdery trail of **sugar and baking soda** (50/50) is said to kill them in a couple of weeks, according to Golden Harvest Organics' tip sheet on pest control (**ghorganics.com**).

Some techniques can be used on multiple creepy crawlies. Try sprinkling straight **natural borax** (which you can buy for a few bucks in the laundry section of your grocery store) on cracks, in garbage cans, and under appliances to kill roaches, water bugs, silverfish, fleas, ants, millipedes—pretty much anything that crawls. Note that borax shouldn't be swallowed by anything or anyone you don't want to make ill.

Diatomaceous earth is a handy all-natural, nontoxic substance (made of crushed marine fossils) to keep around the house, and it won't harm pets (though it can be irritating on the lungs). It kills off all sorts of wigglers, such as earwigs, roaches, ants, and fleas. Sprinkle it around cracks, in crevices, along baseboards, under appliances, and above kitchen cabinets, and roaches, for instance, should be dead soon enough. A layer of this stuff at the base of my back door stopped an ant invasion in its tracks. I also used it successfully on carpenter ants encroaching on my patio door.

Vacuuming is a great nontoxic way to suck up roaches, wasps, and ants. Most will suffocate in the bag, but sprinkling diatomaceous earth in the bag should kill the others. Otherwise, you could soak the bag in soapy water or freeze it for 24 hours (um, yeah, I know—I wouldn't want those things in my freezer either).

Also keep a spray bottle full of **soapy water** on hand to spritz ants, roaches, and other bugs. This surprisingly lethal cocktail also works on garden pests.

Moths: Is your favorite wool sweater riddled with mysterious holes? You've got a moth problem, honey. Whatever you do, do not use mothballs. Not only do they stink up your clothes, but they're made of toxic volatile compounds associated with serious health problems, including liver and neural damage and cancer. Even moth-repellent blocks labeled "cedar" or "lavender" could contain the main toxin found in mothballs. Instead, try **all-natural herbal moth bars**, made with essential oils and eco wax, available at some health stores. Moths do their dirty work in the summer, when our wool clothes are hidden in dark drawers, so lay your woolens out in the sun every so often to kill any sun-loathing larvae.

Before you store your woolens, try washing them with eucalyptus-filled **Eucalan**. Its ingredients are generally plant-derived, though it does contain some synthetics (**eucalan .com**). And if you think you've got a moth infestation in your sweater, stick it in the freezer in a plastic bag for a few days. That'll kill off the larvae and keep your top looking peachy keen.

If the winged things are sprouting up in your pantry, you've got a whole other type of moth. Ditch any sack of flour or rice you may have had sitting open in the cupboard, wash everything down well, and then be sure to keep any new supplies in well-sealed plastic or metallic containers. If your pantry gets really infested with invisible eggs (and eventually, wriggling moth larvae), you'll have to toss everything in there. Sorry.

HOME
IMPROVEMENT

So you want your home to be an eco paradise but you're up to your Adam's apple in environmental sins. Now what? Well, I won't lie to you—you've got a lot of work ahead and most of it won't come cheap. Some of it's fun (like picking out your new cork flooring and recycled-tile backsplash). Other stuff, like installing insulation or saving up for a furnace, isn't quite so sexy but it's what's necessary to really transform your home into a piece of earth-friendly heaven.

RENOVATIONS

Ever fantasize about TV crews demolishing your kitchen and putting in Energy Star appliances and solar panels on the roof? Well, until *Extreme Makeover: Green Edition* comes knocking, it's best to take matters into your own hands. Finding local sources of eco-friendly building materials used to be a nightmare, but times they are a-changin' and by 2010, green remodeling should be a $39 billion business, says the US Green Building Council. You can now punch your zip code into several green directories and find the best flooring, paint, and window options closest to your turf. In all honesty, if you're living in California, you'll still have much more variety within driving distance than does, say, someone living in small-town Georgia; but if you can't find options in your hometown, you can always order online.

On top of letting you search for locally harvested materials in your 'hood, Green Building Pages will pull up detailed background info on your product options (including living-wage policies, whether the product offgasses fumes, and how far the product is shipped to get to the manufacturer) (**greenbuildingpages.com**). Green2Green provides side-by-side chart comparisons so a quick scan will tell you who's got the longest warranty, who has the highest recycled content, and who'll take the product back for recycling at the end of its life (**green2green.org**).

You'll also want to get a copy of *Green Building Products: The GreenSpec Guide to Residential Building Materials* either online or in print. It'll give you access to 2,000 listings for everything from adobe blocks and insulating blinds to solar shingles and wind turbines. And they've all been screened by the authoritative publishers behind *Environmental Building News* (**buildinggreen.com**). GreenHomeGuide promises "unbiased reviews and advice from professionals and homeowners like you," and it has an inspiring directory of green home services and product retailers, but the directory is limited to San Francisco, LA, and New York (**greenhomeguide.com**).

And hey, if you want to see more of these products at mainstream stores near you, pipe up and tell the manager. The store might special-order some for you. And if it gets enough requests, it just might start carrying them.

FLOORING

Starting from the ground up, you've got lots of options for what falls beneath your feet. The greenest of the green is definitely reclaimed wood floors harvested in the US (the closer to home the better). The wood is taken from lake floors, riverbeds, old barns, and construction sites and not only saves a new tree from the chop but revives a little piece of history in your living room. Some companies,

The greenest of the green is definitely RECLAIMED WOOD FLOORS *harvested in the US.*

like **Mountain Lumber**, stick to urban salvage by plucking timber from abandoned factories, demolition projects, and breweries (**mountainlumber.com**). (Buyer beware: flooring labeled "vintage" can actually be new wood that was distressed to make it look old. Ask to be sure.)

If the reclaimed stuff is too pricey for you (it doesn't come cheap) and you want to stick with wood, be sure to look for Forest Stewardship Council–certified flooring. Ideally, the wood would be sourced from American forests. Check out the **SmartWood** directory of certified new and reclaimed wood floors (**ra-smartwood.org**), and there's a ton of FSC-certified and reclaimed wood sources in the *GreenSpec Guide*. You can even access FSC-

HABITAT FOR HUMANITY RE-STORES

Can't afford any major renovations? There's no denying that none of this stuff comes cheap. Try tackling one project at a time. And keep in mind that you can get all sorts of salvaged secondhand items, including lumber, sinks, doors, windows, chandeliers, tiles, mantles, and even nails, hooks, and knobs, from **Habitat for Humanity**'s **ReStores** for about half the retail price. They're like thrift shops for building supplies, full of exciting finds. They also get donations of unwanted extras from builders, contractors, and do-it-yourselfers, as well as scratched and dented items, customer returns, and discontinued stuff from retailers and manufacturers. If you're gutting your home or trashing parts of it, you can call them for free pickup and get a charitable donation receipt in exchange. They have locations in 47 states, and all the money goes to the great cause of building homes for the less fortunate. For more info, go to **habitat.org** and follow the link to ReStores.

certified options at Home Depot and Lowe's home improvement centers, though you might just have to special-order it.

Bamboo is not technically wood (though it acts like it) and isn't exactly local (which means it has to be shipped in from thousands of miles away), but this stuff grows so fast it's almost a weed. Make sure you look for bamboo that's formaldehyde-free (or ultralow in it) so it's not polluting the air in your home. Oh, and keep in mind that cheaper bamboo floors might dent more easily. Look for brands that use more mature bamboo stalks and come with a lengthy warranty to give you a sense of its durability. But also be aware that there's no guarantee natural forests weren't cleared to make way for bamboo plantations. Some more trusted sources included **Teragren** (**teragren.com**) and **Bamboo Hardwoods** (**bamboohardwoods.com**). Smith & Fong's Plyboo is now FSC-certified (**plyboo.com**).

Looking for something with a little give? Warm and cushy **cork** floors can be harvested without damaging the tree. Some rumors were flying around that cork supplies were running low because the trees couldn't keep up with demand, but enviro orgs like the World Wildlife Fund (WWF) say that precious Mediterranean cork forests, and the endangered animals that dwell in them, will actually be threatened if we don't continue to buy cork! Cork and bamboo floors are both available in more and more conventional flooring stores.

Once upon a time, before the vinyl invasion, linoleum actually came from natural sources (imagine that!). Now **natural linoleum** is making a comeback, often going by the name **Marmoleum** (**forboflooringna.com**). The all-natural extra-tough flooring is made of pine resin, cork flour, jute, and, yes, linseed oil (hence the "lin" in "linoleum").

If cool is what you're going for, keep your eyes peeled for ceramic and glass tiles made with high recycled content, like **EcoCycle** by Crossville (**crossvilleinc.com**) and **Terra Classic** by Terra Green Ceramics (**terragreenceramics.com**). Or for more of a mosaic look, check out **Eco-Body** (**quarrytile.com**).

CABINETS

Whether you're trying to cover up your mismatched beer stein collection or you're showing off your matching china, you'll need cabinets to hold it all. Stay away from anything made of pressed sawdust and wood shavings, like medium-density fiberboard (MDF) and particleboard. They sound eco-friendly because they should be made with by-products from the wood-cutting process, but they actually use up to 80% virgin tree content, according to Green Seal. Plus, all that sawdust is bound together with the probable human carcinogen urea formaldehyde, which offgasses air-polluting, headache-inducing fumes into your home. So even if you're buying regular cabinets from mainstream stores, avoid MDF and particleboard unless you know they're formaldehyde-free or have only trace amounts, like **IKEA**'s cabinetry.

Looking for something in a deeper shade of green? You've got a few options. One is **strawboard or wheatboard cabinets**. Made of compressed waste straw or wheat stems, they're basically bio-based particleboard, or MDF, made without formaldehyde and often finished with a pretty veneer of sustainable wood certified by the Forest Stewardship Council (FSC). **Humabuilt** (**humabuilt.com**) and **CitiLog** (**citilogs.com**) both offer cabinets made with formaldehyde-free wheatboard with certified wood exteriors. **EcoCraft** uses FSC veneers on urea formaldehyde–free fiberboard (**ecocraft.com**).

Wherever you end up buying, be sure to ask for water-based finishes, low-VOC stains or paints, or natural oils. Otherwise, get them unfinished and stain them yourself.

COUNTERS AND BACKSPLASHES

You need something that can get messy without messing up the planet. **Recycled glass** is a gorgeous, durable, and stainproof option. **Bio-Glass** makes solid surfacing for countertops, walls, or anywhere else you want to slap it down (**coveringsetc.com**). Want something with a bit more pizzazz? **EnviroGLAS** makes **recycled terrazzo** with glass from discarded bottles, and porcelain from recycled sinks (**enviroglasproducts.com**). **IceStone** (**icestone .biz**) and **Vetrazzo** (**vetrazzo.com**) are two more terrazzolike options made with at least 75%

recycled glass (Vetrazzo uses old traffic lights, windshields, and more). **Eleek** makes slick metallic counter tiles out of 100% **recycled aluminum** (eleekinc.com). Sounds crazy, but you can also get counters made with **recycled paper** that can actually stand up to kitchen use; two sources are paperstoneproducts.com and shetkastone.com. And keep your eye out

THE PVC DEBATE

When it comes to home renovation gear, PVC is in virtually everything: pipes, windows, flooring, horizontal blinds, fake leather couches. Trouble is, the building block of PVC, vinyl chloride, is not only a known carcinogen, but also creates dangerous dioxins (which accumulate in our tissues and the environment) in the manufacturing process and when incinerated at low temperatures (as in crappy municipal incinerators). The additives alone, like potentially hormone-disruptive and carcinogenic phthalates added to make the hard plastic soft, are supercontroversial. Then there are all the heavy metals, like lead and cadmium, used to stabilize the plastic (hence the lead in vinyl blinds and kids' toys).

The industry, of course, says that vinyl is completely safe, that the dangers are exaggerated, and that it has cleaned up its practices since its dirtier days. Enviro groups don't buy any of it, and a couple of years back they demanded that the US Green Building Council take a stand against the vinyl building materials that make up over half of all vinyl purchases. (FYI: many green homes are built with energy-efficient vinyl windows, and many argue that the energy savings they offer are worth the eco price tag.) The council looked into it for 2 years and came out with a draft statement. Its conclusions disappointed many anti-PVCers, who said the council had ignored important studies and used poor source material and questionable methodology. Architects/Designers/Planners for Social Responsibility protested that most of the scientific literature scanned had come from industry sources. When the council issued its final report on the matter in 2007, it stuck by its stance that vinyl windows, for instance, are more efficient than aluminum frames and don't prevent enough of a hazard to homeowners to warrant a switch (unlike the case with vinyl floors, which they trashed). Too bad really, when there are greener choices than both vinyl and aluminum to pick from (see the section on windows, page 238).

Regardless, companies have already started phasing vinyl out. Entire municipalities have also been making moves on this front. A couple years back, Seattle decided to ditch plans to install 34,000 feet of PVC drainage pipes, instead using high-density polyethylene (HDPE) pipes. The move reflects the city's 2002 resolution to reduce or wipe out the purchase of any products with persistent bioaccumulative toxins, including PVC. San Francisco also has an ordinance mandating that all city departments stay away from PVC plastic whenever possible. If you want to get into the nitty-gritty of vinyl-less building materials, head to **healthybuilding.net/pvc/alternatives.html**.

for butcher block surfaces made with **reclaimed and local FSC wood**, as well as **bamboo**. Just note that wood doesn't hold up as well over time and durability is a cornerstone of sustainable renovations.

CARPETS

Remember the plush, shagadelic carpeting of the '70s? Or the wall-to-wall craze of the '80s? Back then, hardwood lost out to carpets, whose soft, padded texture was considered ideal for kids and nice on the feet. Then people started talking about the dark side of carpeting—not only that it's made with polluting petrochemicals, but also that it traps allergens such as dust mites and can create problems for asthmatic children, and that all sorts of mystery fumes offgas from its fibers. For its part, the industry says carpets do trap allergens, but in a good way, keeping them from being airborne, especially if you vacuum with a good vacuum once or twice a week. (Obviously, carpets aren't for lazy people.)

But researchers haven't been convinced. One environmental engineer told *New Scientist* magazine that the dust trapped by carpets contains heavy metals, pesticides, and persistent fire retardants. And you'd have to vacuum 25 times a week for several weeks to bring the level of those contaminants below safety standards! According to one Johns Hopkins University prof, the thicker your carpet pile, the deeper your chemical contamination (if you're set on getting a carpet or rug,

You'd have to vacuum 25 TIMES A WEEK for several weeks to bring the level of contaminants BELOW SAFETY STANDARDS!

get one with a low pile). Another study, out of the University of Southern California in the '90s, found DDT embedded in a quarter of the carpets they tested. Tests by the EPA have corroborated the presence of up to 10 pesticides deeply embedded in carpet fibers. Most of these scientists recommend, at the very least, making sure to check shoes (which often carry pollutants on their soles) at your front door.

Offgassing: What about the chemical fumes said to come off the carpeting itself? The industry says air-polluting, lung-irritating, smog-inducing VOCs dissipate within 48 to 72 hours, after which your floor covering is "essentially" VOC-free. Companies also insist that its carpets are formaldehyde-free. Maybe so, but *Environmental Building News* has reported that VOCs—from, say, painting your house—can get trapped in carpet fibers and will continue to be released into the atmosphere over time. And if your carpet has been tacked down with solvent-based glues, you can factor in even more VOCs rising from your flooring.

Synthetic Carpets: No doubt the carpet industry has done some serious revamping over the last few years to spruce up its green credibility. But carpets are still made mostly of petroleum-based fibers that require a massive amount of energy and water to make, not to mention all the hazardous air pollutants and VOCs released in the process. Turning those fibers into carpeting involves another huge influx of energy and water—about 23,000 BTUs of energy and 10.1 gallons of water per square yard (according to an excellent report by Green Seal that's chock-full of good info cited throughout this section)—although these figures are an improvement over the past.

Nylon carpeting is considered the most durable, but there's no good way to spin the fact that making nylon produces the poison gas hydrogen cyanide, as well as carcinogenic benzene, air-polluting chems, and all sorts of nasty toxins. The good news is that nylon 6 is recyclable, and manufacturers such as **Mohawk** (mohawk-flooring.com) and Shaw (shawfloors.com) include up to 50% recycled content in some products. **Milliken** carries carpeting with as high as 80% refurbished postconsumer nylon, but sadly it's only available to commercial clients. Milliken was also the first company to send zero waste to landfills and go PVC-free

GREEN LABEL

Looking for some guidance—maybe a nice label that tells you the carpet you're about to buy won't put out harmful emissions? The Carpet and Rug Institute (CRI) has developed an indoor air-quality testing program. Rugs that meet its emissions standards have a Green Label logo on the back (for more details and a list of compliant products, check out carpet-rug.com). However, the national coordinator of the *Healthy Building News* openly disses the industry-run program, calling it greenwashing. The **Green Label Plus** program is relatively more hard-core; even the carpet industry says the Plus program uses "the most stringent criteria," while the regular Green Label—well, not so much. Green Label Plus also analyzes carpets for "chemicals of concern" (which aren't otherwise tested for) and tests for them every year. It makes sure carpets meet California's stringent indoor air-quality standards for low-emitting commercial settings. The catch is, Green Label Plus is less commonly available to homeowners.

(**millikencarpet.com**). Both Milliken and **Interface**'s **FLOR** offer **carpet tiles**, which are a great option because you only have to replace heavily worn squares, not the whole carpet (**flor.com**). **FLOR**'s **Fedora carpet tiles** are 80% postconsumer recycled polyester. The **FLOR Terra** line is about 35% GMO-free corn-based plastic (as is **Mohawk**'s **SmartStrand** line).

By the way, when you buy Interface's FLOR or Bentley Prince Street carpeting, tell your sales rep that you want the **Cool Carpet option** on your order so that any climate-changing emissions will be offset.

Although polypropylene and polyester (PET) rugs are more environmentally friendly to produce,

Above all, STAY AWAY FROM PVC backing; although it's recyclable, it could offgas harmful chemicals throughout the life of the carpet.

they aren't as durable, and you can't recycle them when you're done with them. But **Mohawk** produces a PET line made of 100% recycled pop bottles. It's nice to see cola finally doing some good.

Toxic Backing: Like so many things in life, what you see is never what you get. Over half of a carpet's weight comes from the backing. And though the carpets themselves might be getting somewhat more ecologically responsible, almost all of the plastics used as carpet backing are linked to serious eco problems.

Above all, stay away from PVC backing; although it's recyclable, it contains phthalates that could offgas harmful chemicals throughout the life of the carpet. Plus, it releases persistent toxins when it's incinerated after you trash the carpet (or during a house fire). Synthetic rubber is also made with a toxic brew. And popular polyurethane backings, while often deemed a PVC alternative, use a nasty chemical that can make workers really sick, though it isn't supposed to be harmful in a finished product.

Wool and jute backings are, of course, good natural alternatives, but wouldn't you know it, they're harder to find. **Shaw** makes 100% recycled **Endurance II carpet cushioning** using about 25 million pounds of waste from its production each year.

Requesting Greener Glues: Glues, seam sealers, and removable carpet padding can all give off smog-inducing, lung-irritating VOCs, but the glues are probably the worst offenders. Adhesives aren't used in home installations as extensively as they are in commercial spaces, but if any glues will be used in your home, be sure to ask the person laying your carpet to

STAIN-RESISTANT FINISHES

For years, consumers have reached for carpets that come with extra stain protection. Hell, who wouldn't want something that promises to keep dirt, food, and life stains from sinking into your rug? Scotchgard has long been the king of stain-resistant surfaces, but back in 2000 its manufacturer, 3M, decided to quietly phase out production of its original recipe. Turns out the main chemical in Scotchgard, PFOS, is shockingly persistent. It's been found in children and adults, in blood banks, polar bears, dolphins, birds—you name it, they've got it. And Scotchgard records indicate that 3M knew about this sticky side effect for decades. The substance's extreme prevalence is even more upsetting when you look at the data tying it to liver tumors and learn that PFOS killed off rat pups exposed in utero, even second-generation ones that hadn't been directly exposed.

Though the company might have phased PFOS out, it's still using fluorochemicals to make its trademark Scotchgard products, but it swears these aren't so bad. To quote 3M: "3M's 'next generation' formulation has low potential to bioaccumulate, low toxicity and minimal to no environmental impact." Notice they haven't said there's *no* chance that these will build up in your blood—just a low chance. Probably because carpet makers admit to finding traces of PFOA even in newer-generation finishes. It's a by-product they're trying to eliminate, but it's still there. Either way, any Scotchgard-treated product purchased in 2002 or earlier would likely contain the original persistent eco toxins. You might consider pulling the rug out from under your feet, and pronto!

use water-based, low-VOC products. Peel-and-stick carpet tiles also minimize the amount of glue used on-site, although they do get their stick from somewhere.

Recycling Carpets: In an effort to clean up their image, many manufacturers now have take-back programs. That's good news, because a hell of a lot of carpeting is landfilled every year (2 million tons are junked annually in the US alone). Don't worry—they don't expect you to rip up your wall-to-wall and cart it to them. When you buy a new carpet, installers will take your old one away and recycle it (if you're just ripping it out and not putting new carpet in, you'll have to track down a carpet recycler in your 'hood at **carpetrecovery.org**). Some manufacturers, like **Milliken**, **Shaw**, and **Interface**, make old carpets into new ones (the ideal scenario). Others, like **DuPont**, melt old carpets down and turn them into car parts, soundproofing, and all kinds of nifty things.

Carpet Solutions: If you'd rather avoid petroleum-based synthetics altogether, plant-based **jute, sea grass, and sisal rugs** are available at most carpet stores. FYI: wall-to-wall sisal is usually synthetic—the real stuff is tough to install wall-to-wall. **Merida Meridian** offers a stylish selection of rugs made with hemp, jute, sea grass, and abaca (a cousin of the banana plant) for everywhere from sleek living rooms to playful kids' rooms. They even have sexy shag rugs (**meridameridian.com**). **Fibreworks** has coir (coconut fiber), jute, sisal, and more (**fibreworks.com**).

Wool carpets are available pretty much everywhere, but finding ones that are free of chemical treatments and harsh moth-proofers is almost impossible. You pretty much have to head online. **Nature's Carpet** sells insecticide-free wool area rugs and carpeting with jute and natural latex backing (**naturescarpet.com**), as do **EcoChoices** (**ecochoices.com**) and **Earth Weave** (**earthweave.com**).

Child Labor–Free Stamp: Lots of rugs are now essentially machine-made, and while we might ooh and aah over rarer (and pricier) hand-woven rugs, they have been tied to terrible working conditions, long hours, and child labor. Even machine-made rugs have been linked to sweatshops. The **RugMark** label tells you your rug was made in India, Pakistan, or Nepal without the use of child labor; children were instead given access to schooling. For a list of retailers that carry RugMark products, head to **rugmark.org**. Some fair-trade shops carry hand-knotted rugs made by worker co-ops that were paid a fair price. **Ten Thousand Villages**, for instance, has traditional and modern designs made of 100% pure wool or silk-wool blends. Some of the rugs are dyed with natural pigments (just ask to be sure), and they're all sweatshop-free (**rugs.tenthousandvillages.com**).

PAINT

Itching to liven up your digs with a fresh coat of paint? Fortunately, the days of slapping liquid lead onto our walls vanished with the '70s, but today's color concoctions are still a chemical soup. Thousands of chemicals can be used in the mix, including carcinogenic or neurotoxic stuff like toluene, formaldehyde, and benzene. As a rule, alkyd- or oil-based paints are much more toxic than water-based paints. According to the Union of Concerned Scientists, they contain 40% to 60% VOCs, which send polluting smog- and headache-inducing fumes into the atmosphere (not to mention your lungs). Plus, the oil part is a petroleum product.

Just because latex paints are water-based, don't assume they're saints. They're not made with natural latex tapped from a tree; they're made with acrylic—a petroleum-derived plastic. And they still contain up to 10% VOCs. Oh and, um, up until 1991, latex paint makers added mercury as a mold inhibitor. Great.

Low VOC: Most brands make lines of low- and no-VOC paints these days, including **Benjamin Moore, Glidden**, and **ICI Dulux Paints**. To meet EPA standards, paints can't have more than 200 grams of VOCs per liter. The Green Seal logo is a lot stricter. Green Seal–certified paints have to have less than 50 grams of VOCs per liter for flat paints and 150 grams per liter for nonflat paints. **AFM Safecoat** (**afmsafecoat.com**), **YOLO Colorhouse** (**yolocolorhouse.com**), **American Pride** (**americanpridepaint.com**), and **Mythic** (**mythicpaint.com**) all make great zero-VOC wall paint. (By the way, so-called low-odor oil paints aren't any more eco-friendly—they just have masking agents so they don't smell so bad. And low-VOC oil paints don't have to meet the same VOC standards as latex.)

> **B**RIGHTER, SHINIER COLORS *require more petrochemicals, which give off more VOCs.*

Note that no-VOC wall paints are generally limited to flat, eggshell, and semigloss finishes in whites and soft pastels. Brighter, shinier colors require more petrochemicals, which give off more VOCs. Still, you can start with a VOC-free base and add color. **Benjamin Moore** says the **Color Lock** waterborne colorant system in its **Aura** line doesn't add VOCs to its paints and often gets the job done in one coat (unlike most brands). Plus, it's important to realize that VOC-free doesn't mean chemical-free. Some products are still loaded with harsh mildew-fighting fungicides and biocides (a preservative found in most commercial paints). You won't know unless you ask.

Paint Solutions: Want to paint your walls green? (Well, not literally, unless you like green, of course). **BioShield** paints, stains, thinners, and waxes are made from mostly naturally derived raw materials like tree resins, citrus peel extracts, essential oils, mineral fillers, bee waxes, and natural pigments (**bioshieldpaint.com**). **Aglaia** paints, glazes, and primers are 100% plant- and mineral-based, and all their ingredients are listed online (**aglaiapaint.com**). **Green Planet Paints** offers soy paints with clay-based colors (**greenplanetpaints.com**). Luxury organic bedding queen **Anna Sova** is now dishing out wall paint (called **Degussa**) made from up to 99% food-grade ingredients (**annasova.com**).

If you love the southwestern look of plaster walls, you can't get more local or natural than **American Clay**'s products. They use clays, recycled and reclaimed aggregates, and rich natural pigments, all from the US of A (**americanclay.com**). **Silicate mineral paint**, manufactured by **Eco-House**, is particularly suited to use on concrete, stucco, and new drywall (**eco-house.com**). The company tapped into the German concept of using liquid quartz minerals as a base for its extra-durable silica dispersion paint. It works well on both interior and exterior surfaces. Plus, it's naturally antibacterial and solvent-free. Eco-House also makes natural wood stains and artist supplies.

Least toxic of all is **milk paint**, which has been around since the Stone Age (okay, more like ancient Egypt). The modern variety is still a natural, nontoxic stain perfect for antiquing furniture. It can even be used on plaster, drywall, or stucco. And no, it won't sour on your walls (although it does kind of smell like milk when you first put it on). It's basically made of powdered milk protein, lime, and mineral pigments, and it's perfect for nurseries and for anyone with multiple chemical sensitivities. Beware, though, of anyone who mixes milk proteins with formaldehyde or synthetic plastics such as acrylic and calls it milk paint. You can sometimes find milk paint at furniture restoration shops, or you can buy it online from the **Old-Fashioned Milk Paint Company** (**milkpaint.com**). If you're a bit more ambitious and want to get into pioneer mode, you can make your own (for recipes, check out **realmilkpaint.com/recipe.html** and add color with saffron threads, turmeric, or clay-based hues).

Sealants and More: Looking for nontoxic, environmentally preferred sealants, adhesives, caulking compounds, and paints? **AFM Safecoat** is the go-to company. Plus, it makes a natural line of oils, waxes, and thinners (**afmsafecoat.com**).

Paint Cleanup: No one wants to rinse chemicals down the drain, but in general, municipalities say you can wash water-based latex paint out of brushes and rollers in the sink. Just try to wipe off as much paint as you can first using newspaper. Never, ever, ever pour paint down a street gutter or into a storm drain. Storm sewers are generally connected to the nearest body of water, so you could be killing off fish. Plus, paint thinners and strippers are flammable, so you could be contributing to a nasty sewer fire. For the same reason, you should never pour solvents down your own pipes.

Half-empty cans of paint gathering dust in your basement might be RECYCLED BY YOUR MUNICIPALITY.

Oil paint is a whole other ballgame—one where the players can get dizzy, nauseated, and headachy from the fumes. Oil paint should never be rinsed into your sink. (The whole oil-and-water thing wouldn't work out well for you, cleaningwise, anyway.) Again, wipe off as much paint as you can using newspaper, and then soak your brushes in thinner and wipe them with a rag. To condition brushes, soak them in diluted shampoo, and then rinse and dry handle end up. Keep in mind that paint thinner can be reused. Just let the paint settle to the bottom and reuse the clear stuff on top. You can filter it or pour off the clear liquid into a labeled

---

TAKING IT ALL OFF

If you're thinking of peeling paint off furniture or walls, you're bound to bring some seriously hazardous chemicals like methylene chloride into your home, unless you smarten up. Use elbow grease and get sanding instead (unless, of course, you're dealing with lead paint; then call a pro for help). For lead-free situations, you can also try making a thick paste of washing soda (available at health stores and some supermarkets) and water. Spread it on the surface you want to paint and leave it on for several hours, misting it with water now and then. Then rinse it off and strip. (Thanks to **care2.com** for the idea.) There are also some methylene chloride–free paint removers at **environmentalhomecenter.com**, but don't assume they're totally free of harmful ingredients; they're just not as bad.

jar with a tight lid. Take the leftover paint sludge to one of your municipality's household hazardous-waste depots.

If you're halting your paint job partway through, you can wrap soiled paint brushes, rollers—hell, the whole tray—in a plastic bag for a few days to keep them from drying out. (I once left a painting task unfinished in this way for 2 weeks with no troubles, since the bag was pretty well sealed—who has time to do two coats around the trim in one sitting?) That way, you keep the chems you pour down the drain to a minimum.

Paint Recycling: What to do with all those half-empty cans of old paint gathering dust in your basement? Your municipality might recycle paint cans and even the paint itself. Either way, its hazardous-waste depots should be happy to take your old paint. To scout out the paint-recycling options in your neck of the woods, check out **earth911.org**. And ask about paint made from recycled sources at your local paint or hardware store.

WALLPAPER

Wallpaper may add an oh-so-fabulous finish to your living room and animated bears to your nursery, but you need to know what you're getting rolled up in. Wallpaper is made of one of the most reviled plastics around: vinyl (or PVC). Vinyl creates dangerous dioxins in the manufacturing process and is then softened with potentially hormone-disrupting phthalates that can offgas into the air throughout its lifetime. It's all-around bad, bad, bad. Plus, if you apply it in a high-moisture area, you're trapping humidity and welcoming mold. And did I mention that wallpaper glues emit smoggy VOCs? Even low-VOC kinds contain irritating chemicals such as methyl formate.

Why smother your walls when you can go wild with funky green options made of recycled paper, bamboo, cloth, sisal, dried grasses (a.k.a. grasscloth)—even cork—in all kinds of beautiful and interesting designs. **Phillip Jeffries** makes a whole range (**phillipjeffries .com**). For bold designs that would make any hipster (with cash) go weak in the knees, check out **Woodson & Rummerfield**'s recycled-paper wallpaper dyed with vegetable inks, as well as its printed grasscloth (**wandrdesign.com**). **MIO** makes recycled paper go 3D (**mioculture .com**). And just think how great it would be to have walls decked in old phone book fibers when conversation starts to lull at your next dinner party. **Pallas Textiles**' **Dial Tones** wall coverings are made of up to 70% recycled telephone books (**pallastextiles.com**).

HEATING

It's hard to appreciate winters when you don't have a warm, welcoming pad to come home to. Signs of severe heat deficiency include hovering over your oven for warmth, being afraid to undress, and having a paralyzing phobia of getting out of bed in the morning. Don't let this illness take over your life. You can make your home both warm and energy-efficient.

Thermostat: Getting a **programmable thermostat** is an important first step. You can set it so that your furnace kick-starts in the morning before you get up, cools down when you're gone, and warms up again before you come home from work. You can get a good one for upwards of $35, and it'll easily pay for itself within

If your furnace is more than 20 years old, suck it up and sink your cash into a NEW ONE that's 20% to 30% MORE EFFICIENT.

a year. Energy Star–qualified thermostats have four temperature and time settings and should save you about 10% on your power bills. Not bad for one flick of the wrist.

Furnace: If you're a homeowner and your furnace is more than 20 years old, suck it up and sink your cash into a new one. Buying a modern furnace will save you money in the long run, since they're about 20% to 30% more efficient. Look for the Energy Star label when you're shopping—they're up to 15% more efficient than other models in stores (that means they cost more up front, but you'll be making that money back when it comes time to pay your bills). And ask if your municipality or state offers rebates on energy-saving furnaces.

Although natural gas is pushed as the clean energy choice, it's still a polluting fossil fuel. However, it does burn cleaner than oil or coal, so of the mainstream energy options it's your best bet.

Whatever you do, stay away from baseboard heaters. They're supercheap in terms of initial payout, but anyone who's lived with them knows you can crank the bleep out of those babies and still shiver till you're blue in the face. If you're stuck with them, buy some programmable thermostats made for baseboard heaters. And if yours don't come with built-in fans, then try placing a 6-inch fan nearby to help circulate warm air.

Geothermal Energy: Depending on whom you talk to and where you live, geothermal heating is associated with different techniques. Plenty of communities tap into the scalding steam or water in pockets within a mile or so of the earth's surface to heat their abodes. In fact, tapping into just 5% of all that steamy potential in the US could fuel the energy needs of 260 million Americans.

What about humble homeowners living far from gushing geysers and steamy underground springs? Easy—all you have to do is dig a few feet under your daffodils (where the temperature's always 50°F to 60°F) and run some pipes down there to keep your home warm in winter and chilled in summer. It's called a **geothermal heat pump** and will cost you about $10,000 to $30,000 up front. But these systems

Tapping into just 5% of all that steamy potential in the US could fuel the energy needs of **260 MILLION AMERICANS.**

are more efficient than any top-of-the-line gas furnace and will cut your energy use costs by up to two-thirds. Plus, many systems double as central air conditioners in the summer, so basically you're getting a furnace, AC unit, and water heater all in one (did I mention it heats water too?). Pretty damn cool (or hot, depending on what temp you want your house to be). Major brands include **WaterFurnace** (**waterfurnace.com**) and **ClimateMaster**

GREEN RENOVATION BOOKS

- ***Natural Remodeling for the Not-So-Green House:*** *Bringing Your Home into Harmony with Nature*
  by Carol Venolia and Kelly Lerner (part of the "Natural Home & Garden" series)

- ***Eco Deco:*** *Chic Ecological Design Using Recycled Materials*
  by Stewart Walton

- ***The New Ecological Home:*** *A Complete Guide to Green Building Options*
  by Dan Chiras (part of the "Chelsea Green Guides for Homeowners" series)

- ***Green Remodeling:*** *Changing the World One Room at a Time*
  by David R. Johnston and Kim Master

> ### STAYING TOASTY—FURNACE UPKEEP
>
> Furnace filters should be replaced or, if you have washable ones, rinsed out, every 3 months at the very least, though once a month is ideal. This will come as a shock to the vast majority of us who thought an annual filter change was all that was needed. Sorry, kids. Dirt buildup here will mean your furnace can't do its job as well. When my filter was first cleaned after I moved into a new apartment, so much wind started blowing through the vents that curtains began to billow, and the place grew warm for the first time. You also want to make sure you call in a pro for an annual furnace checkup to make sure your system is running safely and at peak efficiency.

(**climatemaster.com**), and even mainstream cooling companies like **Carrier** are getting in on the act (**residential.carrier.com**).

Space Heaters: If you're renting or just can't afford major furnace repairs or replacements, portable space heaters can seem like the only way to warm your home. Trouble is, they're pretty inefficient and can be serious energy suckers. Maybe that's why no models are certified by Energy Star. Space heaters powered by a combo of electricity and natural gas or kerosene emit dangerous carbon monoxide and sulfur dioxides either into your living room (if they're unvented) or into the great outdoors (if they're vented). The first will kill you; the second will kill the planet.

Electric radiant heaters are supposed to be more energy-efficient, and since they don't use fuel they don't emit any nasty fumes, but they warm only the person they're pointed at, not the room.

Weather Stripping: This is your cheapest defense against frigid outside air, so listen up: it's extremely important to fill any and all holes and cracks around windows, doors, baseboards, and electric and plumbing fixtures with caulking or weather-stripping strips. You can either get the cheap, removable plastic or felt kind or invest a little more in durable metal ones, available at any hardware store. A surprising amount of cold air gushes in from these poorly insulated areas. Just put your hand over a light socket and you'll feel it. Holding a smoking incense stick in front of these areas can help you see drafts more readily.

Windows: Though your windows let in warming sunlight, they also have the potential to leak about 25% of your home's heat. If you've weather-stripped your heart out and they

COME ON BABY, LIGHT MY FIRE (ER, MAYBE NOT)

Sitting around ye olde hearth before a roaring fire seems like such an ancient practice it can't be bad for you, right? Unfortunately, burning wood emits climate-changing greenhouse gases like carbon dioxide, the greenhouse gas precursor carbon monoxide, and other smog-forming pollutants that deteriorate the air quality both inside and outside your home (and you thought that was just the smell of winter). In fact, wood smoke can account for about 80% of the air pollution in a residential area, according to the Environmental Protection Agency. Even small towns can get clouds of brown haze over them when wood burning is at its peak. Plus, inhaling this stuff can aggravate health problems such as angina, asthma, and bronchitis, and several of the compounds coming out of that fire are nasty carcinogens (like dioxins, formaldehyde, and benzene).

If split wood has been well "seasoned" (dried in the sun) and cut to the correct length (see **woodheat.org** for details), toxic smoke is reduced. But you'll really cut back on emissions only if you get an **advanced-combustion woodstove or fireplace**. These babies burn 90% cleaner than older models and use a third less wood. They even reburn smoke to create heat.

Try to fuel your fire with sustainably harvested firewood. Look for FSC certification. Or pick up some Java-Logs (**java-log.com**), made of recycled coffee grounds, wood, and vegetable by-products, available at many grocery and hardware stores. They emit about 10 times less carbon monoxide and 6 times less particulate matter than firewood does. Fake logs, by the way, should be burned only in traditional fireplaces, not woodstoves.

If you'd rather skip the whole messy burning-log thing altogether, natural gas fireplaces are a cleaner option, but some can be extremely inefficient. A bad one can generate carbon monoxide and really degrade your indoor air quality (not to mention pollute the planet unnecessarily). Be sure to get an energy-efficient model with an annual efficiency rating of about 70%.

still sap warmth, you have a few options. For one, you can get cheap insulating shrink-wrap. Look for energy conservation kits that come with window film, caulking foam, and sealing liquid—not particularly eco-friendly ingredient-wise, but helpful in this context. Also, **insulating honeycomb or cellular curtains** actually keep the heat in and cool out. Double- or triple-celled models are best and are available at most blinds stores. **Window quilts** are the most insulating window covering on the market; they fold or roll down at night to create a good seal (see **cozycurtains.com** or **windowquilt.com**).

When you've got the funds, look for windows with **low-E films** (the *E* is for "emissivity," which is the ability of a surface to emit warmth). Their thin metal coating (don't worry, it's invisible—you're not buying tinfoil-lined panes here) keeps the heat inside in the winter

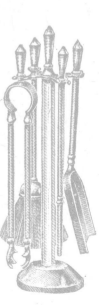

CHEAP TRICKS FOR OLD WINDOWS

- **Apply low-E film to regular windows.** It's an affordable insulator, though scratchable.

- **Seal exterior and interior storm windows well.** A good seal will taper your heat loss by 25% to 50%.

- **Leave south- and west-facing windows uncovered during the day** so you can soak in as much sunlight as possible. It's free heat!

- **If you have any radiators or south-facing windows,** make sure they're clean—dirt and dust absorb heat, robbing you of precious warmth.

and outside in the summer. Be sure to look for the Energy Star label when you're browsing for windows, skylights, and doors (see **energystar.gov** for a directory of retailers). And do try to stay away from PVC and aluminum windows. PVC comes with eco baggage, and aluminum ones aren't that efficient. Better to aim for FSC-certified wood models (like from **jsbensonwoodworking.com** or **loewen.com**) or insulation-filled fiberglass.

COOLING

On extra-sticky summer days, do you ever wish you were small enough to put a lawn chair in your fridge and just chill out in there? Okay, maybe I'm the only one. But come on, if you've lived without air-conditioning, you've no doubt stuck your head in the freezer for one brief, blissful moment and thought, "Man, this is heaven." Of course, it's clearly no long-term solution, so let's get back to reality.

Windows: If you're going to try to stay away from energy-hogging air conditioners, you've got to get strategic. Leave your windows open at night and shut them in the morning before it gets warm. They'll seal in the cooler air, but only if you draw all the blinds too. Up to 40% of heat comes in through your windows. Outdoor shutters and awnings keep the sun's rays from touching the glass, but almost any old blind will help. **Cellular or honeycomb blinds** are better than most. Whatever you do, stay far away from plastic blinds made of toxic PVC or vinyl. The stuff is bad, bad, bad for the environment and has historically been found to contain lead (especially scary if you have kids, since lead builds up in dust on the blinds).

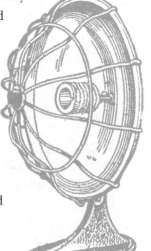

Fans: Moving air across your skin is the key to keeping cool, so get yourself some good fans. They use 90% less electricity than air conditioners. But not all fans are alike. **Energy Star ceiling fans** move air up to 50% more efficiently than standard models. **Reversible window fans** (available at hardware stores) are great because, if you have a couple of them, you can adjust them to pull air from one window and push it out another, creating a much-needed crosscurrent.

Whole-house fan systems are fantastic at sending cooling gusts of air throughout your house. They actually suck air from outside your windows and pull it through your home up into a vented attic. They're ideal for use at night or in the early morning and can really lower the temperature of your house in a hurry, drawing cool air onto stuffy top floors. If your summers don't get too, too hot, you

Fans use 90% LESS ELECTRICITY *than air conditioners.*

can use them in place of air-conditioning, or you can use one in conjunction with AC to cut back on energy costs. They use about one-tenth as much power as air conditioners do. Either head online to sites like **housecooler.com**, **airvent.com**, and **quietcoolfan.com**, or stop to ask about them at your local hardware store.

Swamp coolers, a.k.a. evaporative coolers, also use much less energy than AC, but they're only good for bone-dry climates like Phoenix or Salt Lake City.

Air Conditioners: No matter how many fans you run, one killer-long heat wave can be enough to make many eco lovers cave and buy—gasp!—an air conditioner. Sure, you can blame warmer-than-average summers on climate change, but we're also terrified of breaking a sweat and enjoying the seasons in all their glory. Americans are fortifying their homes and cranking the AC all summer long, regardless of what it's like outside! Try turning it on only when you really need it to stave off heat exhaustion or to sleep, and let windows and fans carry in cooling breezes otherwise.

8 HOT TIPS FOR KEEPING COOL IN JULY

Fan out. Use low-energy fans to keep air circulating. 1

Dig in. Plant a cooling garden and trees to shield your house from the sun. Okay, so this one takes a while to, well, grow into its own, but that's all the more reason to hurry up and get gardening! 2

Don't let the sun shine in. Those rays are cooking your home, and if you've got AC, you're forcing it to work extra hard. Pull those blinds down during the day. 3

Reach out. Install awnings over your windows to keep the sun from hitting the glass. 4

Lighten up. About to redo your roof? Choose light-colored tiles or roofing materials. Black tiles turn your attic into a scrambled egg. 5

Raise the roof. Install a radiant barrier (a thin sheet of aluminum, often lined with craft paper or cardboard) inside your roof to help reduce cooling bills. 6

Get low. Invest in high-quality low-E windows (with an argon or argon-krypton gas fill). A typical double-paned window allows about 75% of the sun's heat into your home. But good-quality windows will seal out the sweltering heat of summer. 7

Cool it. Install energy-efficient compact fluorescent bulbs—regular incandescent bulbs give off more heat. 8

If you're considering an AC unit, this is one of the only times I'll tell you not to buy used. Newer models are much more energy-efficient, especially those certified by **Energy Star**. Energy Star room/window units use at least 10% less energy than other new models.

Try turning on the AC ONLY WHEN YOU REALLY NEED IT *to stave off heat exhaustion or to sleep.*

And Energy Star central-air systems use about 20% less power. Maybe that doesn't sound like much savings, but think of it this way: for every kilowatt-hour of electricity you save, you stop the release of 1½ to 2 pounds of polluting carbon dioxide from local power plants. It adds up quickly when you consider that Americans spend over $22 billion a year and use 183 billion kilowatt-hours of electricity to cool their homes. That according to the US Department of Energy.

Make sure your AC is free of ozone-depleting HCFC refrigerants (which are being

GOT AN AIR CONDITIONER TO DITCH?

If you've decided to get rid of your window air conditioner, don't toss it with your regular trash. The toxic cooling fluids inside can contaminate landfills, leach into the environment, and mess up local groundwater. Nothing cool about that. Call your municipality about proper disposal. They should have hazardous-waste depots where you can drop off your old unit. Stores like Home Depot have also been known to offer rebates on new, more efficient models if you bring in your old clunker. Be sure to ask.

phased out as of 2010). Their replacements (HFCs like Puron) aren't perfect—both HFCs and HCFCs are greenhouse gases—but they're considered the greener option.

Be sure to buy the right unit for your space. There's no need for one that can cool 1,000 square feet when your bedroom is only 200 square feet. And don't be an energy pig. Turn it off (or at the very least raise the temperature) if you're leaving a room or your house for more than 4 hours.

5 TIPS TO IMPROVE EFFICIENCY IF YOU'VE ALREADY GOT AC

Your house isn't a meat locker, so why keep it refrigerated like you're storing sirloin? Set your thermostat to 76°F or 78°F and program it so it turns on an hour before you get home.

Cleanliness is next to coolness. Clean your filter at least once a season to make sure it's working efficiently.

Lock it down. Make sure windows are sealed properly to prevent hot air from coming in. This is especially important for the window the air conditioner is in—those crappy adjustable accordion sides that come with some units won't cut it for most windows.

Dare to repair. If your central AC isn't working well, or if the coils freeze over, you could have a coolant fluid leak. Call a repairperson immediately. Not only is your unit not running efficiently, but you're dripping out harmful greenhouse gases that contribute to climate change.

Inspect your gadget. Have your central AC unit inspected periodically by a professional.

Can't bear the thought of coming home to a warm pad? A programmable thermostat can set the AC to start chilling your space about an hour before you get home. It's a handy dandy tool that'll keep you cool while saving you money and energy.

Solar Air-Conditioning: Imagine cooling your home with the sun's rays. Depending on your vantage point, it sounds absolutely insane or incredibly logical. The day has yet to arrive when air conditioners everywhere run on solar power, but **Solcool One** makes an Energy Star–certified air conditioner that can run on DC power and can thus be used by off-the-gridders. It uses up to 50% less energy than regular air conditioners use, and it has a backup battery that can run up to 12 hours on steamy nights (**solcool.net**).

Geothermal Systems: While we're sizzling aboveground, a few feet down the soil is cool as a cucumber (about 57°F). You can tap into that by drawing the cool air into your home through the liquid-filled coils of a **geothermal system** and reverse it in the winter (for more info on geothermal systems, see page 237).

INSULATION

You need a quality coat to keep warm in winter, don't you? Well, your house does too. There's no doubt that a good layer of insulation has the power to keep energy from escaping through your walls and roof. Although green experts say the energy savings reaped from well-installed insulation offsets the not-so-eco-friendly materials used to make it, if you have the financial means it's best to support products that are green through and through. Fiberglass batting is often bound with formaldehyde. And while polyurethane and polystyrene insulation might no longer be treated with über-persistent PBDE fire retardants, the hexabromocyclododecane used in most extruded polystyrene foam is building up in wildlife and waterways the world over. Plus, polyurethane and polystyrene are still petroleum-based.

Instead, go for blown-in or loose-fill cellulose, made with at least 80% recycled paper content, as from Applegate (**applegateinsulation.com**), Fiberlite (**fiberlitetech.com**), or Tascon (**tasconindustries.com**). If done right, it'll keep cold air at bay better than fiberglass, and it takes as little as a quarter of the energy to manufacture, according to Ecology Action's Green Building Materials Guide. But it can be pretty dusty, so make sure it's well sealed into the wall. **Air Krete** is a nontoxic, inflammable blown-in cement foam made from magnesium oxide, extracted from seawater, and from a ceramic talc mined in New York State. None of that energy- and greenhouse gas–intensive Portland cement business (**airkrete.com**).

THE COOLING POWER OF GREEN ROOFS

Got a boring, flat roof that's just sitting there drawing heat into your home? Why not turn it into a vibrant green setting, full of sun-loving plants that soak up the hot rays and keep them from heating up your pad? Four inches of grass growing on the roof of a typical one-story building cuts its cooling needs by 25%. You could also copy endangered habitats by planting native butterfly gardens or drought-tolerant prairie grasses. You can even plant veggies up there to supply yourself with fresh food (you can't get any more local than that).

Green roofs do the air good by filtering out particles and converting carbon dioxide emissions into fresh, clean oxygen; and they're good for local lakes and rivers because they sop up rain and prevent storm sewer overflows. Rooftop rain barrels can collect the water needed for more water-intensive green roof designs, but some rooftop gardens don't even need watering once the greenery is established.

Before you start throwing dirt down, make sure your roof is structurally sound. Then you need a waterproof barrier, a root barrier, a drainage layer, . . . You know what? You need a professional. A roof contractor with green roof experience can help you get started, even if you want to do your own landscaping. Green Roofs for Healthy Cities lists contractors on its website (**greenroofs.org**). And pick up *Planting Green Roofs and Living Walls,* by Nigel Dunnett and Noël Kingsbury, for some good tips.

Although I just dissed polyurethane (PU), it has some of the highest insulation values around, so it's nice to see some greener PU options. **BioBased 501** is actually 40% soy and was voted outstanding eco-friendly building product of 2003 by the National Association of Home Builders' Green Builders **(biobased.net)**. Heatlok Soya is made of 18% soy and 40% recycled plastic **(demilecusa.com)**.

But if you'd rather avoid these blown-in insulation types, which require

Go for blown-in or loose-fill CELLULOSE, *made with at least 80% recycled paper content.*

professional installation, there's a new product on the block that's been featured in *Newsweek* and elsewhere. Made of recycled denim, **Bonded Logic**'s nontoxic panels are fire-treated with benign borax (the same stuff used as a green cleaner) and can be easily cut with a sharp utility knife **(bondedlogic.com)**.

GREEN ENERGY

It wasn't long ago that "living off the grid" implied that your home was made of logs and you probably hadn't shaved in a while. Now, even concrete dwellers can unplug from the coal/nuke grid with a few solar panels strapped to the roof of a duplex unit, and maybe even a wind turbine. Or you can get really earthy and dig into the soil beneath your house, drawing from the stable temperatures just a few feet underground when the weather outdoors gets a little chilly or sweaty for your taste (for info on this option, see pages 237 and 244). Whatever renewable energy form you choose, you'll need to assess the energy load of your home to figure out how many kilowatt-hours you use on average (online calculators give a rough idea, though many are really antiquated; this is a good one: **nspower.ca/energy_efficiency/energy_calculator**).

Before you go renewable, most companies stress that you make your abode as energy-efficient and insulated as it can be and invest in energy-efficient appliances. Some utilities will even give you cash back if your home energy operation makes more power than you use. Call your local supplier to find out. Also pick up a copy of *$mart Power: An Urban Guide to Renewable Energy and Efficiency* or, for off-the-gridders, *The Renewable Energy Handbook for Homeowners: The Complete Step-by-Step Guide to Making (and Selling) Your Own Power from the Sun, Wind and Water*, both by William H. Kemp.

GREEN RENOVATION REBATES, MORTGAGES, AND INSURANCE

To find out about incentives and rebates in your home state for all things green—new insulation, Energy Star appliances, solar panels, toilets, and more—check out the Database of State Incentives for Renewables & Efficiency (**dsireusa.org**), a comprehensive source for info on state, local, utility, and federal incentives that promote renewable energy and energy efficiency. Home buyers should look into energy-efficient mortgages, also known as EEMs, that make it easier for borrowers to qualify for loans to buy homes with energy-efficient improvements. Look up EEMs at **hud.gov**. You don't even have to have an eco-friendly house to get Fireman's Fund Insurance Company's new premium plan that lets homeowners rebuild their houses with pricier Energy Star appliances, certified wood, and low-VOC paints. You can even rebuild to LEED (Leadership in Energy and Environmental Design) standards! Ask your insurer if it's going to jump on the green train too.

ECO-LABELED HOMES

Shopping for a new home? Sure, they should be more energy-efficient than creaky old houses, but that doesn't make them light on the earth. The majority of home builders are starting to make some green improvements, but keep an eye out for the following eco labels:

- **Energy Star:** Homes with this label are 20% to 30% more efficient than standard homes. They come with Energy Star appliances, better draft-proofing and insulation, and more efficient heating, cooling, and windows.

- **LEED:** This green rating system (LEED stands for Leadership in Energy and Environmental Design), developed by the US Green Building Council, is considered top brass in the green building world. It sets the bar for leading-edge eco design, construction, and building use; and silver, gold, or platinum ratings are awarded on the basis of a point system. The LEED system was first geared more toward office buildings and condos, but there's now a LEED rating system for homes. For more details, including info on mortgage discounts for LEED homes, a list of certified homes nationwide, and Regreen remodeling guidelines, check out **thegreenhomeguide.com**.

Solar Energy: If you're thinking of venturing beyond solar-powered garden lanterns and want to harness the sun's rays to power your home, you need to do a little homework. Typical solar panels are photovoltaic (PV) systems—they convert sunlight directly into electricity. You can buy basic PV modules and install them yourself—but that's not something I'd recommend, since it can get kind of complicated. You generally have to put in an extra two-way utility meter (it costs several

A QUARTER OF YOUR HOME'S ENERGY *goes to keeping your showers steamy and your clothes and dishes clean.*

hundred dollars) and a power cutoff switch (which prevents you from killing the people working on power lines on your street) and ask an electrician for a final stamp of approval. Unless you're qualified to compete on *The Apprentice: Home Improvement Edition*, you might want to call someone to do it for you. For a custom solar estimator and help finding a pro, check out the American Solar Energy Society's site **findsolar.com**.

Costs vary depending on how much of your home you want to power. **Autonomous systems** are completely independent from the grid. This type is generally more popular for country homes with minimal electrical needs. **Hybrid systems** are also off-grid, but they combine solar panels with wind turbines or some sort of generator. The most common and financially palatable system for urbanites is **grid-connected**, meaning you still fuel your home with some regular coal-, hydro-, nuke-fired power, but you reduce your overall reliance on dirty energy. You can get more or fewer panels depending on your budget. Really, it's impossible to estimate price without knowing how much energy you suck back daily. The bigger, and more wasteful, your household is, the more you'll have to cough up.

Solar Water Heaters and Tankless Systems: If you're not ready to commit to the whole-roof concept, consider a **solar-heated hot-water system**, or "thermal solar heating." Since a quarter of your home's energy goes to keeping your showers steamy and your clothes and dishes clean, switching to solar to heat water can really make a dent in your energy bills. You can get such a system pretty cheap. But anyone with cold winters might want to spend a little more on a vacuum-tube model, which is four to five times more efficient at capturing heat energy in the dead of winter.

If thermal solar heating is out of your budget, try a **tankless hot-water system** that heats water up on demand and uses much less energy than typical water heating systems do. A couple of sources are **foreverhotwater.com** and **dotankless.com**.

Pool owners can also install solar-powered water heaters that will let you warm your pool without taxing your utility bills. **Findsolar.com** has more info on this too.

Wind Energy: Leashing wind energy can be a little trickier, especially if you live in an urban center. You could face height and zoning restrictions, and you definitely need a permit from your municipality's building department. Again, a pro can sort this out for you. A small, 1,000-watt turbine itself will cost a few grand, plus the tower, parts, and installation. Turbines are great in the darker months, when solar panels aren't so productive. Plus, the

BUYING GREEN ELECTRICITY

If you dream of being nature-powered but don't have the cash to outfit your house with turbines and solar panels, you might want to look into buying renewable energy from someone who does.

- **Renewable Energy Certificates (a.k.a. green tags/green power certificates):** Feeling bad about all the dirty power your place uses? Offset your home's greenhouse gas footprint by buying wind, solar, or methane certificates from various organizations, like the reputable NativeEnergy (**nativeenergy.com**). Online calculators will tell you your home produces, say, 12 tons of greenhouse gases through its electricity consumption, and being the shamed earth lover you are, you then buy enough wind power to make up for those 12 tons. Critics say that buying offsets gives people an excuse to pollute by making them feel better about their energy usage, but really green tags should be seen as a way of funding clean energy projects when you can't afford to get your house off the grid. Think of it like this: you can get carbon offsets to compensate for the carbon dioxide emissions created by your flight to Mexico, but that doesn't mean you're going to literally be flying a solar-powered plane. Note: with renewable-energy credits, you'll still get a bill from your regular utility provider. (For a critique of carbon offsets, see page 287.) For a list of certified renewable-energy certificates, check out **green-e.org**.

- **Bundled Green Power:** With this option, you can actually replace your regular utility bills with ones from a green power retailer. They don't come and put solar panels on your house, and they can't run a direct power line between you and their wind turbines 200 miles away, but for every kilowatt-hour of energy you use, you'll put your money toward funding renewable energy—in the form of wind, solar, or certified low-impact hydropower (hydropower that's often less than 30 megawatts and ensures that the passage of fish is facilitated, that dams aren't built on fragile ecosystems or where salmon spawn, and so on). You tend to pay a little more a month, but you'll have a clear conscience and will be helping to clean the air. Search under "renewable electricity" for service in your own state at **green-e.org**.

cooler months are exactly when the wind picks up and turbines come into play. For planning tips and helpful info on setting up your own wind turbine, check out the American Wind Energy Association's website: **awea.org/smallwind** (and subscribe to the Home Energy Systems forum).

OUTER
SPACE

*O*nce spring is sprung and the grass is riz, we start digging up our flower beds and firing up the old BBQ with such gusto it might as well be our last day on earth. We also treat the planet like there's no tomorrow. But come on now—our summers shouldn't be defined by gas-guzzling lawn mowers, pesticide-drenched gardens, and air-choking grills. With all the pollutants you're kicking up, your family's bound to suffer from more than just a bad case of sunburn.

GARDEN AND LAWN CARE

Nothin' like working the soil and planting a few daffodils to reconnect us with the earth underneath our feet and help us forget about the 9-to-5. Whether you've got a patch of grass, a sprawling acre of gardens, or a wee balcony, there's a jungle of options out there for the eco-conscious gardener. But just remember, reaching for a bag of synthetic soil, fertilizer, or pesticide could banish you from the Garden of Eden.

Fertilizers: Fertilizer ads promise bigger, fuller flowers in greener, lusher gardens. As tempting as the offer is, stay away from all the mainstream synthetic types that dominate garden centers. They can burn plant roots and kill a significant chunk of beneficial microorganisms in the soil (making your plants more vulnerable to disease and pests). Plus, those fertilizers end up running off your lawn and can seriously pollute groundwater with water-choking phosphates and nitrogen. Many have fossil fuel–derived ingredients and actually strip soil of its ability to retain and release nutrients over time (no wonder you feel like you need to add more and more of the stuff every year).

Scotts, the company behind Miracle-Gro, actually lobbies against stricter environmental health policies on pesticides and fertilizers, according to Boston Common Asset Management, which owns 8,100 of Scotts' shares. Scotts also works with biotech villain Monsanto on distributing genetically engineered lawn seeds (in fact, in 2007 Scotts agreed to pay a $500,000 fine for failing to prevent tests of Roundup Ready generically engineered bent grass for golf courses from contaminating surrounding lands).

The best gift you can give your garden is to spread a layer of nutrient-rich **organic compost** instead. You can either make your own (see page 258) or pick up a few bags from your local garden center (which might be a mix of composted manure, leaves, bark, and the like). It'll also suppress weed growth, especially if you try a no-till approach to your plots, meaning that you don't turn up your dirt every spring. (Tilling is said to disrupt the ecology of soil.) If you want to give trees, shrubs, or plants an added boost, look for **all-natural fertilizers** made from kelp and fish meal, worm castings, or other nonchemical substances (although some might say it's best to leave the fish in the sea).

TerraCycle sells certified organic, odor-free, squirtable liquid worm poop fertilizer in reused soda bottles (available at Home Depot; Walgreens; some Target, Wal-Mart, and OfficeMax stores; as well as online at terracycle.net). Bottles are collected through environmental fund-raisers at hundreds of elementary schools across the US.

The SYNTHETIC FERTILIZERS that dominate garden centers can burn plant roots and KILL a significant chunk of BENEFICIAL ORGANISMS in the soil.

A good **corn-gluten fertilizer** will even fend off pesky procreating weeds before they start (pull existing weeds before you apply it, so you have a clean slate). Plus, unlike fossil fuel–based fertilizers, natural fertilizers actually boost your soil's nutrient-retaining properties. A little **molasses** is great for sweetening tomatoes (trust me, you've never had tomatoes this tasty). Just add a tablespoon to your watering can as the tomatoes get close to ripe. For the lowdown on all the different basic organic fertilizers, plus info on making your own with ingredients you grew yourself (like comfrey and nettle), see the-organic-gardener.com. You can get an even more detailed breakdown of organic fertilizers at basic-info-4-organic-fertilizers.com.

Not sure what your soil needs are? A soil test will tell you its pH and organic-matter content so you can figure out what nutrients you should feed it. Look up "soil testing" in the Yellow Pages.

Pesticides and Herbicides: What if you've nourished your soil properly, but you're already infested with weeds? Before you resort to potent herbicides, consider this: a few weeds won't kill you; toxic pesticides will. Home pesticide use is often fingered as the culprit for the presence of pesticides in humans, and those chemicals are considered especially dangerous for young children, who also happen to spend more time rolling around on the grass than we do. One of the most popular weed killers used on American lawns—2,4-D—is in pretty much everything marked "weed 'n' feed" or "with weed control," including Killex and many Scotts products. Trouble is, it's linked to elevated rates of non-Hodgkin's lymphoma and prostate cancer in humans, not to mention malignant lymphoma in household dogs. Scariest of all, it's found in higher rates in the bodies of young children than adults and California health officials list the stuff as a developmental toxicant. Marvelous. Herbicides also wash off our lawns and gardens in the rain and end up contaminating groundwater and local waterways (the Sierra Club says that over 90% of the 2,4-D used eventually ends up in water).

A *few weeds won't kill you;* TOXIC PESTICIDES WILL.

Still, every year a whopping 70 million pounds of chemical pesticides are spread on our lawns and gardens to keep weeds and bugs at bay. But that's starting to change now that some towns are restricting the cosmetic use of chemical pesticides (for a list of local policies and pesticide-free parks, check out **beyondpesticides.org/lawn/activist/index.htm**). Even if your town hasn't instituted such restrictions, stay away from chemical weed killers and make your peace with the pesky greens. I mean, really—if cancer societies, learning-disability orgs, and physicians for the environment around the globe all urge you not to use the stuff, why would you?

Natural Weed and Pest Control: A healthy lawn will sprout fewer of the wily suckers. I guarantee it. Sprinkle a little **compost** on your grass and throw down some **low-maintenance rye or fine fescue** grass seeds instead of water-sucking Kentucky bluegrass. **Overseeding and mowing high** (so you leave about 2½ to 3 inches of grass) keeps weeds at bay. Leave any grass clippings on your lawn (unless there's over half an inch of the stuff, in

NO-MOW LAWNS

Up there with inheriting a million-dollar cottage and getting 2 months' paid vacation, never having to mow the lawn again has got to be one of the top summertime daydreams. Many rye and fescue grasses make that fantasy come true. Eco lawn seed mixes, once grown, need to be mowed only once a month at most, if you want that clipped suburban look. Left to their own devices, these fescue seeds will form a low, flowing turf that looks like a green golden retriever's coat. The grass's 9-inch roots go much deeper than those of regular Kentucky bluegrass, digging deep for natural nutrients and water instead of relying on external inputs (a.k.a. your hose and a bag of Miracle-Gro). And since it'll stay drier at the surface, you can say goodbye to grubs. You will have to water it frequently in the first year, but next season you shouldn't have to pull out the sprinkler at all except during serious droughts (eco-lawn.com, prairienursery.com).

Want strawberry fields forever? Well, you can get pretty close with the cool drought-resistant, low-mow (not no-mow) **Fleur de Lawn** grass seed mix from a company in Oregon (protimelawnseed.com/about-us/fleur-de-lawn). No actual strawberries, but the mix will give you a yard full of nitrogen-rich strawberry clovers mixed with perennial rye grass (a good alternative to fescues), plus squat, pink English daisies and baby blue-eyes. Basically, a lawn so cute you'll want to hug it.

which case, add it to your flower beds or compost pile); clippings break down into valuable nitrogen and make it harder for weeds to grow. **Aerating** your lawn with one of those rolling aerator thingies, aerator shoes, or a pitchfork will also let it breathe and help nutrients and water reach its roots. And now's a good time to add that weed-inhibiting **corn-gluten fertilizer** I mentioned earlier. For a great cartoon-illustrated guide to going chem-free, pick up *How to Get Your Lawn & Garden Off Drugs: A Basic Guide to Pesticide-Free Gardening in North America*, by Carole Rubin.

As for pests, you can go medieval on their ass without reaching for harsh chemicals. In fact, it's always best to fight fire with fire. Set a bag of **native ladybugs** (not the invasive Asian type) free in your garden to keep aphids under control (be sure to spread them out properly, though, if you want them to be effective). A bag of **praying mantis eggs** will do the same and will nix whitefly too. Spreading good microscopic **nematodes** will get rid of beetle grubs in your grass (to learn which good bugs will help you get rid of the bad ones, visit beneficialinsects101.com). And although they might creep you out, **bats** eat a hell of a lot of insects. Pick up a bat box at your hardware store to keep these helpful bug munchers around. Birds also eat bugs, so put out a birdhouse or feeder to draw them to your yard.

The way the "organic" label is thrown around garden centers, you'd think you were shopping at Whole Foods. Alas, don't be misled into thinking it means your fertilizer is anything close to certified organic standards. The term generally implies that a product came from natural sources, but that's not always the case. In fact, it can contain synthetic urea, synthetic versions of plant nutrients, and human sewage sludge (yes, you heard me right; many municipalities try to pawn this off as a nutrient-rich soil booster), none of which would fly on a real organic farm. Look for ingredients you recognize, like corn, worm poop, fish, and seaweed.

What about bigger garden munchers, such as rabbits? I have to confess that I'm a little biased on this front. I've had three pet rabbits, so I don't really get why anyone would want to discourage these fuzzy wuzzies from frolicking in their yards. But if they're tearing up your lettuce patch, then plant **marigolds** near their favorite foods and sprinkle **pepper** around after every rainfall.

FYI: anthills should vanish once you've sprinkled the area with **cornmeal or instant grits**. Seriously. They'll bring it to their queen, everyone will down the stuff, and next time they go for a sip of water, kaboom!, the cornmeal expands and they explode. I don't recommend attacking anthills, though, unless they're full of the biting kind!

Mulching: We've all heard that spreading wood mulch on your garden is a good thing when it comes to cutting back on water use and suppressing weeds, and that's all true. But did you know that using wood chip mulch (versus bark mulch) in damp, sunny conditions can breed what's called "shotgun" or "artillery" fungi, pesky wood-rot fungi that shoot tarlike spores?

HOMEMADE HERBICIDES

Still freaked out by weeds? Remove them by hand before they go to seed. Or, to kill off those growing on garden paths or between patio blocks, spray a home brew of gin or vodka and water on weeds (carefully avoiding other plants). Straight vinegar also works, plus it's cheaper. Cola gone flat? Pour it on your weeds instead of down the sink. That'll kill them within a week.

DO-IT-YOURSELF BUG KILLERS

Natural insecticidal soap controls all sorts of bugs on fruit, flowers, and veggies. Make your own by combining 1 tablespoon natural dishwashing soap with 1 gallon water. Pour some into a spray bottle and go to town. Crushed garlic steeped in warm water will work on bigger bugs. *You Grow Girl: The Groundbreaking Guide to Gardening*, by Gayla Trail, has tons of great gardening tips (especially for the urban gardener), including a list of natural insecticides that are safe enough to eat (**yougrowgirl.com/garden**).

(They can even spread to your house—talk about a scary B-movie plot!) It's been a major problem in many eastern states, but it's not an issue in dry climes like Arizona.

Wood and bark mulches can also steal nitrogen from the soil as they decay if you till them into the soil (as opposed to leaving them on top), so they can slow the growth of older plants and even starve new ones to death, not to mention attract fire ants and termites. Besides, do you really want to be responsible for knocking down trees just to keep your garden pretty? You especially want to stay away from cypress mulch, whose production contributes to wetland destruction (see **saveourcypress.org** for details).

So what are you supposed to cover your soil with to help it retain water? **Compost**! Yes, according to Ohio State researchers, two inches of compost is just as effective as two of wood chips at keeping weeds at bay, but much healthier for your plants. If you don't make your own (see the next section), head to a garden center. Leaves and lawn clippings also make good mulch.

COMMUNITY GARDENS

Got garden envy? Most urbanites don't have much space to cultivate. If you lack a yard, or your balcony potting just ain't satisfying your need to dig up weeds, look into helping out around your local community garden. Many hold weekly work bees, as well as monthly workshops on eco gardening topics.

Composting: If an apple rots in a landfill, does anybody cry? Well, avid composters do. Once you've seen what food scraps and yard waste can turn into—beautiful, nutrient-rich compost—there's no going back, baby. About a third of what we throw away and truck to the landfill consists of food scraps. Talk about a waste! More and more municipalities are starting composting programs by handing out bins and getting citizens to collect kitchen scraps to boost waste diversion rates. And it's working.

But what if your town hasn't picked up on this yet, or if you want to create your own nourishing compost for your garden? This is where home composting comes into play. Just buy a bin from your local hardware store or garden center (either a rotating one, a regular plastic one with a lid and air holes, or a wooden one), place it on a level spot in a corner of your yard, then start feeding it equal layers of green stuff (food scraps, coffee grounds, tea bags, houseplants) and brown stuff (dry grass clippings, dry leaves, straw, a few wood chips). You'll want to keep meat and fish, dairy products, peanut butter, and fats out (unless you're planning on throwing a raccoon party). Diseased plants, cat litter, and troublesome weeds (such as crabgrass) should be left out too.

About a third of what we **THROW AWAY** *and truck to the landfill consists of food scraps that could be turned into* **BEAUTIFUL, NUTRIENT-RICH COMPOST.**

Everyone seems to recommend a different way to build the compost pile, but here's one way to go: put down a layer of twigs or coarse material, then a four-inch layer of browns, followed by a four-inch layer of greens, then a thin layer of soil. Continue alternating layers, stir it up every couple of weeks, and you should have good compost within a few months. One thing is for sure: if you have too much of one layer or another, you'll end up with weird smells or no compost. For troubleshooting tips, check out Cornell's Department of Crop and Soil Sciences' handy chart at **compost.css.cornell.edu/trouble.html**.

Indoor Composting: Apartment dwellers without municipal composting programs can do their own pint-size composting indoors. How? Okay, now, don't freak—the key to indoor composting is, well, worms (specifically, red wigglers). Yes, vermiculture sounds kind of creepy-crawly for the house, but don't worry: they stay in their bins. Plus, worms eat half their weight in food, and then poop it out into valuable odor-free worm manure called castings. Just think, people pay good money for this stuff in quality garden supply stores (it's even been called "black gold") and you'll be getting it for free. You can mix your finished compost with sand and potting soil in equal parts for indoor pots. If you make too much, just give it away as a hostess gift. For more details on vermiculture, see **gardenguides.com/ articles/worms.htm.**

> **W**orms EAT HALF THEIR WEIGHT *in food, and then poop it out into valuable odor-free worm manure called castings.*

If you can't get past the wiggler thing, look into indoor mechanized composting bins that fit under your sink, by NatureMill (**naturemill .com**). It uses about the same energy over the course of a month as a typical nightlight.

Native Plants: If you want a truly eco-friendly garden, roll up your sleeves and plant some **indigenous or native flowers, shrubs, and grasses.** The Lady Bird Johnson Wildflower Center has a national supplier directory that makes it easier to find businesses that sell native plants or seeds near you (**wildflower.org/suppliers**). Those that are truly indigenous to your ecosystem are extra hardy because they're already adapted to your area's conditions, and they tend to need less water, pest controls, and overall fussing than plants that originate in other climates. They'll also help keep the local ecosystem happy. For example, the elderberry shrub provides food and shelter for many songbirds, and the milkweed plant is much needed by monarch butterflies.

Heritage/Heirloom Plants: Go from garden center to garden center and you'll see pretty much the same plants—hydrangeas, petunias, geraniums—that all look like they came from the same mother. The truth is that there's little genetic variety left in the world of flowers and garden veggies. It's all been whittled down to the few that fly off shelves. Genetically modified seeds, hybridized plants, and flowers grown in dyed water are all common. This is where heritage plants step in to fill a void of authenticity.

Heritage or heirloom gardening is kind of like planting antiques. Essentially, heirloom plants are grown from strains that are at least 50 years old, they're nonhybridized (so they haven't been crossbred, like most modern plants), and they're open-pollinated (which means you can save their seeds and replant them from year to year). For a list of heirloom seed companies, seed swaps, and exchanges, head to **halcyon.com/tmend/heirloom.htm.**

NOT SO NATIVE:
BEWARE OF WILY LABELING

"**W**ildflower" seed mixes may grow wild somewhere, but probably not in your neck of the woods (in fact, some wildflower weeds are actually noxious in your area). Find out if they're native wildflowers before you plant them.

Lawn Mowers: The smell of cut grass just screams summertime, doesn't it? Trouble is, much of what you're inhaling contributes to the smoggy haze that makes the hotter months so hard on the lungs. "Oh, but it's just a little lawn mower, how bad can it be?" you cry. Pretty bad. According to the EPA, a typical push mower cranks out as much hourly pollution as 11 cars. Riding mowers, 34 cars! Multiply that by the 52 million residential mowers being dragged out every other weekend in the summer,

A typical PUSH MOWER cranks out as much hourly pollution as 11 cars.
RIDING MOWERS, 34 CARS.

and we're sucking back 800 million gallons of gasoline a year. Throw in all the leaf blowers and weed whackers firing up in yards across the country, and we're talking a hell of a lot of pollution.

Cleaner **electric options** are 90% less polluting. You can also get rechargeable types, so you're not bound by a cord. Even **four-stroke mowers** are more efficient (70% more) and spew less smog-inducing fumes than two-strokes do. You can also snag yourself a **solar-powered mower** for a little extra cash (**freepowersys .com/sunwhisper.htm**). Home Depot is looking into bringing in some **Solaris mowers** nationwide (**solarispowerproducts.com**). Needless to say, **manual mowers** that run on push power are the greenest of all. Be sure to look for annual lawn mower exchange events in your area (like Dallas, Anaheim, San Diego)—you might just score a rebate for turning in your old beater.

WATER-SMART GARDENS

Yeah, I know. You're wilting. Your flowers are wilting. Everybody wants extra water come summertime. Even the greenest of the green use more H_2O to keep themselves and their yards looking alive when the temperatures soar. You just have to be smart about it all—especially when there's a water advisory on.

Sprinklers: Try to water early in the morning or in the evening to stop the water from evaporating in the hot sun. Forgo the urge to sprinkle frequently; instead, water deeply once a week. If your soil is constantly moist, plant roots will never spread (as they should if they're going to gather moisture well). And resist the temptation to pull out the hose at the sight of plants wilting in the midday sun—plants often send water to their roots during scorchers to prevent evaporation. Relax. They'll send it back up when it cools. If they don't, water them in the evening. If you're dealing with newly planted trees or shrubs, though, they do need to be watered more often than usual until their roots settle in.

RESIST THE TEMPTATION *to pull out the hose at the sight of plants wilting in the midday sun.*

GRAY WATER ON GARDENS

Americans love to toss water around like we're H_2O millionaires. In fact, according to the Organisation for Economic Co-operation and Development (OECD), Americans are the highest per capita water users in the world, when you factor in our home, farm, and industrial uses of the precious resource. Wouldn't you know it, those of us who pay a flat rate use nearly twice as much water as those who pay for each drop used. Why wash all that gray water (used water from nontoilet sources) down into the sewers, when we could be capturing it and putting it on our gardens? It can be as basic as putting a big bowl in your sink as you rinse out lettuce, rice, or coffee mugs or placing a bucket in your shower. (Little bits of food and natural soaps are perfectly acceptable to living greens. Just keep in mind that you don't want to be pouring chlorine or even the eco cleaner borax on your poor plants.)

Gray-water gadgets, like the one made by Envirosink (**envirosink.com**), allow you to pour any water captured in your sink into a funnel that connects to a storage tank. They're great for saving that water you waste when you're waiting for it to warm up or cool down, rinsing produce, or washing dishes. You can use the stored water on your garden or send it to your toilet. You can also get more complicated systems with filters, pumps, and piping from every room that uses water. Best to mull it over with the experts: **greywater.net**.

Rainwater: Any rain that trickles from the sky can be saved and used on your garden. Ask your municipality if it has a downspout disconnection program. If not, call a handyman (or woman) to do it for you, or do it yourself (I did, so it's gotta be easy), so that your downspout can collect any rainwater that funnels off your roof. Pick up a rain barrel with a fine screen to keep bugs out (wouldn't want it to become a mosquito brothel, now would you?), and then use the water you collect on your plants. Warm rainwater is easier on plants than ice-cold chlorinated hose water, any day. And it's free!

Water-Smart Plants: Logic tells you to avoid planting water-intensive flowers, which means steering clear of flower ID tags that say "keep moist" and sticking to the ones that say "water weekly" or "let dry between watering." And generally your instincts are spot-on. Yet lots of people end up watering drought-resistant gardens designed for dry regions more than they water other species. Why? Well, xerophytic plants can survive dry spells, but do they look good trying? Not all of them, according to horticulture myth buster Linda Chalker-Scott, a professor at Washington State University. In fact, some

We all plant one strain of SUPERTHIRSTY grass that needs tons of water and chemical input to look happy and "healthy."

will shed leaves or won't flower unless they get lots of liquid; as a result, well-intentioned people end up using more water than they would use on run-of-the-mill landscape plants. Do your research. And remember that all new trees and shrubs need extra water in their first year or so.

IS YOUR HOSE DRIPPING WITH LEAD?

A hose is a hose is a hose, right? Actually, no. Most cheapie hoses are made of that nasty plastic PVC, and many have been stabilized with lead. In 2003, *Consumer Reports* tested 16 brands of hoses and found that several leached unsafe levels of lead into water. The magazine advised people to stick with hoses labeled "safe for drinking" on the packaging. And although leaky soaker hoses or drip irrigation systems can be much more efficient than old-fashioned sprinklers, that's true only if they're used right. Water loamy soil with these for 30 to 40 minutes once a week, sandy soil more, and clay soil less. Burying the hose under your mulch will help prevent water from evaporating.

Grass is perhaps one of the biggest backyard water suckers. In fact, running the sprinkler for 2 hours can use up to 500 gallons of water! And households with automatic sprinklers tend to use 50% more water than do those that rely on manual sprinklers.

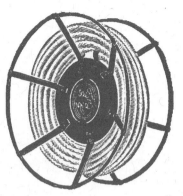

It doesn't have to be this way. Our problem is that we all plant one strain of superthirsty grass that needs tons of water and chemical inputs to look happy and "healthy": Kentucky bluegrass. You (and the planet) would be much better off if you planted some low-maintenance fescues or perennial rye grasses. Don't worry: your backyard won't look like a field of wheat. These breeds are even used on sport fields and golf courses, so your lawn can still be as green as your neighbors' (see the No-Mow Lawns sidebar on page 255).

PATIOS AND BALCONIES

If you've ever lived in an apartment with no outdoor access, you know just how much a patio, balcony, or even a well-placed fire escape means to a person. The access to fresh air, the sun kissing your face, maybe an encounter with a butterfly or a bird—all are a treat. In my case, even nightly visits by a family of raccoons were treasured after I first moved from a dark basement apartment. Of course, once we have such a space, we have to fill it with stuff—pots, patio furniture, a deluxe barbecue. And wouldn't you know it, they all have environmental ramifications.

Pots: Just because something is filled with earth, next to earth, or "of the earth" (think clay, metal, or wood) doesn't mean it's earth-friendly. Take terra-cotta, for instance. This mainstay of the flowerpot world is made of seemingly benign clay. "What could be wrong with clay?" you ask. "It's been sculpted by potters and artisans since the beginning of time." Well, like anything we mine commercially (including those cute tin planters), clay comes with plenty of eco implications, especially in certain parts of the world. Indiscriminate mining of the stuff in areas of India has dried up local wells (leading to severe drinking-water shortages); and paddy fields, once wetland habitats for plants and animals, are being dug up and dried out for the moldable mud. That doesn't mean you'll never buy terra-cotta pots again. But it does mean you should invest in good-quality pots and take good care of them to extend their life. Also, beware of planting edibles in glazed terra-cotta. The finish could contain lead that can leach into your dinner.

Fake terra-cotta and other plastic pots aren't great either. Most are made with polyethylene (a relative of the pop bottle), which, according to Greenpeace's pyramid of plastics, isn't too bad. But like all other plastics, they're petroleum-based and contain chemical UV stabilizers. Cheap plastic planters can easily crack, as can low-grade terra-cotta, so it's best to invest in better-quality containers that you won't have to replace every spring.

So what should you plant your petunias in? Start by hitting secondhand stores, flea markets, and garage sales, where you'll find plenty of weird and wonderful **retro containers**. And think outside the pot. Old boots, wooden crates, and vintage suitcases make great planters. You can also get fibrous pots made out of **recycled cardboard** from any local garden center (speaking of which, try to shop for plants sold in **biodegradable pots** over those sold in nonrecyclable plastic). Even baskets made of fast-growing, sustainable **bamboo** or **rattan** are a sound option. Fair-trade shops tend to have all kinds of planters made of **ceramic** or **wicker**, crafted by worker co-ops with an eye toward sustainable materials.

> **THINK OUTSIDE THE POT.** *Old boots, wooden crates, and vintage suitcases* **MAKE GREAT PLANTERS.**

Patio Furniture: Need a place to sit? Pretty, naturally weather-resistant exotic woods like teak are all the rage, but they're often seriously overharvested, deforesting tropical countries. According to the Rainforest Action Network, at least 75% of logging in Indonesia's rainforests is illegal. And Indonesian plantation teak often comes from 200-year-old, rich second-growth forest. The word from the New York–based forestry watchdog Rainforest Relief is that Indonesia is starting to run low on teak and is now slyly importing Burma's disappearing trees. Too bad most manufacturers aren't keen on the quality of teak from Central America's much more sustainable (though much younger) plantations. Even a Forest Stewardship Council label, says Rainforest Relief director Tim Keating, won't guarantee a tropical table that's old growth–free.

Rainforest Relief tries to pressure retailers like Pottery Barn to stop selling any patio furniture made of teak, nyatoh, kapur, balau, jatoba, garapa, ipê, and other old-growth tropical woods altogether. The group's campaign has already pushed Linens 'n Things, Wal-Mart, and Crate and Barrel to stop using nyatoh wood (**Crate and Barrel** now sells tons of Forest Stewardship Council–certified options that are also old growth–free). **IKEA**'s wooden outdoor furniture isn't all certified, but the company does get the thumbs-up from Rainforest Relief for having responsible forestry policies. Note: just because a store like

Target now has a couple of FSC-certified patio sets doesn't mean they're not still selling endangered tropical woods. **Gaiam** has a decent selection of FSC-certified patio sets and Adirondack chairs (not to mention a hammock made from old soda bottles and a solar patio umbrella) (**gaiam.com**).

Woods that aren't naturally weather-resistant are sealed with petroleum-based finishes that offgas powerful air-polluting volatile organic compounds (VOCs). Even more resilient woods will need to be oiled, so make sure you use a natural one made of natural ingredients like beeswax and tree resins. Some people swear by hemp oil, but I didn't have much luck finishing some outdoor lounge chairs with the stuff. (See the following discussion of decking and fencing for more on waterproof sealants.)

Plastic furniture is made of either PVC (vinyl) or polyethylene, which is considered much more benign than vinyl. But both types tend to break suddenly after a couple of years, potentially giving Grandpa a mini heart attack at your backyard barbecue. (Don't feel bad, the pricier plastics would have cracked too.) Better to get sturdier patio furniture made from **recycled plastic**. As the price suggests—it's nowhere near as cheap as the nonrecycled stuff—it's built to last and it's low-maintenance too. You can find bistro sets, rocking chairs—even club chairs and ottomans—made of milk jugs and water bottles (a.k.a. polywood) at plenty of stores these days. Or shop online at **polywoodinc.com**, **bytheyard.net**, or **millcraftfurniture.com**.

For durability and class appeal, **wrought iron** is great, since it lasts forever. Ideally, you should get the recycled kind (**Gaiam** carries recycled wrought-iron bistro sets). And really any **recycled metal** should be a top choice. But if you're having trouble finding some in your area and you'd rather not ship from California, how 'bout this: we'll forgive the not-so-forgivable eco legacy that mining has given the planet as long as you promise to keep your indestructible metallic patio furniture forever. If your grandkids don't want it when you pass on, antique stores will surely jump at it.

Rustic outdoor furniture made from **willow branches** is in the clear because the branches are fast-growing and usually hand-collected in small quantities, says the Worldwise Wiseguide to sustainable products (**worldwise.com/wiseguide.html**). Plus, willow branches don't need any sealants, since they still have their bark. I've even seen outdoor sleek loungers made of fast-growing water hyacinths (**vivavi.com**).

What about wicker? First of all, you've gotta know your terminology. "Wicker" refers very generally to pliable twigs;

"rattan" refers specifically to a climbing palm plant. Wicker is often made using **rattan**, which is fine, since it's considered renewable, but make sure you're not getting the type that's coated with harsh chemical sealants. Stay away from fake petroleum-based plastic wicker. It's durable and weather-resistant, but I'm still waiting for the day it's made using recycled resin.

Your greenest choice is always the **secondhand** route. You can find tons of gently used patio furniture for a good deal on sites like **craigslist.com**.

Decking and Fencing: Until recently, lumber intended for outdoor use (known as pressure-treated wood) was treated with chromium and arsenic (actually chromated copper arsenate, or CCA), and some of those toxin leachers could still be on shelves. Several towns have ripped out playgrounds built with this kind of wood after realizing that it leaches quite readily into surrounding soil (especially sandy soil, and especially when exposed to sunlight—which is, like, all the time). If your flower beds are framed with arsenic-laced pressure-treated wood, the toxins could make their way into your veggie patch too. (If you decide to toss your old wood, be sure to bring it to your local hazardous-waste depot. Call your municipality for details.)

Alternative pressure-treated woods are already on the market. But the Environmental Protection Agency says little research has been done on the environmental impact of ACQ and copper azole, for instance. Borate-treated lumber might seem less toxic, but many say you shouldn't use it near soil.

If your flower beds are framed with arsenic-laced pressure-treated wood, the **TOXINS** *could make their way into your* **VEGGIE PATCH** *too.*

The best wooden option for decking and anywhere wood touches soil, especially if you are to build, say, an aboveground veggie garden or child's sandbox, is **local cedar**. The natural oils in cedar mean that no sealants or chem treatments are needed. And looking for the Forest Stewardship Council label on that cedar or whatever wood you choose will ensure that it has been sustainably harvested (check out **environmentalhomecenter.com** for FSC-certified American cedar). Beware of deck tiles made of tropical woods, even certified ipê wood (they could contain old-growth trees). FSC-certified deck tiles made of fairly fast-growing **eucalyptus** are considered a better choice, according to Rainforest Relief.

There's also decking and fencing made entirely of **recycled plastic**. It's incredibly durable, being rot- and corrosion-proof. **Trex** manufactures fencing, decking, railing systems, and benches made of 1.5 billion recycled plastic grocery bags a year mixed with waste wood (**trex.com**.) Both Home Depot and Lowe's carry Trex products. Home Depot also sells FSC-certified lumber.

If you need to treat your fence, deck, or what have you, get an all-natural finishing oil, or a plant- and mineral-based wood treatment. For tougher natural wood sealants, check out **SoyGuard Premium Water Repellent and Wood Sealer** at **soyclean.biz** and **Deck Boss** at **weatherbos.com**. **LifeTime Wood Treatment** is another good nontoxic option, and the company swears you have to apply it only once (**valhalco.com**).

BARBECUES

Given the hellish temperature of many kitchens come summer, there's no way we could make it through without an outdoor grill. You can have only so many salads (unless you're on the raw-food diet), so it's either that or packaging-heavy takeout, and barbecuing is definitely the greener way to go. Especially if you do it right.

Hibachis: Anyone with a deep yearning for mesquite or a superlow budget knows the allure of the hibachi. Unfortunately, the most wallet-friendly option is also the dirtiest. Charcoal and wood send soot and smog-inducing carbon monoxide into the air. That applies to both lump charcoal (which is basically unprocessed charred wood) and the pillow-shaped briquettes (made of scrap wood and sawdust). The briquettes may contain coal dust or hidden chems left over from the scrap wood, and the lump kind contributes to deforestation. You just can't win. Better to reach for low-smoke **Cowboy Charcoal** from hardwood scraps free of fillers or chemicals (at Lowe's stores; Cowboy Charcoal goes under the 365 brand at Whole Foods). Stay far, far away from kachi charcoal, if you spot it. It's chopped from threatened mangrove forests.

Grills: Another problem with cheapie barbecues, whether they burn charcoal or propane, is the grill itself. More often than not, low-grade models use chrome-coated aluminum, which chips easily, leaving you with a bare aluminum cooking surface. Not good for the brain cells. You're safer with a **cast-iron** or **stainless steel** grill. The **porcelain-coated** kind, which is quite common, is also good and provides a

Charcoal briquettes may contain COAL DUST, and the lump kind contributes to deforestation.

nonstick surface. If you're buying nonstick grill-top or grill-side trays, rib racks, baskets, and roasting pans, make sure they're coated with ceramic or porcelain. You wouldn't want any Teflon-coated stuff cooking at high temps.

Fuel: In terms of fuel sources, the cleanest, most energy-efficient bet is **natural gas**, **electric**, or **liquid propane** (which is extracted from natural gas). In fact, backyard 'cuing with either of these is more efficient than cooking in your kitchen oven, which takes forever to preheat. Don't get me wrong—natural gas is no saint (think offshore drilling and piping through traditional native lands), but I've yet to encounter a barbie that runs on vegetable oil. An electric barbecue run on solar panels would definitely win the green ribbon at the county fair (at least regular electric grills are fume-free).

CLEANING THE GRILL

Got a chunky, gunky grill caked with last June's basting sauce? Skip the toxic chem-based cleaners. Make your own scrubbing paste with baking soda and water that you apply with one of those wire BBQ brushes. Give the grill a good scrubbing and then wipe with a wet cloth.

There are funky **solar cookers** on the market, but they don't give you that flame-roasted effect. However, advocates swear these contraptions cook a mean casserole and bake some fine cookies in about the same time as your regular oven if it's sunny out, and a little longer if it's partly cloudy. If you're interested in checking them out, **solarovens.net** even sells a solar hybrid oven that you can plug in if the sun goes away. Or make your own with a little foil and plans from **solarhaven.org/SolarCooking.htm**.

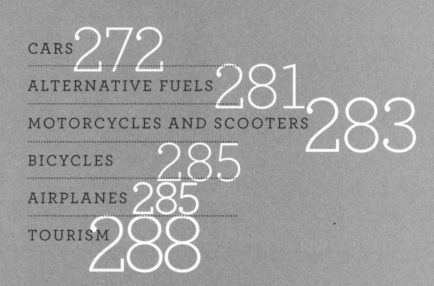

Remember when we had to travel everywhere on horseback and hop in a dugout boat just to get around? Yeah, okay, me neither, though our modern need for speed makes us cringe at how long it must have taken for anyone to get anywhere 100 years ago or so. We've relegated our hikes, boat rides, and equine friends to leisure activities—things we might drive 100 miles out of town to go do. For our real lives, we've got an elaborate network of planes, trains, and automobiles to get us where we want to go in a hurry, with a web of paved roads, rails, and invisible air routes to guide the way. At 90 miles an hour you can lower the roof on your convertible and scream, "Eat my dust, world!" (or rather, "Eat the cloud of particulate matter and greenhouse gases that billows behind me"). Love 'em or hate 'em, modern means of getting around are here to stay—you've just got to know how to pick 'em to make the best of life's nutty journey.

CARS

Maybe it's something about the vastness of the land or the wild fluctuations in our seasons that makes us want to get around in climate-controlled bubbles, but whatever it is, Americans love their cars. Over 250 million vehicles are registered in this country, driving billions of miles a year. If you already own a car, you have to look deep inside and get all

"Montel Williams meets Al Gore" on yourself. Ask yourself, "Do I really need to drive as much as I do? Can I take mass transit or bike to work? Can I even afford to drive at the rate gas prices can skyrocket?" The answers to all three seem to be on everyone's minds—Americans drove 20 billion fewer miles in the first half of 2008 alone.

Exhaust: Wanna know what's spewin' out your tailpipe? Probably not, but pull over and let's talk. The most popular passenger car in the US, the Toyota Camry, might be a little smaller and more efficient than some beasts on the road, but the 2008 model, for instance, still coughs up about 10 tons of carbon dioxide, carbon monoxide, nitrous oxides, and hydrocarbons a year. And that's nothing compared to the 15 tons of pollutants that the country's long-standing

> The most popular passenger car in the US coughs up about 10 tons of CARBON DIOXIDE, CARBON MONOXIDE, NITROUS OXIDES, and HYDROCARBONS *a year.*

sales champ, the Ford F-150, grinds out. All combined, vehicle emissions contribute a huge amount to respiratory infections, ground-level ozone (a.k.a. smog), and climate change. Now put that in your tailpipe and choke on it. Oh wait, we already are.

Mining and Metals: Your car's environmental record doesn't just hinge on its tailpipe. There's a hell of a lot of mining going on (with a quarry full of eco implications) just to dig up enough steel, aluminum, and dozens of other metals to make all those cars. Thirty-five percent of all iron mined in the US, for example, goes to the auto biz, according to an Environmental Defense Fund report. Then there are all the toxic innards, like the mercury switches in pre-2003 North American–made cars and imports from the '90s (thanks to the sloppy recycling of old vehicles, these switches are one of the largest sources of hazardous mercury pollution). Lead starter batteries, according to the Clean Car Campaign, account for the majority of the world's current lead pollution.

In accordance with the much-praised End of Life Vehicle Directive out of Europe, pretty much every car manufacturer has agreed to phase out lead, mercury, and cadmium from all their cars, even outside of Europe, to make them more easily recycled and less toxic in their afterlife (though Chrysler has been dragging its heels about halting the use of lead wheel weights, it will finally do so—in California, at least—by the end of 2009). Check out the state-by-state guide to safely disposing of cars with mercury switches at **elvsolutions.org**.

LOVE THAT NEW-CAR SMELL?

Before you take another whiff, remember, that's partly the scent of chemical phthalates used to soften PVC plastics in the dashboard, door panels, and weather stripping. We inhale them every time we get in our cars (where the average American spends 1½ hours every day). Talk about indoor air pollution! And, scary but true, these chemicals break down even faster in the hot sun. The plastics industry says that phthalates are safe, but six of them have recently been banned from toys. Wouldn't you know it, phthalates aren't the only chemical of concern wafting out of your dashboard (think brominated flame retardants and lead stabilizers in the PVC). Of all the family sedans tested, the 2008 Mazda 6 had the highest overall levels and the **Honda Accord**, the lowest. Of the smaller cars, the Suzuki Forenza flunked out and the **Honda Fit** scored well.

Luckily, **Volvo** banned the use of several PBDEs and phthalates in all its cars. Honda, Toyota, and to some degree Nissan are in the midst of reducing and replacing PVC parts. For more info and details on how different cars rank in terms of their indoor air pollution, check out "Toxic at Any Speed" at **ecocenter.org**.

Oil: If aliens were watching us from outer space, do you think they'd call the planet "Earth"? I doubt it. Given how the human race revolves around the black goopy stuff we dig out of the earth's crust, we'd be known as Slick, Sludge, or maybe Black Gold. And dig for it we do—in the rainforest, on the ocean floor, in wildlife reserves, and in all sorts of ecologically sensitive regions. We knock through wildlands to build roads to remote regions and leave toxic legacies where poorly stored wastewater from drilling leaches into surrounding waterways—polluting rivers, lakes, streams, and local residents. A prime example can be found in an ongoing class action lawsuit representing 30,000 largely indigenous Ecuadorans that claims Texaco dumped over 18 billion gallons of waste products into the local environment throughout the '70s and '80s. The region in question is still appallingly contaminated, say activists, despite Texaco's remediation efforts a decade ago. About 2.5 million acres of rainforest were purportedly lost to contamination and drilling.

Then there's the type of oil mining just to the north, in Canada, where more energy goes into extracting and refining petroleum from the tar sands than is produced. In the process, the tar sand oil creates three to five times more greenhouse gases than conventional oil does, and processing the sticky bitumen shockingly uses more fossil fuels than it puts out! Don't even get me started on how Canada's dirty oil is magically exempt from the 2007 energy bill that otherwise prevents the US government from buying oil that pollutes more than regular oil does. Of course, Americans have their own dirty oil to worry about, what with politicians pushing to tap into 21 billion barrels of US oil offshore.

And all that oil has to be shipped to its destinations. The life-smothering devastation that strikes the seas every time there's an oil spill on tankers or offshore drilling sites is enough to make any dolphin lover weep. In 2007, 10 accidental oil spills leaked somewhere between 7 and 700 tons each, and three leaked even more. If you think the *Exxon Valdez* made a heartbreaking mess sliming the coast of Alaska with 37,000 tons back in 1989, you'll cringe when you realize it was actually one of the smallest of the major oil spills of the last 30 years (in 35th place), according to International Tanker Owners Pollution Federation Limited. A devastating 63,000 tons spilled off the coast of Spain in 2002, and 1991 was particularly bad, with 260,000 tons dumped near Angola and 144,000 off the coast of Italy.

The industry has been painfully slow to take any preventive action. Shipping companies have until 2015 to phase out vulnerable single-hulled ships in European and American waters, but by 2003, only half of the planet's tanker fleets had been converted to double hulls.

America's 150-plus operational oil refineries are also heavy polluters, emitting all sorts of volatile organic compounds (VOCs), including carcinogenic benzene, as well as smog-inducing sulfur dioxide, nitrogen oxides, and carbon monoxide. You don't want to live downwind from one of these babies.

Shockingly, processing sticky tar sands oil uses **MORE FOSSIL FUELS THAN IT PUTS OUT.**

Finally, let's not forget the ecological ramifications tied to waging war in the name of oil (not that this happens—wars are fought for freedom and democracy, of course). Oil fires, often set as acts of sabotage in conflict zones, come with their own special legacy. According to the Worldwatch Institute, the fires set in Kuwait by Iraqi soldiers in the first Gulf War released a ghastly 500 million tons of carbon dioxide into the air, poisoning crops, livestock, and water supplies far and wide. The country is still recovering to this day.

Buying a Car: If you need to buy wheels, think small. The smaller the car, the lighter it'll be, the fewer earthly resources went into it, and the less fuel you'll need to use it. Unless you're hauling cargo up snowy mountain faces, ditch the four-wheel or all-wheel drive—it'll just suck up more fuel (up to 10% more, in fact). Power windows, seats, and mirrors all draw more power and add weight to the car.

I know, I know—you want names. Everyone and his car-loving uncle puts out a list of the greenest rides, but before you buy, look up a car's MPG, estimated annual fuel cost, and carbon footprint at the federal site **fueleconomy.gov**. My favorite ranking site is actually the American Council for an Energy-Efficient Economy (ACEEE), which publishes *ACEEE's Green Book: The Environmental Guide to Cars & Trucks* (available online at **greenercars .org**). The ACEEE assesses automakers for fuel economy and emissions, factors in the pollution from manufacturing the car and producing and distributing the fuel, and then tosses in pollution from the car's tailpipe and evaluates the health problems caused by each pollutant. The group even accounts for the power plant pollution created by plug-in cars. On a scale from 0 to 100, the greenest car of 2008 got a 57. It was the **Honda Civic GX**, which, interestingly enough, beat out the Toyota Prius and the Civic Hybrid for overall eco-ness. The GX runs on natural gas, which burns much cleaner and cheaper, but natural gas

Toyota and Honda produce some of the GREENEST CARS on the market to date.

pumps are harder to come by (though the GX can go about 235 miles on one tank). If you've got natural gas at home, you'll want to get your hands on the GX's home refueling system.

The 2008 list of the "meanest" vehicles for the environment was topped by the Volkswagen Touareg SUV, which scored a dismal 14. The Hummer, GMC Yukon, Jeep Cherokee, and a bunch of luxury cars rounded off the rest of the meanie list. *ACEEE's Green Book* provides rankings for all vehicle types, so you can look up the greenest compact pickup or midsize wagon.

Toyota and **Honda** produce some of the greenest cars on the market to date. American cars, on the other hand, have lagged at the back of the eco pack. According to the Environmental Defense Fund, vehicles produced by the Big Three automakers—Chrysler, GM, and Ford—spew out much more carbon dioxide every year than the largest power company in the States (which includes nearly 60 coal-burning power plants). Chrysler actually forked out a record $30.3 million fine in 2007 for violating federal fuel efficiency requirements.

Ford, in particular, has faced an onslaught of attacks from environmentalists for churning out the biggest gas guzzlers with the lowest overall fuel efficiency (getting fewer miles per gallon than the Model T!), but it gained some credibility when it promised to turn half of its fleet into hybrids by the year 2010. Then, 6 months later, in the summer of 2006, it dropped that pledge like a hot potato. Instead, it promised to double the number of cars it makes that run on alternative fuels, like corn ethanol blend E85—a move many environmentalists consider a cop-out (see page 281 for a discussion of problems with biofuels). Now Ford vows to make fewer large cars and GM is closing four SUV and truck factories. Not for altruistic reasons, of course, but because Americans are growing less and less keen on spending their entire paychecks at the pumps.

If you don't need to drive every day, why shoulder the cost of a car all by yourself? Look into getting joint custody with your sister up the street. Or easier still, check out **auto-sharing programs** near you, which allow you to pay as you drive. Two alternatives are **zipcar.com** and **carsharing.net**. And don't forget to **carpool**. What's the point of three colleagues driving to work from the same part of town in three separate cars? More and more highways even have special carpooling lanes to encourage the practice.

Hybrids: The modern hybrid hit the streets in 1999 with the introduction of the Honda Insight, but it was largely ignored until the price of gas went through the roof. Now hybrids are the hottest cars in Hollywood, and over a million Priuses have been sold. So what are they exactly? Hybrids cross electric motors with gasoline engines to bring you better fuel efficiency—well, most of them, anyway. Most cars, hybrid or not, don't get quite as many miles per gallon as advertised.

And beware of poser hybrids, like the 2008 Chevy Malibu Hybrid, which gets only 2 miles per gallon more than the regular Malibu. Same goes for the Saturn Aura Green Line. Being what's called "mild hybrids," they use the energy generated from the battery for extra oomph and peppy acceleration—not real fuel savings. Mild hybrids can't actually drive in battery mode. Hybrid batteries have a large environmental footprint, so why waste it on a half-assed hybrid?

BEWARE OF POSER HYBRIDS *that get only 2 miles per gallon more than the regular models.*

Don't forget to look into federal and state tax incentives for buying hybrids (**whybuyhybrid.com**). And if you're thinking of buying a used hybrid, find out when the warranty expires, whether it covers the battery, and whether it's transferable. It's a good idea to ask whether the battery has been changed. Be aware that it generally needs to be replaced after about 8 to 10 years—and that's when most warranties expire. Replacing it will cost you a few grand. Make sure yours gets recycled. The nickel metal hydride battery in there may be much less toxic than nickel cadmium batteries, but it still doesn't belong in the landfill.

Electric Cars: GM might have killed the electric car in the '90s, but the good news is it's back from the dead, at least partially. At this point you've got a few types to pick from. First you've got the low-speed types capped at 25 miles an hour. They're often found on campuses and at airports and are being embraced by some earth-lovin' commuters happy to stick to roads with speed limits of 35 miles per hour or less (check out **zenncars.com** or **commutercars.com**). Then you've got the full-speed-ahead types, including the sexy George Clooney–endorsed all-electric **Tesla Roadster**, a sports car with a top speed of 125 miles per hour. It goes 225 miles between charges, though you'll need a fat bank account for this one. At this point the selection of electric vehicles on the road is still pretty limited for Americans, but expect to see more of them at dealerships by 2010.

*The planet would be better off if you bought a car even **A YEAR OR TWO OLD** instead of a new one.*

Or forget waiting for the dealerships to get on board and build your own. It'll run you about $10,000, and it's best to start off with a car that's under 10 years old (though many electric vehicles are old jalopies). According to **evalbum.com** (a great resource-heavy site with links to suppliers), "most conversions are fast enough to get a speeding ticket on any highway." (Order a copy of *Convert It* by Michael Brown and Shari Prange from **electroauto .com** for a step-by-step guide.) Hybrids can also be converted to plug-ins relatively easily and get a good 100 miles per gallon (**hymotion.com**).

Buying Used: Yes, more fuel-efficient models keep rolling onto the lot, but the truth is, unless you're planning on getting an electric car or a hot new model that's vastly more

RENTING A HYBRID

Need to rent a car for a week or the weekend? Most rental companies offer hybrid models these days. If it costs a little more, just think—you'll easily make up the difference with all the gas you save! If a hybrid isn't available, rent a Honda Civic or any of the other fuel-efficient vehicles listed at **greenercars.org**.

efficient than most vehicles, the planet would be better off if you bought one even just a year or two old. That way you're not supporting new-car culture and fueling all the mining and chemical brewing that comes with it.

But you want to make sure that whatever previously owned car you're purchasing (a.k.a. reusing, the second *R* of environmentalism!), you're getting the most fuel-efficient one in its class. Scope out older models at **greenercars.org** for ideas.

Remember: the newer the car, the cleaner it runs. Your 17-year-old Corolla might still get good mileage, but tailpipe emissions have been subject to a massive cleanup operation since then and you're spewing more than your fair share. Pre-1996 models account for only about a quarter of the miles driven on American roads, but they manage to cough up over two-thirds of the total air pollution! And many get off the hook for choking up our air because several states with emissions testing programs (Maine, New Hampshire, Louisiana, North Carolina, and Vermont) don't even test pre-1996 cars. Even if you pass, you're being tested against emissions standards that were in place the year you got your car (say, 1992).

When it's time to put her down, look into scrapping incentives in your area. Colorado has a Repair Your Air Campaign salvage program. California has a vehicle buyback program. Texas's program is called the David McDavid (poor guy) Texas Vehicle Buy Back Program.

Auto Maintenance: Need an oil change? Americans dump about 200 million gallons of used motor oil in the trash, down sewer drains, and on the ground every year. Such a shame, when it could be recycled (in

IDLING CARS ARE THE DEVIL'S TOOL

So you're sitting in your car, waiting. Is your engine running? Hope not. Nationwide, idling slurps back 1.5 million gallons of gasoline and churns out about 40,000 tons of carbon dioxide each and every day! If every American driver cut back on 5 minutes of idling a day, we'd save a heaping 1.4 billion gallons of fuel a year! That's a hell of a lot of dough saved and pollution prevented.

But it takes more gas to turn a car on and off then it does to leave it running, right? Wrong. If you're going to be waiting more than 10 seconds, it's smarter to turn it off. Even if you're more concerned about your cash flow than about ice floes, cutting back on idling makes sense.

TOP 10 TIPS FOR FUEL-SMART DRIVING

Slow down. You'll use 10% more fuel driving at 75 miles an hour than if you stick to 65. **1**

Chill out. Jackrabbit starts, rapid acceleration, and aggressive driving use up to 40% more fuel than following the speed limit. **2**

Stay cool—by rolling down the windows when not on the highway, that is. Switching on the AC ups your fuel needs by 20% in the city. **3**

Pump up. Proper tire pressure can reduce your greenhouse gas emissions by an eighth of a ton a year. Cold temps can decrease air pressure in your tires, so get your gauge out more often in winter. **4**

Partner up. If you've got a 60-mile round-trip commute, carpooling could save you nearly $4,000 over driving alone, according to St. Louis's RideFinders. **5**

Don't tire yourself out. Heavily treaded snow tires suck back more fuel than do all-season tires. Unless you live in serious snow country, there's no need for them. If you're in the market for new tires, ask for **Michelin Energy** **6** MXV4 passenger tires or other low-rolling resistance tires. You'll use up to 5% less fuel and significantly reduce emissions.

Use your feet. Leave your car at home if you're just going to grab a carton of milk around the corner. If you're running around doing errands, walk between stores rather than moving the car three blocks. This is especially important come winter, when engines burn 50% more fuel on short trips than in summer. **7**

Cool it. Newer, computer-controlled engines don't need to warm up for more than 30 seconds. **8**

Dump out your trunk. Driving around with golf clubs in winter and a bag of salt in summer only weighs down your car and uses more fuel. **9**

Create an exit strategy. Get out of your car and hop on a bus, subway, train, or bike. One public bus full of passengers takes roughly 40 cars off the road in rush hour, saving 168 tons of greenhouse gases and over 18,000 gallons of gasoline per year! **10**

fact, re-refining used oil takes 50% to 85% less energy than refining crude oil). Keep your eyes peeled for brands like **America's Choice re-refined motor oil** (**ac-rerefined.com**). If you change your own oil, ask your municipality what you should do with it. Many will take it, as long as it's in a clean, leak-proof container. Plus, most service stations, repair shops, and quick-lube joints will accept used oil and used oil filters. Check with **earth911.org** for options near you.

As for cleaning products, why dish out for heavy-duty cleaning chems when you can make your own nontoxic car cleaners with all-natural ingredients (¼ cup liquid castile soap and hot water will do as a body wash; a blend of vinegar and water works on windows). And watch where you wash! Even if you're using the most biodegradable of suds, water advocates and many municipalities

Americans dump abut 200 **MILLION GALLONS OF USED MOTOR OIL** *in the trash, down sewer drains, and on the ground every year.*

recommend taking your car to an automated car wash where water is recycled and properly treated before it's dumped into sewers. It's much greener than letting your soapy water drip down your driveway, rinsing chemicals that damage aquatic life into nearby waterways. If you insist on doing it yourself, suds up on a grassy surface (often called a lawn) to reduce runoff.

ALTERNATIVE FUELS

It seems like there are a million and one ways you can fill 'er up these days, at least if you've got your eye on prototype cars. But in terms of what's available to most of us as we speak, there are only a few alternative routes to tanking up.

Diesel: Diesel's got a dirty rep, but it's actually more fuel-efficient than gas and, as such, emits less carbon dioxide. Three years ago, I would have told you that diesel is ultimately dirtier than gasoline because it's less refined and emits more sooty particulate matter (kind of obvious when you stand behind an idling tractor trailer). But new regs have mandated the introduction of cleaner diesel. The diesel currently at the pumps contains 97% less polluting sulfur

Any diesel engine can run on **BIODIESEL** *blends.*

than the old stuff. Nonetheless, more crude oil is used to make diesel than to make gasoline, and petroleum is always a bad thing, so diesel will never get two green thumbs-ups.

Biodiesel: Any diesel engine can run on biodiesel blends without being converted. The biodiesel fuels you'll find at rare pumps tend to come in blends of 5% to 20% agriculturally grown soy or other biological matter, and 80% to 95% regular diesel. Cornell's David

WHERE SHOULD I TANK UP?

Figuring out which oil company is the cleanest and greenest is like deciding who was the best lip-syncher, Milli or Vanilli. They're all bad. Pretty much every international oil company has a record of nasty spills and/or exploiting countries in the developing world. But according to rankings by both the Sierra Club and *The Better World Handbook,* ExxonMobil and ConocoPhillips are the bottom of the barrel. ExxonMobil, in particular, has been singled out for boycotts by Greenpeace, Amnesty International, the Natural Resources Defense Council, and more; and it is maligned by enviros for long denying that fossil fuels contribute to climate change and for running ads condemning the Kyoto Protocol.

Though far from blemish-free, **Sunoco** is your best bet. It is the only oil company to sign the Ceres Principles for environmentally sound business practices. **BP** also appears near the top of the list. For more details, check out **sierraclub.org/sierra/pickyourpoison** or **betterworldhandbook. com/gasoline.htm** . And don't overfill your tank! Even small spills contribute to pollution.

Pimental says that making soy-based biodiesel sucks back 57% more energy than it produces. Research out of the University of Minnesota insists that soy-based diesel isn't so bad—that it produces 93% more energy than is used to make it and pumps out 41% less in greenhouse gases than regular gas does (the same study trashed corn-based ethanol as being very inefficient). Obviously, the debate rages on. For more on the biodiesel controversy, see the discussion of ethanol that follows.

Vegan alert: in place of soy, tallow is sometimes used in biodiesel blends.

Ethanol: E10 is regular gas with 10% ethanol, and it's available at pretty much every pump. More and more cars, however, are running on an 85% ethanol blend called E85. Since you get lower mileage on ethanol blends, manufacturers make E85 models with larger fuel tanks. Ethanol is said to reduce your greenhouse gas emissions, in part because corn actually sucks up carbon dioxide as it grows on farmers' fields before it's processed into gasoline, though Cornell's David Pimental says that making corn-based ethanol actually uses 29% more energy than it creates. Also, one 2008 Department of Energy study found that ethanol blends can damage catalytic converters by overheating them.

Either way, getting our fuel from the fields—whether it's corn-based ethanol or soy-based biodiesel—comes with a whole other set of problems. Both crops are largely genetically modified, loaded with pesticides, and heavily treated with fossil fuel–based fertilizers. And turning food into fuel is only driving the global food crisis, triggering serious shortages as well as riots around the world. In a matter of months, onlookers went from calling ethanol the "Holy Grail" to muttering, "Holy crap, did we ever mess this up." Some are working on alternatives, including making ethanol from agricultural residues like straw, cornstalks, switchgrass, and forestry leftovers. We'll have to wait and see who wins at the pumps, but at the rate corn-based ethanol is being subsidized, there's no denying who has a head start.

Straight Vegetable Oil (SVO): If you dream of breaking free from Big Oil and pouring filtered deep-fryer grease from a local burger joint into your diesel tank, you need a straight vegetable oil (SVO) conversion kit; otherwise, you'll end up mucking everything up (to put it technically). You basically need a separate hose and a tank- and oil-warming system, which will cost up to $1,500. Check out **frybrid.com**, **plantdrive.com**, **greasecar.com**, or **goldenfuelsystems.com** for all the greasy details.

Natural Gas and Propane: You may have seen buses, taxis, and commercial vehicles powered by natural gas or propane. Both are fossil fuels, just like gas or diesel, and digging them out and piping them to us comes with heavy environmental implications, but both burn cleaner, produce fewer toxic pollutants and up to 20% less in global warming emissions over their life cycles, and cost less (30% to 40% less). Plus, they're sourced in North America rather than overseas. They're not perfect, but they're an option. And a natural gas tank is why Honda's Civic GX wins greenest car of the year. Conventional gas cars can be converted to run on the stuff for about $4,000 to $6,000, but they don't burn the fuel quite as cleanly as factory-made types. These really only make sense if you have a natural gas source at a station close by or in your own house, if you get a home refueling appliance that hooks up to your natural gas line (**fuelmaker.com** makes some).

MOTORCYCLES AND SCOOTERS

Ever daydream about hitting the open road on a badass cruiser? Sure, the gas tank may be tiny and you might get more miles per gallon from your two-wheeler, but most motorcycles expel 10 times more carbon monoxide and 90 times more polluting hydrocarbon than the average car, according to the EPA. "How can this be?" you cry. Well, cars are subject to much more stringent regulations than either scooters or motorbikes. And most bike makers have been slow to clean up their acts.

With new motorbike pollution standards being phased in starting in 2006, new models of motorcycles and scooters should have pollution-curbing catalytic converters, which can cut hydrocarbon emissions by 60%. Fuel injection systems and oxygen sensors also help with emission reduction. Trouble is, most people take off catalytic converters and emissions canisters after they get their ride home because they think that stuff weighs down the bike. But you would never do such a thing, now would you?

Most motorcycles expel 10 TIMES MORE carbon monoxide and 90 TIMES MORE polluting hydrocarbon than the average car.

Whether you're opting for a scooter or a hog, steer clear of smaller two-stroke engines. Without getting into all the nitty-gritty, two-stroke engines are lighter and relatively peppy, but they're completely unregulated and are literally the dirtiest things on wheels. We're talking the same inefficient, highly polluting types of engines you find in lawn mowers, Jet Skis, and snowmobiles. Although nearly every motorcycle now has a four-stroke, far fewer scooters have made the switch. So scooters, while cute and super–fuel-efficient, can actually be the worst option—polluting even more for their size than large diesel trucks! Unless you get one of the **four-stroke types**. All new **Honda** scooters and motorbikes are four-stroke.

Scooters can actually be the WORST option— polluting EVEN MORE for their size than large diesel trucks.

PSST, HEY YOU THERE, DRIVING TO WORK ALONE

Imagine if your boss offered you free or discounted monthly transit passes, car pool–matching services, subsidized van pools, and strong telework programs—all to discourage you from driving to work alone. Well, the EPA's Best Workplaces for Commuters program facilitates just such initiatives. For a list of participating employers and cities, check out **bestworkplaces.org**

Better yet, get yourself an **e-bike**! These babies can look like slick little scooters, some even look more like speed motorbikes, but their low-powered motors aren't generally able to drive faster than 20 miles an hour. Perfect for inner-city commutes and errand running.

BICYCLES

Something happens to many of us between our early tricycle days and adulthood that makes us shun our two-wheeled friends. Sure a good 100 million Americans own bikes, but are you actually riding yours? If you cycled 4 miles to work instead of driving, you'd stop 15 pounds of climate-changing pollutants from billowing out your tailpipe every day (the only emissions would come from your breath). Plus, it would save you a hell of a lot of money in fuel (and transit passes). It seems people are finally starting to clue in to the advantages of

In 2005, BIKES OUTSOLD CARS in the US for the first time since the oil embargo of the early '70s.

cycling: in 2005, bikes outsold cars in the US for the first time since the oil embargo of the early '70s, and more North Americans are biking to work than ever. Nothing like paying a fortune at the pumps to get people pedaling again! And did you know that 100 bikes can be built with the same amount of energy and resources it takes to build one midsize car?

Buying used is a great, cheap way to give bikes a second life. Or forget buying your own bike if your city has some conveniently scattered around town. For an annual fee of $40, riders in Washington DC can tap into the city's key card–activated **SmartBikes** for up to 3 hours at a time. Denver and Minneapolis both have **bike share programs** of their own, and San Francisco and Chicago are also launching systems. With its network of "bicycle boulevards," locking facilities, and cycling programs, Portland, Oregon, is considered the country's most bike-friendly city.

AIRPLANES

Who doesn't love the feeling you get when you're high in the air on a plane, heading for somewhere—anywhere—different? Well, aviophobes for one, who find nothing but fear in the friendly skies. Or business travelers who spend more time with flight attendants than with their kids. But for most people, flying is kind of magical. Too bad that stuff coming

WHAT'S MORE POLLUTING: DRIVING 200 MILES OR FLYING IT?

Okay, so you live in New York and you have to go to Boston for a wedding next weekend. Environmentally speaking, should you do the 4-hour drive or take the 1-hour flight? Well, my favorite carbon travel calculator, courtesy of **nativeenergy.com**, says your round-trip drive to Boston in a midsize car would put out 400 pounds (0.2 ton) of pollutants. The plane trip would produce 330 pounds (0.165 ton) per passenger. You might initially say, "Aha, I'm better off flying." But not so fast. Don't forget that the plane might be two-thirds full, but it still has to lug those 30 empty seats. And factor in the round-trip cab ride to and from the airport in both cities (about 40 pounds of emissions—more if you're idling in traffic on both ends). Of course, details matter, and if you were doing the road trip in a Prius instead of a regular sedan, those emissions would be slashed by half. If you were on a turboprop plane, your plane emission would drop by nearly a third, but turboprops aren't very common at this point.

Avoid the headache altogether and take the **train** from core to core in 3½ hours flat with little green guilt (a total 172 pounds for the round-trip, or 0.42 pound per passenger mile) and even less stress. Worried about your budget as much as you fret about the planet? Hop a bus for about a meager $12 each way and you'll rack up a measly 76 pounds (0.038 ton) of emissions.

out of the engines isn't fairy dust. Air travel is actually the fastest-growing source of greenhouse gas emissions in the world. It's currently behind at least 3% of man-made greenhouse gas pollution (though eco activists say that number would be doubled or tripled if we factored in the extra impact of spewing emissions in the upper atmosphere, known as radiative forcing).

The industry says airlines have already improved fuel efficiency and CO_2 emissions by almost 20% over the past 10 years and plan to be another 25% more efficient by 2020. And experiments are being done with biofuels and aerodynamics, but hard-cores will tell you that staying grounded is the only green option.

Airlines: Unfortunately, there's no such thing as an eco-friendly airline, but pretty much every company is using the high price of fuel as a good reason to cut back on the amount of weight on board, to add aerodynamic upswept wingtips, and, in some cases, even to paint their fleets a lighter color to draw less heat. If you want to get a seat on one of today's greenest planes, though, make sure it's a turboprop. **Turboprops** are said to have an efficiency rating halfway between a car and a train, and they fly half as high as a modern jet, which means they don't suffer from the same amplifying impact of spewing emissions high in the sky. Continental Airlines announced that it's putting turboprops on short-haul routes out of Newark in 2008, claiming that the airline will save about 30% on fuel per seat. Frontier Airlines also uses a few turboprops on its routes out of Denver. Even China is making turboprops now. If you want to see more of these puppies in the sky, bug the airlines.

.Green Tags: No matter what, flying the skies is never earth-friendly, and many eco heads (especially in Europe) have sworn off it. That's easier said than done in a giant country like the US when you've got relatives 3,000 miles away. But there is one thing you can do to assuage your guilt and ease your impact: get **green tags**, a.k.a. carbon offsets. With green tags, you offset the carbon your flight creates by supporting renewable energy or planting trees for anywhere from $5 to $15 per ton of emissions.

*P*lanting a DOZEN TREES *to neutralize your flight is dissed by eco heads as an* IMPERMANENT SOLUTION.

Just know that all tags are not created equal—nor are they judged equally by environmentalists. Planting a dozen trees to neutralize your flight might seem wonderfully idealistic, but eco heads dis it as an impermanent solution (those trees may be chopped down or die in a drought) and point out that trees take ages to mature to the point where they absorb significant amounts of carbon from the atmosphere. You want to look for offsets that have third-party certification (like

HONEY, DO I LOOK FAT ON THIS PLANE?

You know that extra 10 pounds you snuck on over the last few years? Well, according to the Centers for Disease Control and Prevention, the extra weight Americans put on in the last decade of the 20th century on average caused airlines to burn 350 million more gallons of fuel in 2000. That's a whopping 3.8 million tons in extra CO_2 emissions and other pollutants! Now there's a fresh reason to hit the gym before you hit the beaches of Cancún.

Green-e [green-e.org] or **Gold Standard** [cdmgoldstandard.org]), focus on permanent renewable-energy projects (not just screwing in lightbulbs), calculate radiative forcing on flights (mentioned on page 286), and can attest to "additionality" (basically, ensuring that the money goes to projects that wouldn't have happened otherwise).

Tufts University did a review of carbon offsets, and the only American offsetter that got an unqualified thumbs-up was **NativeEnergy**. Its credits go toward developing renewable-energy projects on Native American lands and farmer-owned wind, solar, and methane projects. Offsets in NativeEnergy's "help build" model go toward funding new projects, and its Vintage offsets/credits go toward creating market demand for existing projects (nativeenergy.com). NativeEnergy also has lifestyle and personal travel calculators, as well as conference and small-business calculators. For more on who Tufts disses and dotes on, check out tufts.edu/tie/tci/carbonoffsets. Want more rankings? See cleanair-coolplanet .org/ConsumersGuidetoCarbonOffsets.pdf.

TOURISM

See the world, they say. So you do. Whether you're saving up your pennies for a 6-month backpacking adventure in the Far East or figuring out how to get as far away as possible from your desk job with your week's vacation, we all need to break away from our daily lives and see what life is like over yonder. But what we think of as a perfect vacation setting can mean just the opposite for locals. We wish away the rain; they call it a drought. We see refreshing swimming pools and green golf courses; they witness a major divesting of precious water sources. Even as the locals are fighting over loaves of bread in countries on the verge of economic collapse, the ripest crops in the land are trucked to hotels to make sure we visitors are well fed. Yes, foreign dollars are wanted; and no, no one's saying you have to stay home for the rest of your life. But it's important to realize some of the impacts of our wandering ways.

Cruises: Cruises are known for their gluttony and extravagance (I mean, really, is a skating rink necessary aboard a boat?), so maybe it's not surprising that they're also extremely wasteful. Still the stats are startling. According to the international eco org Oceana, the average cruise ship produces about 7 tons of garbage and 30,000 gallons of sewage, as well as smokestack and emission pollution equivalent to 12,000 cars, each and every day.

In the winter of 2006, the Cruise Lines International Association and Conservation International announced that sensitive marine areas (including coral reefs, shellfish growing

The average cruise ship produces about 7 TONS of garbage and 30,000 GALLONS of sewage, as well as smokestack and emission pollution equivalent to 12,000 cars, each and every day.

areas, and protected areas) would be incorporated into navigational charts as "no wastewater discharge" zones. Industry reps say they also voluntarily treat all sewage and discharge when ships are within 4 nautical miles of shore. But what about other areas? Environmentalists maintain that even treated wastewater fails to meet federal standards. Hardly a carnival for aquatic life.

Water Usage: Even if you're not cruisin' on water, you're probably going through way too much of it—whether for pools, golf courses, water parks, or even in showers and toilets (many hotels have thousands of guest rooms—when you think about it, that's a hell of a lot of flushing). France, Greece, Italy, and Spain have already lost half of their original wetlands—in large part because of tourist activities, according to a report by the WWF. The report points out that tourists and tourist facilities in the Mediterranean suck up four times more water than locals do. In dry regions, this can be an especially serious problem.

Souvenirs: When you're out and about in the world, make sure that whatever shopping you do isn't leaving a dent in the local ecosystems as well as your wallet. Trinkets and carvings made from elephant tusks may be legal in the country you're visiting (as they are in Hong Kong or South Africa), but you may need special permits to export them, and you definitely aren't allowed to bring them into the US. You can get pretty coral jewelry, shells, and sea sponges from many vendors in the Caribbean, but keep in mind that you're making an ecologically unwelcome purchase. If you spot a giant clam shell on the shores of the Philippines, leave it be. And even if your eco hotel is engaged in protecting sea turtles on the beach, souvenir kiosks are often all too willing to target these endangered creatures for their attractive shells. Also, stay away from carvings made from endangered woods like rosewood, ebony, or African blackwood.

Thinking of getting a nice shahtoosh shawl on your travels in India? What harm could come from wool, right? Well, three of the highly endangered Tibetan antelopes that provide this wool are killed for the making of just one shawl, according to the wildlife trade-monitoring network TRAFFIC. Wherever you plan to go in the world, the old adage "take nothing but photographs, leave nothing but footprints" should be your mantra.

Ecotourism: It's no surprise that the world of ecotourism is booming when we all want to travel but stress out about the greenest way to do it. Just note that the label is casually affixed to any excursion that involves seeing trees or wild animals—any form of nature really. Usually a caravan of SUVs truck well-meaning tourists into pristine locations considered untouched by the masses. Sound magical? The problem is, as wildlife activists will tell you, such areas should remain untouched; daily carloads of people disturb wildlife

The effects of ECOTOURISM *have gotten so bad on certain trails in Peru and Nepal that they've been nicknamed* "COCA-COLA TRAIL" *and* "TOILET PAPER TRAIL."

and degrade fragile ecosystems. It's gotten so bad on certain trails in Peru and Nepal that they've been nicknamed "Coca-Cola trail" and "toilet paper trail."

So, whether you're planning a homegrown American adventure or a trip around the world, how do you know if you're picking a responsible tour operator? Ask the tour company for its environmental and social policies. A group that discusses conservation and ecosystem education is more likely to be a true ecotour company, rather than a plain old adventure or

nature tour company. Ecotours should include local and indigenous communities in their planning, development, and operation (you don't want all the money leaving the country or community). Ask whether local guides are used. Prod ecotour operators about whether any of the tour fee goes to local conservation groups. And note that ecotours should allow only small groups.

It might seem a little unsavory, but the International Ecotourism Society suggests that you ask your hotel how it disposes of its waste and sewage. It's a huge problem, even in ecotourism meccas such as Costa

AMERICA'S GREENEST HOTELS

You don't have to leave the country to check into an ecologically inspired room for the night. You just have to decide what mood you're in. Hipsters looking for funky boutique hotel vibes should check out (or check into) the many incarnations of **Kimpton Hotels** and their EarthCare commitments (**kimptonhotels.com**). You can't go wrong when you bed down at a hotel that's certified by LEED (Leadership in Energy and Environmental Design), like the sleek 'n' green **Orchard Garden Hotel** in San Francisco (**theorchardgardenhotel.com**). Even bigger chains are getting in on the act. **Starwood Hotels & Resorts** are opening 20 eco-chic, LEED-certified **Element Hotels** in New York, Chicago, Vegas, and elsewhere (**starwoodhotels.com**).

Looking for something a little more quaint? The solar and wind-powered, straw-bale **Las Manos B&B** nestled at the foot of the Rockies in Buena Vista, Colorado, should do the trick (**lasmanosbandb.com**). How 'bout more of a secluded sanctuary that's still in harmony with the earth? The **El Monte Sagrado** living resort and spa in Taos, New Mexico, has got that one pegged (**elmontesagrado.com**). If that's still too manicured for you, snuggle up on the natural latex and wool beds of Maiden Rock, Wisconsin's, farmhouse-style **Journey Inn** (**journeyinn .net**). Or splurge a little (okay, a lot) to get lost in nature with one or two wonderful nights at the **Lodge on Little St. Simons Island**. You literally need to take a boat to get to this private island off the Georgia coast, which has 10 wild acres to wander through (**littlestsimonsisland.com**). For serious honeymoon luxury without boundaries, the conscientious cliffside opulence of Big Sur's **Post Ranch Inn** should leave you drooling (**postranchinn.com**).

For more ideas on ecologically minded places to hang your hat, from ecological trailer rentals and adorable inns to corporate chains and resorts around the globe, check **greenhotels .com**. **Organicholidays.com** is a great guide to small hotels, bed-and-breakfasts, and farm accommodations where organic food and produce is used, from Canada to Crete. The respected third-party body Green Seal generally certifies more mainstream lodgings (**greenseal.org**).

WWF EXPEDITIONS

For that extra green stamp of approval, travel with one of the most trusted wildlife protection groups on the planet—the **World Wildlife Fund**. Through this nonprofit, you can sail to the Antarctic, glide down the Amazon on a riverboat, or visit the monarch butterflies of Mexico. All the while your guides will teach you about conservation efforts, feed you with local ingredients whenever possible, and put you up in charming, sustainable accommodations. And all the profits go to the WWF's conservation efforts (**worldwildlife.org/travel**).

Rica. Sewage runoff can wreak havoc on coral reefs, as well as on all sorts of flora and fauna in local lakes and rivers—wherever the dumping occurs.

Germany's TO DO! awards are a highly reputable measure of sound ecotourism models. Check **to-do-contest.org** for inspiring award winners. Green Globe 21 is a green certification body that supposedly does on-site visits, but note that hotels with a Green Globe Affiliate stamp haven't necessarily taken any action to improve their property. All the stamp signals is that the hotel has paid a certain amount to Green Globe, that it's aware of its environmental problems, and that it hopes to improve—but it doesn't have to prove that it will.

IT'S ALL FUN AND GAMES

(UNTIL SOMEONE LOSES A PLANET)

Do you get through trying Mondays by dreaming of your week off in the woods? Do you break away from it all on weekends to cut fresh powder down a snowy slope or play a round on some breezy greens? Maybe you bliss out on a yoga mat to burn off a little stress. Now, I bet you're thinking, "Here comes Ms. Buzz Kill, ready to ruin my fun. Do I really have to worry about the ecological ramifications of my one joy in life?" Relax. I know there's no coming between you and your favorite source of pleasure. Just know that there's a dark side to everything—but if the biggest shopping season of the year can be turned into an earthy event, even your golf game can get greener.

SPORTS

Most athletes are well aware of how the environment affects them—smog, for instance, can make biking a bummer and an unusually warm winter can make snow sports a no-go. However, few enthusiasts have thought about the ecological ramifications of their arena, pool, or ski hill on the earth, despite all the chemical use, energy consumption, and habitat destruction that may be involved. Well, that's all starting to turn around. The NFL is planting thousands of trees every year to offset the million pounds of CO_2 created by the Super Bowl. NASCAR is finally phasing out leaded gas. Now it's time for a pep talk on how to improve our own game.

Ball Sports: Nearly gone are the days when balls were made of natural rubber. Soccer balls, basketballs, and volleyballs are made mostly of that eco outlaw PVC. Polyurethane is also polluting to manufacture but not quite so bad. Real leather is no saint, but at least it eventually breaks down. There's also been plenty of scandal around soccer balls—in particular, being stitched by 10-year-olds in the developing world. You can play with a clear conscience if you order eco-certified, fair-trade soccer balls, basketballs, volleyballs, footballs, and ultimate Frisbees through **fairtradesports.com**. It's not certified fair-trade, but **Wilson** has come out with a Rebound "green" recycled-rubber basketball, so keep your eyes on the ball (**wilson.com**); you'll find it at **sportsauthority.com**.

Watercraft: Some water sports, like the art of gliding across the skin of a lake in a carved-out kayak, are perfectly sustainable; others, not so much. Take personal recreational watercraft like Jet Skis. A 1998 report by the state of California Air Resources Board calling for tighter regs on marine engines states that a full day of jet-skiing on a 100-horsepower watercraft releases more polluting hydrocarbons and nitrogen oxides than driving a 1998 passenger car 100,000 miles! No joke. The Earth Island Institute reports that the pollution from personal watercraft actually causes chromosomal damage in fish.

Ultrapolluting two-stroke engines power the vast majority of motorboats in this country, which affects you, water-skiers, and wakeboarders. Investing in **four-stroke** boats and personal watercraft makes an

> A *full day of jet-skiing on a 10-year-old, 100-horsepower watercraft releases* MORE POLLUTING HYDROCARBONS *and nitrogen oxides than driving a 1998 passenger car 100,000 miles!*

enormous difference, ecologically speaking, since they put out 97% less airborne pollution than the two-strokes do. But however many strokes they have, they still make a hell of a lot of noise, and they're still bound to piss off the shore-bound.

Swimming Pools: Swimming, of course, produces zero emissions when you're just flapping your arms around in a lake or ocean, but factor in the impact of heating and chlorinating pools, and you've got a whole other kettle of fish. When chlorine mixes with carbon-containing material like leaves, bugs, dirt, and skin flakes (yum), toxic trihalomethanes like carcinogenic chloroform can form. Belgian researchers found that young kids who swam regularly in chlorinated pools had increased risks of asthma.

Competitive swimmers were at higher risks too. But don't panic, backstroke enthusiasts! There are **chlorine-free pool systems** out there that use UV light, ozone (popular in Europe), and even hydrogen peroxide. And plenty of American pool owners are making the switch to **salt water**. You just need a chlorine generator, about 50 pounds of salt, and soon you'll be testing salt levels, not chlorine levels.

Still, pools require a lot of water to fill, which isn't great during water advisories, and they need frequent topping off in really hot, dry weather. Plus, many of us refuse to swim in anything below 80°F, so wasteful hot-water heaters come into play. If you already own a pool, you can offset some of this by getting a good **solar blanket** and a **solar hot-water heater** (see the American Solar Energy Society's renewable resources directory for solar thermal dealers near you that might do pools: **ases.org**). The rest of you, just visit a community pool.

Golf: They call golf courses "greens," but there's nothing green about these bad boys other than the color. To carve courses out of the natural landscape, acres of forests, wetlands, and wild habitats are often cleared. They're then replaced with non-native grasses that are drenched in pesticides and so much water that rural water tables are lowered and nearby creeks and streams contaminated. I'm

The average American golf course uses about 312,000 GALLONS OF WATER *per day.*

not kidding—the average American golf course uses about 312,000 gallons of water per day, according to the Audubon Society—yes, I said *per day* (and in ultradry areas like Palm Springs, courses suck back closer to a million gallons a day).

But all that's starting to change. More and more courses are reining in their bad behavior. Some spray pesticides only as required rather than every 10 days, water only at night to prevent wasteful evaporation, cut their grass less often, and plant drought-resistant grasses, among other things. A few even collect storm water and purify wastewater to keep the fairways green. Shouldn't all this just be par for the course?

Instead of clearing pristine lands to put in a course, a surprising number of planners are reclaiming contaminated sites, capping them, and then building greens over them. Chicago's **Harborside International Golf Center**, New Jersey's **McCullough's Emerald Golf Links**, and Houston's **Wildcat Golf Club** all turned old landfills into rolling courses.

Audubon International certifies golf courses in its Audubon Cooperative Sanctuary system for water quality protection, resource conservation, and providing wildlife habitats. Not many are certified "gold" (just over a dozen in the US). But a couple thousand courses meet minimal "certified Audubon Sanctuary" standards. Talk to your golf course about taking it up a notch.

Yoga: Even the ancient Indian art of stretching yourself into a pretzel is not immune to modern eco problems. I-am-one-with-the-universe yoga bunnies tend to have no idea that most of the mats they tote to class are made of what Greenpeace calls the most ecologically harmful plastic on the planet—PVC. And don't assume that because a PVC mat is labeled as "100% closed-cell," no chemicals will escape the plastic surface. Come on, you can smell the fumes coming off those pretty pink, purple, and blue things. You're inhaling the chemical softeners—phthalates—that make those mats so squishy. The industry insists phthalates are safe, but the family of hormone disrupters has been banned from kids' toys all across the country.

You might spot mats made from thermal plastic elastomers (TPEs) or polymer resins. These may still be petroleum-based, but they're phthalate-, PVC-, and heavy metal–free yet still have that sticky PVC-style grip. **Barefoot Yoga** carries tons of greener mats, including some made of jute and natural rubber blends, jute and resin blends, as well as TPE mats (though you'll want to avoid the Sticky Mats, since they're made

Most yoga mats are made of what Greenpeace calls the most ECOLOGICALLY HARMFUL PLASTIC on the planet—PVC.

of PVC) (**barefootyoga.com**). On top of selling cork and bamboo yoga blocks, and hemp mat slings, **Gaiam** sells natural rubber and cushy cotton yoga mats, but beware of its PVC-based Yoga Essentials line (including the cute patterned ones) (**gaiam.com**). And note that natural rubber mats are much heavier than PVC (weighing about 5 pounds). You can also get 100% organic hemp mats from **Rawganique.com** or certified organic, fair-trade cotton mats from **Intent** (**intentusa.com**), but these don't have much traction.

Skiing and Snowboarding: Multiply the soil erosion that can happen at a popular kids' sledding spot by a thousand, add superwasteful snowmakers, glaring lights, and heated chair lifts, and you've got yourself a ski hill. Not to mention that every new resort or run destroys many animals' homes, snowmakers can divert valuable water from local streams, and bioaccumulative snow-hardening chemicals end up polluting soil and water.

Some resorts are trying to green up their act, especially since slope lovers are realizing the impact that global warming is having on their favorite activity. Keep Winter Cool warns skiers and snowboarders that climate change could mean fewer ski days, less real snow, more snow guns, wetter seasons—even fewer mountains (**keepwintercool.org**). The National Ski Areas Association's Sustainable Slopes charter acknowledges that greenhouse gases are a real threat to the industry, so the NSAA lobbies government to take broader action and encourages members to cut their emissions (through energy, water, and waste conservation). For details on which hills have been helping to conserve local wildlife, which have eco-friendly snowmakers, and which have water- and energy-saving initiatives, check out **nsaa.org/ nsaa/environment/the_greenroom**.

Keep in mind, though, that the NSAA did come in tenth on a list of America's worst greenwashers in 2005 because its Sustainable Slopes program doesn't put poor performers on probation or have third-party audits. Western

Aspen Mountain has the industry's largest system of SOLAR PANELS.

US slopes are perhaps most honestly and scathingly reviewed by the Ski Area Citizens' Coalition (**skiareacitizens.com**). Its website lets you compare ski resorts by state and ranks the top 10 greenest hills, as well as the top worst hills in the US (graded on their impact of roadless areas, logging, renewable-energy purchases, and more). Scoring A's in the '07/'08

SUSTAINABLE SNOW/SURF/SKATEBOARDS

Dude—you, like, totally need to stop buying boards made with uncool, earth-bashing woods and plastics and get something sustainable instead. **Arbor** makes beautiful snow- and skateboards from bamboo and well-managed woods (**arborsports.com**). Seriously gnarly (do people still say "gnarly"?) **Venture** snowboards are made in a wind-powered Colorado factory with wood certified by the Forest Stewardship Council. You can even get yours with organic hemp or cotton top sheets to help cut back on the use of plastics and solvents (order online at **venturesnowboards.com**).

As for all you water-bound surfers, avoiding the usual boards made of polystyrene foam laced with neurotoxic toluene can be tough, but **Neilson Surfboards** has created a series of boards from soy-based Biofoam (**tomneilsonshapes.com**). Eco surf store **Green Wave** carries those, as well as nontoxic board wax, organic surf gear, and more (**greenwaveeco.com**).

> ## PLAY IT AGAIN
>
> **B**esides carpooling or taking transit to practice, one of the best ways to green your game is to buy your gear used. Trolling craigslist online is one option. And you'll definitely want to track down the nearest **Play It Again Sports** store. Play It Again has everything from golf clubs and wakeboards to baseball bats and football pads. And if sports aren't your thang, they even have treadmills, elliptical machines, and home weights.

report were **Sundance Resort** in Utah (**sundanceresort.com**), **Park City Mountain** in Utah (**parkcitymountain.com**), as well as **Buttermilk** and finally **Aspen Mountain** (two of four Aspen Snowmass hills in Colorado; **aspensnowmass.com**) in the top slot. This tree-hugging resort has the industry's largest system of solar panels, it subsidizes public transit, and it built a low-impact hydro plant that, on its own, prevents the emission of half a million pounds of carbon dioxide.

If you're a fan of **cross-country skiing**, you can glide in peace, knowing you're doing much less damage to the ecosystem than downhill skiing does—as long as the trails don't go through known feeding areas or nesting or breeding grounds. Conservation areas and provincial parks can be great places to ski and often offer other winter activities, such as snowshoeing (which is super-low-impact) and ice-skating at frozen lakes. For great places to cross-country ski and snowshoe across North America, search the Cross Country Ski Areas Association's database at **xcski.org**.

CAMPING

The crackling fire, the starry sky, peeing in the woods—it's enough to dupe you into thinking you're one with nature. Alas, just because your tent is green doesn't mean you are. In fact, honest camping-supply stores will tell you that most of their goods are far from eco-friendly. Seems a tad hypocritical, really, considering how much campers love the outdoors. Of course, if you forage for green supplies as deftly as bears forage for berries, you should be in the clear.

Gear and Tents: Most of the camping world's waterproof synthetic stuff is made with toxic solvents that emit polluting volatile organic compounds (VOCs) and dioxins in production. Lots of backpacks (and even sleeping bags, like Marmot's old Pinnacle Gossamer bags) are coated with Teflon, which is made with a superpersistent chemical, PFOA, found in rivers and bloodstreams everywhere. Whatever isn't coated with Teflon is made with its sister chem, perforated PTFE, found in Gore-Tex. We're surrounded! Now, that's not to say you should toss out your old Gore-Tex gear. W. L. Gore & Associates (the maker of Gore-Tex fabric) says PTFE is so "stable" it won't leach or offgas in landfills. (See page 32 for more on Gore-Tex.)

A lesser evil is nylon waterproofed with silicone, neither of which seems to ruffle as many eco feathers as Gore-Tex and Teflon do. It can be tough to find tents that aren't made with synthetics—and most people really wouldn't want the soggy heavy canvas tents of yesteryear. Still, if that rings your bell, army surplus stores are a good place to look for these (though most have PVC bottoms or have been treated with fungicides).

Honest camping-supply stores will tell you that most of their goods are FAR FROM ECO-FRIENDLY.

As for sleeping bags, your options are looking up. **Marmot** makes an **EcoPro sleeping bag** with 100% recycled fabric and 80% recycled insulation (marmot.com). **Sierra Designs** sleeping bags have recycled insulation made from reclaimed polyester and PET bottles, as well as a coconut husk–based lining (sierra-designs.com). **REI** (rei.com) also carries inflatable sleeping pads made from recycled polyester by **Big Agnes** (bigagnes.com) and nifty bamboo-based **ECO Thermo pads** from **Pacific Outdoor Equipment** (pacoutdoor .com) so that you can bed down with a clear conscience.

Water Purifying: Rather than dropping nasty chlorine or iodine tabs into a bottle of lake water and masking the god-awful taste with some sugary artificial powder, why not invest in a portable filter and truly enjoy that fresh water taste? **Katadyn** ceramic and activated carbon filters are touted by outdoor enthusiasts for removing all harmful bacteria, fungi, cysts, and parasites and a long list of dangerous diseases without any chemicals (katadyn.com). And be sure to pack it in polycarbonate-free canisters like those made by Klean Kanteen (kleankanteen.com).

Alternative-Powered Tech: **Solar-powered, pump-up, shake-up, or windup flashlights** are much wiser options for the woods than the battery-operated kind. If you're rolling your eyes at the prospect of pumping and shaking to get a few minutes of flashlight time, lighten up—you can even make a little dance of it. Although really, 2 minutes of easy cranking will give you a good 80 minutes of light with **Freeplay**'s self-powered **Sherpa Xray LED flashlight** (available at rei.com). Good camping stores like REI should also have solar chargers for your MP3 player, cell phone, or any other portable electronics (not that you really need these out in the wilds, but hey, to each his own). **Crank AM/FM shortwave radios** are also handy when you need a ditty (or a weather forecast) in a jiffy. **Etón** makes some that come with a built-in emergency siren, flashlight, and cell phone charger (etoncorp.com).

Food: All that fresh air and hiking can create a Sasquatch-size appetite. Try to minimize packaging by bringing bulk items such as couscous or rice in big PVC-free baggies (made by **Ziploc** or **Glad**). If you're looking for ideas on what to cook on the trail, pick up the *Leave-No-Crumbs Camping Cookbook* from your local or online bookstore. Individually packaged camp foods create

No BURNING PLASTICS IN THE CAMPFIRE, *unless you want to suck back noxious and* DANGEROUS CARCINOGENS.

a lot of waste—which, by the way, should never be burned. I repeat: no burning plastics in the campfire, unless you want to suck back noxious and dangerous carcinogens, like dioxins, that build up in the food chain! If you're going to buy ready-to-heat camp food, at least go for organic brands like **MaryJanesFarm**, which also comes in burnable packaging (maryjanesfarm.org).

HOLIDAYS AND CELEBRATIONS

I must admit I love a big celebration (hence my 3-day-long birthday party); and while I'm outing myself, I also secretly love Bing Crosby's rendition of "Silver Bells" and think a holiday dedicated to chocolate rabbits isn't so terrible (hey, who doesn't love bunnies?). What's so wrong with events that bring families and friends together for a big meal and maybe a bottle or two of wine? Well, if we were actually taking these moments to savor our relationships and the flavors of life, absolutely nothing. The problem comes when the holiday season warps into the high holidays of consumer culture. Aren't we putting the emphasis on the wrong syl-LA-ble?

Gift Giving: No matter how much you hate malls and the shop-till-you-drop philosophy, there are certain times of the year—birthdays, Christmas, showers, weddings, Hanukkah—when people just expect presents. So why not let your gifts reflect your concern for the environment? For one thing, you can cut back on fossil fuels by supporting **local artisans** and all their wonderful handmade crafts. Hunt down stores that sell hand-dyed scarves or recycled steel sculptures rather than mass-produced imports. Your regional crafts council or association will often have an online list of local guild shops and artist galleries. Or hit a **craft show**, where you'll be able to buy work

GIFT DONATIONS

Tired of giving (or getting) unappreciated gifts that sit unused in dusty closets? Give something that actually means something—a goat. No, seriously. If you give a needy family in the developing world a goat through an organization like **Changing The Present** (changingthepresent.org) or **World Vision** (worldvision.org), they'll get about a quart of fresh milk a day, great fertilizing manure for vegetable gardens, and about two or three offspring a year. Changing The Present has an especially huge range of gift donations: $60 buys 10 midwife supply kits for Afghan women; $100 will pay for someone's legal defense in Burma; $25 can help mount solar panels on affordable housing. You can feel good knowing your holiday presents actually mean something to someone somewhere, unlike that purple beret you got from Grandma last year.

(RE-)GIFT EXCHANGE

Having a gift swap with friends or co-workers? Make it "recycled": everyone wraps up an old unwanted gift, and participants can either draw from the unopened pile or steal someone else's. You might be surprised by how popular that tea cozy your aunt gave you for your birthday is.

directly from the artist. Buying locally is even better if you can find craftspeople who work with recycled and eco-friendly materials. Keep your eye out for them and ask how they made their products.

Fair-trade shops are also great one-stop gift shops. Though the items for sale are not made locally, they are made under good working conditions by artisan co-ops paid a fair price—a refreshing change from all the cheap imports made in sweatshops. Online shops like **Global Exchange** (**globalexchangestore.org**) and national storefronts like **Ten Thousand Villages** (**tenthousandvillages.com**) are crammed with gift ideas—teapots, toys, jewelry, picture frames, chess sets,

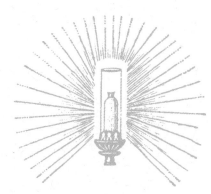

HOLIDAY LIGHTS

Whether you celebrate Christmas with a rainbow of lights or Hanukkah with blue and white ones, December ain't December without a few strings of these. And no doubt all you folks who are trying to rival Chevy Chase's house in *National Lampoon's Christmas Vacation* know what a seasonal drain they can be on your energy bills. Sure, those little bulbs might be only 2½ or 5 watts each, but they add up. Think of it this way: California uses about 1,000 megawatts on these minilights alone, which, according to **grist.org**, is enough to power 1 million homes. No, I'm not asking you to spend the holiday season in the dark, but do you really need so many lights? If your house can be spotted by overhead planes, you know you've gone too far.

Switch to efficient strings of **LED lights**, available at any hardware store. They use up to 95% less energy and last up to 20 times as long. Plus, they don't get hot, so you won't burn down the Christmas tree. Some municipalities are even holding free festive lighting swaps, where you bring in your old, inefficient strings, and get new LED ones. Now that's the spirit!

GREEN GIFT IDEAS

- **For the foodie:** Make your own gourmet food basket by hitting a health store and buying all sorts of yummy local organic jams, salsas, and crackers and fair-trade organic cocoa. Or if you're handy in the kitchen, include some of your own homemade preserves or cookies.

- **For the beauty buff:** Hit the personal-care aisle of your local health store and grab an armful of great organic goodies, like lip gloss, bath salts, and lotions.

- **For the host:** Why not take the opportunity to introduce friends and family to some of the more enjoyable fruits of organic agriculture? Look for organic labels like **Bonterra Chardonnay** (one of my faves). Introduce beer fans to a local organic brew. And forget Tanqueray; serious gin heads will love **Juniper Green Organic London Dry Gin**, made with organic coriander, savory, and angelica root (**junipergreen.org**).

- **For friends and family:** Create homemade coupons. These could be anything, depending on your time and talents. You could promise an hour of babysitting to a new mom or a three-course meal to an overworked friend, or offer to teach a pal how to snowboard, samba, or strum a guitar. An hour massage is always nice when it comes from a main squeeze who's normally too tired to spend more than 3 minutes on your neck.

chimes, chocolates—each with its own inspiring story. Plus, the goods tend to be made with an eye toward sustainability and sometimes contain recycled or eco-friendly materials.

If there are hard-core environmentalists in your life, why not give them a tree? Well, if not an actual tree (though that's not a bad idea, if they have somewhere to plant it and the ground isn't frozen outside), then how 'bout a symbolic one? The **Rainforest Alliance** has an **Adopt-A-Rainforest** program through which your gift will support the purchase and sustainable management of tropical forests (**rainforest-alliance.org**). You can also **adopt an acre** of Costa Rican wildlife habitat in someone's name through the **Nature Conservancy** (**nature.org**). Or just give your enviro friends a **national-parks annual pass** to explore nature on their own time (**nps.gov/fees_passes.htm**).

Kids will love the idea of saving the polar bears or whales through the **World Wildlife Fund**'s **adoption kits**—especially since they come with a plush teddy, a personalized adoption certificate, a sticker, and a report on the work you'll be supporting (**worldwildlife**

THE GREAT CHRISTMAS TREE DEBATE

You want a tree, but you're torn as to whether you should chop down a live one or go with long-lasting plastic. Some will tell you to save a perfectly healthy living tree from the chop and go fake. Trouble is, artificial trees are made of lead-tainted PVC plastic. Sure, they last 10 or more years, but they clog our landfills for centuries to come and leach while they're at it. Real trees, on the other hand, are almost all harvested from tree farms. Those in the industry say trees are often grown on soils that can't support other crops and for every tree chopped another 2 to 10 are planted. They also note that farmed trees suck up greenhouse gases like carbon dioxide and pump out oxygen—before they face the chop, of course, at 7 or so years old. (This is of any good only if real forests aren't cleared for tree plantations, since pine plantations, for instance, don't hold as much carbon as a natural forest does.)

But here's the hitch—and it's a big one: the vast majority of Christmas trees are sprayed. All sorts of chemicals, including nasty insecticides and rodenticides, are used to keep them looking pretty. Although Christmas tree groves often provide habitats for all sorts of wildlife, these chems can cause serious harm. And organic Christmas trees, Charlie Brown, are sadly hard to find (though you should definitely take the time to look for them in your area!).

If you go for the live tree, note that many municipalities have tree composting or mulching programs, so be sure to put yours out on the right day. Another option is to buy a potted version. These are great because they can be planted in your backyard when the holiday is over. Just note that they require lots of TLC at first and are easily killed. Talk to a greenhouse for tips, or go to **christmastree.org/livecare.cfm**. The main thing is not to let your potted tree dry out, and don't keep it inside for more than a week.

Easier still, get yourself a potted Norfolk Island pine that stays inside year-round (eventually, it grows to the height of a regular Christmas tree; repot every 4 years). Just deck it out with cranberry strings come December, and bam, instant festivity.

.**org**). And what kind of uncle would you be if you handed your niece a toy molded with lead and hormone-disrupting phthalates? Lucky for you, a national ban on six phthalates in toys is coming into effect in 2009 and the feds have promised to crack down on lead levels in playthings as well. If you're still nervous, best to stay away from PVC plastic. All **Plan Toys** are made of wood from rubber trees that have stopped producing latex. There are whole worlds of Plan cities, Plan dollhouses, and Plan toys geared toward preschoolers (**plantoys.com**). **HaPe** makes a line of sustainable bamboo games (**educo.com**). You can get fairly traded dolls, instruments, and toys from **Ten Thousand Villages** or at many fair-trade shops listed at **fairtradefederation.org**. For more on green kids' presents, see page 141.

When buying a gift for a gadget geek, look for the Energy Star symbol—it lets you know your electronics aren't sucking up gobs of excess energy. And keep your eye on Greenpeace's latest guide to greener electronics (see page 185 for more on electronics). It's also a good idea to include rechargeable batteries (and a charger) when giving gadgets, gizmos, and tech toys of any kind (for battery tips, see page 190).

Gift Wrap: Wondering what to do about gift wrap? There's no need to reach for that fresh-cut-tree variety. Make your own from old road maps, cartoons, pictures, calendars, greeting cards, or even unwanted fabric. Or pick up some plain brown recycled paper from your local art supply store and tie a leaf, fallen twig, or wildflower onto it with twine.

Candy and Chocolates: That candy you buy in drugstores or supermarkets for Valentine's Day or Halloween might come in cute shapes, but it's also made with lots of cheap chemicals, preservatives, and low-grade chocolate grown with highly toxic pesticides and picked by workers for appalling wages (see page 105). And of course, we can't forget the harmful contaminant melamine, found in sweets like lollipops and chocolate gold coins in late 2008. In the UK in the late '90s, Friends of the Earth found residues of lindane, a pesticide banned in dozens of countries, in several supermarket chocolates.

Larger health stores often carry organic fair-trade seasonally inspired chocolates, as well as Halloween treats. If you can't find these goodies near you, local chocolatiers tend to create holiday treats in-house using all-natural ingredients.

Flowers: Oh, Poison, you were right: every rose does have its thorn. But we still love the prickly flowers, and we're compelled to show our feelings for our wives, girlfriends, mothers, party hosts, and even ourselves with a big bouquet of them, or some sort of brightly colored arrangement. Over 100 million blooms are grown and wrapped in cellophane for your buying pleasure every year. And each one is trucked and jetted thousands of polluting miles to reach your local flower shop.

But the real ecological horror show happens in fields and greenhouses. Flower cultivation sucks back more pesticides than any other agricultural product, according to the Sierra Club. To create flawless buds, hundreds of different pest-killing chems are used—

many of them neurotoxins, others suspected endocrine disrupters, still others probable carcinogens that are considered either extremely toxic or just plain illegal in the US. All the groundwater used on needy plants has led to dropping water tables. And the quest for perfect, pest-free flowers often means that the supertoxic and ozone-depleting fumigant methyl bromide is applied to greenhouse soil (although an increasing number of countries have either banned or are trying to phase out the nasty substance).

Not only are flower farm chemicals contaminating groundwater through runoff or straight-up dumping (reports from Costa Rica document direct discharges into waterways, for instance), but workers aren't given much protection either. The distressing reality is they're often asked to go into greenhouses an hour or two after toxic spraying without any protective gear, and some have been forced to keep working while the spraying goes on. No wonder over 50% of Costa Rican flower laborers and nearly two-thirds of those surveyed in Ecuador complained of headaches, nausea, blurred vision, rashes, and dizziness. And can we be surprised that pregnant workers have been found to have increased risks of birth defects, premature births, and miscarriages, according

F*lower cultivation sucks back* MORE PESTICIDES *than any other agricultural product.*

to a study by the Colombian National Institute of Health? This is particularly troublesome because 70% of Colombia's flower workers are women—women who are paid about 58 cents a day (covering less than half a family's basic needs), putting in long hours, especially before Valentine's Day and Mother's Day. Kind of ironic when you think about it: we honor the women in our lives with bouquets picked by women who are treated with little to no respect.

Sure, all this is happening, for the most part, in lands far away (though pesticide-heavy American flower farms have also been tied to contaminated wells and waterways), but if we're demanding exotic bouquets of perfect flowers, we have to own up

LOCAL, ORGANIC BLOOMS

Looking for something that doesn't have to hop on a plane to brighten up your day? All you have to do is punch in your zip code at **localharvest.org/organic-flowers.jsp** and you'll tap into a network of amazing homegrown pesticide-free flowers picked by LocalHarvest family farmers. You'll find lavender farms, lots of community-supported produce farms that offer up seasonal cut flowers, hanging baskets, and more. Some even invite you to come pick your own wildflowers. Now that's a breath of fresh air.

to our role in fueling unsustainable practices. If you've wondered why flowers have grown so cheap in recent years, the answer is that we switched from buying pricier petals from places like northern California and the Netherlands to flying in cheaper roses and carnations from Latin America—countries with lax worker and environmental regulations.

And all those chemicals are still sitting on that bouquet when you bring it home to your dining-room table. Environmental Working Group tests found that even flowers grown in the US had up to 50 times more carcinogenic pesticide residues than food products have.

Flowers grown in the US have up to 50 times more **CARCINOGENIC PESTICIDE RESIDUES** *than food products have.*

Are you going to lick your petunias? I hope not, but your kids or pets might, and we all bury our noses in them to get a deep whiff of the sweet aromas. And florists have been known to develop rashes and allergic reactions from arranging stems all day. (I've eerily broken out myself after handling floral gifts.) To be safe, make sure you wash your hands well after handling a bouquet, or wear gloves.

Floral Solutions: Okay, so organic flowers aren't a dime a dozen. You won't find them at every corner shop and they'll cost you more when you do, but they're definitely worth it. Plus, it's easy now that all you have to do is jump online to order a gorgeous organic and fairly grown bouquet (wrapped in biodegradable cellophane or a recycled glass vase) and have it delivered straight to your mom's door through **Organic Bouquet** (**organicbouquet .com**). For lovely field-grown, USDA organic flowers from a small family farm in Sacramento, check out **California Organic Flowers** (**californiaorganicflowers.com**). Whole Foods sells some organic, fair-trade, and local blooms—but it also sells a lot of conventionally grown plants (though all such flowers are supposedly tested to make sure they don't exceed set levels of pesticide residues). Best to ask.

No matter where you live, tell your local florist you'd like to see a blossoming selection of pesticide-free blooms that you can feel good about buying.

YOU WORK HARD
FOR YOUR
MONEY

(SO YOU BETTER GREEN IT RIGHT)

*J*ust like Dolly said: working 9 to 5 is no way to make a living. But most of us don't have much choice in the matter (and slaving away on a graveyard shift can be such a drag it isn't even song-worthy). We spend at least half of our waking hours at work—and if you're out of a job, you probably spend almost as much time looking for one. After a long week, the energy you put into the process feels about as renewable as a tank of gas. But how does the job itself fair? Is your workplace an energy hog or keen on conservation? Maybe you're tired of your office's flagrant paper wastage and would rather apply your accounting skills to wind turbine inventory instead of disposable-mop accounts. And if all of your hard-earned cash isn't instantly swallowed by bills, diapers, and dog food, you've gotta figure out where to put it (a bank, for one, and mutual funds if you're moderately ambitious). Might as well make it all as earth-friendly as possible.

FINANCES

The world of finance may be dripping in green, but that's not because of its heartfelt allegiance to the sustainability of double-crested cormorants. Still, even though the banking and investment biz may have a bad rep for its nefarious connections to the dirtiest industries this side of Jupiter, that doesn't mean your money can't be different. From where you store your cash to how you invest it and what credit card you use to spend it, there are tons of ways to green your greenbacks.

Banks: We all groan about how banks gouge the hell out of us. But what doesn't get muttered around the watercooler quite so often is that they're also putting your money to work financing dirty gold mines, oil digs, and ecologically devastating dams around the world. Still, a few banks have made some green inroads (though they're still miles from perfect). In 2008, Ceres (a national network of investors and enviro orgs working with companies on climate change issues) ranked 40 global banks on their green performance. Ceres gave **HSBC**, the first bank to go carbon-neutral, the top score (70 out of 100). **Citibank** and **Bank of America** were the highest-ranking American banks, with scores of 59 and 56, respectively.

For its part, Bank of America has earmarked $20 billion to support the growth of eco-friendly businesses, it has a detailed forest practices policy, and it has set voluntary

Even though the banking and investment biz may have a bad rep for its NEFARIOUS connections to the dirtiest industries this side of Jupiter, that doesn't mean YOUR MONEY can't be DIFFERENT.

greenhouse gas targets for its internal operations and its utilities lending portfolio. It was also the first bank to become part of the Environmental Protection Agency's Climate Leaders program.

Citibank started getting its act together after having been dogged by full-page ads in the *New York Times* and TV spots that targeted its poor record a few years back. It's now coughing up $50 billion to finance alternative energy and carbon-reducing projects. It has best practices around endangered forest protection, illegal logging, carbon reduction, Native American rights, and renewable energy and is making all its new banks LEED-certified.

Regardless of all the green-policy showcasing, Co-op America and the Rainforest Action Network say that both Citibank and Bank of America, among others, are still financing polluting coal projects; and the groups have been asking their members to send protest letters to both institutions.

Credit Unions and Community Development Banks: A smarter place to store your coin is with a **credit union** or a **community development bank**. They offer all the same services as banks but do business with a lot more integrity. Credit unions are actually not-for-profit co-ops in which every "member" has a share. They tend to offer lower loan rates, higher savings rates, and fewer service fees. There are thousands of them across the US. Many have ethical policies and won't invest in corporations with ecologically destructive practices, or with poor labor relations or

CREDIT UNIONS *and community development banks offer all the same services as banks but do business with a* LOT MORE INTEGRITY.

human rights standards. Not all credit unions have these policies, though, so it's best to ask before joining. To find a credit union branch near you, check with the Credit Union National Association (**creditunion.coop**).

CREDIT CARDS AND CHECKS

Okay, so you've almost got your finances in order. Now it's time to open that wallet and peek at your credit cards. Instead of handing all that interest straight to Visa, why not share a little with your charity of choice? A **Nature Conservancy Visa** will automatically donate $65 to the charity when you open the account, and the org gets 0.25% of your purchases (**nature.org**). **Chase Bank** offers a range of cards dedicated to enviro causes, including a World Wildlife Fund (WWF) platinum Visa card that coughs up $50 up front and 1% of sales (since 1995, the WWF has gotten over $10 million through this program).

Not so keen on the idea of being rewarded with air mileage points that pollute high in the skies? **Bank of America**'s **Brighter Planet credit card** lets you score one "EarthSmart" point for every dollar you spend. For every 1,000-point increment, the bank will offset 1 ton of carbon dioxide emissions through renewable-energy projects (**brighterplanet.com**). About the same as taking a car off the road for a month.

Less popular with enviros is GE Money's Earth Rewards platinum MasterCard, which contributes 1% of your purchases to greenhouse gas offsets. The executive director of the Rainforest Action Network has slammed this particular card because GE actually supplies parts for polluting, coal-fired plants. Oh, the irony.

Check manufacturers aren't as big givers, but the good ones do offer a little chunk to charity every time you order a new batch. **Message!Products** offers checks affiliated with the Sierra Club, WWF, Ocean Conservancy, Greenpeace, and more, where 10% goes to the charity (see **messageproducts.com**). Just be aware of personal-affinity checks that let you pick green-themed logos without actually giving any money to an enviro cause. Whatever card or checks you choose, always ask for specifics about where the money goes and what percentage is donated.

Though there aren't as many of them, community development banks (CDBs) are federally insured banks that focus their efforts on all kinds of feel-good stuff, including stimulating the local economy, creating jobs, and improving the quality of life in low-income neighborhoods. For info and links to CDBs across the country, see **communitydevelopmentbanks.org**.

Investing: Most of us start thinking about financial investments only come IRA season, or maybe when we see pension fund payments coming off our paychecks. But whether you're planning for your retirement, dabbling in stocks, or

By 2007, Americans had $2.7 trillion involved in SOCIALLY RESPONSIBLE INVESTING.

just looking to invest without polluting the planet, ethical funds are an excellent option. By 2007, Americans had $2.7 trillion in **socially responsible investing** (SRI). Okay, so these took a hit in the recent market collapse along with everything else, but green investments are, without a doubt, the light at the end of the tunnel.

The majority of the eco-conscious investment funds out there are branded as ethical/social rather than just green. However, almost all say they factor environmental issues—along with other concerns, like human rights—into investment decisions. Plus, they all stay away from nuke-, military-, and tobacco-related companies.

Socially responsible investors essentially want to reward good behavior. Socially

ARE YOU A GREEN SHAREHOLDER?

Already got investments that ain't exactly easy on the earth? Don't dump them. Go to annual general shareholder meetings and demand action through shareholder resolutions, which you're free to submit. If more than 50% of shareholders agree with your proposal, the company has to do what you say. No kidding. Write letters to the company and lobby other shareholders to take action too. For info on shareholder actions, head to **ceres.org**.

conscious funds generally invest in corporations whose management commits to making labor, ecological, or human rights improvements (even if they're not saints). The funds leverage their buying power to push corporations to clean up their acts. And if they don't, those corporations will eventually be dumped. Overall, it's way beyond what mainstream funds offer; these sink their cash anywhere the money blows, with little regard for the planet and the people who have to live on it.

Nonetheless, if you look closely at the list of investments on many socially responsible funds, you'll probably notice some surprising choices, like Coca-Cola, PepsiCo, Proctor & Gamble, and Microsoft (slammed in Greenpeace's electronics ranking). Not the kind of businesses all tree huggers love to sink their cash into. Still, insiders argue that if your filters are too stringent, you'll be cutting out half the market and upping your portfolio risk. After all, all of these companies are on the Domini social investment index of 400 ethically screened American companies (see the sidebar on Domini).

If none of that sits well with you, there are greener investment options out there, just not as many. The **Sierra Club Stock Fund** (**sierraclubfunds.com**) and **Green Century**

Funds (**greencentury.com**) are two choices that get the green thumbs-up. On top of screening out the basics (nukes, tobacco, etc.), they filter out things like pesticide use, fossil fuels, GMOs, factory farming, animal testing, urban-sprawl pushers, and more. The **New Alternatives Fund** invests heavily in biomass, solar, wind, geothermal, and hydro alternative energies, as well as hybrid car batteries and companies like Whole Foods (**newalternativesfund.com**). The **Winslow Green Growth Fund** invests in smaller businesses set to take off, like Green Mountain Coffee Roasters, Chipotle Mexican Grill (big on naturally raised meat), Gaiam (green online retailer), Interface (a carpeting company championed by greens for sustainable practices), and more (**winslowgreen.com**). (Note: the fund does finance a few smaller, cutting-edge pharmaceutical companies, which likely test on animals.)

Mainstream banks, by the way, don't always carry ethical funds, especially the more hard-core ones. If you're shopping around for ethical mutual funds, know that there are about 170 across the country. It's probably best to talk to a financial planner well versed in SRI first. For a financial services directory of socially and environmentally responsible financial planners, mutual funds, retirement options, mutual-fund performance charts, and more, go to the Social Investment Forum's site: **socialinvest.org**. Credit unions are another good place to find these funds.

INVESTING IN YOUR COMMUNITY

Got a big heart and a little cash to spare? You can help finance social services and green projects in your 'hood through community investing. The money goes to loans to not-for-profits, co-ops, social housing, and all sorts of inspiring social enterprises. And your deposit and interest are often guaranteed so you can't lose money. Ask your local credit union and community development bank about community development loan funds and venture capital funds accessible to individuals like you. So far, community investing institutions have about $25 billion in assets, and that number is growing. For more details, including a community investing database, go to Co-op America's Community Investing Center at **communityinvest.org**.

CAREER

So you need a job, do ya? Who doesn't? Last I checked, my father was still right: lots of wonderful green things grow on trees, but not money. If only we could work for leaves instead of coins. Oh wait, you can—just work for the environment! All those who are willing to dedicate their entire professional lives to an environmental cause of some sort deserve our support. Green headhunters should be chasing you down in your home and throwing enticing benefit packages at you. But until that day, plenty of resources are at your fingertips to help you find the job you're looking for.

Hunting for Environmental Jobs: You can contact each and every eco-bent company and organization you can think of to see if it happens to have a slot to fill—if you have all the time in the world. Or you can try more of a one-stop shopping approach and check out online employment databases specifically for earth-lovin' people like you. **EnvironmentalCareer.com** has well-organized listings that give you the lowdown on working as an environmental planner or as a green teacher, everywhere from Vegas to Wyoming. You can search

Check out ONLINE EMPLOYMENT DATABASES specifically for EARTH-LOVIN' people like you.

by categories (such as "Academic," "Accounting," "Activism/Advocacy," or "Architecture") or by city or state. You can post your résumé or, if you're an employer, post jobs. Or set up a free search agent (a program that'll do the job hunting for you) and get offers by e-mail. The site also has a publication dedicated to the topic: the *Green Careers Journal*.

DEGREES OF GREEN

Looking to start a career of tree hugging and earth saving but don't have the qualifications? If you're ready to hit the books (maybe for the first or second time) and want to try your hand at a new degree or masters in greener studies, scope out your options at **EnviroEducation.com**. It lets you search for schools that offer programs ranging from oceanography to environmental entrepreneurship (yep, green MBAs do exist). You'll find everything from Ivy Leaguers like Yale and Duke, to cozier spots like the Audubon Expedition Institute.

STARTING YOUR OWN GREEN BIZ

Perhaps you have visions of starting your own sustainable company—maybe an organic sock bunny store or a paper clip recycling center. The US government's **Green Business Guide** has info on enviro regs, incentives, and loans for energy efficiency projects, green commuting programs for your employees, as well as supplements on e-labeling and certification and tips for marketing your green biz (**business.gov/guides/environment**). Consider joining **Co-op America**'s network of green businesses and your recycled sock bunny business will be posted on its popular National Green Pages directory. You'll also have access to its green business conference and Green Festival consumer shows, and if you pass the screening process, you'll even receive the trusted Co-op America seal of approval (**coopamerica.org**).

EcoEmploy's site (**ecoemploy.com**) is less slickly designed, but it lists government openings as well as postings at enviro agencies, nongovernmental organizations (NGOs), and corporations looking for everything from foresters and oceanographers to media relations people and executive directors. **SustainableBusiness.com** lets you search green dream jobs (**sustainablebusiness.com/jobs**) by skill set (senior-level, entry-level, or volunteer). You'll also find career listings at **Jobs.greenbiz.com** and **greenjobsearch.org**. **Greencollarblog.org** connects you to even more sites (like **jobs.treehugger.com**) through its green-job board and listing of eco recruiters.

Volunteering: If you're having trouble finding work, I have three tips for you: volunteer, volunteer, volunteer. Even if you're not looking to pad your résumé and just want to get off the couch and put your spare time to good use, there are countless organizations out there that could use a helping hand, whether you're willing to lick stamps or wash oil slicks off seabirds. For a state-by-state list of environmental orgs nationwide, head to **eco-usa. net**. Browse through the lists to find groups that interest you, and then give them a call. For those open to a little globe-trotting, **greenvolunteering.org** is loaded with info on nearly 500 conservation and wildlife projects worldwide, with long- and short-term commitments.

Idealist.org has over 13,000 volunteer opportunities posted. You can search its database by punching in your area of focus and it will let you scan for opportunities in your home state or as far away as Africa.

Are you a student hoping to spend a term studying, oh, I don't know, maybe real life abroad? **Living Routes** lets you learn about sustainable development, green building, organic

**GREAT GREEN BOOKS ON BUSINESS,
JOBS, AND THE NEW ECONOMY**

- *Natural Capitalism: Creating the Next Industrial Revolution* by Paul Hawken with Amory Lovins and Hunter Lovins

- *The Eco Guide to Careers That Make a Difference: Environmental Work for a Sustainable World* by the Environmental Careers Organization

- *Cradle to Cradle: Remaking the Way We Make Things* by Michael Braungart and William McDonough

- *Designing the Green Economy: The Postindustrial Alternative to Corporate Globalization* by Brian Milani

- *The Sustainable Company: How to Create Lasting Value Through Social and Environmental Performance* by Chris Laszlo

agriculture, and more while living in Ecovillages around the world. And you score a college credit too (**livingroutes.org**).

Want to get really down and dirty with Mother Nature? WWOOFing has nothing to do with canine mating calls, but it does involve digging up gardens. WWOOF stands for **World Wide Opportunities on Organic Farms**, an organization that provides volunteer opportunities to visit an organic farm anywhere in the world, get some fresh air, and learn all about organic agriculture through enriching hands-on experience. You get free room and board in exchange. You can WWOOF for a week, a month, or a year—it's up to you. Wherever there's an organic farm in the world, you can probably be a WWOOFer. Visit **wwoofusa.org** if you want to sign up.

THE OFFICE

When we're trying so hard to be conscientious in our own homes, it can be pretty frustrating to get to the office and see so much waste—lights blazing 24/7, endless photocopies destined for landfill, disposable cups piling up by the watercooler (most of which can't be recycled). Just because we're overworked doesn't mean the planet should be.

Talk to your office manager (or whoever's in charge of this kind of thing) about bringing in more responsible options. Sure, most will gripe about the extra cost of buying recycled materials, but point out that they can offset the expense with energy-saving measures. You can make a nice spreadsheet (or whatever it is you number crunchers do) to demonstrate that greening your office makes good fiscal sense. For more resistant types, start by suggesting small steps that will save them money, like turning off lights and computers at night and turning down the heat by a few degrees. Once they've warmed up to the benefits of going green, you can hit them up for new Energy Star computers. And, of course, lead by example—even if it's just from your little cubicle.

Lighting/Energy: A quarter of a building's energy bills go to lighting. Your company can save coin by switching to **compact fluorescent bulbs**, which use up to 80% less energy than regular incandescents. In terms of tubular fluorescents, switching to T8 types (which produce more light per watt and are a third more efficient than standard T12s) and adding **electric ballasts** (which regulate the current flow) will save 10% to 15% on energy bills. Switching to T6s will save you even more. For detailed reports on which commercial fluorescent lighting to buy, see **greenseal.org**. Your office manager will want to consider purchasing **timers** and **occupancy sensors**. Why waste power lighting a room when no one's there but the photocopier?

Also, ask your building manager or landlord to spend 50 bucks on a good energy-saving **programmable thermostat** certified by Energy Star. You can set it so that the temperature drops to 60°F or so at night in the winter and turns off the AC altogether at night in the summer, then kicks back into a comfortable but energy-saving temperature during business hours: 78° in the summer and 68° to 70° in the winter. And lowering the thermostat on the water heater from 130° to 120° can save 5% on water heating.

Office Equipment: In the market for new computers? Printer dying on you? Be sure to look for the **Energy Star** label when you're shopping for new technology (including faxes, scanners, mailing machines, copiers, and more). A home office using an Energy Star computer, printer, and fax machine saves enough electricity every year to light your house for over 4 years. Just think about how much energy a whole office building

COMPUTER MYTHS

Heard the one about how you save more power by leaving your computer on than by shutting it down and restarting it? Yep, well, totally bogus. Computers use about 2 seconds' worth of power to start up, according to the US Office of Energy Efficiency and Renewable Energy. So turn off your electronic equipment when you leave the office for lunch (or at least put it into sleep mode). FYI: pretty screen savers of the Amazon don't save energy; in fact, fancy graphics often suck more power than just letting the screen go dark in screen-saver mode.

can save. In fact, if every computer sold in the US were Energy Star, we could pocket over $2 billion in energy savings each year, eliminating as many CO_2 emissions as taking 2 million cars off the road would do. And it doesn't end there. Energy Star laser printers and copiers use 25% less, and both can do double-sided printing. Even an Energy Star watercooler will save your office about $30 a year. For details on qualified office equipment (including mailing machines, scanners, etc.), as well as savings calculators and more, check out energystar.gov.

If every computer sold in the US were ENERGY STAR, we could pocket $5 billion in savings each year!

Machinery on the fritz? Don't toss it; contact the manufacturer. If you purchased wisely—say, from Xerox—companies will not only provide you with the maintenance help

AIR QUALITY FACELIFT

If your office is so dated it looks like Melanie Griffith in *Working Girls* could show up any minute, the air inside probably feels just as old. Ideally, you would get rid of dust-trapping carpets and switch to FSC-certified wood, but if wall-to-wall is nonnegotiable, stick to a sustainable company like Interface or Milliken. Be sure to slap on low- or no-zero paints to avoid giving anyone a headache. And avoid particleboard cubicles and desks that keep offgassing formaldehyde fumes for years (Baltix Sustainable Furniture makes VOC-free workstations from wheat straw, sunflower hulls, recycled wood, and steel) (baltix.com). Add a VOC-absorbing houseplant on every desk or so, and you might even be able to breathe deeply again.

you need to keep your equipment running, but they'll take it back when it dies and convert it into new equipment. By 2007, Xerox had kept 2 billion pounds of waste out of landfill, thanks to such a program. Apple, Dell, and Hewlett-Packard also have take-back programs. Ask your manufacturer if it has one, and keep asking as you shop around for new gear (this applies to computers too). Also, don't forget about charities in your area that refurbish old computers and donate them to the needy (see page 185).

Ditching Old Data: Got a stack of floppy disks from the early '90s lying around? Send old diskettes to GreenDisk for recycling (**greendisk.com**). You can also send them old data-storing CDs if they're scratched or are just plain useless to you now. And next time, be sure to buy rewritable CDs so they can be used more than once.

Paper: Did you know that the average office worker goes through about 10,000 sheets of paper every year? Pretty appalling really, considering it takes 24 full-grown trees to make a ton of virgin office paper (as well as 5,690 pounds of CO_2 and 19,075 gallons of water), according to the Environmental Defense Fund's paper calculator (**papercalculator.org**). Lots of businesses have recycling bins in place (if yours doesn't, this

> **T**he average office worker goes through about **10,000 SHEETS OF PAPER** *every year.*

is the first thing you should look into), but not enough pay attention to the type of paper they're buying. Switching to 100% recycled printing and photocopy paper would save about 2,100 pounds of greenhouse gases and 8,750 gallons of water, not to mention all those trees, for every ton of paper.

Ideally, you'd be buying 100% **postconsumer recycled (PCR), chlorine-free paper**. (Bleaching paper is an incredibly toxic process that emits dangerous persistent dioxins that accumulate in our tissues. Elemental chlorine–free paper is better but not totally dioxin-free. Processed chlorine–free is best.) If that's too costly for your stingy office, even 30% PCR content would be a start. You can also find hanging file folders, files, envelopes, portfolios, Post-it notes, and adding-machine rolls with as much as 100% PCR content these days, so don't limit your green paper supplies to what spits out of your printer.

Writing Tools: We buy, toss, and lose millions of pens and pencils a year in North America, and they all end up in landfill at the end of the day (although I swear little gnomes are stealing pens from my desk and using them as back scratchers). Pen chewers should ditch

TRACKING DOWN GREEN OFFICE SUPPLIES

So just where do you get your hands on recycled-rubber briefcases or recycled paper clips? Though more and more eco-friendly gear can be found in mainstream office supply stores, there are a few one-stop eco office shops online that have all kinds of cool stuff. Beyond the basics, **Green Earth Office Supply** carries binders and business card holders made of old circuit boards, biodegradable corn-based coffee mugs and pens you can print your corporate logo on, eco kitchen and cleaning supplies, earth-friendly art supplies, and more (**greenearthofficesupply. com**). **The Green Office** has smaller stuff like recycled paper products and green pens, as well as bigger items like Energy Star phones and fax machines (**thegreenoffice.com**). Note that this site carries plenty of conventional, not-so-green products too, including vinyl banner paper and vinyl chairs.

those petroleum-derived plastic ones and reach for **refillable ballpoint pens** made with recycled plastic. Pencil pushers should be scribbling with pencils certified by the Forest Stewardship Council (FSC), like **ForestChoice pencils** (**forestchoice.com**).

Reach for REFILLABLE *ballpoint pens* *made with* RECYCLED PLASTIC *and* FSC-CERTIFIED *pencils.*

The greenest options, though, don't involve any trees or petroleum at all, so keep an eye out for pencils made of reclaimed wood and recycled newspapers (like **Earthwrite**; **papermate.com**) or pens made of old lunch trays and denim instead. As for markers, the permanent ones are full of air-polluting VOCs (you can kind of tell by the fumes). Better to get **water-based markers**. Same goes with correction fluid (get correction tape instead). With dry-erase markers, look for alcohol-based, low-odor brands.

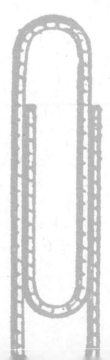

Coffee/Mugs: We all know coffee is the ultimate office supply— no doubt, productivity would plummet without it. But why would anyone want to brew up low-grade, pesticide-laden beans for which coffee pickers are paid starvation wages when several office coffee suppliers offer fair-trade java? Even American Coffee Services carries certified fair-trade organic coffees like **Green Mountain**'s **PBS Blend**,

7 PAPER-SAVING STRATEGIES

Use print preview religiously. I can't stress this one enough. It lets you see what you're about to print so you can assess whether you can make it fit on fewer pages or whether you need only the first three sheets.

1

E-mail everything. Even pay stubs can be encrypted and sent to every worker's inbox.

2

Don't print out a whole 60-page report willy-nilly. Take a quick look on-screen to decide which sections you really need.

3

Photocopy and print on both sides of the page. Get the tech guy to change everyone's default settings to double-sided.

4

If you use an extra-large on-screen font to avoid eyestrain, make sure you shrink it down before you press the print button; otherwise, you'll turn a 2-page document into 10 pages.

5

Use an e-fax program—there might even be one set up on your computer. If not, ask your office manager to order **eFax** or **Comodo TrustFax** or, for high-volume corporate accounts, something like **Faxage**. Small businesses can even get free e-faxing. (And if your office insists on having a fax machine, make sure it uses regular paper, not chemically treated fax paper, which isn't always recyclable.)

6

Hold on to paper that was printed on one side only and use the other side to take notes—or to turn into paper airplanes to throw at people who don't recycle.

7

Newman's Own, and more. Trouble is, they come only with ultra-packaging-heavy K-Cup systems. **Van Houtte** has drip systems for offices that brew up organic, fair-trade beans (**vanhoutte.com**).

And get everyone to bring in reusable mugs while you're at it. Those foam cups aren't recyclable in most towns, and they take forever to break down in landfill. If your workplace has a kitchen, talk to the office manager about supplying reusable mugs, dishes, and cutlery. Say goodbye to individual sugar packets and creamers too. Buying in bulk is always greener.

The TROUBLE *with some organic office coffee is that it comes with* ULTRA-PACKAGING-HEAVY K-CUP SYSTEMS.

TOP 10 TIPS FOR GREENING YOUR OFFICE

Find strength in numbers. Sure, one person can make a difference, but join up with a few other people and suddenly you're a mighty earth-loving force to be reckoned with. Especially if you call yourself the "green committee" (anything with the word "committee" in it is important). Map out what needs greening and start with the free initiatives first. **1**

Be a pusher man (or woman). Advocate for a strong paper-saving strategy using 100% recycled paper with high postconsumer content. Do we really need to kill 178 million trees a year for memos and internal reports destined for the dustbin? **2**

Don't waste your energy. Reduce office hum and energy bills by switching to energy-efficient lights and installing programmable thermostats, sensors, and timers. **3**

Be water-wise. Instead of drinking from bisphenol A–leaching plastic watercoolers, talk to your boss about getting a carbon filter for the kitchen sink or a tankless water cooler. And while you're talking H_2O, suggest adding cheap water-saving toilet dams to all the bathrooms. **4**

Waste not. Eating takeout lunches everyday doesn't just take a toll on your hips. You're clogging landfills with unrecyclable plastics that could easily be avoided if you brought your own reusable food containers to takeout counters. My containers go to Chinese restaurants, Caribbean joints, and more and get a warm reception every time. **5**

Out, damn ink spot! Recycle your ink cartridges for printers and photocopiers. Over a billion a year are used worldwide, and we don't want those needlessly clogging landfills. **6**

Bin recyclin'? Make sure all employees have recycling bins at their desks, and place one in the office kitchen. (And if your town collects food scraps from homes, ask if businesses can access the program. Some progressive offices even have composting bins at every workstation, or at least in the kitchen.) NatureMill makes some superefficient automatic indoor composters that can handle 120 pounds of food a month (**naturemill.com**). **7**

Give a hoot; green your commute. Set up carpooling and bike-to-work programs with sign-up boards or Listservs. Make sure your office has bike racks. **8**

Suit yourself. Talk to your bosses about ditching ties and jackets in the summer so the AC doesn't have to be blasting. Japan's prime minister has asked the whole country to do this, so you've got an entire nation to back you up. **9**

Don't move. If you drive to the office, talk to your employer about working from home one day a week to cut back on travel emissions, or about working from home altogether (this even has an official name: telework). Bonus: you spend less time and money shopping for office clothes! **10**

FUEL-EFFICIENT FLEET

If your company has a fleet of cars—even if it's just three—it can save bigtime on gas bills by switching from gas-guzzling SUVs or sedans to more efficient models, including hybrids (see **greenercars.org** for recommendations). The fleet can even be converted to run on more efficient natural gas (see page 283 for more info).

Cleaning: Tired of coming to work and choking on the chemical trail the cleaners left behind? Encourage your employer to consider greener, healthier alternatives. If you have a small business and don't need massive quantities, just wander into a health store and pick up some green cleaners. Green Seal certifies a bunch of commercial cleaners; check the website for listings (**greenseal.org**). Many cleaning companies will use whatever products you ask them to, as long as you supply them. Others market themselves as strictly green to begin with, but eco-friendly cleaners willing to do large offices are hard to find. If you have an office kitchen, make sure it's equipped with environmentally friendly dishwashing soaps, like **Ecover**, and that washrooms have natural soap dispensers, like the kind **EO** offers in bulk (**eoproducts.com**).

BIG
ISSUES

We can chat all you want about the value of compact fluorescent bulbs and which kitty litter is more eco-friendly, but there's no denying that there are larger issues at play. I'm not talking about theological musings like whether God is a woman or a blanket of molecules or whether Angelina Jolie can single-handedly adopt all the world's needy children. I'm talking climate change, mass deforestation, wiping out wildlife—you know, end-of-the-world stuff.

Not to propagate fear, but we should be freaked out—the United States ranks worse than every other industrialized nation in energy consumption, water use, greenhouse gas emissions, air pollutants, and pesticide use. But change is in the air, which means rather than hang our heads in shame, it's time for some "participaction"—where we shake our fists, pick up the phone, write letters, take to the streets, and work together to turn America into the green leader it could be. Hell, if we're rigorous enough about it, we could tackle obesity rates at the same time.

Enough of the rant. Here's a breakdown of the major eco hurdles we face and some tips on how to stay informed, get involved, and get our politicians and polluting corporations on the greener path.

CLIMATE CHANGE

The term "climate change" may be synonymous with "The planet is melting! The planet is melting!" but this is no imaginary concoction of some children's-book chicken. Despite the clucking of a dwindling number of oil company–backed naysayers, carbon dioxide levels haven't been this high for, oh, at least 650,000 years, and the temperature keeps climbing along with them. If things heat up another 2 or 3 degrees, we'll be experiencing global temps not seen since 3 million years ago when sea levels were 80 feet higher, according to NASA's Goddard Institute for Space Studies. Thank mass fossil fuel burning, industrial and agricultural pollution, and rampant clear-cutting of the world's carbon-trapping forests for that. Along with other greenhouse gases, all those CO_2 emissions build up in the earth's atmosphere, trapping the sun's heat (hence the "greenhouse" effect).

The ramifications? Glaciers around the globe are melting faster than they have in 5,000 years. One scientist at the National Snow and Ice Data Center noted that "arctic ice is in its death spiral." Low-lying islands in the South Pacific are being evacuated because of rising sea levels. Starving polar bears are resorting to cannibalism. And although it's also called "global warming" (which sounds deceptively peachy to snow-bogged Alaskans), climate change is perhaps more aptly associated with

Carbon dioxide levels haven't been this high for at least 650,000 YEARS, and the temperature keeps climbing along with them.

catastrophic storms: Ohio-size floods, California-style wildfires, Dust Bowl-esque droughts, sizzling temps, freak cold snaps, and pretty much any extreme weather à la Hurricane Katrina and worse. Luckily, consensus has finally arrived in the global arena: climate change is the single gravest issue facing humanity. Let's hope this year our politicians and corporations start acting like they care about the fate of our grandchildren, and the planet we all call home.

Action Needed: The US has hogged the honor of being the world's largest emitter of greenhouse gases (although China is now sliding into top spot). It has also trailed at the very back of the G8 and 56 countries ranked on climate action (at least we beat out China and Saudi Arabia—phew!). And yes, we blew our chance at the Kyoto Accord (at this point there's no way we could slash our emissions to 6% below 1990 levels by 2012 even if Obama *wanted* to sign it). But we have to make sure we're leaders in pushing the next climate change accord.

The president says he'll commit to reducing emissions by 80% by 2050. Make sure he sticks to that.

With Barack Obama now running the White House, the country will no doubt be taking major steps forward, but that doesn't mean it's time for the rest of us to get lazy. Be a climate change watchdog. Stay on top of your representatives to make sure climate change legislation doesn't get watered down. Whoever's in charge at your city/state/federal level needs to know that Americans are ready for meaningful action. No window dressing, please. And remember that everything's interconnected. Energy activists, forestry campaigners, wildlife advocates, and water keepers have all been unified by the threat of climate change. So your struggle to save your neighborhood's thatch of trees or a nearby patch of wetlands is actually helping us all in the greater planetary fight.

ENDANGERED SPECIES

Sure, many species came and went long before humans arrived on the scene (any *Jurassic Park* fan knows that), but since the 1500s humans can take the blame for the vast majority of recorded extinctions. Destruction of habitat, pollution, climate change, and hunting have meant that we've put animals, birds, fish, and plant species at risk of permanent obliteration around the globe. The World Wildlife Fund reports that global biodiversity has dropped by almost a third in the past 35 years. And today in the US, 609 animal species and 744 plant species are listed as threatened or endangered. Some, like the sea mink, the passenger pigeon, and the blue pike, are already gone forever. But that's just the beginning.

Climate change's rising temperatures and changing rainfall patterns could wipe out TWO-THIRDS *of California's 2,300 one-of-a-kind* plant species. AND THAT'S JUST IN ONE STATE.

A 2008 report from Berkeley and friends said that climate change's rising temperatures and changing rainfall patterns could wipe out two-thirds of California's 2,300 one-of-a-kind plant species. And that's just in one state. We could be here all day if I get my crystal ball out and start predicting the impact of climate change on species nationwide.

Politicians have had a bad habit of assuring us that they love and protect our wildlife in one breath, and then selling off wildlife rights in the next. Yes, polar bears were declared a threatened species, but the final rules authorize the "nonlethal, incidental, unintentional take of small numbers of Pacific walruses and polar bears." Sounds harmless, but by "take" they mean "to harass, hunt, capture, or kill." Enviros cry the whole loophole was designed to give seven oil and gas companies some leeway in disrupting the threatened bears as they dig around for fossil fuels.

Of course, it's not the first time that energy's been prioritized over nature. The utter collapse of western salmon populations has forced the closure of sport and commercial fishing off California and Oregon, but the previous government repeatedly ignored environmental pleas to remove four eastern Washington dams to help save the endangered fish. Sure, all that dam power is cheap as can be, but the Bush administration spent $8 billion on trying to minimize the dams' impact on baby salmon, according to CBS's *60 Minutes*. Environmental orgs charge that officials have been effectively throwing money into the wind to save the dams and barely giving a damn about the endangered species. Talk about fishy.

Action Needed: Environmentalists are counting on the new administration to undo a lot of damage done by the previous government. Now is a good time to call up your elected reps and remind them that the Endangered Species Act legally binds them to protect animal habitat. Otherwise they might just end up in court, like the US Fish and Wildlife Service did when 10 enviro orgs filed a legal challenge against it in the fall of 2008 for failing to protect wolverines and their habitat. In fact, the Bush administration protected the fewest new species under the Endangered Species Act of any previous administration (about 60 compared to over 500 under former president Clinton, according to Defenders of Wildlife). Make sure the new administration knows this can't happen again.

ENERGY CRISIS

Our hyperindustrial society would be nowhere without power—not the hierarchical kind you find in boardrooms, but the type that fuels our cars, our hot-water tanks, and pretty much every plug-in apparatus you can imagine. Trouble is, our addiction to oil, coal, and natural gas is a deadly double-edged sword. They not only spew out nasty air-clogging pollutants as we use them (particularly oil and coal), but digging for them comes with all kinds of disturbing ecological ramifications.

Drilling for natural gas is hurting wildlife and their habitats. Digging for coal ravages the land whether you're slicing off mountaintops in Appalachia or mining in the Rockies (not to mention the serious stream and groundwater contamination, as well as greenhouse gas and mercury pollution it creates). Liquid coal not only produces twice the global warming pollution of conventional gasoline, but the plants needed to process the stuff cost over $4 billion each to build, according to the Natural Resources Defense Council. Large hydro dams often flood wild habitats and seriously disrupt aquatic life. And the uranium that fuels nuclear power plants isn't just polluting to mine; its dangerous radioactive waste is with us forever (and already bursting at the seams from aging storage tanks in Washington State). And who's running these joints? Homer Simpson? Illinois, the state with the greatest number of nuke reactors, has experienced nearly a dozen irradiated tritium leaks since 1996 but kept them hush-hush for a decade. Plus, let's not forget that uranium is another finite, nonrenewable fuel that we'll run out of sooner or later.

Then there's oil. Our dependence on the juice of million-year-old fossils is clearly unsustainable, and our hankering for it makes our other fuel addictions look like child's play. Wars (both covert and overt) are waged in its name; fragile habitats are ravaged to excavate it and ship it. Oh, but digging for new oil on American turf would free us from the international headache and price gouging that happens when we have to import 15 million

We can't DRILL OUR WAY OUT *of the energy crisis.*

out of 20 million barrels a day, say drill-more-oil-on-American-soil types. Well, even if we overturned the offshore drilling ban that's been in place since the '80s and we started slicing up our ocean beds in the hopes of striking black gold, experts estimate that, at best, we'd score 2 to 4 million barrels a day. Hardly enough to loosen our dependency on foreign oil and definitely not enough to drop prices at the pumps. Bottom line: we can't drill our way out of the energy crisis. Why risk our waters and wildlife for so little?

Action Needed: Forget sniffing around ocean bottoms and wildlife reserves for buried oil or carving off mountaintops for coal. We need to make conservation a top-tier national priority. And politely asking Americans to switch their lightbulbs to CFLs won't cut it. We need tough regulations mandating ambitious energy efficiency standards for manufacturers and all industry; for the products we buy; for builders, home renovators, landlords, and utility companies.

Tell your representative you won't buy into so-called clean coal, clean nukes, or any other Pandora's box for that matter. While you're on the topic of dodgy energy, remind your rep that the government should have nothing to do with dirty Canadian tar sands oil that's three to five times dirtier than regular fuel. Don't hang up just yet! Obama may have been smart enough to promise billions toward renewable energy initiatives to kick-start green jobs. But you need to remind your state and local politicians that you want to see investments in renewable energy from their pockets, too.

WATER SHORTAGE

Most Americans have had a certain cockiness about their water supply. After all, the crystal clear fluid flows freely from our taps and toilets on command for mere pennies, even when it's dry as a bone outside. Now we're finally starting to sweat about just how clean and plentiful that water really is. Southwesterners know they've been on the frontlines of some serious H_2O struggles, but hold on to your drinks, folks—things are about to get a lot drier thanks to climate change, warn the experts. Not good when you consider that the states suffering the worst water shortages are also some of the fastest-growing in the country. But even if your home's sitting on the shores of a big green lake, what good will our fresh water do us if it's chock-full of contaminants? Despite cleanup efforts, the Great Lakes are still a chemical bath tied to elevated cancer risks and premature births (in fact, the government tried to suppress a 2008 Centers for Disease Control and Prevention report raising these very concerns).

Of course, it's not just the Great Lakes. Poorly treated sewage is turning the Gulf of Mexico into "Florida's toilet." Flushed drugs are tainting our waters with antibiotics, mood stabilizers, and sex hormones. Nitrogen-heavy fertilizer runoff is fueling a 7,900-square-mile dead zone from the mouth of the Mississippi (one of 200 oxygen-starved dead zones in the world, according to the United Nations Environment Programme). Even phosphate-heavy dish soaps help breed toxic algae-clogged

A THIRD OF THE WORLD'S POPULATION *doesn't have enough clean water.*

lakes that could kill your dog if it drank from them. No wonder our fish are so overloaded with toxins: we treat the ocean like a garbage bin.

Clean water becomes especially precious when you consider that a third of the world's population doesn't have enough. That's a position we weren't expected to be in until 2025, but a report released in the summer of 2006 by the International Water Management Institute in Sri Lanka says we're already there. That's enough to have some people calling water the "new oil," and speculating that the wars of the future will be waged for access to the "blue gold." (Just pray that Kevin Costner doesn't make a film about *this* water world!)

Action Needed: Yes, our water has gotten somewhat cleaner since the dead-lake scares of the '70s, but more than 20,000 bodies of water, according to the EPA and US PIRG, are too polluted to meet basic water quality standards. Enforcement of the Clean Water Act is spotty and shoddy. It's time for a crackdown on standards. The act itself needs to be pried open and strengthened, insists the Clean Water Network so that it can be directed at sneaky "non-point-source pollution" from agricultural runoff and storm water overflows, and not just straight-up '70s-style dumping. It's also time for the feds to start treating streams and tributaries like they matter. We need to overturn a Bush-era directive telling EPA field staff to stop applying the act's protections to "isolated" waters without consent from Washington headquarters.

We need a national "Healthy Oceans Act." We need nationwide policies that require water bottlers to pay for the H_2O they take from our taps and springs and then charge us two bucks for. We need to build gray-water recycling into building codes so that we can stop flushing so much coal-heavy energy and life-giving H_2O down the toilet (pumping water to southern California for instance, is the single largest use of energy in that state).

Get moving in your own 'hood. Want to prevent wild flooding? Fight to keep wetlands safe. Want to stop the degradation of a nearby waterway? Start a neighborhood watch program for your local river or marsh through an organization like Waterkeeper Alliance. For effective ideas on how to get involved in your home state, head to **cleanwateraction.org**.

DEFORESTATION

Up there with water wealth is our perception that the US is covered with an endless canopy of trees. In truth, we do have a hell of a lot of forest (about 1.2 million square miles of it), but we also have the seventh highest deforestation rate in the world, according to the UN Food and Agriculture Organization. Sure, we might be making up for some of our losses with plantation trees, but nothing can replace the rich animal and plant diversity that's woven into old-growth forests. And sadly, less than

Nearly 80% of the planet's forests have been PARTLY OR FULLY DESTROYED.

5% of American old-growth forests remain, according to the Rainforest Action Network. Considering that nearly 80% of the planet's forests have been partly or fully destroyed, we need to make sure we hold on to what we've got (as Joni says, you don't know what you've got till it's gone). But do we care? Nah. We just raze it for furniture and toilet paper. It's shameful, really. Without a second thought we blow our noses on and order bras off ancient trees that were once home to countless numbers of animal species.

Action Needed: First off, we need to ban all logging in the US's disappearing old-growth forests. We could very well create a market niche by mandating that every piece of lumber we sell be old growth–free. Encourage your town to pass on old growth– and tropical wood–free ordinance when it comes to municipal purchases like public benches (which are one of the largest consumers of tropical old-growth trees in this country). Our private forests should also be certified by the Forest Stewardship Council (FSC). The program is backed by eco activists like Greenpeace and ensures that environmental impacts are minimized. It's not a perfect system, but it's the best certifier on the market. About 5% of America's managed forests are already FSC-certified; we just need to go further.

Even more important, we need to start freeing ourselves from our tree addiction and actively support tree-free alternatives like hemp and agricultural waste (which can be used to make products like strawboard cabinets, furniture, and newsprint). Pushing for minimum-recycled-content regs for paper products would also be of help—that is, if we want to have any forest around in 100 years. Cutting global deforestation rates by just 10% around the world could earn us a stockpile of carbon credits too.

CHEMICALS

We're surrounded. There are nearly 10 million synthetic chemicals out there and about 100,000 in commercial use. They're in our homes, beauty and baby products, clothing, food—and now they're in our bodies, rivers, soil, and wildlife. Fine, you say, but they've all been tested for safety. Wrong. A shocking 95% of all chemicals on the market have never been tested for toxicity or their impact on the planet. About 62,000 chemicals that were in use before 1979 were grandfathered in under the Toxic Substances Control Act (TSCA), meaning they were exempted from safety-testing standards because they were around before the act came in. "Age before brains" was clearly the motto there. Since then, the EPA has tested fewer than 200 of these grandfathered chems, banning a mere handful.

Part of the problem, say critics, is that the TSCA allows the Environmental Protection Agency to restrict chemicals only if they present "an unreasonable risk to human health" (versus a more easily proven "significant risk") and dictates that the costs to industry must be considered. Also, the burden of proof is placed on the EPA to prove a chemical is unsafe, rather than forcing industry to demonstrate that their products won't give us cancer before they go to market. Combined with aggressive industry lobbying, all this explains why it has taken so long to get dangerous chemicals like asbestos off the market.

A *shocking 95% of all chemicals on the market* *have* **NEVER BEEN TESTED FOR TOXICITY** *or their impact on the planet.*

Even when reviewing questionable chemicals, the EPA is not always considered neutral. In 2006, union leaders representing 9,000 government scientists, managers, and employees publicly complained that the EPA was pressuring them to rush safety reviews and skip steps in the agency's review of 232 old pesticide ingredients already on the market. In the spring of 2008, the US Government Accountability Office, a congressional watchdog, said new changes to the way high-risk toxins are assessed is letting nonscientists in the Pentagon, NASA, Department of Energy, and other agencies seriously delay and hamper chemical reviews.

Action Needed: We need to overhaul our system of evaluating chemicals so that it prioritizes human and environmental health over industry profits (gee, imagine that). Ideally, that system would look more like Europe's new REACH initiative, which is forcing all chemicals to be evaluated for toxicity and puts the burden of proof on manufacturers. Fifteen hundred chemicals will be yanked from the marketplace if manufacturers can't prove that they can be "adequately controlled."

North Americans bear the dishonor of having 10 times the amount of chemicals in our systems as Europeans have. Clearly we need to start picking up the pace on purging the country of persistent chemicals. Lead and DDT bans have proven that the faster we get rid of these things in our world, the sooner we can eliminate them from our bodies, so that maybe our grandchildren and their children have a fighting chance.

FOOD CRISIS

Toss food in basket. Lift fork to mouth. It's all so automatic there's nary a thought to what that food had to go through to get to you. Most of us don't even do a little "thank you, Lord, for this KFC" (although I believe a quick "thank you, farmers, for the food we are about to eat" would go a long way). Yet suddenly, food has become front-page news and people around the globe are rioting because they can't afford a sack of rice or a bag of corn. Crops are failing, surpluses are dwindling, countries are hoarding, and the price of basics is skyrocketing, as is the cost of fossil fuel–based fertilizers and shipping. Doesn't help matters that we're filling our gas tanks with food-based fuel meant for hungry mouths (in fact, a surprising World Bank report blamed biofuels for 75% of the price rise) and the globe's growing middle classes are demanding more grain-intensive

CROPS ARE FAILING, *surpluses are dwindling, countries are hoarding, and the price of basics is* SKYROCKETING.

meat. Add to the mix the imminent collapse of world fish stocks (thanks to our unfortunate practice of vacuuming the oceans bare) and the wilder weather coming with climate change, and you just watch those hunger pangs really kick in, mister.

We start to lose our appetites, however, when we find out that antibiotic-tainted manure runs off farmland and leaches from giant storage lagoons into rivers and streams on a daily basis. We reconsider our beef jerky intake when we realize we've been feeding cow parts to cows (who are vegetarian, by the way) and it's—surprise, surprise—making them, well, mad. We look at our peaches funny when our lips start to tingle, knowing that 73% of fruits and veggies in the US have tested positive for pesticide residues. Maybe it's no surprise that we're so out of touch with our food when you consider that our meals come from thousands of miles away, and most of us have no clue about the origins of our dinner.

Action Needed: So what can you do about it? Well, besides buying local and organic with minimal packaging, you need to start harassing your politicians about a thing or two.

For one, tell them to stop subsidizing ethanol so aggressively. We don't need to jack up the cost of corn to crisis levels by fueling the growth of an especially inefficient biofuel. Talk to your state representatives about sustainable land use policies that protect local farms from developers (genuine greenbelt protection nationwide would help preserve farmland and should boost reliable access to healthy local food when the shit hits the fan). Talk to your school board about a farm-to-schools program that brings in farm-fresh, local organic food. Talk to your workplace, local hospitals, and institutions about going farm-to-cafeteria. Push for community gardens and farmers markets in neighborhoods otherwise saturated with fast food and concrete. Fight to keep the greasy chains out and bring healthy food in.

And while you're fighting for greener food, here's a thought: if we're going to subsidize farmers so heavily, we should be doing the same for organic growers, since they not only feed our bellies, but do our bodies—and the environment—more good than any pesticide-laden genetically modified patch of refined white wheat ever could.

WHAT YOU CAN DO

"Oh, but the world's problems are so big, what can I really do to make a difference?" you say. Fear not, I have some handy tips to make it nice and easy. Reclaiming the reins of power from the oil companies, lumber mills, and chemical corporations that seem to run this joint is not as hard as it seems if we all grab our elected representatives by the lapels and remind them that we the people hold the ultimate power in a democracy. You've just gotta take that first step. Start by picking a cause that's dearest to you and get informed.

Start by picking a cause that's DEAREST TO YOU and GET INFORMED.

Lobbying: Okay, so you're mad as hell. Now what? Time to take that frustration out on some politicians. I'm not saying you should be throwing spitballs at your local representatives, but you do want to make sure they remember that their job is to represent those who elected them. That includes you. You don't have to wear an alarmingly expensive suit and work for a shady corporation to be a lobbyist. Every letter you write and every petition you sign is an act of lobbying.

Better still, get on the phone and tell your elected reps your thoughts on the US's appalling pollution record or horrendous water safeguards. No doubt they'll talk a good game, trying to convince you that plenty of impressive steps have already been taken to rectify the situation, but don't back down! You can argue your position best if you do your research beforehand. And google your politicians to dig up their environmental records or public positions on the issue.

If you're really gung ho, book an appointment to chat face-to-face. Bring along a minidelegation of two or three others who back your sound, earth-lovin' views. You'll get about 15 minutes to present your points, so be prepared with a written brief and printouts of any good research, charts, or reports you can find. If you bend their ear enough, you can get them to hold community meetings, ask probing questions in the legislature, or even submit private bills.

You don't have to wear an alarmingly expensive suit to be a lobbyist. Every LETTER YOU WRITE and EVERY PETITION YOU SIGN is an act of lobbying.

Using many of the same techniques—phone calls, letters, e-mails—you can also direct your lobbying efforts at the corporations doing the damage. For instance, the Union of Concerned Scientists, Natural Resources Defense Council, US PIRG, and Sierra Club all encourage gas buyers to boycott climate change naysayer ExxonMobil (**exxposeexxon.com**). If you own shares in the company, use that foot in the door to launch a shareholder action (see page 317 for more info). You can even kick it up a notch by taking it to the streets. Help organize or participate in public protests outside the company's office. If you're actually a victim of a corporation's ecological recklessness (like, say, you live next door to a leaky plant), make like Erin Brockovich and file a class action lawsuit!

Joining Clubs: It can be hard (not to mention lonely) to take effective action as just one person. So why not join an environmental organization? There are countless to choose from (see the resource guide, page 359, for national listings; and page 321 for more info on volunteering), and whether you want to save the unicorned snails, picket an oil company, or help with a revitalization project in a sensitive wetland close to home, there's one out there for you. Making that first call can be a challenge if you've been spending most of your free time watching *Seinfeld* reruns or knitting, but once you go to a group meeting and get hooked on that feeling of accomplishment, of community, of hope you get from being involved in changing the world with a posse, you'll never look back.

Voter Power: Don't like what your politicians are doing? Don't think they're standing up for the planet often enough or loud enough? Maybe they've sided one too many times in favor of developers over green space and polluters over communities? That little X you make in the ballot box is mighty powerful. Maybe it's time you changed your vote.

Make sure all your family and friends are REGISTERED TO VOTE *and know why their* VOTE MATTERS.

And make sure all your family and friends are registered to vote and know why their vote matters. If you know your local rep supports a new coal plant or voted in favor of paving through sensitive wetlands, tell people about it. Especially come election time. Print up flyers (on recycled paper, of course) with bullet points on the politician's dodgy record and slip it in your neighbors' mailboxes. If you join up with a group of like-minded citizens, you'll make a bigger splash.

Consumer Power: Buy, buy, buy—it's all we do. In fact, some rank shopping as their favorite pastime. And who am I to judge? I have a closet full of clothes and drawers full of necklaces and bangles that I'd no doubt want firefighters to save if flames were ever licking at my apartment. The point is, we all spend money on way too much stuff, even if you think you're a miser conservationist. And while we tend to focus on how a

Why not use your CONSUMER POWER *for good? You can lend your dollars to products made with* ETHICAL POLICIES *and* YANK *money away from corporations that are* UNRESPONSIVE *to earthy considerations.*

product will meet our needs (as in, "I need a bigger TV"; "I need a new cell phone"; "I need a teak coffee table"), we've got to own up to the fact that these purchases are fueling chemical pollution, habitat destruction, and landfill clogging. Why not use your consumer power for good? You can lend your dollars to products made with ethical policies and ecologically sound materials and yank money away from companies that are unresponsive to earthy considerations (check out Co-op America's *Boycott Organizer's Guide* at **coopamerica .org/programs/boycotts**). Lest we forget, money talks. And boy, do corporations speak its language.

Now, put the book down, get off that couch/chair/futon and start your own planet-saving chapter of Ecoholics Anonymous (well, you can scan the resource guide first, if you like).

Appendix: Plastics Exposed

This petrochemical invention has enveloped nearly everything on the planet in a nonbiodegradable sheath. The US produces nearly 30 million tons of plastic a year and most of it gets trashed. There's even a garbage patch the size of Texas swirling in the Pacific. But no matter how planet-conscious you are, sometimes you just can't get away from using plastic, so it's best to size up which type causes the least harm.

KNOW YOUR NUMBERS

(Those little triangular recycling logos are there for a reason.)

Polyethylene Terephthalate (PET): Soda bottles, shampoo bottles, and water bottles. Probably the most commonly recycled plastic. Contains UV stabilizers and flame retardants, but has fewer harmful additives that will leach into landfills and your meal. PET disposable water bottles have been known to leach antimony, however. In 2008, a *Milwaukee Journal Sentinel* investigation found that even some #1 containers leached bisphenol A in the microwave. The news didn't spread.

High-Density Polyethylene (HDPE): Milk jugs, cleaning-product bottles, shopping bags (which aren't necessarily recycled in municipalities that recycle #2 plastic—best to check). Most municipalities accept narrow-nose containers, but not all take wide-lipped ones such as margarine tubs. HDPE is not a bad plastic, compared to the others, though the 2008 *Milwaukee Journal Sentinel* investigation found that even some #2 containers leached bisphenol A in the microwave.

Polyvinyl Chloride (PVC): Greenpeace ranks this one as the biggest eco villain of all. PVC, or vinyl, is made with vinyl chloride, a known human carcinogen. It's said to emit persistent dioxins in both its manufacture and incineration (especially in crappy municipal incinerators). Hormone-disrupting phthalates added to soften it have been found to offgas from the plastic. Lead and cadmium are commonly used as stabilizers and have also been found to migrate from the plastic (think lead in toys). Though it's used mostly by the construction biz (yes, your pipes just might be PVC), it's also the basis of vinyl records, old car seats, those shiny black outfits worn by the fetish crowd (sorry, guys!), and, scary but true, toys. The plastics people stand by its safety. If your plastic bottle has the number 3 or a *V* on the bottom, it's PVC. Rarely recycled.

Low-Density Polyethylene (LDPE): Like its high-density sibling, #4 plastic isn't as toxic to manufacture as other plastics are, but it's not commonly recycled.

Polypropylene (PP): Not always recyclable in every municipality, but it's considered the safest plastic in terms of leaching potential. Shocker of all shockers, in the *Milwaukee Journal Sentinel* investigation some #5 containers were also found to leach bisphenol A when microwaved.

Polystyrene (PS): A category best known by the trade name Styrofoam. Tied with polyurethane for second worst plastic, because making the stuff involves carcinogenic benzene; plus, it's very rarely recycled.

Mixed Bag: Basically any plastic other than #1–6. Not readily recyclable. Under this broad umbrella sits polycarbonate (the hard plastic used for refillable baby and water bottles), which used to be marketed as nonleaching, not to mention indestructible—perfect for outdoorsy types. Turns out it does leach the hormone-disrupting chemical bisphenol A (found in the lining of food and beverage cans and polycarbonate bottles, including baby versions). For more on the controversy, see page 133. Polyurethane is also a #7, and though considered greener than PVC, it still emits toxins like methylene chloride during production.

GREEN PLASTICS

Bioplastic: Made from plant-based oils, starches, or fibers. Could come from genetically engineered crops, so it's always best to ask.

Biodegradable Plastic: Needs only naturally present bacteria to dissolve back into natural elements. Given that decades-old apple cores can still be found in dumps, it's no surprise that even these plastics have a hard time breaking down in dark, airless landfills.

Compostable Plastic: Certified to break down in a municipal composter as fast as other compostable goods, with no toxic residue. It may or may not break down in your backyard composter, so read the fine print.

Degradable or Oxo-degradable Plastic (Often Petrol-Based): Designed to decompose when exposed to UV light or oxygen, both of which are rarely found in landfills.

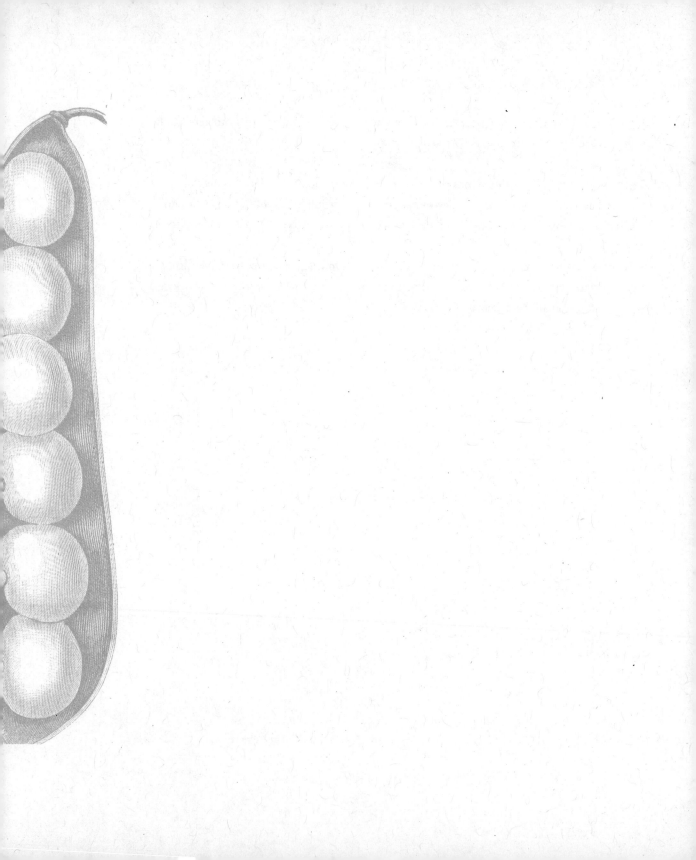

Glossary

1,4-dioxane: A petroleum-derived contaminant considered a probable human carcinogen by the Environmental Protection Agency (EPA), and a definite animal carcinogen. It's a by-product of chemical processing found in many sudsy products, like shampoo, bubble bath, and dish soap. Potentially contaminated chemicals include polyethylene, polyethylene glycol (PEG), polyoxyethylene, polyethoxyethylene, and polyoxynolethylene.

ammonium nitrate: Made famous by its use in explosives (widely used in World War II), but mostly purchased as a fertilizer because it's a cheap source of nitrogen. Large spills can kill vegetation, and runoff from farms into waterways can create large algal blooms that choke rivers and bays and kill off fish.

bioaccumulation: Buildup of chemicals in the tissues of a living thing, whether human, wildlife, or plant. (Chemicals enter our bodies through the food we eat, the air we breathe, and the water we drink.) Bioaccumulation explains why larger, older fish have higher levels of mercury, for instance, than do smaller, younger ones.

biomonitoring: A way of testing what happens to chemicals in the environment (for example, scientists use this method to test for persistent organic pollutants in polar bears and for dozens of chemicals in human blood, urine, and saliva). Since 2001, the Centers for Disease Control and Prevention has been biomonitoring thousands of Americans.

bisphenol A: Found in polycarbonate plastic bottles (the ones with the little #7 on the bottom), ceramic dental fillings, paper products, and food and beverage can linings. It is an estrogen-mimicking hormone disrupter found to leach from products. Numerous studies have tied low exposure levels to birth defects, breast and prostate cancer, and more (a study released in 2008 by the *Journal of the American Medical Association* said that adults exposed to higher amounts of the chemical were three times as likely to suffer from heart disease and 2.4 times as likely to have type 2 diabetes).

Manufacturers argue that the levels are so low they're not a health risk, but in 2008 Nalgene stopped using the plastic and many retailers, like Toys"R"Us, pulled polycarbonate baby bottles from shelves. Although Canada has deemed the compound dangerous and vowed to remove it from kids' products, the EPA, to date, continues to stand by it. Attorneys general in states like Connecticut, New Jersey, and Delaware have asked manufacturers to stop using bisphenol A when making baby bottles and formula containers.

brominated fire retardants (a.k.a. polybrominated diphenyl ethers, or PBDEs): These babies might make your mattress, couch, and electronics less likely to erupt in flames, but they're a family of chemicals that are incredibly persistent and tend to accumulate in human and animal tissue. Skyrocketing levels have been found in everything from arctic animals, lake trout, whales, and waterbirds, to human breast milk. PentaBDE and octaBDE production in the US ceased at the end of 2004, but they might still be found in imported products. Canada now says decaBDEs are so dangerous that it won't let companies manufacture them there, but deca is still common in consumer electronics, wire insulation, draperies, and upholstery on both sides of the border.

Bt (a.k.a. *Bacillus thuringiensis*): A naturally occurring bacterium that's toxic to certain insects. Its gene has been cloned and spliced into plants, such as cotton, to make them insect-resistant.

C8: See "PFOA."

cadmium: A metallic element that is considered a probable human carcinogen.

carcinogen: Anything that may cause cancer.

chemical sensitivities (a.k.a. multiple chemical sensitivities): A chronic syndrome caused by a person's intolerance to chemicals. Even low doses of the offending chemicals can stimulate a negative reaction. Symptoms vary but can include headaches, a runny nose, aching joints, confusion, fatigue, and sore throat. Symptoms generally improve or disappear when the chemicals are removed. A team of researchers recently found that people with multiple chemical sensitivities are missing certain enzymes that help metabolize chemicals.

chlorinated tris: A carcinogenic fire retardant banned from children's PJs 30 years ago but still used on furniture foam. Deemed a health hazard by the World Health Organization, the National Cancer Institute, and the National Research Council.

chloromethane (a.k.a. methyl chloride): A potent neurotoxin and possible human carcinogen found in air, water (including ground- and drinking water), and soil samples. Sources include burning PVC and silicone rubber, as well as cigarettes, chlorinated pools, and polystyrene insulation.

chlorpropham: A pesticide used on many fruits and veggies to control weeds. It inhibits sprouting in potatoes. Long-term exposure to very high doses triggered tumors and stunted growth in lab animals, and in some instances caused death, but it is generally considered to be of low toxicity.

chlorpyrifos: A pesticide used on farms, on lawns, in pet collars, and in home pest control. It is very toxic to animals, fish, and birds and is a suspected endocrine disrupter, which is especially harmful for young children. Phased out for residential use in the US. Still allowed on crops.

closed-cell: Used in reference to plastics found in products like yoga mats, as in "100% closed-cell PVC mat." The term may imply that the product doesn't offgas, but all it really means is that its plastic cells are sealed within their own little bubble, making it highly water-resistant.

DDT: Considered the first modern pesticide. DDT was first used during World War II to combat mosquitoes, and then was commonly used on crops and sprayed in residential areas to combat tree infestations. It is extremely toxic to fish and birds, accumulates in the food chain, and is classified as a probable human carcinogen. Most uses were phased out in the '70s, when its environmental impacts first came to light, and it was banned in the US in 1972. It's still found in breast milk and in the bloodstreams of North American adults and, to a lesser extent, children. DDT is still used to fight insect-borne malaria and typhoid in some developing countries.

DEHP: See "phthalates."

diethanolamine (DEA): A suspected carcinogen common in shampoos, body washes, and makeup. Cocamide DEA, MEA, and TEA may be contaminated with DEA.

dimethyl ditallow ammonium chloride: Found in antistatic products, fabric dyes, fertilizers, and lubricating oil. Made from animal fat, it is toxic to fish and algae, and it isn't readily biodegradable.

dioxins (a.k.a. furans): Carcinogenic, endocrine-disrupting neurotoxins. There are lots of different types of dioxins, but they all contain chlorine, and they're all bad. The largest source of dioxins in the US is the burning of municipal and medical waste (mainly from burning PVC products). Burning plastics in your backyard releases dioxins too, as does burning chemically treated wood. Dioxins build up in animal tissues, which explains why the main way humans ingest dioxins is by eating meat, milk products, and fish. The pulp and paper processing biz was historically also a big source of dioxins, but the industry says it has seriously reduced dioxin pollution.

diphenylamine: A fungicide used to prevent discoloration in apples. It contains an impurity that is considered a known carcinogen.

endocrine disrupters: Chemicals that interfere with the endocrine system, which secretes development-guiding and reproductive hormones. See also "hormone disrupters."

formaldehyde: Commonly found in pressed woods (particleboard and medium-density fiberboard), permanent-press fabric (clothing and curtains), and insulation. There are two types: urea formaldehyde releases volatile formaldehyde gas, but the phenol type tends to offgas less, according to the National Safety Council. Formaldehyde may cause cancer in humans, as well as wheezing, fatigue, rashes, and eye, nose, and throat irritations. Some people are especially sensitive to it. It's also a major component of smog.

formic acid: See "methyl formate."

furans: See "dioxins." (Though not exactly the same, these two are usually lumped together and often given the same description.)

Gore-Tex: See "PTFE."

grandfathered: Exempt from new regulation.

high-density polyethylene (HDPE): See the appendix on plastics.

hormone disrupters: Chemicals that mimic or block hormones, potentially throwing off normal body functions and triggering behavioral, reproductive, and developmental problems. See also "endocrine disrupters."

low-density polyethylene (LDPE): See the appendix on plastics.

malathion: An organophosphate pesticide in use in the US since 1956. It's sprayed mostly on crops but is perhaps best known for its use to control adult mosquitoes in residential areas. It's not really persistent in the environment, but it is deadly to all insects, including good ones such as honeybees, as well as fish and aquatic life. Health officials say it's not dangerous to humans, but environmentalists say it can cause kidney problems, intestinal problems, and cancer in lab animals.

mercury: The shiny stuff in old thermometers and the only metal that's liquid at room temperature. Mercury is used in dental fillings and batteries and as a preservative in some vaccines. Most of the mercury in landfill comes from car switches. Most human exposure to the potent neurotoxin comes from eating mercury-contaminated fish, according to the EPA. Developing fetuses are most at risk and can develop severe disabilities from exposure—hence the 2004 EPA warning to women who want to become pregnant, pregnant or nursing moms, and young children to curb their tuna intake (enviros say to ditch it altogether). The EPA estimates that 300,000 newborns each year have an increased risk of learning disabilities thanks to exposure to mercury in the womb. How do fish get so full of mercury to begin with? Emissions from coal plants and other factories send mercury up into the air, where it can travel great distances on wind currents and come down as rain or snow over bodies of water. It then collects in the bodies of aquatic animals and moves up the food chain. See also "bioaccumulation."

methyl chloride: See "chloromethane."

methyl formate (a.k.a. formic acid): A suspected neurotoxin. Exposure can trigger eye, nose, and skin irritations; shortness of breath; dizziness; and headaches.

methylene chloride: Emitted in polyurethane production and found in paint thinners and strippers, shoe polish, fabric protectors, and pesticides—and, oh yes, used in the production of decaf coffee and tea. The EPA classifies it as a probable carcinogen. It doesn't dissolve well in water and can be found in drinking water.

multiple chemical sensitivities: See "chemical sensitivities."

neurotoxin: A toxin that affects the central nervous system, harming neural tissue.

nitrogen oxide: A gas present in car exhaust and a major component of smog.

offgassing: Not a bodily function, but the release of chemicals into the air.

organochlorines: A notorious group of chemicals that includes all kinds of bad boys, such as DDT, PCBs, and dioxins. Some are carcinogens, and most accumulate in fatty tissues.

organophosphates (OPs): An old-generation family of chemical pesticides that mess with an insect's nervous system. OPs are the most widely used pesticides in the world and are often quite toxic. They are also used for head lice, in sheep dips, and as nerve gas in chemical warfare (in fact, the use of OPs as an insecticide was discovered in Germany during World War II in the production of nerve gas). OPs don't so much accumulate in the environment as make wildlife and workers that come in contact with them sick. They're popular in the developing world, where they're cheaper than newer pesticides. But of a short list of pesticides that developing nations' governments are advised to restrict, all five, according to the Pesticide Action Network, are OPs.

parabens: All types of parabens (methyl-, ethyl-, etc.) have been found to be estrogenic—meaning they mimic female hormones. They have been found in breast tumor samples but haven't been conclusively linked to cancer.

PBDEs: See "brominated fire retardants."

PCB (polychlorinated biphenyl): An extremely persistent environmental contaminant. The industrial chemical was introduced in 1929 and used in the making of electronic equipment. The US banned the substance in 1979, but it's still turning up in human tissues and farmed salmon.

permethrin: A suspected hormone disrupter and possible carcinogen. Permethrin is toxic to fish and tadpoles and can cause all sorts of physical reactions in humans, from nausea to asthma attacks.

persistent: Referring to a chemical that does not readily biodegrade but instead accumulates in the environment and living tissues. See also "bioaccumulation."

petrochemical: Any chemical derived from petroleum, whether crude oil or natural gas. Petrochemicals are used to make plastic, fertilizers, paint, cleaning products, asphalt, and synthetic fabrics such as polyester. All the ecological problems that arise from petroleum excavation, processing, and shipping are also associated with its offshoots, plus the extra pollution created by refining and manufacturing each chemical.

PFOA (a.k.a. C8): An ingredient used to make nonstick surfaces on cookware, microwave popcorn bags, candy wrappers, fast-food french-fry containers, cardboard pizza trays, and burger wrappers. It does not break down in the wild (even DDT breaks down eventually) and has reportedly accumulated in 95% of Americans' tissues and in high levels in wildlife, including polar bears. In early 2006, the EPA announced that it had reached an agreement with DuPont and seven other major manufacturers to cut their emissions and PFOA-containing products by 95% by 2010 and to eliminate PFOA altogether by 2015. (EPA documents show that DuPont has known about PFOA's persistence in the broader population since 1976.) Part of a slippery and persistent class of chemicals called PFCs (perfluorinated chemicals) that keep your eggs from sticking, repel stains, and make rain bead off your jacket. For a shopper's guide to what products contain PFCs and detailed reports on the topic, check out **ewg.org**.

PFOS (a.k.a. perfluorooctanesulfonate): A chemical commonly found on older stain-repellent carpets, furniture, and clothing. PFOS was the basis of Scotchgard's and Stainmaster's original formulation, until 3M stopped production of the chemical in 2000 after the EPA threatened it with regulatory action. Studies found that PFOS was turning up everywhere in the environment, and that it killed some rat pups even though it was their mothers that had been exposed while the pups were in the womb, not the pups themselves. Like PFOA, it was also used as a grease-repellent surface in fast-food wrappers, popcorn bags, candy bars, and beverage containers. PFOS use has been phased out in the US. PFOS is part of the persistent PFC (perfluorinated chemicals) family.

phthalates: Chemicals often added to PVC plastic as softeners, found in everything from kids' toys to sex toys, as well as all sorts of personal-care products and perfumes. The industry insists they're safe, but the feds have now banned six from baby toys. One type of phthalate in particular, DEHP, has been found to cause birth defects in lab animals and is classified as a probable human carcinogen. Harvard researchers found that another, DEP, can cause DNA damage in the sperm of adult men. Many toy companies had already phased them out in toys intended for younger children. Also found in water, household dust, breast milk, and wildlife—showing that phthalates clearly migrate from their source.

polybrominated diphenyl ethers: See "brominated fire retardants."

polyethylene terephthalate (PET): See the appendix on plastics.

polypropylene (PP): See the appendix on plastics.

polystyrene (PS): See the appendix on plastics.

polyvinyl chloride (PVC): See "PVC."

polyvinylidene chloride (PVDC): Used to make some cling wrap. Ten percent of PVDC wrap can be made up of potentially hormone-disrupting, liver-damaging phthalates, which have been found to drift into food.

PTFE: Generally considered a PFC (perfluorinated chemical) (though a chemist might argue the point and say it's in the fluoroplastic family). The trade name for PTFE, owned by DuPont, is Teflon. Gore-Tex products are basically PTFE with micropores. Gore-Tex swears its gear is so stable it'll never break down, but you wouldn't want to, say, accidentally throw your rain gear in a fire. A few groups of scientists found that using PTFE-coated heat lamps to warm chicks and ducklings killed up to 52% of them within 3 to 5 days. Considered to be the compound in nonstick pans that may kill pet birds if a pan is heated to extremely high temperatures.

PVC (polyvinyl chloride, a.k.a. vinyl): Found in pipes, windows, toys, flip-flops, garden furniture, flooring, plastic bottles (check the bottom for recycling symbol #3), venetian blinds, umbrellas, fake leather couches, and even the puffy 3D cartoon on your kid's T-shirt. Just the additives—phthalates, lead, and cadmium—are supercontroversial. In the late '90s, after 2 years of investigation, Greenpeace concluded that vinyl is the absolute worst plastic for the environment. The building block of PVC, vinyl chloride, is not only a known carcinogen, but creates dangerous dioxins in the manufacturing process and when incinerated. The industry, of course, says vinyl is completely safe and claims it has cleaned up its practices since its dirtier days and now emits very few dioxins and furans. Even so, many companies, such as Adidas, Reebok, Puma, Nike, Microsoft, Hewlett-Packard, Toyota, and Honda, are committed to reducing or limiting the plastic. IKEA outlaws the substance altogether, and several municipalities have been making moves to do the same. See also the appendix on plastics.

sodium laureth sulfate: Similar to sodium lauryl sulfate, but somewhat gentler. Still, maligned for the same reasons. Processing could create harmful 1,4-dioxanes and the by-product could be found in final products.

sodium lauryl sulfate (SLS): A sudsing surfactant found in shampoos, soaps, and toothpaste, and a known skin and eye irritant that may aggravate dandruff and mouth ulcers. Rumors of its being a carcinogen are considered urban myths. Health food products often contain SLS made from coconut oil.

surfactant: A type of chemical found in cleaning products, dish and laundry detergents, shampoos, and washes. Surfactants make things lather, spread, and penetrate well. Hundreds of surfactants are in existence, many petroleum-based. Most surfactants biodegrade in sewage treatment plants, but nonylphenol ethoxylates (NPEs) are of environmental concern because they don't really biodegrade, are toxic to algae and aquatic life, and have been associated with hormone-disrupting effects.

Teflon: See "PTFE" and "PFOA."

toluene: A common solvent used in paints, glues, disinfectants, and rubber, as well as in tanning leather and manufacturing polyurethane foam. Inhaling toluene regularly over time can lead to brain and kidney damage. Even low doses can cause confusion, as well as memory, hearing, and vision loss. Pregnant women should minimize exposure. Toluene is a petroleum by-product.

triclocarbon: A chemical disinfectant found in some antibacterial soaps, though it's less common than triclosan. Triclocarbon is persistent and has been known to survive the sewage treatment process and turn up in lakes, rivers, and streams.

triclosan: The active ingredient in many antibacterial soaps, deodorants, and toothpastes. Beyond accumulating in fatty tissues (it's been found in fish and in breast milk), it has made its way into lakes, rivers, and streams (the US Geological Survey found triclosan to be one of the top 10 stream contaminants). When it's exposed to sunlight in water, a mild dioxin forms. And when you throw chlorinated water into the mix, it could turn into a much nastier dioxin. Scientists also say it acts as a harmful hormone disrupter in aquatic life. *E. coli* that survived being treated with triclosan became resistant to 7 of 12 antibiotics.

vinyl: See "PVC."

volatile organic compounds (VOCs): Found in paint, glue, gasoline, cleaning products, ink, permanent markers, correction fluid, pesticides, and air fresheners. Don't be fooled by the word "organic" in the name—VOCs aren't good for us. They're carbon-containing gases and vapors that evaporate readily into the air, contributing to air pollution. VOCs can even offgas from nonliquid sources, such as office furniture, that contain formaldehyde and cause serious indoor air pollution. Exposure can cause dizziness, headaches, and nausea. Some VOCs are more toxic than others and are tied to cancer and kidney and liver damage. Some react with nitrogen oxide to form smog-inducing compounds.

Resource Guide

NATIONAL ENVIRONMENTAL ORGANIZATIONS (GET INVOLVED!)

Environmental Defense Fund

edf.org
Membership and Public Information
1875 Connecticut Avenue, NW, Suite 600
Washington, DC 20009
1-800-684-3322

Friends of the Earth

foe.org
1717 Massachusetts Avenue, Suite 600
Washington, DC 20036
1-877-843-8687

Greenpeace USA

greenpeace.org/usa
702 H Street, NW
Washington, DC 20001
(202) 462-1177

National Audubon Society

audubon.org
225 Varick Street, 7th floor
New York, NY 10014
(212) 979-3000

National Wildlife Federation

nwf.org
11100 Wildlife Center Drive
Reston, VA 20190
1-800-822-9919

Natural Resources Defense Council

nrdc.org
40 West 20th Street
New York, NY 10011
(212) 727-2700

Nature Conservancy

nature.org
4245 North Fairfax Drive, Suite 100
Arlington, VA 22203-1606
(703) 841-5300

Ocean Conservancy

oceanconservancy.org
1300 19th Street, NW, 8th Floor
Washington, DC 20036
1-800-519-1541

Oceana

oceana.org/north-america
1350 Connecticut Avenue, NW, 5th Floor
Washington, DC 20036
1-877-7-OCEANA

Rainforest Action Network

ran.org
221 Pine Street, 5th Floor
San Francisco, CA 94104
(415) 398-4404

Sierra Club

sierraclub.org
85 Second Street, 2nd Floor
San Francisco, CA 94105
(415) 977-5500

Waterkeeper Alliance

waterkeeper.org
50 South Buckhout, Suite 302
Irvington, NY 10533
(914) 674-0622

KICK-ASS ECO WEBSITES

Grist: My personal fave. These guys deliver gloom and doom with a sense of humor (that's actually their official motto). grist.org

Green Guide: Full of practical reports on green problems and solutions for everyday things. thegreenguide.com

E Magazine: A great eco magazine with both online and hard-copy versions available by subscription. Some online content is free. emagazine.com

Environmental Health News: Check it every day to stay on top of extensive enviro news coverage from around the globe. environmentalhealthnews.org

Treehugger: Get the scoop on all the latest and coolest green designs, gizmos, and policies. treehugger.com

Care2: It's got a news section and a petition section, but the "Healthy & Green Living" section crammed with do-it-yourself tips on everything is the most handy. care2.com

OTHER RESOURCES

For a list of state groups, go to eco-usa.net. For a listing of organizations by topic, head

Acknowledgments

Who would have thought a little column from Toronto could make its way to the US in the form of this book? And there are a few people I have to thank for that (wait, let me slip into my gown and rented diamonds first). First I have to thank Angela for agreeing to take on *Ecoholic* to begin with (not to mention the whole team at Norton, including Erica and Stephanie). My agent, Denise, for making it all happen. My *NOW Magazine* publishers and column editor for supporting *Ecoholic* in every incarnation. My readers, who write in every week with probing questions that fuel every page of this book. My out-of-this-world researcher Tonya, who took a mountain of research on with grace and ease (and, of course, my kick-ass tri-coastal research queens, Dara, Melissa, and Alex). Dustin, for donating his amazing creativity and vision to the cover. Bryan, for edging the cover into the home stretch. And of course, this book couldn't have been written without the unyielding love, encouragement, and zaniness of my incredible family and friends. No stretch of writing could ever be accomplished without my muse, a.k.a. The Mews. But most of all I have to thank the man who brings a smile to my face even when the woes of the world are weighing on me, Brad. You are my sunshine, you are my rock, you are my deep blue sea. And lastly I have to thank the earth, for hanging in there while the ecoholics of the world organize a rescue op.

Index

Ecoholic was printed with the proprietary and exclusive eco-friendly, ultralow Volatile Organic Compound (VOC) THINKTech™ printing process, at a plant that has received both Forest Stewardship Council (FSC) and Sustainable Forest Initiative (SFI) Chain-of-Custody certifications. THINKTech™ slashes the percentage of VOC emissions released by the ink down to 2–3%, which is less than a tenth of the emissions generated from standard petroleum-based inks. This process also reduces the energy needs for printing this book on a web press by 70%, and eliminates the natural gas and electricity typically required for oven curing and the operation of chill rollers. This special ink also dries quickly and is odor free.

The paper used to print Ecoholic contains 100% postconsumer fiber, and is certified EcoLogo, Processed Chlorine Free (PCF), and FSC Recycled. It is manufactured at a mill that uses biogas energy. Using recycled paper for the first printing of this book, instead of virgin fibers, reduced our ecological footprint by:

Trees: 213
Solid waste: 13,503 pounds
Water: 127,450 gallons
Suspended particles in the water: 85.4 pounds
Air emissions: 29,652 pounds
Natural gas: 30,900 cubic feet

The cover was printed with non-petroleum-based inks on an uncoated, 100% postconsumer, FSC-certified and PCF-certified stock, made with 100% certified renewable energy. The cover was coated with a liquid varnish instead of nonbiodegradable plastic film.

Adapted from the "Ecoholic" columns previously
published in *NOW Magazine*, Toronto, Canada.

Previous edition published as *Ecoholic: Your Guide to the Most
Environmentally Friendly Products, Information and Services in Canada*

For information about special discounts for bulk purchases,
please contact W. W. Norton Special Sales at
specialsales@wwnorton.com or 800-233-4830

Manufacturing by The Maple Vail Book Manufacturing Group
Book design by Judith Stagnitto Abbate / Abbate Design
Production manager: Devon Zahn

Library of Congress Cataloging-in-Publication Data

Vasil, Adria.
Ecoholic : your guide to the most environmentally friendly
information, products, and services / Adria Vasil. — 1st American ed.
p. cm.
Adapted from the Ecoholic column found in Now magazine, Toronto,
Canada.
Includes index.
ISBN 978-0-393-33428-9 (pbk.)
1. Home economics—Handbooks, manuals, etc. 2. Green
products—Handbooks, manuals, etc. 3. Sustainable living—
Handbooks, manuals, etc. 4. Environmental protection—
Handbooks, manuals, etc. I. Now (Toronto, Ont. : 1981) II. Title.
TX145.V4 2009
640—dc22

                                                    2009004499

W. W. Norton & Company, Inc.
500 Fifth Avenue, New York, N.Y. 10110
www.wwnorton.com

W. W. Norton & Company Ltd.
Castle House, 75/76 Wells Street, London W1T 3QT

1 2 3 4 5 6 7 8 9 0